This is the first in-depth critical appraisal in English of the political, legal, and cultural writings of Carl Schmitt, perhaps this century's most brilliant critic of liberalism. Moreover, it offers an assessment of this most sophisticated of fascist theorists without attempting either to apologize for or demonize him.

Schmitt's eventual collusion with the Nazis has long discouraged any serious engagement with the critique of liberalism that he undertook during the crisis-ridden Weimar Republic. However, contemporary political conditions, such as disaffection with liberalism and the rise of extremist political organizations, have rendered Schmitt's work both relevant and insightful.

Schmitt's Weimar writings confront the role of modern technology as it finds expression through the principles and practices of liberalism. Just as technology is characterized by both the abstractly formal logic of Enlightenment science and the irrational will toward domination generated by mass exhilaration and fear, so liberalism, according to Schmitt, lays out abstractly neutral rules to govern a social reality comprising a plurality of mutually irrational and incommensurable subjective perspectives. John McCormick examines why technology becomes a rallying cry for both right- and left-wing intellectuals at times when liberalism appears anachronistic, and he shows the continuities between Weimar's ideological debates and those of our own age.

By setting Schmitt's work in the context of contemporaries such as Weber, Lukács, Benjamin, Heidegger, and Adorno as well as earlier figures such as Machiavelli, Hobbes, Hegel, Marx, and Nietzsche, John McCormick has furnished philosophers, historians, and political theorists with the most comprehensive account of Schmitt available.

CARL SCHMITT'S CRITIQUE OF LIBERALISM

MODERN EUROPEAN PHILOSOPHY

General Editor
Robert B. Pippin, University of Chicago

Advisory Board
Gary Gutting, University of Notre Dame
Rolf-Peter Horstmann, Humboldt University, Berlin
Mark Sacks, University of Essex

This series contains a range of high-quality books on philosophers, topics, and schools of thought prominent in the Kantian and post-Kantian European tradition. It is nonsectarian in approach and methodology, and it includes both introductory and more specialized treatments of these thinkers and topics. Authors are encouraged to interpret the boundaries of the modern European tradition in a broad way and in primarily philosophical rather than historical terms.

Some Recent Titles

Frederick A. Olafson: *What Is a Human Being?*
Stanley Rosen: *The Mask of Enlightenment: Nietzsche's Zarathustra*
Robert C. Scharff: *Comte after Positivism*
F.C.T. Moore: *Bergson: Thinking Backwards*
Charles Larmore: *The Morals of Modernity*
Robert B. Pippin: *Idealism as Modernism: Hegelian Variations*
Daniel Conway: *Nietzsche's Dangerous Game*

CARL SCHMITT'S CRITIQUE OF LIBERALISM

AGAINST POLITICS AS TECHNOLOGY

JOHN P. McCORMICK

University of New Hampshire

CAMBRIDGE UNIVERSITY PRESS

PUBLISHED BY THE PRESS SYNDICATE OF THE UNIVERSITY OF CAMBRIDGE
The Pitt Building, Trumpington Street, Cambridge CB2 1RP, United Kingdom

CAMBRIDGE UNIVERSITY PRESS
The Edinburgh Building, Cambridge CB2 2RU, United Kingdom
40 West 20th Street, New York, NY 10011-4211, USA
10 Stamford Road, Oakleigh, Melbourne 3166, Australia

First published 1997

Printed in the United States of America

Typeset in Baskerville

Library of Congress Cataloging-in-Publication Data
McCormick, John P., 1966–
Carl Schmitt's critique of liberalism : against politics as
technology / John P. McCormick.
p.   cm. – (Modern European philosophy)
Includes bibliographical references and index.
ISBN 0-521-59167-8
1. Schmitt, Carl, 1888–   .   2. Liberalism.   3. Technology and
civilization.   I. Title.   II. Series.
JC263.S34M385   1997
320'.092 – dc21   97-12109
                                                      CIP

*A catalog record for this book is available from
the British Library.*

ISBN 0 521 59167 8 hardback

FOR MY PARENTS,
J.M. AND B.T. MCCORMICK

CONTENTS

vii

III Liberalism and Fascism/Technology and Politics

ACKNOWLEDGMENTS

There are many people and institutions who aided and encouraged me to undertake and carry out this project. During my years as a graduate student I was fortunate to benefit from the learned guidance and unfailing support of perhaps the best mentors and colleagues in the world. I especially thank Stephen Holmes, Bernard Manin, Robert Pippin, Moishe Postone, Dan Carpenter, Ann Davies, Neil Brenner, Gia Pascarelli, as well as particular members of the Workshop in the History of Political Thought, the Interdisciplinary Social Theory Forum, the Modern European History Workshop, and the Political Theory Sunday Night Group at the University of Chicago. All were enthusiastic in their engagement with this book in earlier incarnations, ruthless in their criticisms of it, as well as faithful in prodding me to bring the various versions of it to completion.

Other scholars whose help with the manuscript as a whole has proven indispensable over the years include Richard J. Bernstein, Carl Caldwell, David Dyzenhaus, Michael Geyer, Charles Larmore, George Schwab, Tracy Strong, Leo Walsh, and Richard Wolin. Specific portions of the manuscript have benefited markedly from the critical attention of Susan Buck-Morss, Renato Cristi, Adam Daniel, Gary Herrigel, Ellen Kennedy, Matthias Konzett, Reinhart Koselleck, Pasquale Pasquino, Lloyd Rudolph, Susanne Hoeber Rudolph, Bill Scheuerman, and Gary Ulmen. The final manuscript has been drastically improved by the diligent, creative, and always expedient editorial and production efforts of

Terence Moore, Andrew Roney, Gwen Seznec, and Lisa Lincoln of Cambridge University Press, as well as the copyediting work of Carol Roberts. The shortcomings that remain in the finished product are of course my own responsibility.

Without the financial support of the following institutions, I would have been able to complete this manuscript in neither a moderately timely nor a tolerably competent manner: The Mellon Foundation and the Division of the Social Sciences and the Department of Political Science of the University of Chicago provided generous dissertation funding; the William J. Fulbright Foundation provided a grant to conduct research in Germany at the University of Bremen during 1994–95; and the European University Institute awarded me a Jean Monnet postdoctoral fellowship to reside in Florence, Italy, during 1995–96.

Moreover, I thank the many scholars in Europe at the time of my stay who improved this project by reading and commenting on its chapters, by discussing its contents, by providing public forums for it at their institutions, or by simply offering friendship and community to a scholar abroad: Perry Anderson, Marina Calloni, Dario Castiglione, Richard Dienst, Klaus Eder, Michelle Everson, Andrea Gavriel, Christian Joerges, Christian Joppke, Axel Honneth, Stephan Leibfried, Steven Lukes, Ingeborg Maus, Reinhard Mehring, Jo McKendry, Peter Niesen, Claus Offe, Gianfranco Poggi, Ulrich Preuß, Peggy Somers, Yasemin Soysal, John Torpey, and Bruce Western.

I must also express my gratitude to the late Michael Harrington for first impressing on me how essential German philosophy could be for understanding political power, historical change, and social justice in modernity.

To Gia Pascarelli I owe a special acknowledgment for all the support – emotional, intellectual, and otherwise – that she has afforded me over the years as a friend, a spouse, a partner, a colleague, and in so many other capacities for which, fortunately, there do not exist categories. Simply, thank you.

This book is dedicated to my parents, who encouraged me unconditionally in this as in all endeavors.

Permission to reprint the following is gratefully acknowledged: An earlier version of Chapter 2 appeared in *Philosophy and Social Criticism* 21: 4 (Copyright © 1995 by Sage Publications); parts of Chapter 3 appeared in the *Canadian Journal of Law and Jurisprudence* 10: 1 (Copyright © 1996, Faculty of Law, University of Western Ontario); and parts of Chapter 6 appeared in *Political Theory* 22: 4 (Copyright © 1994 by Sage Publications).

ABBREVIATIONS

Listed below are abbreviations of the works by Carl Schmitt most frequently cited in this study.* The publication dates of the original German editions appear in brackets.

N   *Theodor Däublers "Nordlicht": Drei Studien über die Elemente, den Geist und die Aktualität des Werkes* ([1916] Berlin: Duncker & Humblot, 1991).

PR   *Political Romanticism,* trans. Guy Oakes ([1919] Cambridge, Mass.: MIT Press, 1986).

D   *Die Diktatur: Von den Anfängen des modernen Souveränitätsgedankens bis zum proletarischen Klassenkampf* ([1921] Berlin: Duncker & Humblot, 1989).

PT   *Political Theology: Four Chapters on the Theory of Sovereignty,* trans. George Schwab ([1922] Cambridge, Mass.: MIT Press, 1986).

RC   *Roman Catholicism and Political Form,* trans. G. L. Ulmen ([1923] Westport: Greenwood Press, 1996).

P   *The Crisis of Parliamentary Democracy,* trans. Ellen Kennedy ([1923] Cambridge, Mass.: MIT Press, 1986).

V   *Verfassungslehre* ([1928] Berlin: Duncker & Humblot, 1989).

*Works by other authors that may be abbreviated in the study are listed in the notes of the particular chapters.

ND   "The Age of Neutralizations and Depoliticizations" (1929), trans. Matthias Konzett and John P. McCormick, *Telos* 96 (summer 1993).

CP   *The Concept of the Political*, trans. George Schwab ([1932] New Brunswick: Rutgers University Press, 1976).

LL   *Legalität und Legitimität* (1932), in *Verfassungsrechtliche Aufsätze aus den Jahren 1924–1954: Materialien zu einer Verfassungslehre* (Berlin: Duncker & Humblot, 1958).

L   *The Leviathan in the State Theory of Thomas Hobbes: Meaning and Failure of a Political Symbol*, trans. George Schwab and Erna Hilfstein ([1938] Westport: Greenwood Press, 1996).

PJ   "The Plight of European Jurisprudence" (1943/44), trans. G. L. Ulmen, *Telos* 83 (spring 1990).

INTRODUCTION

Over the last decade, there has been a veritable explosion of Anglo-American interest in the works of Weimar constitutional and political theorist, Carl Schmitt.[1] Even before joining the National Socialist party in 1933,

---

1 Recent full-length studies on Schmitt include the reissue of George Schwab's *Challenge of The Exception: An Introduction to the Political Ideas of Carl Schmitt between 1921 and 1936* (Westport: Greenwood, 1989); Schmitt's intellectual-political biography by Joseph Bendersky, *Carl Schmitt: Theorist for the Reich* (Princeton: Princeton University Press, 1983); as well as Paul Edward Gottfried's *Carl Schmitt: Politics and Theory* (Westport: Greenwood, 1990). Perhaps surprisingly, it has been scholars on the Left who have been the most active in promoting Schmitt in the English-speaking world. The journal *Telos* devoted a whole issue to Schmitt (no. 72, summer 1987) and regularly publishes translations of, and commentaries on, his work by G. L. Ulmen. The following monographs by veterans of the new Left also confront Schmitt's work seriously: Jean Cohen and Andrew Arato, *Civil Society and Political Theory* (Cambridge, Mass.: MIT Press, 1992); Paul Hirst, *Law, Socialism and Democracy* (London: Routledge, 1986); and Chantal Mouffe, *The Return of the Political* (London: Verso, 1993). Jürgen Habermas, Stephen Holmes, and Richard Wolin, on the other hand, express dismay over, and advise caution toward, this new enthusiasm for Schmitt. See Habermas, "The Horrors of Autonomy," in *The New Conservatism: Cultural Criticism and the Historians' Debate,* trans. Shierry Weber Nicholsen (Cambridge, Mass.: MIT Press, 1989); Holmes, "The Scourge of Liberalism," *The New Republic* 199 (August 22, 1988); and Wolin, "Carl Schmitt, Political Existentialism and the Total State," in *The Terms of Cultural Criticism: The Frankfurt School, Existentialism, Poststructuralism* (New York: Columbia University Press, 1992). For a critical survey of the recent literature on Schmitt, see Tracy B. Strong's "Foreword: Dimensions of the New Debate around Carl Schmitt," in the most recent edition of Schmitt's *Concept of the Political,* trans. George Schwab (Chicago: University of Chicago Press, 1996).

Schmitt launched incessant theoretical assaults against liberalism in the twenties and early thirties. He depicted the principles of pluralism, publicity, discussion, and representation; the practices of separation of powers, judicial review, and majoritarian elections; and such institutions as the Western European parliament as misguided and dangerous endeavors that ultimately only paralyze the modern state. Such principles and practices inhibit a state's ability to decide on the unavoidable question of friend and enemy, what he termed "the political,"[2] as well as leave it vulnerable to an unforeseen emergency, which he called the "exception."[3]

Almost concurrently there has been a revival in the treatment of technology as a subject worthy of social-philosophical inquiry. Attention is again being devoted to the theoretical and political implications of technology's seemingly ever-expanding role in contemporary Western postindustrial societies and to the arguments developed to address this issue in twentieth-century German theoretical traditions: recent efforts explicitly draw on Edmund Husserl and phenomenology, Martin Heidegger and existentialism, Georg Lukács and critical theory, as well as the thought of Hannah Arendt.[4]

Yet the two scholarly movements have surprisingly passed each other by. Surprisingly because, as I will demonstrate, the German critique of technology is crucial for understanding the works of Carl Schmitt, especially his criticisms of liberalism. Vice versa, theoretical confrontations with technology, often dismissed as excessively abstract, overly metaphysical, or hopelessly "mystical," might benefit in certain ways by observing how Schmitt incorporated a theoretical engagement with technology into practical-political treatises, as well as by witnessing how the issue of technology can be put to reactionary political ends at particular historical moments. In this way, the conjuncture of the critiques of liberalism and technology in Schmitt's writings may shed fresh light on the once again relevant problem

2 Carl Schmitt, *The Concept of the Political* (1932), trans. George Schwab (New Brunswick: Rutgers University Press, 1976), hereafter *CP*.
3 Carl Schmitt, *Political Theology: Four Chapters on the Concept of Sovereignty* (1922), trans. George Schwab (Cambridge, Mass.: MIT Press, 1985), p. 5; hereafter *PT*.
4 For a fair sample of this literature, consult the titles in *The Indiana Series in the Philosophy of Technology*, directed by Don Ihde, such as Michael E. Zimmerman, *Heidegger's Confrontation with Modernity: Technology, Politics, Art* (Bloomington: Indiana University Press, 1990); and Andrew Feenberg and Alastair Hannay, eds., *Technology and the Politics of Knowledge* (Bloomington: Indiana University Press, 1995). Not in this series but also of note are Andrew Feenberg, *Critical Theory of Technology* (Oxford: Oxford University Press, 1991); Roger Fellows, ed., *Philosophy and Technology* (Cambridge: Cambridge University Press, 1995); David J. Hess, *Science and Technology in a Multicultural World: The Cultural Politics of Facts and Artifacts* (New York: Columbia University Press, 1995); and Bruno Latour, *Aramis, or the Love of Technology* (Cambridge, Mass.: Harvard University Press, 1996).

of "technocracy" in liberal democratic regimes and the potential for authoritarianism that is latent within it.[5] Why does technology become the object
of political-philosophical contestation during times of structural socioeconomic change, such as that of Weimar Germany and our own as well? How
does technology become a rallying cry for both right- and left-wing intellectuals during such moments?[6] What are the continuities between that earlier
moment's ideological debates and those of our own, especially the often-
unacknowledged relationship between interwar German fascism and postwar American "conservatism?" Is there cause for alarm in the fact that
Schmitt's work has been revived simultaneously with a reemergence of the
kind of right-wing political activity that Schmitt himself endorsed? These
are some of the questions I address in this study of Schmitt, liberalism, and
technology.

   Schmitt's Weimar works are rightly viewed as some of the most stunning
critiques of liberalism and parliamentary democracy ever penned and certainly deserve the aforementioned scholarly attention that they have received in North America, however late. Yet, although this scholarship does
indeed concentrate on such themes as Schmitt's famous "friend/enemy"
distinction, his fascination with the political "exception," and his claim that
liberalism is incapable of successfully realizing substantive democracy, by
neglecting the technology question in Schmitt's thought, this scholarship
has not completely examined the theoretical grounds for such arguments
and has consequently missed, to some extent, the fuller implications of
Schmitt's critique. For instance, Chantal Mouffe recognizes that Schmitt
criticizes the institutions of "liberal parliamentary democracy" as "mere in-

---

5   The chief example of how the technological determinism of orthodox Marxism was appro-
    priated in the seventies to justify the revival of traditional values by "neoconservatism" is the
    work of Daniel Bell: see *The Coming of Post-Industrial Society* (New York: Basic Books, 1972);
    and *The Cultural Contradictions of Capitalism* (New York: Basic Books, 1978). The attempt to
    impose a cultural asceticism by appeals to supposedly irresistible technological imperatives
    is quite dominant today. For a lucid and now classic account of how state functioning in
    Western mass democracies has become increasingly governed by the questions of efficiency
    and control at the expense of the normative principles of democratic accountability – a
    description that does *not* lapse into neoconservative excess – see Claus Offe, *Contradictions of
    the Welfare State,* ed. John Keane (Cambridge, Mass.: MIT Press, 1984). See also the more
    recent book by Carol J. Hager, *Technological Democracy: Bureaucracy and Citizenry in the German
    Energy Debate* (Ann Arbor: University of Michigan Press, 1995).
6   For an early sociohistorical analysis of such questions, see Charles Maier, "Between Taylor-
    ism and Technocracy: European Ideologies and the Vision of Industrial Productivity in the
    1920s," *Journal of Contemporary History* 5 (1970); and for a more recent socio-aesthetic one,
    see the essays contained in Andreas Huyssen, *After the Great Divide: Modernism, Mass Culture,
    Postmodernism* (Bloomington: Indiana University Press, 1986).

strumental techniques"; Ellen Kennedy declares that "the dilemma of modern jurisprudence in Schmitt's thinking is a result of its place between theology and technology"; Joseph Cropsey observes that in Schmitt's worldview, "Liberalism is . . . complicitous with communism in standing for the withering away of the political and replacing it with the technological"; and Keith Tribe observes that for Schmitt politics is "not simply a product of political machinery."[7] Yet despite illuminating other important aspects of Schmitt's thought, these scholars, like most others, neglect to sufficiently follow through on these observations.[8] As already mentioned, the literature dealing with twentieth-century German perspectives on technology has done little to fill this void.[9]

My claim is that Schmitt's critique of liberalism – particularly as it is directed at modern parliamentarism and constitutional law – is based on a broader criticism of modern thought that he sees as having been infiltrated by the technological, which he often equates with the economic and the positivistic. Therefore, the criticisms of liberalism in such influential Weimar works as *The Concept of the Political, Political Theology, Parlamentarismus,* and *Verfassungslehre,*[10] are extensions, or even applications, of the more general criticisms of modernity put forth most powerfully in such less-discussed works as *Political Romanticism, Roman Catholicism and Political Form,* "The Age of Neutralizations and Depoliticizations," and *Theodor Däubler's "Northern Lights."*[11] Thus, to appreciate fully Schmitt's enterprise, one needs

7   Mouffe, *The Return of the Political,* p. 120. Kennedy, "Carl Schmitt and the Frankfurt School," *Telos* 71 (spring 1987): 41. Cropsey, foreword to Heinrich Meier, *Carl Schmitt and Leo Strauss: The Hidden Dialogue,* trans. J. Harvey Lomax (Chicago: University of Chicago Press, 1995), p. x. Tribe, introduction to *Social Democracy and the Rule of Law: Otto Kirchheimer and Franz Neumann,* ed. Keith Tribe (London: Unwin & Allen, 1987), p. 10.

8   Jerry Z. Muller and Richard Wolin, on the other hand, present Schmitt as a rather unmitigated *advocate* of technology: see Muller, "Carl Schmitt, Hans Freyer and the Radical Conservative Critique of Liberal Democracy in the Weimar Republic," *History of Political Thought* 12:4 (winter 1991); and Wolin, "Carl Schmitt, the Conservative Revolutionary: Habitus and the Aesthetics of Horror," *Political Theory* 20:3 (August 1992).

9   There is little mention of Schmitt at all in the philosophy of technology literature except for Jeffrey Herf's *Reactionary Modernism: Technology, Culture and Politics in Weimar and the Third Reich* (Cambridge: Cambridge University Press, 1984), which relies too heavily on the misinterpretation of Schmitt's attitude toward technology put forth by Karl Heinz Bohrer in the otherwise excellent *Die Aesthetik des Schreckens: Die pessimistische Romantik und Ernst Jüngers Frühwerk* (Munich: Carl Hanser, 1978).

10 *CP* and *PT;* Carl Schmitt, *The Crisis of Parliamentary Democracy* (1923), trans. Ellen Kennedy (Cambridge, Mass.: MIT Press, 1985), hereafter *P;* Carl Schmitt, *Verfassungslehre* ([1928] Berlin: Duncker & Humblot, 1989), hereafter *V.*

11 Carl Schmitt, *Political Romanticism* (1919), trans. Guy Oakes (Cambridge, Mass.: MIT Press, 1985), hereafter *PR; Roman Catholicism and Political Form* (1923), trans. G. L. Ulmen

to see more clearly – in total, and beyond mere apology and polemic – what it is that Schmitt is actually trying to refute and combat.

Title and Methodology

The title of this book is somewhat deceiving. In the first place, it potentially misleads with regard to the exact status of technology within Schmitt's thought. The German language has several words that may all, to some degree or another, be accurately translated as "technology": *Technik, Technizität,* and *Technologie.* Early in his career, Schmitt employed the first two terms more or less interchangeably but later differentiated between the two, eventually criticizing the second, *technicity,* more intensely than the first, *technology.* I will elaborate on the significance of these distinctions at length in the book, especially in Chapters 1 and 2.[12] What will become clear is that for Schmitt technology is something much more than the commonplace notion of "applied science."

My title might also lead one to believe that liberalism is Schmitt's chief or sole intellectual-political nemesis, when in fact this may not be so. Socialism, domestically manifested in revolutionary and reformist parties and externally manifested in the Soviet Union, is the political ideology that clearly most rouses Schmitt's ire. However, the fact that to Schmitt's mind liberalism as a hegemonic political theory and as a ruling political order in the Weimar Republic weakened Germany's position vis-à-vis socialism internally and internationally indeed made liberalism an unavoidable object of his

---

(Westport: Greenwood, 1996), hereafter *RC;* "The Age of Neutralizations and Depoliticizations" (1929), trans. Matthias Konzett and John P. McCormick, *Telos* 96 (summer 1993), hereafter *ND; Theodor Däublers "Nordlicht": Drei Studien über die Elemente, den Geist und die Aktualität des Werkes* ([1916] Berlin: Duncker & Humblot, 1991), hereafter *N.*

12   Here it can be said that the distinction between *Technik* and *Technizität* for Schmitt corresponds fairly closely to the differentiation discerned by R. L. Rutsky in an analysis of Weimar dispositions towards technology: the former, "a rationalist, functionalist notion of technology" and the latter, "a notion that emphasizes the irrational, chaotic, and even the destructive aspects of technology, that sees it as a dynamic, shocking, almost libidinal force." Rutsky, "The Mediation of Technology and Gender: *Metropolis,* Nazism, Modernism," *New German Critique* 60 (fall 1993). Miriam Hansen and Reiner Schürmann helpfully explicate the use of terms pertaining to technology in the work of two representatives of the intellectual traditions between which I seek to situate Schmitt as a procedural point of departure – T. W. Adorno and Martin Heidegger, respectively: see Hansen, "Introduction to Adorno's 'Transparencies on Film' (1966)," *New German Critique* 24–5 (fall/winter 1981–2); and Schürmann, "Technicity, Topology, Tragedy: Heidegger on 'That Which Saves' in the Global Reach," in *Technology in the Western Political Tradition,* ed. A. M. Melzer, J. Weinberger, and M. R. Zinman (Ithaca, N.Y.: Cornell University Press, 1993).

critical attention. Moreover, because it is liberalism that stands "victorious" over state socialism today, it is this aspect of Schmitt's project that is my principle focus.

I do however believe that my title, *Carl Schmitt's Critique of Liberalism: Against Politics as Technology,* specifies certain crucial aspects of Schmitt's thought that I wish to emphasize in this study. The oppositional preposition "against" reflects the confrontational quality of the theorist of the friend/enemy distinction. "Politics" has a special connotation for the theorist of "the political," which in Schmitt's sense implies the ever-present possibility of conflict that modern "technology," as a supposedly neutral force, attempts to suppress. As I will show, Schmitt explicitly equates liberalism – that is, governmentally, the constitutional and institutional guarantee of limited government and individual rights; culturally, the emphasis on compromise over conflict, and the individual over the group – with this neutralizing technical force. I do not use "critique" in the sense of mere criticism but rather in the philosophically dialectical sense of analyzing something from within its own categories, such that the rational core of the object of investigation is preserved. As I hope to show, Schmitt's critique of liberalism does indeed indicate elements that are potentially problematic with the theory and practice of liberalism, *as well as* that which ought to be preserved from liberalism in changing historical contexts. This last fact will come as a surprise to many, as it certainly would have to Schmitt himself. Furthermore, my own critique of Schmitt will indicate not only the elements of his theory that are not adequate to modern democratic theory but also that which is worth taking seriously in his thought. In my estimation, the North American reception of Schmitt's work has been too often characterized by an insufficiently theorized staking of positions. Schmitt is either denounced almost out of hand from a liberal or neoleftist standpoint[13] or positively appropriated perhaps a bit too unreflectively for a leftist or rightist political agenda.[14]

In the course of this study, it will often appear as though I merely recon-

13 See Martin Jay, "Reconciling the Irreconcilable?" *Telos* 71 (spring 1987); and Jeffrey Herf's contribution to "Reading and Misreading Schmitt: An Exchange," *Telos* 74 (winter 1987–8).

14 The editors of the journal *Telos* draw on Schmitt to fill the apparent lacunae in the state theory of the Frankfurt School tradition of critical theory, and Chantal Mouffe deploys Schmitt in a poststructuralist critique of liberalism in *The Return of the Political.* See Richard Bellamy and Peter Baehr, "Carl Schmitt and the Contradictions of Liberal Democracy," *European Journal of Political Research* 23 (February 1993) for a left-liberal use of Schmitt. The major effort to revive Schmitt for a contemporary right-wing theoretical orientation is Gottfried's *Carl Schmitt: Politics and Theory.*

struct Schmitt's arguments in relatively mute agreement. However, I actually hope to allow Schmitt's theoretical categories to emerge themselves through my textual explication so that I may criticize him more fundamentally by negating these categories against each other further along in my analysis. I choose not to "refute" him from an a priori liberal or leftist standpoint that holds him up to some external ideals to which he never held himself. I hope to avoid such a potentially artificial method of critique that unfortunately characterizes most of the literature on Schmitt by proceeding more immanently to his theory – even if initially risking the perception that I stand in silent agreement with all that he claims, often fantastically. By the conclusion of each chapter, I hope to have shown how one can better criticize Schmitt by reading him against himself, rather than by holding him up to, for instance, a Kantian standard derived from either of its currently predominant Rawlsian or Habermasian varieties. However, this does not mean that I will fail to hold Schmitt accountable for the many distortions and misrepresentations of the Enlightenment tradition to which he so often resorts in his writings. On the contrary, there is much to be learned from such misreadings; however, they will not be the major source of my criticisms of Schmitt.

So much of political theory of the last twenty years – particularly that associated with the question of liberalism – has followed a by-now-tired course: One inevitably turns to *A Theory of Justice*[15] and either proceeds to employ it as a yardstick by which to measure a liberal-challenging alternative or, conversely, holds Rawls's political philosophy up to some other standard so as to judge liberalism's adequacy for that particular agenda (e.g., Aristotelianism, communitarianism, perfectionism, utilitarianism, neoconservatism, feminism, environmentalism).[16] Again, this is not the mode of procedure of this project. I will not be comparing and contrasting Schmitt's theory with that of any liberals to whom he did not explicitly compare himself in the hope of demonstrating the respective advantages and deficiencies on each side. Rather, I attempt to carefully read Schmitt's Weimar texts in light of the many kinds of thinkers from his "context," broadly defined, to help demonstrate the fuller ramifications of his thought for the relationship between

15 John Rawls, *A Theory of Justice* (Cambridge, Mass.: Harvard University Press, 1971).
16 Robert Nozick began this trend with *Anarchy, State, and Utopia* (New York: Basic Books, 1974), after which followed countless "critiques" of "Rawlsian" liberalism. It should be noted here that Mouffe and David Dyzenhaus undertake challenging theoretical juxtapositions of Schmitt and Rawls; see Mouffe, *The Return of the Political;* and Dyzenhaus, "Liberalism after the Fall: Schmitt, Rawls and the Problem of Justification," *Philosophy and Social Criticism* 22:3 (1996).

technology and liberalism, technocracy and fascism.[17] Most often I read
Schmitt in light of his Weimar contemporaries, liberals like Hans Kelsen, as
well as others on the Left and the Right, including Georg Lukács, Martin
Heidegger, T. W. Adorno, and Walter Benjamin, or intellectual figures from
a previous era whose influence still resonated in Weimar, such as Karl Marx
and Friedrich Nietzsche. Sometimes I read Schmitt in light of his own
curiously self-understood "contemporaries" from earlier ages, such as
Niccolò Machiavelli and Thomas Hobbes. Throughout the work, however, I
make constant reference to a figure who had perhaps the most profound
influence on Schmitt and to whom Schmitt referred as that "German professor of liberal provenance," Max Weber (*RC*, 5).[18] I hope that what might
superficially appear as a rather cluttered collection of cross-readings will be
theoretically justified by what follows in the study and that it will help bring

17   In this way I hope that the study will serve as what Axel Honneth calls "a history of theory
with systematic intent"; see Honneth, *The Critique of Power: Reflective Stages in a Critical Social
Theory*, trans. Kenneth Baynes (Cambridge, Mass.: MIT Press, 1991), p. xiii. Of course I do
not wish to emphasize *intellectual* context to the exclusion of *social* context. Among the
major historical works consulted in the research of this study are David Blackbourn and
Geoff Eley, *The Peculiarities of German History: Bourgeois Society and Politics in Nineteenth-
Century Germany* (Oxford: Oxford University Press, 1984); Karl Dietrich Bracher, *Die
Auflösung der Weimarer Republik: Eine Studie zum Problem des Machtverfalls in der Demokratie*
(Düsseldorf: Droste, 1984); Gordon A. Craig, *Germany, 1866–1945* (Oxford: Oxford
University Press, 1980); Geoff Eley, *Reshaping the German Right: Radical Nationalism and
Political Change after Bismarck* (New Haven: Yale University Press, 1980); Charles S. Maier,
*Recasting Bourgeois Europe: Stabilization in France, Germany, and Italy in the Decade after World
War I* (Princeton: Princeton University Press, 1975); Charles S. Maier, *The Unmasterable
Past: History, Holocaust and German Identity* (Cambridge, Mass.: Harvard University Press,
1988); Heinrich August Winkler, *Weimar 1918–1933: Die Geschichte der Ersten Deutschen
Demokratie* (Munich: C. H. Beck, 1994); Geoff Eley, ed., *Society, Culture, and the State in
Germany, 1870–1930* (Ann Arbor: University of Michigan Press, 1996); Hans Mommsen,
The Rise and Decline of Weimar Democracy (Chapel Hill: University of North Carolina Press,
1996); and especially Detlev Peukert, *The Weimar Republic: The Crisis of Classical Modernity*,
trans. Richard Deveson (New York: Hill & Wang, 1992).

18   For examinations of the issue of Weber's liberalism, see David Beetham, "Weber and the
Liberal Tradition," and Tracy Strong, "Max Weber and the Bourgeoisie," both in *The
Barbarism of Reason: Max Weber and the Twilight of Enlightenment*, ed. A. Horowitz and T.
Maley (Toronto: University of Toronto Press, 1994). The work of Stephen Holmes, which
has had a profound impact on this book, perhaps best exemplifies a contemporary
"Weberian" liberalism: Holmes prioritizes as a central task of liberal politics the contain-
ment and redirection of the multifarious expressions of human irrationality, in *Passions
and Constraint: On the Theory of Liberal Democracy* (Chicago: University of Chicago Press,
1995), and he ruthlessly assails romantically inclined critics of liberalism and the Enlightenment whom he identifies as dangerous expressions of this irrationality, in *The Anatomy of
Antiliberalism* (Cambridge, MA: Harvard University Press, 1993). These are aspects of
Weber's political orientation and Schmitt's reception of them that will be discussed and
criticized in the course of this book.

to the fore the issues of technology and politics more provocatively than a crude comparison and contrast of Schmittianism and liberalism.[19]

The late *Kaiserreich* and the Weimar Republic itself were characterized intellectually by a divide between forms of neo-Kantianism and strands of what can be identified for heuristic purposes as kinds of neo-Nietzschean *Lebensphilosophie.* There was the abstract concern with normative formalism, on the one hand, and with existential substance as such – that is, positivism versus existentialism – on the other. The two poles can be interpreted as reactions to a changing political and socioeconomic situation from the laissez-faire arrangement of state and society of the nineteenth century to the state-interventionist scenario of the early twentieth, in which technology was perceived in varying ways as the agent of change.[20] This scenario should not sound altogether unfamiliar to students of the political philosophy, social theory, and intellectual history of the last twenty-five years in North America and Europe. In the midst of a present transformation from a welfare-state configuration to what has been variously described as a postindustrial, post-Fordist, flexible accumulation, or economically globalized configuration, in which technology has again been assigned a central role,[21]

---

19 Recently published or forthcoming monographs that situate Schmitt within the broader context of other Weimar constitutional lawyers, such as Kelsen, Hermann Heller, Otto Kirchheimer, Franz Neumann, Rudolph Smend, and Richard Thoma, are Peter C. Caldwell, *Popular Sovereignty and the Crisis of German Constitutional Law: The Theory and Practice of Weimar Constitutionalism* (Durham, N.C.: Duke University Press, 1997); David Dyzenhaus, *Truth's Revenge: Carl Schmitt, Hans Kelsen and Hermann Heller in Weimar* (Oxford: Oxford University Press, 1997); and William E. Scheuerman, *Between the Norm and the Exception: The Frankfurt School and the Rule of Law* (Cambridge, Mass.: MIT Press, 1994). See also, Arthur J. Jacobson and Bernhard Schlink, eds., *Weimar: A Jurisprudence of Crisis* (Berkeley: University of California Press, 1998).

20 For one of the most profound accounts of this shift, see Jürgen Habermas, *The Structural Transformation of the Public Sphere,* trans. T. Burger with the assistance of F. Lawrence (Cambridge, Mass.: MIT Press, 1989).

21 As just a small sampling of the literatures on post-Fordism, multilateralism, internationalization, and, most fashionably, globalization, see Michael Piore and Charles Sabel, *The Second Industrial Divide: Possibilities for Prosperity* (New York: Basic Books, 1984); Scott Lash and John Urry, *The End of Organized Capitalism* (Madison: University of Wisconsin Press, 1987); Alain Lipietz, *Towards a New Economic Order: Postfordism, Ecology and Democracy* (New York: Oxford University Press, 1992); John Gerard Ruggie, ed., *Multilateralism Matters: The Theory and Praxis of an Institutional Form* (New York: Columbia University Press, 1993); Ash Amin, ed., *Post-Fordism: A Reader* (Cambridge, Mass.: Blackwell, 1994); and Robert O. Keohane and Helen V. Miller, eds., *Internationalization and Domestic Politics* (Cambridge: Cambridge University Press, 1996). A recent grappling with the broader intellectual ramifications of these changes is Moishe Postone, "Contemporary Historical Transformations: Some Theoretical Considerations," unpublished manuscript, Department of History, University of Chicago (1995).

we have likewise witnessed a revival of Kantian normative theory in the political liberalism of Rawls and the communicative social democracy of Habermas, as well as a resurgence of Nietzsche- or even Heidegger-inspired neoexistentialism in the form of the deconstruction and postmodernism of Jacques Derrida, Michel Foucault, and many of their devotees.

Besides ossifying these two intellectual antinomies, the first industrial transformation in this century also opened up the opportunity for Hegel-derived theoretical attempts that did not merely opt for one of the opposing Kantian/Nietzschean poles of the changing dynamic but rather sought to mediate the two antitheses and embed them within the historical transformation itself and understand the technological change for neither the irresistible "iron cage" of bureaucratic rationalization or abstract normative imperatives, nor the opportunity for expressing a concrete primordial will – the extremes expressed by the two formerly mentioned modes of thinking.[22] It is my hope that an analysis of a central figure of that initial transformation in its German context, Carl Schmitt, and the place of technology in his thought, will aid in the ever more pressing theoretical apprehension of the scope and ramifications of the present technological, intellectual, and political change, including the possibility for progressive democratic practice as well as the danger of reactionary, authoritarian regression.[23]

Carl Schmitt, rivaled perhaps only by Martin Heidegger, is commonly understood as the representative par excellence of one wing of the dualities just mentioned: Nietzschean existentialism or *Lebensphilosophie* and the will-driven project to seize technology in a supernationalistic reactionary project. This is not an altogether inaccurate characterization, but it is certainly a rather undifferentiated account of Schmitt's theoretical efforts. I attempt to show that Schmitt quite often simultaneously sought the route of a Hegelian mediation of the intellectual poles of modernity and their relationship with technology, alongside the more commonly acknowledged

22 The left-Hegelianism of Lukács and his "Western Marxist" heirs are perhaps the best representatives of this methodology that sought to overcome the Kantian/Nietzschean divide. For excellent general accounts, see David Held, *Introduction to Critical Theory: Horkheimer to Habermas* (Berkeley: University of California Press, 1980); Martin Jay, *Marxism and Totality: The Adventures of a Concept from Lukács to Habermas* (Berkeley: University of California Press, 1984), and Raymond Geuss, *The Idea of a Critical Theory: Habermas and the Frankfurt School* (Cambridge: Cambridge University Press, 1981).

23 Two accounts of left-Hegelian methodology that preserve its viability as a contemporary theoretical-political orientation are Robert B. Pippin, *Hegel's Idealism: The Satisfactions of Self-Consciousness* (Cambridge: Cambridge University Press, 1989); and Moishe Postone, *Time, Labor and Social Domination: A Reinterpretation of Marx's Critical Theory* (Cambridge: Cambridge University Press, 1993).

Nietzschean thrusts of his work. I explore both of these moments of his thought to demonstrate the highly complicated road to fascism taken by one of interwar Europe's most brilliant intellectuals. My motive in doing so is not by any means to resuscitate Schmitt (a charge that those who turn their attention to Schmitt must face from the many who polemicize against the theorist). Rather I hope to demonstrate the sophistication of his authoritarianism, so that the stereotyped picture of it afforded us by the Cold War era (and its general treatment of fascism as conquered past or repressed memory) will enable us to recognize this phenomenon in its already-reemerging form in the current transformations around the world, including Europe *and* the United States.[24] To be sure, many of the specificities of contemporary regressive responses to structural transformation and technological change will necessarily differ from those of the initial one in this century, the current transformation of the role of the state itself, after all, differs qualitatively from the first in its extranational as opposed to intranational character (e.g., international multilateralism vs. nation-state Fordism).[25] But there will certainly be important similarities just as there were among fascism and its earlier, exclusively modern, authoritarian godfathers: early-modern absolutism and nineteenth-century Bonapartism, movements for which Schmitt more frequently and explicitly expressed admiration than he did for fascism, at least during the life of the Weimar Republic.[26]

Liberalism and Fascism – Or, Why Carl Schmitt?

In the postwar era, Schmitt's writings have often been segregated into well-defined categories, such as "reactionary modernism," "decisionism," "revolutionary conservatism," or "counter-Enlightenment thinking."[27] This strat-

---

24 Several recent reevaluations of fascism that are inspired by contemporary trends include Peter Baldwin, "Social Interpretations of Nazism: Renewing a Tradition," *Journal of Contemporary History* 25 (1990); Roberto Vivarelli, "Interpretations of the Origins of Fascism," *Journal of Modern History* 63 (March 1991); Roger Griffin, *The Nature of Fascism* (New York: St. Martin's Press, 1991); and Zeev Sternhell, *The Birth of Fascist Ideology*, trans. David Maisel (Princeton: Princeton University Press, 1994).

25 On this transition, especially see the essays contained in Amin, ed., *Post-Fordism;* Keohane and Miller, eds., *Internationalization and Domestic Politics;* and Ruggie, ed., *Multilateralism Matters.*

26 Schmitt was, however, known to speak well of Italian fascism. For an excellent study of the latter, see Mabel Berezin, *Communities of Feeling: Culture, Politics and Identity in Fascist Italy* (Ithaca, N.Y.: Cornell University Press, 1996).

27 See Jürgen Fijalkowski, *Die Wendung zum Führerstaat: Ideologische Komponenten in der politischen Philosophie Carl Schmitts* (Cologne: Westdeutscher, 1958); Christian Graf von Krockow, *Die Entscheidung: Eine Untersuchung über Ernst Jünger, Carl Schmitt, Martin Heidegger*

egy may serve to help upstanding, progressive intellectuals feel secure from
the threat and influence of the likes of this radical authoritarian and, further, may serve to superficially keep other realms of thought, such as liberalism or social democracy, sanitary from what is understandably perceived as
Schmitt's fetid influence.[28] But such a potentially coerced quarantine in
fact serves mostly to distort history. Fascism, as Schmitt and others theorized
it, drew on, and interacted with, many intellectual sources.[29] To deny this
with an attempt to pack Schmitt in a box affixed with a warning label and
indefinitely store him away will only yield further regressive outcomes. Such
a policy of containment toward fascism will prove – indeed has proven –
unsuccessful, a fact to which any halfway sensitive observation of the globe
today will attest. Fascism, as defined in the course of this study, has not been
locked away forever but rather lives on – not only in "developing" areas of
South America, Africa, and Eastern Europe, but elsewhere in Europe and in
the United States. Avoidance of, as well as the purely polemical lashing out
against, Carl Schmitt will only ensure that what is necessarily repressed in
such approaches will strike back with ever more forceful vengeance and will
possibly contribute to the reemergence of fascism in the nineties and
beyond.

Fascism is often understood as a phenomenon cordoned off historically
by the dates 1918 and 1945, and geographically by the territorial borders of
Germany and Italy (and perhaps Vichy France and Franco's Spain). Because
of these starkly drawn boundaries, it is generally considered scholastically
idiosyncratic, not to say also politically suspect, to undertake a study of a
subject like the work of Schmitt. But as the emerging political realities of the
nineties suggest, fascism has not been so successfully contained as the assertion of the temporal and geographical borders mentioned suggests: As
parliamentary institutions and practices reach an almost unparalleled low in

([1958] Frankfurt a. M.: Campus, 1990); George L. Mosse, *The Crisis of German Ideology:
Intellectual Origins of the Third Reich* (New York: Grosset & Dunlap, 1964); and most recently Herf, *Reactionary Modernism.* Bendersky justifiably criticizes the interpretive excesses
of this literature but in so doing goes too far in understating the radical nature of
Schmitt's thinking; see "Carl Schmitt and the Conservative Revolution," *Telos* 72 (summer
1987).

28 Liberal political theorist Charles Larmore, for instance, approximates an offhand
dismissal of Schmitt in "Carl Schmitt's Critique of Liberal Democracy," in *The Morals of
Modernity* (Cambridge: Cambridge University Press, 1996). After discussing only one of
Schmitt's works, *Parlamentarismus,* Larmore finds Schmitt's critique of liberalism "aston-
ishingly weak" and concludes that Schmitt's work does little more than affirm liberalism's
near invincibility (pp. 186, 188).

29 See the helpful source book edited by Roger Griffin, *Fascism* (Oxford: Oxford University
Press, 1996).

popular esteem in parts of the Northern Hemisphere; as mainstream politicians unashamedly suggest dismantling the separation of powers in the name of populism, efficiency, or both, irrespective of the potential damage to principles of rights; as social groups, whether self- or, more often, elite-defined in terms of the supposedly irreducible "concrete being" of ethnic, religious, or cultural identity compete for control of power apparatuses all over the world; as states, less and less sovereign in their authority over their citizens and borders, either abdicate responsibility or resort to more extreme measures of control in a world of economic globalization; as detainment camps once again mar the spiritual and physical landscape of Central Europe, and governments seek to "homogenize" their populations in the name of territorial "integrity"; as paramilitary groups increasingly threaten the state monopoly on violence in even the most advanced liberal-democratic industrial regimes, in this context Carl Schmitt becomes less the object of purely perverse interest. The "triumph" of liberalism over fascism in 1945, long taken for granted as fact, now must be thoroughly reconsidered in the wake of the former's recent "triumph" over communism.[30]

Indeed the relationship of liberalism to fascism may not ultimately prove to be one of two separate or even opposite entities, the latter conquering the former in Germany in 1933, only to be cast off with external aid by the former in 1945. As scholars affiliated with the Frankfurt Institute of Social Research had argued so brilliantly, in early essays that dealt explicitly with Schmitt, Heidegger, and other right-wing intellectuals,[31] there is a certain fluidity between liberalism, with its apparently insurmountable categorical contradictions, on the one hand, and the phenomenon of fascism, on the other, which may not be an altogether distinct alternative to liberalism, but which itself appears to be a product of, and solution to, liberalism's theoretical-practical impasses. This is illustrated by the Weimar thinking of Carl Schmitt that takes as its starting point the antinomies of Enlightenment

30 See Herbert Kitschelt and Anthony McGann, *The Radical Right in Western Europe: A Comparative Analysis* (Ann Arbor: University of Michigan Press, 1995); and Ulrich Wank, ed., *The Resurgence of Right-Wing Radicalism in Germany: New Forms of an Old Phenomenon?* (Atlantic Highlands, N.J.: Humanities Press, 1996).

31 See Herbert Marcuse, "The Struggle against Liberalism in the Totalitarian View of the State" (1934), reprinted in *Negations: Essays in Critical Theory,* trans. Jeremy Shapiro (Boston: Beacon Press, 1968); and Siegfried Kracauer, "Revolt of the Middle Classes" (1931), in *The Mass Ornament: Weimar Essays,* ed., T. Levin (Cambridge, Mass.: Harvard University Press, 1995). See also another classic critique of Schmitt recently made available to English-speaking audiences: Karl Löwith, "The Occasional Decisionism of Carl Schmitt," in *Heidegger and European Nihilism,* trans. Gary Steiner (New York: Columbia University Press, 1995).

rationality in a new, twentieth-century, mass-democratic, welfare-state historical moment and seeks to negate the oppositional moments in liberal theory. But instead of moving beyond such dead ends, as is his professed
intention, Schmitt theologizes or mythologizes that which seems to have
been taken as far as it can go within the purview of "reason." Interestingly, as
we will see, Schmitt rarely claims that something wholly or externally
different from liberalism is necessitated by the present historical moment,
but rather he valorizes one of the results or outcomes of the "progressive"
movement of Enlightenment rationality so as to show that there is apparently no other alternative than his authoritarian one that has been spawned
by the very transformations of liberalism. Liberalism itself has brought us to
this point, and the conclusion is "self-evident." This argument and a methodology that cleverly and carefully ensures that Schmitt's fascist alternative
is inextricably bound with the particular moments of his critique of liberalism show not where liberalism and fascism are separated but where they are
conjoined – and the question of technology is absolutely central to this
conjunction. Along these lines, it is ultimately the tension between what
many commentators have identified as the liberal Hobbes and the absolutist
Hobbes[32] that proves to be the point of departure for Schmitt's most radical
Weimar phase.

The today shocking and, no doubt to some, scandalous assertion that
fascism was indeed a radicalization of liberalism arises out of the analysis of
the intersection of the two aforementioned intellectual-political poles. The
more generally familiar tracing out in the thought of Max Weber of the
technological determinism of neo-Kantian positivism as well as the exalting
of charismatically imbued political will associated with Nietzschean existentialism is an example of this kind of analysis. Another way to explicate this
subterranean relationship between liberalism and fascism would be to trace
the origins of the policy prescriptions of contemporary "neoliberal"
devotees of F. A. Hayek and Leo Strauss through the writings of those figures
to Schmitt. After such a genealogy, the assertion above might not seem so
utterly outrageous (see Chapter 6).[33]

A goal of this study, then, is to move beyond the apologetic and polemical
approaches to Schmitt that have dominated discussions of his work.[34] Al-

---

32 See, most recently, Jürgen Habermas, *Between Facts and Norms: Contributions to a Discourse
    Theory of Law and Democracy* (Cambridge, Mass.: MIT Press, 1996), p. 90.

33 On Hayek's debt to Schmitt, see Bill Scheuerman, "The Unholy Alliance of Carl Schmitt
    and Friedrich A. Hayek," *Constellations* 4:2 (October 1997); and Renato Cristi, "Hayek and
    Schmitt on the Rule of Law," *Canadian Journal of Political Science* 17:3 (1984).

34 Reinhard Mehring considers the status of these two interpretive poles in the recent

though the apologetic stance toward Schmitt has been intensely and extensively attacked in the literature, there are definite drawbacks to bald polemics as well. Sympathetic approaches to Schmitt's authoritarianism may
indeed encourage cynical appropriation of his thought for contemporary
"conservative" agendas.[35] But insufficiently theorized attacks may also aid in
an illegitimate rehabilitation and sanitizing of his dangerous positions.
Again, the lack of subtlety necessarily involved in polemicizing against
Schmitt's often quite nuanced and complicated theories may result in
caricatures of his positions that themselves invite the illegitimate resuscita-
tion of Schmitt by those who would point out misinterpretations simply in
the name of "clarity." Moreover, when critics resort to friend/enemy approaches in confronting the author of the "concept of the political," they
unwittingly draw themselves into adopting Schmitt's own pathological
methodology in an attempt to criticize him. By engaging such an opponent
on his own familiar terrain, who do they suppose will have the ultimate
advantage? The fact that North American academics in the nineties could
be so naive as to think they can emerge victorious from such a confrontation
with the cunning sage of modern tyranny suggests that the over-inflated self-
image of intellectual elites that proved disastrous in Schmitt's own Weimar
context persists today. If one wishes to ascertain the deficiencies of liberalism that still make fascism an immanent sociopolitical alternative, as well as
technology's central role in this dynamic, neither apologies nor polemics
with respect to Carl Schmitt will prove sufficient. Moral outrage toward
Schmitt the historical, intellectual, and political figure, and cautious suspi-
cion toward those who would devote attention to him is appropriate and
warranted – but not at the expense of theoretical rigor and textual fidelity.

German literature: "Raffinierter Meister des Anstößigen. Versuch jenseits von Apologie
und Polemik: Carl Schmitts Werk und seine Wirkung," *Die Welt* (May 21, 1994). Publications on Schmitt in German indeed abound, yet each decade seems to produce at least
one outstanding work; see Hasso Hofmann, *Legitimität gegen Legalität: Der Weg der politischen Philosophie Carl Schmitts* (Berlin: Hermann Luchterhand, 1964); Ingeborg Maus,
*Bürgerliche Rechtstheorie und Faschismus: Zur sozialen Funktion und aktuellen Wirkung der The-
orie Carl Schmitts* ([1976] Munich: C. H. Beck, 1980); and Mehring's own *Pathetisches
Denken. Carl Schmitts Denkweg am Leitfaden Hegels: Katholische Grundstellung und antimarx-
istische Hegelstrategie* (Berlin: Duncker & Humblot, 1989).

35   Schwab's *Challenge of the Exception* and Bendersky's *Carl Schmitt: Theorist for the Reich* are
     most frequently and violently criticized as apologetic, yet they do not in fact promote
     Schmitt for any particular political ideology. In contrast, as mentioned earlier, Gottfried's
     Carl Schmitt: Politics and Theory unabashedly incorporates Schmitt into a right-wing
     project – a project *so* conservative that Gottfried dismisses the prefix "neo" in his develop-
     ment of the notion of "*paleo*conservatism." See Paul Gottfried, *The Conservative Movement*
     (New York: Twayne, 1993).

Carl Schmitt: Critical Theorist of the Right?

Stephen Holmes detects a certain tension in Schmitt's writings: "Characteristic of Schmitt's artfully crafted prose is an unremitting oscillation between the cold and the feverish, the academic and the prophetic, the analytical and the mythical. . . . His books plait together sober theoretical observations with near-ecstatic political intimations. . . . [H]e can make even discussions of constitutional technicalities glow incandescently."[36] I would suggest that this tension between the analytic and the mythic runs deep in Schmitt's thought and is entwined inextricably with the issue of technology. As will become clearer in this summary of the project as a whole, Schmitt's work reflects a dualism that he himself attributes to modern thought – a dualism he initially attempts to surmount.

Schmitt often characterizes modernity as an apparent opposition between, on the one hand, the abstractly formal elements of science, technology, and economics and, on the other, a concretely content-oriented fascination that is expressed most notably in romanticism, that often manifests itself in neomythology. As we will see, he consistently points out this opposition, suggests that the two poles are in fact intrinsically related in a structural manner, and argues that any intellectual endeavor that privileges one over the other is only an inadequate "negation" of modernity and not a theoretical apprehension of it. Yet, as the quote from Holmes suggests, this tension between the analytically formal and the mythically substantive is maintained within Schmitt's own writings – maintained, that is, until he invariably exalts the latter aspect over the former one.

For instance, in *Roman Catholicism and Political Form* (1923), Schmitt rationally criticizes this ostensible opposition between the positivistic and the romantic in modernity – the abstractly formal and the substantively mythic – and yet in conclusion himself erupts into a call for mythic battle with the technoanarchic "enemy," the Soviet Union. In *Parlamentarismus* (1923), he follows an apparently neutral historical-analytical treatment of the principles of liberal parliamentary government with an arrestingly approving account of the new politics of "irrationality" promoted by Sorel, Bakunin, and Mussolini. In *Political Theology* (1922), in the midst of an

---

36 Holmes, "Schmitt: The Debility of Liberalism," in *The Anatomy of Antiliberalism*, p. 39. Others who have commented on this aspect of Schmitt's prose are Reinhard Mehring, *Carl Schmitt: Zur Einführung* (Hamburg: Junius, 1992); and Caldwell, *Popular Sovereignty and the Crisis of German Constitutional Law.*

attempt at mediating between pure jurisprudential formalism and pure decisionism – theories of the judge as "vending machine" versus the judge as sovereign legislator – Schmitt aestheticizes what at first is presented as an analytical category, the exception, into an occasion of almost divine will. In *The Concept of the Political* (1927) and its companion piece, "The Age of Neutralizations and Depoliticizations" (1929), after criticizing the modern, random, and theoretically ungrounded ascription of foundational meaning to various entities (the "individual," Catholicism, the French Revolution, economics, history, etc.) Schmitt, in just as theoretically unreflective a manner, "grounds" universal meaning in "the political," the transhistorically legitimated human propensity toward violent existential conflict. This tension between the rational and the mythical and Schmitt's consistent opting for the latter will be central to each of my chapters and runs as a common thread throughout the book.

In Part One, I entertain the notion that Schmitt be considered a critical theorist of sorts because of this theoretical sensitivity to intrinsically bound, structurally grounded oppositions in modernity that other exclusively existentialist or positivist thinkers choose to view separately as the positively or negatively valorized essence of modernity or as the very answer to the problems of modernity. But the lapsing into the irrational that consistently characterizes Schmitt's philosophy and the lack of emancipatory potential concomitant with this theoretical-political move effectively forecloses the viability of such a characterization.[37] Although Schmitt's stunted dialectics may allow for no democratic emancipation, my analysis of the *aporiai* of his initially promising approach will demonstrate further the relationship, of myth and rationality in modernity, the centrality of technology to that rela-

---

37 It is perhaps the close proximity of Schmitt's methodological orientation to that of members of the Frankfurt School and the vast abyss between his political orientation and their own that has provoked some rather strong reactions to his work by North American proponents of critical theory. Note the tenor of the response by Martin Jay to Ellen Kennedy's provocative, if perhaps somewhat overstated, "Carl Schmitt and the Frankfurt School." See also Richard Wolin, "Carl Schmitt, The Conservative Revolutionary"; and Bill Scheuerman, "Carl Schmitt and the Nazis," *German Politics and Society* 23 (summer 1991). However the subsequent turn to more objective treatments of Schmitt by both Wolin and Scheuerman bespeaks the necessity of this perspective's engaging him in a rigorous manner; see Scheuerman, "The Unholy Alliance of Carl Schmitt and Friedrich A. Hayek"; and Wolin's reworked version of "Carl Schmitt, the Conservative Revolutionary," as it appears in *Labyrinths: Explorations in the Critical History of Ideas* (Amherst: University of Massachusetts Press, 1995). An early exception in this literature was Cohen and Arato, *Civil Society and Political Theory*, which contains an illustrative and unbiased chapter on Schmitt, Reinhart Koselleck, and Jürgen Habermas.

tionship and the prospective and relative likelihood of liberal, fascist, or more substantively democratic political results.[38]

Project Overview

Part One attempts to ascertain exactly what technology is for Schmitt. I interpret his work from various stages of his Weimar career, drawing out his notion of technology by accentuating its affinities and oppositions with two sets of theoretical contemporaries, who might be somewhat vulgarly categorized as Nietzschean existentialists and Marxian critical theorists. Central to this part is Schmitt's reception of Weber's theory of rationalization, for it is in confrontation with this that Schmitt develops his theory of technology. Like Weber, who recognizes that the problem of technology does not lie essentially with the proliferation of machines as such, Schmitt sees technology as inherently linked with a way of thinking that he calls "economic-technical thought." This phenomenon is concerned primarily with the manipulation of matter, one that saps the world of meaning, and establishes the possibility for novel and harsher modes of domination. Schmitt holds these views in common with the more existentialist of his contemporaries, who view technology as an overly quantitative and abstract force that eradicates the concrete and qualitative particularities of human existence. However, as mentioned earlier, I will suggest that Schmitt has more in common on this issue with the critical theorists of his era who argue that this abstract and quantitative characteristic is only one side of modernity, and that modern technology also elicits a purely modern fixation on the qualitative and the particular. As I will demonstrate in Chapter 1, this eludes the existentialists as well as Schmitt's mentor, Weber. But again, Schmitt's recognition of this unreflective privileging of the concrete in Weber (e.g., the irreducible *will* behind the "warring gods" thesis of modernity), or in romanticism (e.g., the aesthetic enrapture with the "occasion"), does not prevent Schmitt himself from engaging in it. I show in Chapter 2 that his attempt to infuse the technologically disenchanted world with meaning through "the concept of the political" or the "friend/enemy" distinction (especially as expressed in a doctrine of cultural conflict versus

---

38 In *Pathetisches Denken*, Mehring also theoretically interrogates the rarely noticed dialectical methodology employed by Schmitt and emphasizes the anti-Marxian ends to which he put it. A recent work in the German literature on Schmitt that focuses on the role of technology in Schmitt's work is Thomas Vesting, *Politische Einheitsbildung und technische Realisation: Ueber die Expansion der Technik und die Grenzen der Demokratie* (Baden-Baden: Nomos, 1990).

Soviet Russia, or quasi-theological conflict against what emerges again and again in his writings on technology – the Antichrist) is Schmitt's own succumbing to the obfuscating dichotomies of the technological modernity he criticizes.

Part Two focuses more specifically on the relationship between technology and politics. Chapter 3 examines the issue of technology and emergency powers and takes up Schmitt's claim that a constitutional regime characterized by institutional diversity that does not have recourse to a constitutionally unimpeded executive agent is an overly technified complex that, as such, cannot withstand the challenge of a political exception. I compare Schmitt's *Die Diktatur,* in which he praises the Roman constitutionally *limited* practice of temporary dictatorship in time of crisis, with *Political Theology,* written only a year later in 1922, in which he advocates an all-powerful, potentially constitution-abrogating "sovereign" to confront the "exception." This strange, subtle, and rapid shift, for which I attempt to account, hinges on the question of technology. I demonstrate how in the earlier work Schmitt promotes Roman dictatorship precisely on technical grounds; he admires the fact that it is a purely technical means to a functionally specific end: the immediate emergency it is called forth to address. This "commissarial" dictatorship is a technique that restores a regular constitutional order that is itself something more than political technology. In the later work, Schmitt reverses his evaluations. The regular constitutional order is that which is deemed "mechanical," and the exception as well as the sovereign action that must deal with it are the quasi-charismatic phenomena that must restore substance to the wholly formal order.

Chapter 4 examines Schmitt's criticisms of liberal parliamentarism. His critique centers on the notion of representation that, according to Schmitt, has become more like mechanical reproduction in modernity, due to the influence of technology. Liberal representation re-presents in parliament *not* the democratic substance of the people but a quantitative replication of them in their number; the public forum necessary for representation in any meaningful sense is undermined by the technobureaucratic workings of closed committees and mass-party politics. I demonstrate how Schmitt tacitly employs the Catholic, quasi-medieval, "substantive" theory of representation that he explicates in *Roman Catholicism and Political Form* when denouncing modern parliamentary representation in *Parlamentarismus,* written later the same year, in 1923. Yet the political alternative suggested by his critique is not a revival of a neomedieval estatist notion of representation but rather the very modern notion of plebiscitarily legitimated executive rule, coupled with an endorsement of irrational, nationalist myth, at the conclusion of his quite rational analysis of parliamentarism in the book on that subject.

Chapter 5 deals with Schmitt's criticisms of liberal jurisprudence and constitutional law. For Schmitt, the rise of modern natural science and technology has infiltrated the law to the extent that gaps in statute law and exceptions in constitutional law have become ignored, with deleterious results for the state. Drawing on Weber's sociology of law and setting up Kelsen's legal positivism as his principle target, Schmitt argues in *Political Theology* that the commitment to a rationally scientific worldview that characterizes nature as a regularly functioning "system," and to a technology that seeks to violently enforce this regularity, eliminates the important role of judges, endangers regimes to what has not been constitutionally foreseen, and dissipates the power of modern sovereignty. Besides elaborating and assessing these claims, I also examine some of Schmitt's other constitutional works from the Republic to evaluate his strategy of denouncing the abstract legal ideology of the nineteenth century while seeking to coordinate the concrete socioeconomic reality of the twentieth century into a more "stable," that is, fascist, orientation.

Chapter 6 concerns Schmitt's appropriation of the central intellectual figure of early-modern European state building, Thomas Hobbes. I show how Schmitt and a young student of his named Leo Strauss undertake the project of reviving the Hobbesian theory of the state, but with important "emendations." To restore order to a German society on the brink of civil war in the late twenties and early thirties, Schmitt and Strauss revive the great seventeenth-century civil war theorist so as to refound the chaos-suspending and order-establishing Leviathan state. According to these scholars, Hobbes's theory encouraged people to accept the "protection for obedience" proposition at the base of the liberal state by guaranteeing them a subjective freedom that could be expressed in commerce and the scientific-technological development of civil society. This was a mistake, according to Schmitt and Strauss, because civil society, subsequently armed with the weapons of technology, comes to threaten the authority of the state itself. Schmitt and Strauss seek to replace the inducement of subjective and scientific freedom with another suggested by the Hobbesian theory: fear. And in order to instill this fear without relying too extensively on the technological apparatus that itself threatens the state, Schmitt endorses the revival of myth. The ramifications of myth, conceived either in opposition to, or entwined with, the question of technology, will be addressed at the end of this chapter and in Part Three, which concludes with general reflections on fascism and liberalism.

Weimar and What Then?

Why deal less extensively with Schmitt's National Socialist and post–World War II works than with his Weimar ones? That Schmitt certainly continued to be a staunch critic of liberalism after the collapse of the Weimar Republic is a point well taken. But there are reasons besides considerations of project scope that justify my particular focus on Weimar. Although Schmitt was often engaged in furthering the practical causes of conservative and authoritarian politicians in his writings during Weimar, particularly during its crisis years of 1929–33, I would claim that there is still a greater degree of intellectual independence reflected in these works than in his later National Socialist ones. The latter are to some extent constrained by Schmitt's – undoubtedly willing and eager – efforts to keep his reflections within the confines of party dogma.[39] And although his postwar work is so deeply influential for the intellectual context of the Federal Republic of Germany, it is also so intricately entangled with his subtle yet elaborate attempt at self-exculpation that there is questionable utility for my purposes in attempting to recover its political-philosophical core.[40]

Thus, I view Schmitt's critique of liberalism as it is expressed in Weimar as sustaining a kind of purity that makes it helpful for contemporary considerations of liberal democratic theory and the threat of neoconservative technocracy, and worse, neofascist authoritarianism. Of course, I do not mean "pure" in any normative sense; although Schmitt's Weimar work is not intrinsically Nazi, as some would claim, it is undoubtedly fascist as it reaches

---

39 Regarding Schmitt's work under National Socialism, see, in the German literature, Bernd Rüthers, *Carl Schmitt im Dritten Reich: Wissenschaft als Zeitgeist-Verstärkung?* (Munich: C. H. Beck, 1989); and in the English, Peter C. Caldwell, "National Socialism and Constitutional Law: Carl Schmitt, Otto Koellreutter, and the Debate over the Nature of the Nazi State, 1933–1937," *Cardozo Law Review* 16:2 (December 1994).

40 On the subject of Schmitt's influence on both the Right and the Left in the BRD, see Hans Lietzmann, "Vater der Verfassungsväter?: Carl Schmitt und die Verfassungsgründung in der Bundesrepublik Deutschland," in *Carl Schmitt und die Liberalismuskritik* (Opladen: Laske & Budrich, 1988); R. Mußgnug, "Carl Schmitts verfassungsrechtliches Werk und sein Fortwirken im Staatsrecht der Bundesrepublik Deutschland," in Helmut Quaritsch, ed., *Complexio Oppositorum: Ueber Carl Schmitt* (Berlin: Duncker & Humblot, 1988); Ulrich K. Preuß, "Vater der Verfassungsväter?: Carl Schmitts Verfassungslehre und die verfassungspolitische Diskussion der Gegenwart," *Politisches Denken Jahrbuch 1993*, ed. V. Gerhardt, H. Ottman, and M. Thompson (Stuttgart: J. B. Metzler, 1993); Dirk van Laaks, *Gespräche in der Sicherheit des Scheigens – Carl Schmitt in der Geistesgeschichte der frühen Bundesrepublik* (Berlin: Akademie, 1993); and Reinhard Mehring, "Carl Schmitt und die Verfassungslehre unserer Tage," *Archiv des öffentlichen Recht* 55 (1995).

maturity in the early to mid twenties.[41] There is clearly some degree of theoretical continuity from his Weimar to his National Socialist and even Federal Republic works. However, the precise and fine delineation required to specify these strands would make this book more of an effort in intellectual history and political biography than I actually intend.[42]

Technology and Politics

Throughout this book, I more often than not treat technology as a cultural artifact of the Weimar era and, implicitly, of our own, in order to draw out the sociopolitical ramifications of intellectual constructions of the phenomenon. However, in so doing I do not wish to dismiss or treat superficially the content of Weimar and contemporary debates on technology; after all, the twentieth-century German theoretical tradition has produced some of the most incisive critics of the infiltration of politics by technology.

Most familiar to North American audiences is the work of Max Horkheimer, T. W. Adorno (and other scholars affiliated with the Frankfurt Institute for Social Research), Hannah Arendt, and Jürgen Habermas.[43] In much of the discourse on technology, the practical-normative questions are often formulated as follows: Is modern technology merely the more readily applied instrument of a disposition toward nature that has always existed in humanity? Or has the rise of modern technology resulted from, and reciprocally resulted in, a fundamentally changed view of nature? If indeed technology is part and parcel of a changed conception, has this change been beneficial or dangerous? Is technology the powerful liberating force it

41 As Chantal Mouffe articulately explains, "It is incorrect to assert, as some do, that Schmitt's thinking was imbued with Nazism before his turnabout of 1933 and his espousal of Hitler's movement. There is, however, no doubt that it was his deep hostility to liberalism which made possible, or which did not prevent, his joining the Nazis." Mouffe, *The Return of the Political*, p. 121.

42 On this question, see Volker Neumann, *Der Staat im Bürgerkrieg: Kontinuität und Wandlung des Staatsbegriffs in der politischen Theorie Carl Schmitts* (Frankfurt a. M.: Campus, 1980); and Ingeborg Maus, "Zur 'Zäsur' von 1933 in der Theorie Carl Schmitts," in *Rechtstheorie und politische Theorie im Industriekapitalismus* (Munich: Wilhelm Fink, 1986).

43 See Horkheimer and Adorno, *Dialectic of Enlightenment* (1944), trans. John Cummings (New York: Continuum, 1989); Arendt, *The Human Condition* (Chicago: University of Chicago: 1958); and Habermas, *Toward a Rational Society: Student Protest, Science and Politics*, trans. Jeremy Shapiro (Boston: Beacon Press, 1970); Habermas, *The Theory of Communicative Action*, vol. 1: *Reason and the Rationalization of Society*, trans. Thomas McCarthy (Boston: Beacon Press, 1984); and Habermas, *The Theory of Communicative Action*, vol. 2: *Lifeworld and System: A Critique of Functionalist Reason*, trans. Thomas McCarthy (Boston: Beacon Press, 1987).

was thought to be in the Enlightenment, or is it rather an instrument for the further enslavement, in mind as in body, of humanity?

Contemporary commentators have, however, called into question the very notions of technology with which those esteemed theorists have operated. Consequently, their respective critiques of the technification of politics have been to some extent undermined.[44] Moreover, all of those theorists have been accused of abstracting too distantly from the practicalities or potentialities of modern politics.[45] This same critique is leveled against the most influential German philosopher of technology, Martin Heidegger,

44 Horkheimer and Adorno have been criticized for reducing *all* human activity to the instrumental domination of nature. See, for instance, Honneth, *The Critique of Power,* chaps. 2 and 3. Arendt privileges the political *praxis* she attributes to the ancient Greek polis over modern, technified political action, and hence – her admiration for modern political revolutionaries notwithstanding – it is potentially problematic to derive a modern theory of political action from her theory. See Richard J. Bernstein, *Beyond Objectivism and Relativism: Science, Hermeneutics and Praxis* (Philadelphia: University of Pennsylvania Press, 1988), pp. 207–20. Habermas has been besieged on many fronts for espousing a transhistorical notion of technology that compromises the attempt to grasp the specificities of modern technology. See Postone, *Time, Labor and Social Domination,* chap. 6; and Robert B. Pippin, "On the Notion of Technology as Ideology: Prospects," in *Technology, Pessimism and Postmodernism,* ed. Y. Ezrahi, E. Mendelsohn, and H. Segal (Boston: Kluwer, 1994), pp. 107–10. It should be noted that although Thomas McCarthy provides a more sympathetic account of Habermas's theory both in this regard and in general, in *The Critical Theory of Jürgen Habermas* (Cambridge, Mass.: MIT Press, 1978), he also lays out quite articulately the problem of technology and politics in the first subsection of the work, "The Scientization of Politics."

45 As Sheldon Wolin observes, Horkheimer's and Adorno's theory of technology "meant the loss of a political context." They "refused to recontextualize their politics around the fate of democratic politics. They made no effort to develop a theoretical defense of even the troubled form of it in the liberal regime of Weimar or, later, the more robust social democratic politics of New Deal America." Wolin, "Reason in Exile: Critical Theory and Technological Society," in *Technology in the Western Political Tradition,* p. 181. Arendt's well-known distinguishing of the "political" from the "social" that disparages the latter in the name of the former may render her theory insufficiently equipped to deal with issues that most persons interested in democratic theory would not be willing to abandon in a *political* theory. See Bernstein, *Beyond Objectivism and Relativism,* pp. 214–20. Habermas is a more complicated case, as he has always been quite willing to "descend" into discussions about the practicalities of liberal-democratic politics. However, even his most recent work, *Between Facts and Norms,* which purports to mediate the concrete "facticity" of sociopolitical reality with the normative "validity" of ethical-political theory, is still a bit too much of the latter, with insufficient attention to the former; see Veit-Michael Bader, "Viel Geltung und immer weniger Faktizität: Zur Kritik an Jürgen Habermas' diskurstheoretischer Rechts- und Demokratietheorie," in *Produktion und Klassentheorie: Festschrift für Sebastion Herkommer,* ed., H. Ganßmann and S. Krüger (Hamburg: VSA, 1993); and Neil Brenner, "The Limits of Civil Society in the Age of Global Capital: A Critique of Jürgen Habermas' Mature Social Theory," master's thesis, Department of Political Science, University of Chicago (1993).

whom I discuss at various junctures in the book. It is worth mentioning here that Heidegger harbored ulterior motives in ceasing to speak explicitly about political action in the years after World War II.[46]

Schmitt, as we will see, is not free from all of the theoretical *aporiai* that plague these often more sophisticated, and with the exception of Heidegger, certainly more ethically palatable theorists. However, where Schmitt is potentially more useful than the others is in his willingness to engage technology in the nuts and bolts of modern political theory and practice: in the realm of liberal institutions and constitutional law. In one apologia from among the many that he would have to make in his lifetime – unfortunately, never in a fully satisfactory manner – Schmitt described his constitutional thought: "My constitutional expositions are entirely concerned with the attempt to convey recognition of the meaning and consequences of the German constitution, without regard to changing party interest, and to oppose degrading it to a tactical instrument and tool. I . . . struggle against a misuse of the concept of legality and against a value- and reality-neutral functionalism."[47]

It is my argument that Schmitt's derogatory references to what is "tactical" or is a reflection of some kind of narrow "functionalism," as well as his disdain for what he describes as an instrument or tool, are not merely rhetorical. They are indications of a deep-seated connection within Schmitt's political theory between liberalism and modern technology. It is my hope that an analysis of this connection will begin to open new and

---

46   See Heidegger, *The Question Concerning Technology and Other Essays*, trans. William Lovitt (New York: Harper and Row, 1977). If one reduces all action to technology-driven activity, one no longer needs to take responsibility for one's own political actions, whatever they may have been. Unlike Heidegger, however, Schmitt, even in his postwar writings, never considers technology a fate or a destiny to which humanity must resign itself. See Schmitt, "Die Einheit der Welt," *Merkur* 6:1 (January 1952); and "Der Neue Nomos der Erde," *Gemeinschaft und Politik* 3:1 (1955). This distinction is important, because it demonstrates that Schmitt's influential student, Ernst Forsthoff, a well-known German theorist of technology and politics, is actually closer to Heidegger in this regard. It is ironic that a critique of technology that lapses into resignation emerges ultimately as an apology for neoconservative technocracy. Again, however, this is the intellectual trajectory of Schmitt's student, not of Schmitt himself. A study of postwar German conservatism that understands this distinction is Peter C. Caldwell, "Ernst Forsthoff and the Legacy of Radical Conservative State Theory in the Federal Republic of Germany," *History of Political Thought* 15:4 (winter 1994); and one that does not is Jerry Z. Muller, *The Other God That Failed: Hans Freyer and the Deradicalization of German Conservatism* (Princeton: Princeton University Press, 1987).
47   Letter from Schmitt to Prelate Kass, head of the Catholic Center Party (Jan. 30, 1933), quoted from Bendersky, *Carl Schmitt*, p. 187. Kass had – quite prophetically, as it turned out – accused Schmitt of constitutional relativism and a willingness to resort to illegality in matters of state.

perhaps more productive avenues for understanding each of these important entities. The problem of technocracy has become a persistent issue in the practical reality and public discourse of liberal democracies. A careful study of Schmitt's work – where liberalism and technology inexorably intersect – might provide some provisional insight into this problem.

The context in which fascism first emerged in Europe was characterized by a structural transformation – a fusion – of the economy, society, and politics, while welfare-state conditions eclipsed the nineteenth century's supposedly separate state/society configuration. As the perceived agent or means of this transformation, technology consequently aroused exhilaration, awe, and fear, irrespective of whether it was perceived as wholly beneficial or detrimental. The analyses on the part of the intellectuals who engaged technology in this context were often hysterical but also sometimes quite perspicacious. Soviet Communism, fascism, and liberal technocracy were all posed as potential solutions to this situation. Since the early seventies, industrial societies have been undergoing another structural transformation, as a Fordist welfare-state configuration gives way to an economically internationalized one. This process may have helped to bring down Soviet Communism, but fascism has reemerged, and liberal technocracy transmutes itself in not necessarily progressive ways. The considerations of these political alternatives in the wake of this century's first technological transformation by fascism's most brilliant promoter and liberalism's most relentless critic, Carl Schmitt, may not provide facile answers in the midst of this century's second transformation. But we must properly understand the past in order to accurately assess the present and ensure that the disastrous outcomes that befell a fragile liberal democracy like Weimar's are not replicated in any context.[48]

48 A few years ago, before he undertook the business of governing a fledgling government, Václav Havel spoke of technology and liberal democracy together: "Technology, that child of modern science . . . is out of humanity's control, has ceased to serve us, has enslaved us, and compelled us to participate in the preparation of our own destruction. And humanity can find no way out: we have no idea and no faith, and even less do we have a political conception to help us bring things back under human control. . . . [Parliamentary democracies] can offer no fundamental opposition to the automatism of technological civilization and the industrial consumer society." Havel, "The Power of the Powerless," in *Living in Truth* (London: Faber & Faber, 1987), pp. 114–16. Recently the editors of a volume on technology and politics expressed similar concerns: "Because of the intimate connection [of technology and liberalism], it does seem peculiarly difficult for thinkers working within the liberal democratic tradition to confront the problem of technology in its most radical forms, as the relative silence on the topic by liberal theorists – John Rawls, Ronald Dworkin, and Robert Nozick, for example – would seem to indicate. But for the same reason it is above all necessary for liberals to address it. The problem of technology

Prefatory Remarks on Part One

I analyze Schmitt's theory of technology as it appears in four important but understudied works that are spread out chronologically across his Weimar career: *Theodor Däubler's "Northern Lights"* (1916), *Political Romanticism* (1919), *Roman Catholicism and Political Form* (1923), and "The Age of Neutralizations and Depoliticizations" (1929). I present his theory in light of the two most influential philosophical grapplings with technology to arise out of Weimar Germany. The first is dealt with in Chapter 1: The Marxian tradition of critical theory is most notably represented in the twenties and thirties by Georg Lukács and his heirs in the Frankfurt Institute for Social Research, such as Max Horkheimer and T. W. Adorno. The second is detailed in Chapter 2: the more Nietzschean tradition referred to as "existentialism," which finds its most famous early-twentieth-century exponent in Martin Heidegger.

I am not directly concerned with the question of whether Schmitt had been overtly influenced by, for instance, *Capital* or *Beyond Good and Evil* or had read the writings of his Frankfurt School or existentialist contemporaries. What is more interesting, I think, is the fact that his work is one of the most sophisticated amalgams of the very themes and concerns that find expression in these two very different philosophical schools and is therefore an excellent site for a theoretical engagement with the phenomenon of modern technology. By the twenties both schools of thought and Schmitt himself had come to see Enlightenment rationality as something technological, that is, ultimately contentless, blindly manipulative of, and potentially threatening to, human existence. As a result, both sought theoretical and practical responses to it. Like the critical theorists of his time, Schmitt, in *"Northern Lights," Political Romanticism, Roman Catholicism,* and the "Neutralizations" essay, undertakes a philosophically dialectical approach to the apparent dualities associated with technological thinking: Technology is not only the objectively rational, precalculated manipulation of inanimate nature with material instruments but can also be characterized by an irrational, subjective elevation of specific aspects of the world to the status of myth. But despite this relatively sophisticated mode of analysis, explicated in detail in Chapter 1, Schmitt himself, as elucidated in Chapter 2, like his

is, to a very great extent, the problem of liberal democracy." A. M. Melzer, J. Weinberger, and M. R. Zinman, Preface, to *Technology in the Western Political Tradition*. Schmitt's political theory is in its own terms hardly friendly to liberalism. Yet it might be of more than just perverse interest to study it with an eye toward addressing a problem becoming ever more salient in liberal democracies.

existentialist contemporaries in the other camp, ultimately resorts to the irrational element of myth to confront and challenge the threat of technology in the modern world. It is the dissection of these entwined elements of myth and rationality in his thought that I hope will prove fruitful for theoretical analyses of technology – particularly those with an eye toward politics. I hope to highlight both the promise and the shortcomings of his theory of technology in Part One before delineating and analyzing his location of technology in liberal institutions and theories of law, in Part Two.

In both *"Northern Lights"* and *Roman Catholicism,* Schmitt likens technology to the Antichrist, and even in the "Neutralizations" piece, written after he had officially abandoned Catholicism, he still employs negative theological terms, such as "demonic" or "satanic," to describe the phenomenon. Yet he was certainly not the first author to use such theological or mythic language to deal with elements related to modern technology. In the "Fetishism" section of chapter 1 of *Capital,* Marx refers to the "theological," "mystical," "mysterious," and "phantasmagorical" attributes of that which transforms qualitatively different entities into quantitatively equivalent ones, the commodity form. In the next chapter, as soon as Marx has introduced the "socially recognized" embodiment of this "universally equivalent" form, namely, money, he quotes, within the body of the text, several Latin verses from Revelation that invoke the image of "the beast," the Antichrist.[49] Three decades later, in a work bearing that very name, Nietzsche pronounces himself the Antichrist, the antithesis to what *he* considers the ultimate leveler, that which for him is the "universally equivalent form," Christianity.[50] With this stance, Nietzsche purports to "revaluate" the nihilistic values of the Socratic-Christian tradition, including its modern culmination in what is commonly called "science" but for Nietzsche is ultimately not worthy of that name.

For Schmitt, it is something quite closely related to modern economics and science – technology – that is the twentieth-century manifestation of the Enlightenment's process of "neutralization," the process that, echoing the authors cited earlier, renders all things "equivalent." Ultimately, the important question to try to answer is this: Why do these authors, and for our concerns, Schmitt, use the image of the Antichrist in regard to such a process? Thus, Chapter 1 examines Schmitt's "critical" engagement with

49 Karl Marx, *Capital: A Critique of Political Economy* (1867), vol. 1, trans. Ben Fowkes (London: Vintage, 1976), p. 181.
50 Friedrich Nietzsche, *The Antichrist* (1895), in *The Portable Nietzsche,* ed. and trans. Walter Kaufmann (New York: Viking, 1954).

technology – in Hegelian-Marxist terms, his dialectically rational deciphering of what appears "demonic" in the workings of modern technology.
Chapter 2 shows how, despite the critically rational moments of Schmitt's
analysis, he ultimately succumbs to the Nietzschean reversion to myth in an
attempt to fend off the encroachments of a demonized technology.

I

BETWEEN CRITICAL THEORY AND POLITICAL EXISTENTIALISM

SCHMITT'S CONFRONTATION WITH TECHNOLOGY

ANTINOMIES OF TECHNICAL THOUGHT

ATTEMPTING TO TRANSCEND WEBER'S
CATEGORIES OF MODERNITY

In his cultural-political treatises from the years 1916 to 1923, Schmitt attempts to formulate a critique of modernity that properly apprehends technology's role within it, without either aesthetically valorizing or fearfully fleeing from it – responses characteristic of many of his contemporaries.[1] His first effort at this, in his commentary on the poem "Northern Lights" in 1916, is followed by another socioliterary study from 1919, *Political Romanticism*.[2] He then takes up this task more rigorously in *Roman Catholicism and Political Form* in 1923.[3] Schmitt confronts the problem that modernity seems to have two opposite intellectual poles: the one, economic-technical

1 Despite certain interpretive deficiencies with respect to Schmitt and others, Jeffrey Herf's *Reactionary Modernism: Technology, Culture and Politics in Weimar and the Third Reich* (New York: Cambridge University Press, 1984) provides many vivid examples of attitudes toward technology in this context. More generally reliable studies within the realm of cultural studies are Andreas Huyssen, *After the Great Divide: Modernism, Mass Culture, Postmodernism* (Bloomington: Indiana University Press, 1986); and a friendly criticism of the latter by R. L. Rutsky, "The Mediation of Technology and Gender: *Metropolis*, Nazism, Modernism," *New German Critique* 60 (fall 1993). See also in the German literature Karl Heinz Bohrer, *Aesthetik des Schreckens: Die Pessimistische Romantik und Ernst Jüngers Frühwerk* (Munich: Carl Hanser, 1978).

2 Schmitt, *Theodor Däublers "Nordlicht": Drei Studien über die Elemente, den Geist und die Aktualität des Werkes* (Berlin: Duncker & Humblot, 1991), hereafter *N*; *Political Romanticism*, trans. Guy Oakes (Cambridge, Mass.: MIT Press, 1985), hereafter *PR*.

3 Schmitt, *Roman Catholicism and Political Form* (1923), trans. G. L. Ulmen (Westport: Greenwood, 1996), hereafter referred to as *Political Form* and cited as *RC*.

thought, the abstractly formal rationality associated with economics, technology, and positivism; the other, the many strands of romanticism, the highly subjective and aesthetic enrapture with specifically concrete objects. For the early Schmitt, the task of a rationality not beholden to either one of these particular opposites of modernity would be one that understands their interrelatedness in the specific historical moment of the present and attempts to move beyond them in practice, as we will see, in a particular understanding of political practice.

It is noteworthy that in the same year as the publication of *Roman Catholicism and Political Form,* the centerpiece of Schmitt's early cultural-political confrontation with technology, Georg Lukács published *History and Class Consciousness,* a Marxian attempt to deal with much the same problem.[4] Yet the relationship between the two works and the two authors themselves is generally overlooked.[5] This is somewhat surprising, given that both Schmitt and Lukács were intellectually and personally influenced in such profound ways by Max Weber. Schmitt attended Weber's famous "Science as a Vocation" and "Politics as a Vocation" lectures in Munich, in the years 1917–20.[6]

4   Lukács, *History and Class Consciousness* (1923), trans. Rodney Livingstone (Cambridge, Mass.: MIT Press, 1988), hereafter *HCC.*

5   An otherwise excellent account of the young Lukács's intellectual context does not mention Schmitt at all: Mary Gluck, *Georg Lukács and His Generation: 1900–1918* (Cambridge, Mass.: Harvard University Press, 1985). Notable exceptions in this regard are Norbert Bolz, *Auszug aus der entzauberten Welt* (Munich: Wilhelm Fink, 1989); Stefan Breuer, "The Illusion of Politics: Politics and Rationalization in Max Weber and Georg Lukács," *New German Critique* 26 (summer 1982); and especially G. L. Ulmen, *Politische Mehrwert: Eine Studie über Max Weber und Carl Schmitt* (Weinheim: VCH Acta humaniora, 1991). See also Agnes Heller, "The Concept of the Political Revisited," in *Political Theory Today,* ed. D. Held (Stanford: Stanford University Press, 1991). The connection between Schmitt and Lukács's theoretical progeny in the so-called Frankfurt School has been more widely discussed, however; see the debate on the topic engaged in by Ellen Kennedy, Ulrich K. Preuß, Martin Jay, and Alfons Söllner in *Telos* 71 (spring 1987); more recently, see William E. Scheuerman, *Between the Exception and the Norm: The Frankfurt School and the Rule of Law* (Cambridge, Mass.: MIT Press, 1994).

6   Both appear in *From Max Weber: Essays in Sociology,* ed. and trans. H. H. Gerth and C. Wright Mills (New York: Oxford University Press, 1958). Schmitt was in the audience for the "Science" lecture (Nov. 7, 1917), a speech on "Germany's New Political Order" (Nov. 14, 1918), and the "Politics" lecture (Jan. 28, 1919). In the winter of 1919–20, he attended Weber's course, "Outline of a Universal Social and Economic History." Throughout these years, Schmitt had several private conversations with Weber. See Ulmen, *Politische Mehrwert,* pp. 20–1.

    In a controversial statement, Jürgen Habermas remarked that Schmitt was a "true student," or at least a "natural son," of Weber; see *Max Weber and Sociology Today* (1965), ed. Otto Stammer, trans. K. Morris (New York: Harper & Row, 1971), p. 66, n. 4. Regarding Weber's influence on Schmitt more elaborately, see Wolfgang Mommsen, *Max Weber and German Politics, 1890–1920* (1959), trans. M. S. Steinberg (Chicago: University of Chicago

Indeed, much of the fury that Schmitt directs at romantics and romanticism in his book of 1919 on that subject parallels Weber's denouncement of the contemporary forces of irrationalism and passivity in the "Vocation" lectures. Lukács was a member of Weber's *Kreis* from 1911 to 1915, participating in his Sunday afternoon discussion group.[7] Like Schmitt, Lukács comes to his 1923 critique via socio-aesthetic studies of literature.[8]

Both young scholars were deeply affected by Weber's rationalization thesis, particularly as it appeared in *The Protestant Ethic and the Spirit of Capitalism*. A juxtaposition to Lukács's own coming to terms with Weber will provide the best alternative example for assessing Schmitt's confrontation with technology and politics in this chapter. What is perhaps most potentially fascinating about a comparison of these two theorists is the startling similarities, as well as important differences, that it highlights on the issue of technology and liberalism between Schmitt, the great anti-Marxist, and the tradition of Western Marxism or critical theory inaugurated in no small degree by Lukács; the theoretical flaws that it magnifies in the neo-Kantianism of Weber's simultaneously technocratic and technophobic "liberal" social science and political theory; and the political dangers it exposes in even the most brilliant critiques of Kantian liberalism that too readily endorse political action as an alternative.[9]

Press, 1984); Rune Slagstad, "Liberal Constitutionalism and Its Critics: Max Weber and Carl Schmitt," in *Constitutionalism and Democracy*, ed. J. Elster and R. Slagstad (Cambridge: Cambridge University Press, 1988); Matthias Eberl, *Die Legitimität der Moderne: Kulturkritik und Herrschaftskonzeption bei Max Weber und Carl Schmitt* (Marburg: Tectum, 1994); and, most extensively, Ulmen, *Politische Mehrwert*.

7   The intellectual relationship of Lukács and Weber is well covered in the better English-language studies of the former's social and political theory; see Andrew Arato and Paul Breines, *The Young Lukács and the Origins of Western Marxism* (New York: Pluto Press, 1979); Breuer, "The Illusion of Politics"; and Andrew Feenberg, *Lukács, Marx, and the Sources of Critical Theory* (Oxford: Oxford University Press, 1986). Their personal relationship is examined in biographical studies of the respective figures: e.g., Arthur Mitzman, *The Iron Cage: An Historical Interpretation of Max Weber* (New Brunswick: Transaction Press, 1985); and Arpad Kadarkay, *Georg Lukács: Life, Thought and Politics* (Cambridge: Basil Blackwell, 1991).

8   Lukács, *Soul and Form* (1910–11), trans. A. Bostock (Cambridge, Mass.: MIT Press, 1974); "Zur Soziologie des modernen Drama," *Archiv für Sozialwissenschaft und Sozialpolitik* (1914); and *Theory of the Novel* (1916), trans. A. Bostock (Cambridge, Mass.: MIT Press, 1971).

9   These affinities between Schmitt and Lukács might help account for the fact – mentioned in my introduction – that over the last ten years an impressive array of ex-, post-, and neo-Marxists have felt compelled to appropriate or confront Schmitt: Andrew Arato, Norberto Bobbio, Jean Cohen, Paul Hirst, Martin Jay, John Keane, Chantal Mouffe, Paul Piccone, Gary Ulmen, and Richard Wolin. Cohen and Arato, although justifiably critical of Schmitt, laud his "dialectical virtuosity" in their book *Civil Society and Political Theory* (Cambridge, Mass.: MIT Press, 1992), p. 236. Mouffe identifies Schmitt as "a rigorous and perspicacious opponent," in *The Return of the Political* (London: Verso, 1993), p. 118.

Both Schmitt and Lukács find Weber's thesis susceptible to the same criticism of excessive formalism cum underlying irrationalism as the Kantian philosophy on which it is based. Weber's theory generally perceives the elements of irrationality that inevitably confront modern rationalization in three ways: either as external or prior to the system of rationalism itself – "old gods" who "ascend from their graves" to "resume their eternal struggle"; as simply reactions to rationalization; or as deviations from the rational.[10] In their respective works from this period, Schmitt and Lukács cautiously incorporate, while exploring the limits of, Weber's thesis and illustrate how the supposedly premodern or extrarational irrationality that remains impenetrable to Enlightenment rationality is an inherent part of that very rationality.

By 1923, however, they come to view Weber's approach as insufficiently one-sided, for it cannot adequately account for the existence of the concrete, qualitative manifestations of social reality and, relatedly, the persistence of the irrational, the romantic, and the mythical in modern society. Whereas Weber generally claims that the phenomena associated with this latter category are either modern remnants of an irrational past or contemporary flights from an overly rationalized present, Lukács and Schmitt attempt to show that such irrationality and neomythology are intrinsically linked to the abstract rationality that Weber describes and practices. In other words, modernity, rather than fostering the "disenchantment" of politics or the banishment of cultural superstition, itself manufactures them; concomitantly, Weber's Kantian methodology and politics, rather than promoting Enlightenment rationality, instead harbors a potentially dangerous irrationality. They derive much of the evidence for this argument from Weber himself: The battle of the many "warring gods" to which the discussion of values is reduced in Weber's theory of pluralism is eventually understood as the latent, irrational, subjective will that serves as a mere comple-

---

10   On irrationality as a reaction, see Weber, "Science as a Vocation," p. 149. Modern religious irrationalism, for instance, is conceived by Weber as an almost mechanical response to secularization: "This reaction is the stronger the more systematic the thinking about the 'meaning' of the universe becomes, the more the external organization of the world is rationalized, and the more the conscious experience of the world's irrational content is sublimated." See "Religious Rejections of the World and Their Directions," in *From Max Weber,* p. 357. The new emphasis on mystical experience, according to Weber, is a backlash to an increasingly dominant "rational cognition and mastery of nature." See "The Social Psychology of the World Religions," in *From Max Weber,* p. 282. Cf. also "Science as a Vocation," pp. 143, 154. On irrationality as a "deviation," see Weber, *Economy and Society: An Outline of Interpretive Sociology* (1920), 2 vols., ed. Guenther Roth and Claus Wittich (Berkeley: University of California Press, 1978), p. 6; hereafter *ES.*

ment to the irresistible, objectively rational structures of the "iron cage" of modernity. I hope to explore these themes in a way that transcends the terms of the well-known debates over the normative and historical ramifications of the later Weber's theorizing of charisma and *Führerdemokratie* – issues that I take up again in Chapter 4. However, what one must not forget in the course of this analysis is that Schmitt and Lukács themselves – each in his own different way, to be sure – eventually endorsed twentieth-century political mythologies that quite vigorously championed political "will": left- and right-wing authoritarianism in the forms of, respectively, Soviet Communism and National Socialism. I take up more extensively Schmitt's particular road to such an endorsement in the next chapter and subsequent ones.

The parallels between Schmitt and Lukács exceed the shared influence of Weber, however much the latter's intellectual-spiritual presence clearly permeates almost all of what concerns the two in this period. For instance, both young scholars adopted short-length works or collections of essays as their preferred vehicles of expression rather than the traditionally Germanic volume-length tome.[11] Both recognized the kernel of truth in Weber's association of modernization and Protestantism yet sought to compensate for its exaggerations and broaden its scope from the standpoint of their own critical, outsider, theological-political perspectives – political Catholicism for Schmitt and secular messianic Judaism for Lukács.[12] Both began

---

11 Besides the brief and forceful thrust of such a medium, which matches Schmitt's prose, Reinhard Mehring points out how the pamphlet expresses Schmitt's philosophical suspension between "system and aphorism," between "Hegel and Nietzsche." See *Pathetisches Denken: Carl Schmitts Denkweg am Leitfaden Hegels: Katholische Grundstellung und antimarxistische Hegelstrategie* (Berlin: Duncker & Humblot, 1989), p. 21. Arato and Breines remark on Lukács's essayistic approach: "[T]he essay and the fragment, in their brevity and incompleteness, remain true to the living reality of their objects. Incompatible with intellectual synthesis and resolution of actual antagonisms, the essay and the fragment are, in an antagonistic world, the dialectical forms of expression par excellence." *The Young Lukács*, p. 4.

12 With respect to the influence of Catholicism on Schmitt's early career, consult his biographies: Joseph Bendersky, *Carl Schmitt: Theorist for the Reich* (Princeton: Princeton University Press, 1983); Paul Noack, *Carl Schmitt: Eine Biographie* (Berlin: Propyläen, 1993); and Andreas Koenen, *Der Fall Carl Schmitt: Sein Aufstieg zum "Kronjuristen des Dritten Reiches"* (Darmstadt: Wissenschaftlichen Buchgesellschaft, 1995), although the latter may overemphasize the importance of Schmitt's confessional disposition over the course of his entire life. Schmitt was certainly a believing Roman Catholic in the early twenties, writing frequently in the Catholic press but never officially joining the Catholic Center Party. He was excommunicated by the Church in 1926 because of the complexities of his marital situation. He apparently grew quite bitter toward the Church in the late Weimar Republic, publicly feuding with the more moderate Center party. His antipathy reached its peak under National Socialism, as he is quoted to have said in 1938: "If the Pope excommuni-

their careers practicing the methodological neo-Kantianism dominant at the time, and yet both became two of its most radical critics.[13] Neither seemed to be unconscious of the other's intellectual activities: Schmitt was an admirer of Lukács' essay, "Legality and Illegality," which was added to *History and Class Consciousness*,[14] and Lukács eventually wrote a serious review of Schmitt's *Political Romanticism*.[15] In fact, long after Lukács had become a Soviet apologist, he was careful to distinguish Schmitt's intellectual efforts from those of other, more vulgar Weimar conservatives in his account of German philosophical irrationalism, *The Destruction of Reason*.[16] For his part, just a year before he was to become a Nazi activist, Schmitt devotes the longest and most substantive footnote in *The Concept of the Political* to Hegel and to Lukács as the one who has kept the "actuality" of Hegel "most vitally alive."[17]

cates a nation so therefore does he only excommunicate himself." After the war, Schmitt seemed to have made some peace with Catholicism once his excommunication was lifted, remarking years later, "I am as Catholic as the tree is green, but have my own ideas on it"; elsewhere, even more provocatively, "I am Catholic not only by confession, but rather also by historical extraction – if I may be allowed to say so, racially." See Helmut Quaritsch, *Positionen und Begriffe Carl Schmitts* (Berlin: Duncker & Humblot, 1989), pp. 33–4; and Reinhard Mehring, *Carl Schmitt: Zur Einführung*, p. 169, n. 113.

   Regarding Lukács's own "sectarian-messianic," political-theological orientation, see Joseph B. Maier, "Georg Lukács and the Frankfurt School: A Case of Secular Messianism," in *Georg Lukács: Theory, Culture and Politics*, ed. J. Marcus and Z. Tarr (Oxford: Transaction, 1989); Anson Rabinbach, "Between Enlightenment and Apocalypse: Benjamin, Bloch and Modern Jewish Messianism," *New German Critique* 34 (winter 1985); and Richard Wolin, "Reflections on Jewish Secular Messianism," in *Labyrinths: Explorations in the Critical History of Ideas* (Amherst: University of Massachusetts Press, 1995). For Lukács's own account of the relevance of his Jewish background to his work, see "Gelebtes Denken: Notes Toward an Autobiography," in *Record of a Life: An Autobiographical Sketch*, ed. I. Eörsi, trans. R. Livingstone (London: Verso, 1983). Also note the way Lukács and Ernst Bloch are described in Weber's official biography: Marianne Weber, *Max Weber: A Biography* (1926), trans. H. Zohn (New York: Wiley, 1975), p. 466.

13   On Schmitt's early neo-Kantianism, see Bendersky, *Carl Schmitt: Theorist for the Reich*, pp. 8–11.

14   On this as well as other reflections on the parallels between Schmitt and Lukács, see Ulmen, *Politische Mehrwert*, pp. 86, 115–24.

15   Lukács, "Carl Schmitt: *Politische Romantik*" (1928), in *Georg Lukács Werke*, vol. 2: *Frühschriften II* (Berlin: Hermann Luchterhand, 1964).

16   Observing the "special nuances" of Schmitt's thought, Lukács remarks that "the overtly reactionary" yet "superior" Schmitt "perceived in the antithesis of liberalism and democracy an important present day problem." See *The Destruction of Reason* (1962), trans. Peter Palmer (Atlantic Highlands, N. J.: Humanities Press, 1980), pp. 652–54. Lukács is specifically referring to Schmitt's *Die geistesgeschichtliche Lage des heutigen Parlamentarismus* (Munich: Duncker & Humblot, 1926). Lukács had written his own critique of liberal parliamentarism in 1920: "Zur Frage des Parlamentarismus," in *Georg Lukács Werke*, vol. 2.

17   Schmitt, *Der Begriff des Politischen: Text von 1932 mit einem Vorwort und drei Corollarien* (Berlin:

Indeed, it is the similar and not-so-similar relationship to Hegel or at least a Hegelian method that proves the most interesting cross-comparison of Schmitt and Lukács as theorists of modernity and critics of technology and liberalism.[18] Schmitt once spoke of "a different lineage from Hegel," alluding of course to the leftist one that can be traced back from Lukács and critical theory through Marx, and at the same time intimating the existence of another one that can be traced back on the right.[19] One may then view Schmitt as the chief example of what might be called the dialectical Right. It is the early practice of dialectics by Schmitt and Lukács that at once points out the deficiencies of a Weberian liberal account of modernity and technology as well as the dangers of totalitarianism in attempts to transcend those deficiencies that are not themselves sufficiently dialectical.

Technology and Political Action as Weberian Categories

It is most appropriate to begin to frame the technology question with respect to Schmitt, as well as Lukács, by examining the issue in the thought of their teacher, Weber. As we will see in this chapter and the next, Schmitt's theory of technology has marked affinity with those of Nietzsche, Heidegger, and Lukács, for instance, but it is Weber who most singularly establishes the problematic for Schmitt.[20] Modern technology, according to this account, is in fact something much more than just applied science.

Duncker & Humblot, 1963), pp. 61–3, n. 22. Under National Socialism, Schmitt either refrained from citing Lukács altogether or denounced him as a Jew and a Marxist; see "Der Staat als Mechanismus bei Hobbes und Descartes," *Archiv für Rechts- und Sozialphilosophie* 39 (1937). He returned to serious considerations on Lukács after the war; see *Verfassungsrechtliche Aufsätze aus den Jahren 1924–1954: Materialien zu einer Verfassungslehre* (Berlin: Duncker & Humblot, 1958), pp. 425–6, 450.

18 On Schmitt's debt to Hegel or "Hegelian strategy," see Mehring, *Pathetisches Denken*. I focus more on this strategy as it was practiced in Weimar in particular rather than in nineteenth- and twentieth-century German philosophy, broadly conceived. Moreover, I do not immediately focus on the "antimarxism" of Schmitt's approach but rather initially on its similarities to Lukács's particular Marxism. See Lukács's own work on the philosopher, *The Young Hegel* (1938), trans. R. Livingstone (Cambridge, Mass.: MIT Press, 1976); as well as his remarks on the Hegelian quality of *History and Class Consciousness* in the 1967 preface to the work.

19 See Schmitt "Die andere Hegel-Linie: Hans Freyer zum 70. Geburtstag," *Christ und Welt* 30 (Jul. 25, 1957).

20 To mention just a few recent works from the enormous literature on the "Weberian" framing of these questions, see Lawrence A. Scaff, *Fleeing the Iron Cage: Culture, Politics and Modernity in the Thought of Max Weber* (Berkeley: University of California Press, 1989); Gilbert G. Germain, *A Discourse on Disenchantment: Reflections on Politics and Technology* (Albany: State University of New York Press, 1995); John Patrick Diggins, *Max Weber: Politics and the Spirit of Tragedy* (New York: Basic Books, 1996); as well as the essays included

The narrative of modernity offered by Weber in *The Protestant Ethic and the Spirit of Capitalism,* which structures the technology question in so many ways, centers on a value transformation in the Western Christian worldview.[21] At the risk of perhaps crudely summarizing Weber's well-known thesis, Reformation Protestants rebel at what they perceive to be the excessive formalism of Roman Catholicism: its overemphasis on ritual, dogma, and, in general, extrasubjective criteria. Radical Protestantism turns inward generating, unbeknownst to itself, in a tragically ironic fashion, the structures of the most "formally" dominating society the world has ever known: the modern West, a culture dominated by capitalism, bureaucracy, science, and technology. The turn away from external, clerically imposed sanctions liberates Protestants from priestly domination but simultaneously enslaves them to a self-imposed domination actualized in anonymous social structures. Thus, Weber contrasts the "very human Catholic cycle of sin, repentance, atonement, release, followed by renewed sin" with the "tremendous tension" of the Calvinist's psychological state, which lacks immediate "atonement, hope of grace, certainty of forgiveness," and hence any "release."[22] This tension is sublimated into activity in a world now free of the magic attributed to it by Catholicism, activity that quantitatively calculates and rationally manipulates this world, furthering the process that Weber calls "disenchantment." The more dynamic conception of the Christian as the "tool" of God's will in radical Protestantism supplants the relatively static one of the Catholic as "vessel" of God's grace. In Roman Catholicism, activity, good works, allowed one to *attain* salvation; some arbitrary, Church-imposed number of works could guarantee admittance to the kingdom of heaven. In Calvinism, good works *confirmed* a salvation that was already established through predestination, but because no authority could determine or guarantee when or if that status had been in fact attained, there ensues the compulsion to sublimate the consequent anxiety more and more into one's economic vocation, one's "calling," in order to demonstrate salvation.[23]

in Hartmut Lehman and Guenther Roth, eds., *Weber's Protestant Ethic: Origins, Evidence, Contexts* (Cambridge: Cambridge University Press, 1995). For perhaps the most serious engagement with the Protestant ethic thesis, see Gianfranco Poggi, *Calvinism and the Capitalist Spirit: Max Weber's* Protestant Ethic (Amherst: University of Massachusetts Press, 1983).

21   Weber, *The Protestant Ethic and the Spirit of Capitalism* (1904–5), trans. Talcott Parsons, (New York: Scribner's, 1958).

22   Ibid., p. 117.

23   Ibid., pp. 114–15.

Hence, a religiously driven economic fervor that in the Middle Ages was consigned to monasteries, and thus otherworldly directed, in modernity enters everyday life through the "inner-worldly asceticism" of radical Protestantism and generates the processes of modern commercial and industrial activity – capitalism. According to Weber, the result is a world that comes to be viewed as a *machine:* In its rejection of Catholicism, "ascetic Protestantism" rejects metaphysical or superstitious interpretations of the world in favor of solely empirical ones, thus reducing it "to a causal mechanism."[24] In this way, Protestant asceticism is bound with the "technical and economic conditions of machine production" that drive the mechanism that is the modern world. When the religious motivations dissipate, the rational processes continue to drive on, and aid in, the construction of the famous "iron cage."[25] Life itself becomes no more serious than sport, and death loses its resonance as "science and scientifically oriented technology" take the place of religion, but science unlike religion can provide humanity with no substantive meaning.[26] It offers only the emotionally, psychologically, and spiritually unsatisfactory means for "mastery" through "calculation."[27] This mastery entails domination not only of nature but of human beings as well; bureaucracy, itself an "animate machine," in Weber's estimation, has the potential for unprecedented human enslavement: "Together with the inanimate machine [the factory] it is busy fabricating the shell of bondage which men will perhaps be forced to inhabit someday, as powerless as the fellahs of ancient Egypt" (*ES,* 1402). Weber at times offers this as the "inescapable fate" of Western civilization and, alas, the world.[28]

There are, additionally, ethical-political ramifications of Weber's sociological account of modernity which Schmitt initially struggles with and eventually radicalizes. According to Schmitt and Lukács as well, just as Kant poses an irresistibly formal rationality that exists prior to, and is ultimately

24   Weber, "Religious Rejections of the World and Their Directions," p. 350.
25   Weber, *The Protestant Ethic,* p. 181.
26   Ibid., p. 182; and Weber, "Science as a Vocation," p. 140.
27   Weber, "Science as a Vocation," p. 139.
28   In his more analytical writings, Weber distinguishes between "instrumentally rational action," which is conditioned by solely manipulative considerations, and "value rational action," which is conditioned by external substantive norms (*ES,* 24–25). In his historical-philosophical reflections, however, it is clear that he believes that the former has come to dominate the latter, although the latter make their stand, as we will see, in Weber's tendency toward certain strands of subjective decisionism, which Schmitt inherits from his teacher. Weber also distinguishes between "technical rationality" and "economic rationality" in his social-scientific writings (*ES,* 65–7), only to collapse the distinction in his political works; again a move followed by Schmitt, as we will see.

unaffected by, the explicit subjectivity of his ethics, Weber's calls to responsible individual stands in his political tracts remain ineffective vis-à-vis the objectively formal structures of society, whose development he so carefully delineates in his account of modernity.[29] Weber insists that one must act ethically in order to legitimately attempt to seize the "wheel of history."[30] But given the irresistible nature of the technorationalized process of modern history as described by Weber, it remains unlikely that such ethical activity can substantively affect it. This "necessity versus freedom" opposition is of course completely consistent with what replays itself to this day in the more familiar language of mainstream social science as the opposition of fact and value, or of structure and agency.[31]

Moreover, the normative status of these personally subjective stands remains ultimately indeterminate, as they are inaccessible to the hegemonic, technical rationality of the objective forms they are severed from and posed against. Modernity is hence characterized by Weber as a multiplicity of value assertions, all mutually indefensible from a rational standpoint.[32] His distinction between an ethics of conviction and one of responsibility, and his endorsement of the latter as a way to negotiate this "pluriverse" of "warring gods," cannot ultimately be sustained in practice. Although Weber scorns the unreflective practitioners of conviction who act solely on the basis of a particular issue or cause, with little or no regard for the consequences of their actions, his preferred politics of responsibility ultimately collapses into a similar or even identical position. So long as adherents of the latter value orientation take into account all of the possible and likely ramifications of their actions and experience them "inwardly," according to Weber, he gives them license to take the secularized Protestant stance: "Here I stand; I can

29 Weber's complicated relationship to Kantianism is examined in Christian Lenhardt, "Max Weber and the Legacy of Critical Idealism," in *The Barbarism of Reason: Max Weber and the Twilight of Enlightenment,* ed. A. Horowitz and T. Maley (Toronto: University of Toronto Press, 1994). On the Kantian origins of value stances like the ones promulgated by Weber, see Charles Larmore, *Patterns of Moral Complexity* (Cambridge: Cambridge University Press, 1987), pp. 149–50.; and on German neo-Kantianism more generally, see Thomas Willey, *Back to Kant: The Revival of Kantianism in German Social and Historical Thought, 1860–1914* (Detroit: Wayne State University Press, 1978).

30 Weber, "Politics as a Vocation," p. 115.

31 On the Kantian foundations of these oppositions and the Hegelian attempt to overcome them, see Robert B. Pippin, *Hegel's Idealism: The Satisfactions of Self-Consciousness* (Cambridge: Cambridge University Press, 1989), e.g., pp. 12, 180. On this problem in social science more generally, see the essays contained in Jürgen Habermas, *Theory and Practice,* trans. John Viertel (Boston: Beacon Press, 1973).

32 See Weber, "Politics as a Vocation."

do no other."[33] Weber requires no further substantively normative criteria to be met by his responsible ethic, hence allowing it to still harbor a certain propensity toward irrationality. In a similar spirit, he repeatedly equates even a responsibly sought-after cause with the theological terms "gods" and "demons," further betraying a latent irrationality in the disposition, a fact confirmed by his definition of the "ethical locus" of politics: "Here, to be sure, ultimate *Weltanschauungen* clash . . . [and] one has to make a choice" – a choice whose normative content remains deliberately underspecified.[34]

What Weber's students, Schmitt and Lukács, will want to know is how their master's paradigm – methodological and political, although Weber claims to keep the two orientations distinct – provides for meaningful and effective political activity in an age dominated, in precisely Weberian terms, by a seemingly autonomous technology and an apparently irresistible process of rationalization. They attempt to expand this paradigm while their teacher is alive but then replace it with more radical ones of their own in the wake of his death in 1923. In Weber's (in)famous call to *politics* (to leadership, to charisma, to elites) as a response to the impact of the rationalization he had theorized in his social-scientific works and then applied to the context of post–World War I Germany,[35] Schmitt and Lukács ultimately observe the romantic counterpart to the bureaucratization that Weber's

33 Ibid., p. 127; Weber does not pose these types of ethics as absolute opposites, however, nor does he reflect on their propensity to dissolve into one another.

34 Ibid., p.117. The "subjective" and "objective" poles of Weber's thesis still manifest themselves in contemporary debates. Normative liberal theory, especially in its Rawlsian form, replays the search for a political standpoint that can be legitimately maintained in a "pluriverse of values"; see John Rawls, *Political Liberalism* (New York: Columbia University Press, 1993). Re-Kantianized as a "just" or "neutral," as opposed to a more modestly "responsible," stand, the purportedly biased, prejudiced, and ethically problematic quality of these positions is repeatedly "unmasked" by poststructuralist and postmodernist critiques. On the other hand, the rationalization thesis has been revamped by the imposing theories of "societal complexity" or "systems differentiation," inspired by the work of Niklas Luhmann, theories within which there is little room for normative considerations or substantively meaningful action; see Luhmann, *Social Systems* (Stanford: Stanford University Press, 1995). The respective dead ends of these positions make the contemporary revival of Schmitt's corpus particularly chilling, because, as we will see in what follows, it had been quite similar dead ends in the first part of this century that inspired his work and his proposed reactionary "way out." On these issues, consult David Dyzenhaus, "Liberalism after the Fall: Schmitt, Rawls and the Problem of Justification," *Philosophy and Social Criticism* 22:3 (1996).

35 Cf. Weber, "Politics as a Vocation," as well as the "Parliament and Government" lecture appended to *Economy and Society*.

prescriptions are intended to solve.[36] Whether they adequately address the *aporiai* of Weber's orientation or, especially in the case of Schmitt, only exacerbate its regressively ethical-political potential, as described earlier, is a central question of this and the next chapter.[37]

Technology and Economic-Technical Thinking

In 1916, Schmitt undertakes an analysis of the epic poem penned by Theodor Däubler in 1910, "Northern Lights."[38] Although Schmitt exhibits much sympathy with the poet's depiction of modernity, he actually reconstructs this view in terms of the primacy of technical functionality and loss of meaning that is more reminiscent of Weber: "This age characterizes itself as capitalistic, mechanistic, relativistic; as the age of commerce, technology and organization. In fact the 'factory' appeared to give the age its signature. As *the imposing of functional means toward some wretched or senseless purpose,* as the universal urgency of means over ends, the factory so nullified the individual that not once did he recognize his own eradication" (*N*, 59; emphasis added). What most disturbs Schmitt about the way of thinking that characterizes modernity is a blind domination of nature and what has come to be called "instrumental rationality": "functional means" toward a "senseless purpose." Products, whether the outcomes of a capitalist assembly line or the results of a bureaucratic decision-making apparatus, are spurted out quickly and efficiently without any serious consideration of their ethical worth. Rationality is equated with efficient production, on the one hand, and consumption is driven by irrational impulses, on the other. Substantive reflection finds no place in the equation. This "disastrous path" leads everything toward "relativism" (*N*, 66–7). According to Schmitt, the secularization that emerged with the outset of modernity eventually neutralized any

36 For instance, Weber characterizes charisma as pure substance and charismatic authority as the concrete opposite of abstract bureaucratic authority (*ES*, 1112, 1116) and hence an object for the aesthetic preoccupation of the masses.
37 I do not compare Lukács's more Weberian/neo-Kantian literary studies from the years during and immediately after the Great War with Schmitt's nearly identical efforts from the same period here. For such an exegesis and analysis, see my "Transcending Weber's Categories of Modernity?: The Early Lukács and Schmitt on the Rationalization Thesis," *New German Critique* (1997).
38 Theodor Johannes Adolf Däubler (1876–1934), born in Trieste, was known for his celebration of southern European life and culture over its northern counterpart. Young Schmitt, a German Catholic with certain pretensions about his cultural ties to France and Italy, must have found in the poet a kind of role model. See Schmitt's biographies: Bendersky, *Carl Schmitt: Theorist for the Reich;* Noack, *Carl Schmitt: Eine Biographie;* and Koenen, *Der Fall Carl Schmitt.*

kind of moral substance, and hence produced a vacuum in moral guidance: "Law became power; loyalty, calculability; truth, generally recognized correctness; Christianity, a pacifist group. A widespread confusion and falsification of values governed souls. In place of the distinction between good and evil appeared a sublime discrimination between usefulness and uselessness" (*N*, 61).[39]

Years later, in *Roman Catholicism and Political Form,* Schmitt, still a believing Catholic, claims that in the valueless rationality of economic-technical thought is found the "fundamental antithesis to the political idea of Catholicism" (*RC*, 13). Countering Weber's now chauvinistic/now repentant attributing to Protestantism the glories and horrors of modern rationality, Schmitt asserts that Catholic rationalism is not indifferent to what persons are or what they do, as are the "laws" of the market and of science. In fact, Roman Catholicism's "substantive interest is the normative guidance of human social life" (*RC*, 12). The economic-technical rationality that is characteristic of modernity maintains rules that pertain not to people as such but to objects in a scheme of production and consumption – mere "matter." For Schmitt, there is a difference between rules that govern human behavior and those that deal with the inanimate, that which is without life. Economics and technology, according to Schmitt, obscure this distinction, are indifferent to "life," and thus "arouse a specific Catholic anxiety":

> Modern technology easily becomes the servant of this or that want or need. In modern economy *a completely irrational consumption conforms to a totally rationalized production.* A marvelously rational mechanism serves one or another demand, always with the same earnestness and precision, be it for a silk blouse or poison gas or anything whatsoever. (*RC*, 14–15, emphasis added)

The logic of efficient production and wanton consumption will render whatever is called for, regardless of its impact on people. The imperatives of economics and of technology are mere forms that ignore the significance of the substance they act on – humanity (*RC*, 14). Because technology and economics remain normatively indifferent to the real nature of the demands they serve (i.e., the demands of human beings), what Weber calls "rationality," according to Schmitt, is reason become "warped fantastically"

39 Such expressions against the technological nature of modern society also appear in Schmitt's early legal treatises. In *Der Wert des Staates und die Bedeutung des Einzelnen* (Tübingen: J. C. B. Mohr [Paul Siebeck], 1914), Schmitt speaks of "the age of the machine, of organization, the mechanistic age . . . the age that objectively exhibits its lust and desire" (p. 5).

(*RC,* 15). As we will see, for Schmitt, Catholicism stands beyond the irrationally subjective pole manifested in consumption and the rationally objective one expressed by technological production.

In the influential "Neutralizations" essay of 1929,[40] Schmitt is even more precise about the issues of economics, technology, mastery of nature and indifference to humanity. He situates the rise of modern technology within the broader process of neutralization that drives modernity. According to Schmitt, since the religious wars of the sixteenth century, the West has been seeking a neutral sphere in which agreement could be reached and conflict diminished. This project was sponsored by intellectual elites who sought neutrality in various conceptual principles, *Zentralgebiete* or "central spheres." Europe moved from the controversial sphere of theology in the sixteenth century to the apparently neutral one of metaphysics in the seventeenth and, successively, to humanitarian morality in the eighteenth, to economics in the nineteenth, and finally to technology in the twentieth. I return to the issues of elites and the historical process of neutralization in Chapter 2. Here it is important to note how Schmitt treats technology in the essay.

Schmitt seeks to emphasize the fact that the truly compelling problem posed by the primacy of the technical in the modern world is *not* the machines that characterize technology so much as the way of thinking and the spirit that creates and continues to drive those machines. To this end, he distinguishes between the machine-specific realm of technology [*Technik*], which is "dead," and the intellectual-spiritual [*geistige*] realm of technicity [*Technizität*], which is very much "alive":

> it is not permissible to represent a result of human understanding and discipline simply as dead and soulless, as is the case with every, and particularly, modern technology, and confound the religion of technicity with technology itself. The spirit of technicity that has led to the mass belief of an antireligious this-worldly activism, is nevertheless spirit, perhaps a more evil and demonic spirit, but not to be dismissed as mechanistic and not to be attributed to technology as such. It is perhaps something terrifying, but is not itself technical or machinelike. It is the belief of an activist metaphysics, the belief in a limitless power and domination of man over nature, even over human nature, in the unlimited "receding of natural boundaries" . . . concerning the natural

40 Schmitt's, "Das Zeitalter der Neutralisierungen und Entpolitisierungen" appears in *Der Begriff des Politischen* (Berlin: Duncker & Humblot, 1963); the English renderings are drawn from the translation by Matthias Konzett and John P. McCormick, "The Age of Neutralizations and Depoliticizations," *Telos* 96 (summer 1993).

and worldly existence of man. This belief can be called fantastic and satanic, but not simply dead, spiritless or mechanized soullessness. (*ND*, 140–1)[41]

Thus, Schmitt describes technicity in the same terms that he employed to describe the more general phenomena of economic-technical thought, or Weberian rationalization, in *"Northern Lights"*: It is a "metaphysics" of activity concerned solely with the material world; it is practiced through the "limitless" and "unbounded" domination of nature, including human nature. What *is* new is his claim that although it may be responsible for modern technology and the "splendid array of [its] instruments" (*ND*, 140), unlike the latter, technicity is not simply "technical" or "machinelike." His conception of technicity is, hence, akin to Heidegger's account of Western metaphysics or his notion of "enframing" [*Gestell*] in that an entity that can be considered almost *alive* in itself is actually the driving force behind the emergence and continued functioning of the basically *lifeless* machines of modern technology.[42]

Having established a brief overview of Schmitt's conception of technology and economic-technical thought throughout his Weimar career, I return to his early commentary on Däubler: Given this power of economic-technical thinking, Schmitt finds it quite understandable that the crisis of modernity should often be cast in terms of "the opposition of mechanics and soul," the lifeless forms and the life that rebels against them, as it is in "Northern Lights" (*N*, 63). But there are theoretical problems with this position that pertain to the very possibility of making such an assertion or acting to address it. As in the Gnostic view of the world, which sees the earth only as "the complete work of the devil, in which eternal spiritlessness is triumphant over spirit," in the "mechanics versus soul" worldview there is no room for human activity or reflection that is then free of such condemnation (*N*, 63). In such a scenario, "we would be beyond help; we must at least see out of our prison to escape, so as to save the soul"(*N*, 64). A theme that returns time and again in these works is that "dualisms," like the one be-

41   Jeffrey Herf, among others, has interpreted this passage as proof of Schmitt's supposed protechnology stance in order to group him in a reductionist manner with such figures as Ernst Jünger, Hans Freyer, Werner Sombart, and Oswald Spengler; see Herf, *Reactionary Modernism*, pp. 3, 42, 44–6, 118–20. For a criticism of Herf on this point, see my "Introduction to Schmitt's 'The Age of Neutralizations and Depoliticizations,'" *Telos* 96 (summer 1993).
42   Martin Heidegger, "The Question Concerning Technology" (1954), in *The Question Concerning Technology and Other Essays*, trans. William Lovitt (New York: Harper & Row, 1977), p. 20. I deal with Heidegger somewhat more specifically in Chapter 2.

tween soul and soullessness, left as such, will do nothing to help one theoretically apprehend the age for what it is, or actively change it (*N*, 70).

Thus, despite his admiration and respect for the poet Däubler, "who grasps and portrays the present more comprehensively than a critical historian," Schmitt ultimately finds his work theoretically lacking because "a critical-historical standpoint cannot be found present in 'Northern Lights' " (*N*, 66). Because Däubler relies so heavily on dualisms, such as the mechanical world versus living soul and spirit, his work can be little more than "a compensation to the age of spiritlessness . . . a counterweight to a mechanistic age" (*N*, 64). It is a negation of the age – perhaps "the last and most universal negation" – but not a real critique of modernity, because it cannot itself transcend the dualism of soul versus soullessness that is itself characteristic of the age (*N*, 65). Unlike Dante's *Commedia* or St. Thomas's *Summa*, which are "fruits" of their age, "Northern Lights" is a negation of its age but, most significantly for Schmitt, the negation of an age that structurally produces its own negation.

Schmitt does not himself offer an alternative to such a negation in *"Northern Lights."* Instead, in his next cultural-political treatise, *Political Romanticism* of 1919, he follows up his critique of Däubler's insufficient response to technology and provides an in-depth case study of the most pervasive form of undertheorized negation of modernity: romanticism. He then tries to bring both poles together – abstract technical rationality and concretely obsessed irrational aesthetics; that is, production and consumption – in *Political Form.* These two sides that Weber had related to each other in a somewhat mechanistic stimulus-and-response fashion are theorized as more intricately related in that work from 1923 that will be juxtaposed with Lukács's effort from the same year, *History and Class Consciousness,* in the next section.

Romanticism, Aestheticism, Dualism

Schmitt acknowledges that romanticism as a movement, like Däubler the poet, has legitimate complaints against capitalism, science, and technology but ultimately provides only a complementary structure to them. He employs the Weberian method of "ideal types" (*PR*, 57) and subtly draws on the recently delivered "Vocation" lectures in carrying out his analysis.[43] He does

43 For a contemporary discussion of liberalism and political romanticism influenced by Weber and informed by Schmitt, see Stephen Holmes, "Romanticism and the Rancor against Modernity," in *Benjamin Constant and the Making of Modern Liberalism* (New Haven: Yale University Press, 1984).

ANTINOMIES OF TECHNICAL THOUGHT

not yet, as he later will, more explicitly implicate Weber within the theoretical complex of technology-romanticism.

Schmitt traces this antinomial structure in which Däubler had participated to the very foundations of modern thought: Early-modern rationalism had already compromised a unifying vision of the world in the split between abstract scientific thinking, characteristic of Copernicus's objective approach, on the one hand, and the inward, individualistic rationality characteristic of Descartes's subjective approach, on the other (*PR*, 52). This culminates in the formal rationality of Kant that, in order to maintain its universalism, must impute an inaccessible irrationality to concrete reality – the world exists only as the product of human senses, as a collection of things-in-themselves whose quality is derived solely from the observing subject and not from or by the objects themselves:

> Natural Science ceased to be geocentric and sought its focal point beyond the earth. Philosophy became egocentric and sought its focal point in itself. Modern philosophy is governed by a schism between thought and being, concept and reality, mind and nature, subject and object, that was not eliminated even by Kant's transcendental solution. Kant's solution did not restore the reality of the external world to the thinking mind. That is because for Kant, the objectivity of thought lies in the consideration that thought moves in objectively valid forms. The essence of empirical reality, the thing in itself, is not a possible object of comprehension at all. Post-Kantian philosophy, however, made a deliberate attempt to grasp this essence of the world in order to put an end to the inexplicability and irrationality of real being. (*PR*, 52)[44]

Hegel, according to Schmitt, is the only thinker to nearly resolve this "duality of abstract concept and concrete being characteristic of abstract rationality," the "mechanistic worldview" most vigorously practiced by Descartes, Hobbes, and Kant (*PR*, 53–4): "As early as 1801, Hegel, with an unerring sense of genius had already recognized that the connection with the rationalism of the previous century, and thus the historical inadequacy of the system, lay in the causal relationship between the ego and the non-ego. The Romantics were incapable of this sort of philosophical insight" (*PR*, 82). Hegel recognized that any account of the objective world and the subjective self would have to demonstrate that the latter was not discreetly separate from, nor ideally creative of, but rather a part of, the former in

---

44 See Robert B. Pippin, *Kant's Theory of Form: An Essay on the* Critique of Pure Reason (New Haven: Yale University Press, 1982) for an excellent explication and interrogation of the formalism of Kantian transcendental philosophy.

order for either to be understood.[45] The romantics either accelerated the moment of subjective ego or related the two phenomena to each other in a purely literary way.

Because the very "structure" of modern thought renders concrete reality irrational, the unrestrained, subjective ego picks out various instances of it and imparts meaning to it; however, this meaning, freed as it is from the confinement of the kind of religious or cultural prohibitions that obtained in the West before modernity, is *not* derived from any reflective thought process but is basically arbitrary whim. Harmless objects, such as a jewel, a book, a lock of hair, become objects of intense, subjective aestheticization, but so, too, do political-philosophical concepts, such as "humanity" by the revolutionary Left, or "history" by the conservative Right (*PR*, 59–60), with each side accusing the other of romanticism (*PR*, 25). In the manner that Rousseau aestheticized "children" or "primitive peoples," revolutionaries positively aestheticize "the people" and negatively aestheticize Jesuits, Illuminati, and Freemasons (*PR*, 28–32, 38). Culturally conservative romantics may seek to escape the positivism of the present by taking refuge in the past, in history, but their only ultimately subjective interest in it and their strategic deployment of it replicates the positivism they oppose: "The temporally or spatially remote romantic object – regardless of whether it is the glory of classical antiquity, the noble chivalry of the Middle Ages, or the powerful grandeur of Asia – is not of interest for its own sake. It is a trump card that is played against the commonplace, actual reality of the present, and it is intended to negate the present" (*PR*, 70).

In romanticism, according to Schmitt, the object is still given substantive content only by the subjects themselves and is subsequently manipulated for an external strategy – this is the very definition of positivism. In fact, Schmitt refers to the romantic's mode of procedure in such a way as to underscore its mechanistic quality; he calls it "romantic productivity" that manipulates objects of the material world as if they were interchangeable, in much the same way as the technology of industrial production:

> Surrender to this romantic productivity involves the conscious renunciation of
> an adequate relationship to the visible, external world. Everything real is only
> an *occasion*. The object is without substance, essence and function. It is a
> concrete point about which the romantic game of fantasy moves. As a starting
> point, this concrete point always remains present, but without any commen-

45   On Hegel's understanding of these deficiencies of Kantian rationality and the relative
success of his attempt to overcome them, see Pippin, *Hegel's Idealism*, pp. 17–19, 27–8,
31–8, 180, 253–4.

surable relation to the romantic digression, which is the only thing essential [to the romantic]. In consequence, there is no possibility of distinguishing a romantic object from the other object – the Queen, the state, the beloved, the Madonna – precisely because there are no longer any objects but only *occasiones*. (*PR*, 84–5, emphases added)

As noted earlier, in *Political Form* Schmitt identifies the abstract processes of technological production as rendering all matter commensurable such that there was no longer a distinction between the production of "a silk blouse or poison gas" (*RC*, 14). Four years earlier, here in *Political Romanticism,* he identifies the romantic's arbitrary, concrete ascription of quality to objects – romantic products – as also encouraging a commensurability of objects. Every particular instance of the sensual world becomes ultimately the same, because the individual's whim is the determining factor in defining reality such that "forms without substance can be related to any content. In the normative anarchy, everyone can form his own world, elevate every word and every sound to a vessel of infinite possibilities, and transform every situation and every event in a romantic fashion" (*PR*, 76–7). Activity that drains concrete specificity from the actual world so that it may manipulate its components, technology, is mirrored by activity that endlessly imputes a random concrete specificity to aspects of that world in a subjective scheme of manipulation, romanticism.

No matter how devoted they may seem to the object of their attentions – whether the affection of a beloved, the preservation of tradition, or the emancipation of the people – romantics are in the end "always occupied with themselves" (*PR*, 75). Romantics are incapable of substantially interacting with others or the world because of their fundamental self-absorption. For instance, Schmitt asserts, "Fichte's absolute ego, revamped in an emotional and aestheticized fashion, results in an altered world, not by means of activity, but by mood and imagination. . . . [I]t can be absolutely creative in absolute subjectivity, namely, by producing chimeras, by 'poeticizing'" (*PR*, 84).

The romantic's own emotions or affectations and the intensity thereof are all that lend importance to the objects that arouse, or serve as occasions for such responses (*PR*, 94, 100). The object in fact ideally ought not protrude anything of itself into the enraptured trance of the romantic, "who has no interest in really changing the world, [and] regards it as good if it does not disturb him in his illusions" (*PR*, 98). The essence of romanticism, and political romanticism especially, for Schmitt, is passivity (*PR*, 115). As he declares in the chapter added to *Political Romanticism* in 1920, despite its

feigned intense engagement with the world, romanticism is "the unconditional passivism that destroys all activity" (*PR*, 116). As Weber remarks in the
"Politics" lecture of the practitioners of the unreconstructed ethic of absolute conviction: They are ultimately not interested in their political action
or their cause or issue but only their own egos; they are what Schmitt would
soon call political romantics: "windbags who do not fully realize what they
take upon themselves but who intoxicate themselves with romantic sensa-
tions. . . . and mystic flight from reality."[46]

Schmitt declares that romanticism is passive because the superiorly subjective, aloof, and unengaged disposition of the romantic is inherently
linked with an actual enslavement to the objective environment itself:
"When the isolated subject treats the world as an *occasio* . . . the activity of
the subject consists only in the fanciful animation of its affect. The romantic
reacts only with his affect. His activity is the affective echo of an activity that
is necessarily not his own" (*PR*, 94; cf. 162). The romantic is both superior
to his or her objects of choice in attribution or accentuation of contents that
are the subject's, but also subservient to the object that arouses the emotional response.

The romantics who are somewhat sensitive to the presence of a dualist
structure to which they may be a part do not simply remain in subjective
passivity. Schmitt describes how they attempt to account for the dualism not
in any theoretical sense but in an exclusively aesthetic one. Rather than
interrogate their sources, this type of romanticism "transforms the oppositions it sees into an aesthetically balanced harmony. . . . [I]t does not produce a unity from the dualism, it reduces the opposition to aesthetic or
emotional contrasts in order to fuse them" (*PR*, 55). The results are always
formulated in a "pithy and striking" manner, but none of the "antithetical
constructs" can be traced to "a science or to ethics. . . . The only productivity that the subject can develop in this situation is of an aesthetic sort" (*PR*,
104). Schmitt identifies Adam Müller's "rhetorical contrasts" as examples of
posited oppositions that are not substantive antinomies:

> Müller's arguments can be judged only as an oratorical performance. The
> antitheses he expounds are not objective differences or oppositions, the su-
> perlatives are not substantive enhancements, and the "ternary" is not an accu-
> mulation of ideas, but rather of words. The antitheses are rhetorical. They are
> oratorical pendants, and with the help of rhythm and the effect of sonority,
> they have a suggestive force. This is how the high-romantic assertions and

46   Weber, "Politics as a Vocation," pp. 127–8.

blending of every imaginable "antithesis" are justified: man and woman, city and country, . . . body and soul, person and thing, . . . and so on. They are interchanged. Sometimes they are treated as parallel contrasts, sometimes as antitheses, and sometimes as identities. They always however remain mere sounds and chords that blend, contrast, or harmonize in accordance with the oratorical effect in a single case. . . . [E]very idea is construed in opposition. (*PR*, 137–9)

Even though Schmitt expresses reservation regarding the mechanical and the technical in modernity, he is not prepared to accept the particular antithesis of "life versus mechanics" posed by the romantics, because it is not properly considered (*PR*, 101). Consistent with his position in *"Northern Lights"* and, as we will see in Chapter 2, in the "Neutralizations" essay, he regards such a position as merely an intellectual negation, not a philosophical conclusion, that is in fact itself a rather mechanical formulation.

If they attempt at all to transcend the rhetorical "thunder" of their posed oppositions (*PR*, 104), romantics often do so by appealing to a "higher third" (*PR*, 66, 85): "[T]he occasionalist does not explain a dualism, but rather lets it stand. He makes it illusory, however, by shifting into a comprehensive third sphere" (*PR*, 87). Adjectives like "true," "real," and "genuine" are often attached to one of the entities opposed to one another as a substitution for resolution (*PR*, 92): For example, "*real* soul" is meant to incorporate everything that is contrasted by the terms "body and soul." Such maneuvers, although appearing profound, serve to "conceal the simple structure of the romantic mode of being" (*PR*, 91; translation amended).

Although carefully exposing the romantic's ineptitude in dealing with these oppositions and suggesting that one must address them with "mediation and interaction" (*PR*, 88), Schmitt does not actually do so in the main text of *Political Romanticism*. He writes briefly in the introduction about the need "to ascertain what is systematically essential by means of a conscious delineation to a specific historical complex" (*PR*, 31; translation amended). Yet each time he seems poised to undertake such an historicization, each time he appears prepared to show how such oppositions are grounded in the structural social realities of their particular moment, he cites yet another example of romantic deficiency, against which he proceeds to polemicize (e.g., *PR*, 91). In the new preface published in 1923, Schmitt describes the kind of historical contextualization that it would take to ground the oppositions the romantics play with and are an inadequately self-understood component of. The problem with the contemporary attempt to account for romanticism is that it does not constitute historical knowledge. Its defect is that, as a result of a dogmatic and moralistic abstraction, it fails to recognize the historical distinctiveness of the movement. . . . We have to take every intellectual movement seriously, both metaphysically and morally, not as an instance of an abstract thesis, but as a concrete historical reality in the context of a historical process. . . . [The point is] not to unmask a fraud or to "hunt down a poor rabbit" . . . [but rather] to give an objective answer to a question that is seriously intended. (*PR*, 5, 21)

The need to historicize phenomena rather than transtemporally generalize them, such that their specificity is lost, is a sophisticated critical-theoretical point. To examine an intellectual position such that one properly understands its place in history, and so that one can be sure that it is not just an ideological product, reflection, or affirmation of the moment, is one of the most important tenets of any kind of critical thought after Kant. To truly effect change that does not unreflectively reinforce history as it is but understands one's particular moment in a way that conditions the possibility of participating in history, that makes *practice* possible, is the essence of an active Hegelianism.[47]

But when Schmitt provides examples of who has most seriously practiced such an approach, it is no longer Hegel he cites but the Catholic counterrevolutionaries, such as Joseph de Maistre, Edmund Burke, Louis Bonald, and Donoso Cortés (*PR*, 8–9). Until we examine Schmitt's counterproposal to the "passivity" engendered by romanticism, it does not become clear why they would be different from the German conservatives he previously criticized for romanticizing history or simply negating it.

The passivity encouraged by romanticism that so rouses Schmitt's ire is normatively evaluated in negative terms by him. Echoing Weber's warringgods formulation, he claims that "the essential feature of the intellectual situation of the romantic is that in the struggle of the deities he does not commit himself and his subjective personality" (*PR*, 64). The romantic shirks the responsibility of engaging in the struggle of ideologies that *is* modernity and of choosing between right and wrong. Following Weber closely here in 1919 while he was still alive, the essence of nonromantic activity, according to Schmitt, is normatively responsible, as opposed to aesthetically whimsical, decision: "[I]t should not be difficult to differentiate [romantic] organic passivity from the restraints of an active statesman that result from political experience and objectives. The criterion is

---

47   See Seyla Benhabib, *Critique, Norm and Utopia: A Study of the Foundations of Critical Theory* (New York: Columbia University Press, 1986).

whether the ability to make a decision between right and wrong is present" (*PR*, 116). Romantics shy away from politics, which means making value judgments that cannot be deferred into the quest for an ephemeral "higher third" (*PR*, 117).

This necessity of deciding and acting on what is right and wrong leads Schmitt to the bizarre position of employing Don Quixote as the model of political activity: Quixote is superior to such romantics as Adam Müller and A. F. Schlegel, because "he was capable of seeing the difference between right and wrong and of making a decision in favor of what seemed right to him," even if he was driven "to a senseless disregard of external reality" (*PR*, 147–8). Now performing the collapse into incoherence that inevitably awaits Weber's distinction of politics of responsibility versus politics of conviction, Schmitt blurs the two such that "fantastically absurd" practice is considered better than romantic activity, because it is not inherently passive and is willing to act for what it perceives as right (*PR*, 148). By this standard only do the often ecstatic theoretical efforts of Burke and especially Donoso Cortés and Maistre – efforts that could easily be seen as extreme examples of political romanticism – qualify as nonromantic because of the deeply convicted quality of their political attachments. Through the examples of these figures, Schmitt attempts to Catholicize the seemingly essentially Protestant-like quality of the "here I stand" orientation advocated by Weber. In commitment to a cause that is both responsibly considered and absolutely unyielding, Catholics can be as resolute as Protestants. In fairness to the Left, Schmitt is willing to make concessions to your average revolutionary or conservative who hold such convictions and have thoroughly considered the consequences of their actions (*PR*, 147–8).

I draw conclusions about the ramifications of these insights for Schmitt's theory in general as he spells out his own theoretical-political convictions in *Political Form* and the "Neutralizations" piece later. Here we may observe that in *"Northern Lights"* Schmitt focused on how the technoscientific aspect of modernity abstracts away from all reality, such that it can manipulate it, rendering all objects the same and hence meaningless, whereas in *Political Romanticism,* he interrogates the opposite side of this rationality that arbitrarily infuses all objects with aesthetic meaning, such that it is equally irrational. The point of his early theoretical endeavor is to formulate a rationality that can overcome both, but not in the purely rhetorical or sentimental way of the romantics. What is clear from Schmitt's account is the extent to which Weberian ethical stands, no matter how "responsible," may foster irrational activity by what Schmitt calls elsewhere "a senseless disregard of external reality" when that reality is depicted as irresistible, unchangeable, and impenetrable, as it generally is by Weber.[48] A rationally justifiable normative viewpoint may not remain such within the dynamic that renders it inherently ineffective vis-à-vis the "real world." On the other hand, once Schmitt fully sheds Weberian neo-Kantianism because of its depiction of reality, it is questionable to what extent he has any recourse at all to the Kantian categories of right and wrong.

Georg Lukács's own initial theoretical confrontation with modernity in his studies of literature and aesthetics, particularly in *The Soul and the Forms,* "The Sociology of Modern Drama," and *The Theory of the Novel,* has been well documented;[49] Schmitt's almost-identical early approach elucidated earlier has not, at least in English.[50] Therefore, I do not want to comment as extensively here on these early works of Lukács as I do on his masterpiece of 1923, *History and Class Consciousness,* and compare it with *Roman Catholicism and Political Form.* Some remarks on Lukács's socioliterary work are nonetheless warranted.

Lukács in these writings, like Schmitt in his own, appropriates not only the objective side of Weber's narrative – the "spirit of capitalism" component – but the subjective one as well, more specifically, his concern with personal, individual dispositions like the Protestant "ethic." Therefore, in Lukács's case, long before making these opposing objective and subjective categories famous in his "Antinomies of Bourgeois Thought" section of *History and Class Consciousness,* he was already juxtaposing these theoretical moments of modernity in his studies of literature. However, still within the realm of the neo-Kantianism that he shared with Weber in these literary analyses before the twenties, Lukács's orientation toward these antinomies was different from the way they would appear in his Hegelian-Marxist writings a few years later. The crucial opposition of abstract, objective form and concrete, subjective content is more or less treated in a way that actually privileges the former in Lukács's early literary works. For instance, in *Soul and Form,* he pursues a marriage of the timeless elements of his collection's title – "the mystical moment of the union of internal and external, the soul

48 See Schmitt, *Political Theology: Four Chapters on the Concept of Sovereignty* (1922), trans. George Schwab (Cambridge, Mass.: MIT Press, 1985), pp. 147–8.

49 See the collection, *Die Seele und das Leben: Studien zum frühen Lukács,* ed. Agnes Heller et al. (Frankfurt a. M.: Suhrkamp, 1977); and in English: *Lukács Reappraised,* ed. A. Heller (New York: Columbia University Press, 1983). G. H. R. Parkinson's *Georg Lukács* (London: Routledge & Kegan Paul, 1977) nicely integrates the concerns of the early aesthetic studies and those of *History and Class Consciousness.*

50 See my "Transcending Weber's Categories"; and in the German literature, Mehring, *Pathetisches Denken.*

and the form" – but he does so in a way that prioritizes the latter, abstract *forms* over the substantive content of *soul*.[51] Just as Weber deploys the formal, often transhistorically applied, categories of the "ideal type" to impart meaning to empirical reality in his methodology,[52] Lukács views literary genres, for example, as the frameworks that allow the substance of literary reality to emerge: "[F]orm sets limits round a substance which otherwise would dissolve like air."[53] Moreover, much like Weber's famous social-scientific observer – the impartial, neutral, impersonal subject – who in effect creates meaning through interpretive analysis of material reality by means of the techniques of the atemporal formal types,[54] Lukács's literary critic likewise draws reality from the chaos of literary material: "The critic is one who glimpses destiny in forms: whose most profound experience is the soul-content which forms indirectly and unconsciously conceal within themselves."[55]

As is well known, in Weber the neutrality and atemporality of the methodology does not, however, prevent the expression of a prejudiced disposition over historical specificity: for example, the melancholy ruminations at the conclusions of *The Protestant Ethic* and the "Science" lecture, which fuels the call for responsible personal stands in the "Politics" and "Parliament and Government" lectures. Lukács's early writings betray a similar lament over, and desire to actively transcend, the alienation brought on by a rationalized modernity. In this regard, he frequently exhibits an existential pathos derived often explicitly from Kierkegaard, Nietzsche, and Dostoyevsky. *The Theory of the Novel*, for instance, much like Schmitt's "Northern Lights," repeatedly praises the artists and thinkers of the Middle Ages for capturing what is simultaneously transcendent and finite in their world: Giotto, St. Thomas, St. Francis, and, most important, Dante, are praised for expressing a "wholeness" that is inaccessible to modernity.[56] Weber lifts from Tolstoy the biblical image of the contented Abraham to contrast with the alienated citizen of modernity;[57] curiously, Lukács, again like Schmitt, employs the title character of Cervantes's *Don Quixote* to make an even more profound

51 Lukács, *Soul and Form,* p. 8.
52 Cf. in theory: Weber, *The Methodology of the Social Sciences,* trans. and ed. G. Roth and C. Wittich (New York: Free Press, 1949), p. 90; and in practice: "Types of Legitimate Authority" in *ES,* pp. 212–301.
53 Lukács, *Soul and Form,* p. 7.
54 For a discussion of the intricacies of Weber's "ideal types" and his "objectivity" thesis, see Susan Hekman, "Max Weber and Post-Positivist Social Theory" in *The Barbarism of Reason.*
55 Lukács, *Soul and Form,* p. 8.
56 Lukács, *Theory of the Novel,* pp. 37, 101–2.
57 Weber, "Science as a Vocation," p. 140.

point: In Cervantes's novel, Lukács finds the last historical instance when objective reality and subjective experience, moments of the eternally unchanging and the fleetingly ephemeral, coexisted in the West before disintegrating in modernity. Lukács laments that after Cervantes the relationship of subjective disposition and objective reality, correlates to what he had theorized as "soul and form," is fractured, leaving individual consciousness alienated from the outside world and condemned to an "all-devouring concentration on a single point of existence," a "narrowing of their souls."[58] This is the same frivolous enrapture with internal moods characteristic of romanticism and *Lebensphilosophie* that Schmitt criticizes in *Political Romanticism*

In their earliest literary studies then, both Lukács and Schmitt adopt Weber's theory of modernity as the culmination of a rationalization process driven forward by modern capitalism. They also reiterate Weber's frequent laments over the quantitatively impersonal forces that eradicate what is qualitatively specific about human existence. In *Soul and Form*, Lukács had criticized modern aesthetics, particularly as manifested by romanticism, as the appropriate expression of capitalism, despite its often self-understood opposition to it. Romantics promote an "aesthetic culture" whose passivity conforms perfectly with the helplessness of the bourgeois and the unreflective activity of industrial production that, for all its apparent frenzy, is still deemed passive by Lukács.[59] Lukács thus thoroughly criticizes the same interiority and subjective preoccupation that fosters the social passivity identified by Schmitt, in his own literary studies.

Commentators find in the conclusion of Lukács's *Theory of the Novel* a turn from Kant to Hegel.[60] Others have found in Schmitt's post–*Political Romanticism* work a dramatic declaration of independence from neo-Kantianism.[61] It is quite likely that the dissatisfaction with the opposition of subject and object elucidated in their early works, its manifestation in the theory of their mentor (individual ethic versus societal rationalization), and its apparent inability to be transcended by "bourgeois" thought and reality foster this

58   Lukács, *Theory of the Novel*, pp. 104–6.
59   Ibid.
60   See, e. g., Parkinson, and Arato and Breines. On the question of continuity and discontinuity between Lukács's literary works and *History*, see Gyorgy Márkus, "Life and the Soul: The Young Lukács and the Problem of Culture," in *Lukács Reappraised*.
61   Jacob Taubes, for one, identifies the first chapter of *Political Theology* of 1922 as just such a declaration; see *Die Politische Theologie des Paulus* (Munich: Fink, 1993), pp. 141–2. See also the fine volume edited by Taubes, *Der Fürst dieser Welt: Carl Schmitt und die Folgen* (Munich: Wilhelm Fink, 1983). On the trajectory of Schmitt's early thought in general, see Reinhard Mehring, *Carl Schmitt: Zur Einführung* (Hamburg: Junius, 1992), pp. 55–77.

turn: the transition to political perspectives that explicitly seek to overcome these impasses, and the composition of some of the most important essays in non- or antiliberal thought intended to foster this overcoming.

Left- and Right-wing Hegelianism versus Kantian Liberalism

By 1923, the publication dates of the two works that serve as the centerpiece of this chapter, both Lukács and Schmitt had only recently undergone conversions of sorts. Lukács had joined the Hungarian Communist party by 1919, and Schmitt had shifted from conservative neo-Kantianism to a more radical theoretical position, the specific account and analysis of which I undertake toward the end of this chapter and in subsequent chapters. Moving away from a quasi-Kantian approach to the form/content, production/consumption dualities, by means of the formally privileged method of ideal types in socioliterary studies, Schmitt and Lukács seek to overcome the divide in concrete political practice and historical reality in their works from 1923. The Weberian narrative of history, in which historical time is posited as space to be filled by increasingly rationalized complexity and subsystem differentiation, is perceived by the two theorists as rendering implausible the prescribed responsible, original, and meaningful activity of Weberian ethics. A new conception of history and a new understanding of action is developed by Weber's students to rectify and overcome the limitations of their teacher's worldview.

This new theoretical-political orientation and new evaluation of Weber is signaled by a comparison of the titles of the two works from 1923 with that of Weber's most famous effort:

> *The Protestant Ethic and the Spirit of Capitalism*
> *History and Class Consciousness*
> *Roman Catholicism and Political Form*

The significance of Lukács's title lies in the suggestion that capitalism has *not* in fact facilitated the once-and-for-all constructed iron cage that permanently arrests historical development, over which Weber laments at the conclusion of his work. Rather "history" continues to foster qualitative social transformation because the agent of this change is not the, in Weber's estimation, now-exhausted Protestant sects and their "ethic" or "values" but the still immanently active agency of productive labor now embodied in the proletarian "class."

Schmitt's title, on the other hand, does not so much refute the specifics of Weber's historical account of modernity as much as suggest a possible way out of the petrified theoretical-practical dead end that Weber's thesis, its process and its agents, brought about: The residue of the inward perspective of Protestantism that had generated a process of social change through activity – whose results it can no longer control – now seeks refuge more and more in types of privacy, manifested aesthetically in romanticism and politically in liberalism. This passive and stagnant retreat from the social world is countered by Schmitt with a Catholicism that supposedly transcends objective and subjective antinomies rather than perpetuates them, and whose public, as opposed to private, disposition is manifested in the primacy of politics rather than a sacred domestic or economic realm. Both qualities restore substantive meaning to the world.[62]

Both theorists support their new positions by reassessing the form/content, object/subject relationship that they tried to navigate within neo-Kantianism during Weber's lifetime. Rather than attempting to effect the liberation of the qualitatively concrete aspects of social life by applying the appropriate formally abstract a priori categories to it, as with the use of ideal types in their socioliterary studies, both theorists pursue explicitly *practical*, that is, not *passive* approaches that allow qualitative reality, especially social reality, to emerge and itself determine and interact with the forms of specific concrete existence. Political activity entails identifying the political forms of social life's substantive expression. Schmitt and Lukács perceive themselves as carrying out this agenda without lapsing into a romantic enrapture with such concrete reality that cannot itself apprehend the latter's qualitative existence. To properly pursue such a strategy, the individualistic characteristics of Weber's subjective standpoint – political and methodological – must give way to a theorizing of a collective standpoint that will not *participate* in a subject/object dualism but will itself *be* the identical subject-object that transcends it philosophically and politically. An intersubjective standpoint, made viable by changes in consciousness delivered through dramatic and dynamic historical change, will supposedly overcome the metaphysical *aporiai* of Kantian derived notions of an individual subject that interacts indeterminately, artificially, and "passively" with an objective world, and of history as interpreted in terms of a linear progression of ever-increasing rationalization and complexity. The former aspect of this worldview renders impossible the attempt to act in the world, and the latter precludes the

---

62   See Ulmen, *Politische Mehrwert*, pp. 179–211; and his introduction to *Political Form*, for his own discussion of the significance of this set of titles.

possibility of qualitative change within the world. But before condemning or dismissing Schmitt and Lukács for the excesses that already might seem so obviously invited by such a reorientation – the move from the individual to the collective and from sober progress to radical change – it is necessary first to grapple with the seriousness of the political-theoretical dilemma that faced them and to apprehend the critical-theoretical aspect of their approaches.

In both works, the phenomenon of rationalization is not abandoned as a social problem despite Schmitt's and Lukács's self-understood departure from Weber's method. Both acknowledge the obvious hegemony of abstract-quantitative analysis in the social sciences and its ties to societal rationalization writ large. As Schmitt observes, its influence is nearly all-pervasive: "In almost every discussion one can observe the extent to which the methodology of the natural-technical sciences dominates contemporary thinking" (RC, 12). And Lukács remarks on the infiltration of thought by the purely technical and the increasing "quantification" of rationality (HCC, 98) in modern society: "[T]he demand that mathematical and rational categories should be applied to all phenomena. . . . interacts fruitfully with a technology becoming increasingly more rationalized" (HCC, 113). But he now attributes the genesis of this rationality to a Marxian category and no longer to a Weberian one: "The modern modes of thought already eroded by the reifying effects of the dominant commodity form" encourage purely "quantitative" analyses of society and not "qualitative" ones (HCC, 84).

Schmitt reiterates his reservations regarding a mode of production that offers no normative accounting for the products of that process, whether they be used for decoration or death, a silk blouse or poison gas: "A mechanism of production serving the satisfaction of arbitrary material needs is called 'rational' without bringing into question what is most important – the rationality of the purpose that can make use of this supremely rational mechanism" (RC, 15). One of the main theses of both works is still the fact that human beings themselves, in their potentially limitless qualitative uniqueness, become commensurable material objects for manipulation by an economic-technical rationality. Lukács remarks how this rationality imposes on society "a second nature" that is "a more soulless, impenetrable nature than feudalism ever was" (HCC, 19). Although this might sound reminiscent of Weber's description of bureaucratized modernity as a "shell of bondage" (ES, 1402), Lukács and Schmitt both offer alternatives to this new form of domination that are not available to Weber and his categories.

At the outset of the central essay of History and Class Consciousness, "Reification and the Consciousness of the Proletariat," Lukács embeds his analysis of modern rationalization no longer primarily in terms of Weber's sociology but now explicitly in terms of Marx's commodity form: It is the "commodity structure" of modern capitalism that facilitates the situation in which "relations between people take on the character of things" (*HCC*, 83) and generates the consequent "progressive elimination of the qualitative, human and individual attributes of the worker" (*HCC*, 88). The commodity form is "the central, structural problem of capitalist society in all its aspects" (*HCC*, 88).[63] The total commensurability of commodities in capitalism – the fact that for Schmitt a silk blouse can be equated unproblematically with poison gas – is grounded by Lukács in Marx's analyses of the exchange and use values of the commodity: "The formal act of exchange which constitutes the basic fact for the theory of marginal utility likewise suppresses use-value as use-value and establishes a relation of concrete equality between concretely unequal and indeed incomparable objects" (*HCC*, 104). It is the exchange value that conceals what is qualitatively specific about objects – a reduction of qualitative difference to the relative quantitative amounts of labor hours it took to produce them and ignoring what is "organic, irrational and qualitatively determined" about them (*HCC*, 88).[64] Sounding more like fellow anticommunist and fellow future Nazi, Martin Heidegger,[65] in this particular instance, than Lukács (who would later endorse Stalinist Russia), Schmitt, however, asserts at one point that the same economic-technical thinking governs Soviet Communism as Western capitalism:

> The world-view of the modern capitalist is the same as that of the industrial proletarian, as if one were the twin brother of the other. Thus they are of one accord when they struggle side by side for economic thinking. Insofar as socialism has become the religion of the industrial proletariat of big cities it contraposes a fabulous mechanism to that of the capitalist world. . . . The big industrialist has no other ideal than that of Lenin – an "electrified earth." They disagree essentially on the correct method of electrification. American financiers and Russian Bolsheviks find themselves in common struggle for economic thinking. (*RC*, 13)[66]

63 Cf. Karl Marx, *Capital: A Critique of Political Economy*, trans. B. Fowkes (London: Vintage, 1976) vol. 1, chap. 1.
64 For a more comprehensive analysis of the commodity form, see Moishe Postone, *Time, Labor and Social Domination: A Reinterpretation of Marx's Critical Theory* (New York: Cambridge University Press, 1993).
65 See Victor Farias, *Heidegger and the Nazis* (Philadelphia: Temple University Press, 1989).
66 Cf. Heidegger's famous statement on the similarity of the United States and the Soviet Union: "From a metaphysical view, Russia and America are the same; the same dreary

Although both Schmitt and Lukács criticize the romantic obsession with concrete particularity and its own manipulation through subjective aesthet_icization, both are sensitive to the vulnerability of qualitative reality in the face of the power of abstract rationality. According to Lukács, under the imperative of "technical" and "economic autonomy" in the sphere of pro_duction, "the human qualities and idiosyncrasies of the worker appear in_creasingly as mere sources of error when contrasted with . . . abstract special laws functioning according to rational predictions" (*HCC*, 89). The princi_ple of rationalization "must declare war" on the "organic," the "irrational," and the "qualitatively determined" (*HCC*, 88).

Schmitt, in the mode of Catholic apologetics, asserts that the rationality of the Roman Church, despite its universalism, has actually defended local particularities of many sorts from various forms of universalization, even when the enemy of the former was not necessarily an enemy of the Church (*RC*, 6). Schmitt finds it ironic that Protestant opponents of Catholicism would identify it as a mechanical force, "a papal machine," "a monstrous hierarchical power apparatus" (*RC*, 4).[67] Appropriating Weber into his apol_ogia and turning against Weber's political-theological standpoint and Web_er's own social scientific conclusions, Schmitt declares that it is of course Protestantism and its accompanying rationality that actually level all the particularities of nature mechanically:

> The Huguenot and the Puritan has a strength and pride that is often inhu_man. He is capable of living on any soil. But it would be wrong to say he finds roots in every soil. He can build his industry far and wide, make all soil the servant of his skilled labor and "inner-worldly asceticism," and in the end have a comfortable home; all this because he makes himself master of nature and harnesses it to his will. His type of domination remains inaccessible to the Roman Catholic concept of nature. (*RC*, 10)

To discerning observers, this abstract domination that accompanies the rationalization process is only part of the story: "The rationalization of the world *appears* to be complete," says Lukács (*HCC*, 101). This only apparently omnipotent reign of rationalization is in fact merely a component within a dualism that itself obtains in reality. It is a dualism that, according to

technological frenzy, the same unrestricted organization of the average man." *An Introduc_tion to Metaphysics* (1953), trans. Ralph Manheim (Garden City, N.J.: Doubleday Anchor, 1961), p. 37. Lukács was as positively obsessed with Russia (see Arato and Breines, *The Young Lukács*, p. 69) as Schmitt was negatively so obsessed, as we will see in Chapter 2.
67 Weber refers to the "machinery of the papacy" (*ES*, 809).

Schmitt, has a structural basis in fact and takes on many incarnations. Rationalization is merely a part of the same dualistic structure, a part that confronts its opposite whether that opposite be a romantic valorization of nature, Weber's emphasis on charisma, or even Däubler's elevation of soul: "Though it sounds improbable [these dualisms] are completely in harmony with the spirit of our age because their intellectual structure accords with a reality. Their point of departure is actually a real cleavage and division: an antithesis which calls for a synthesis" (*RC*, 9). The economic-technical rationalism of modernity, so entirely devoid of content, is interrelated with the very opposite of that rationalism, which in its role as opposite has as little valid pretense to "reality" as the rationality it opposes. One cannot apprehend the whole by privileging one side as the superior or truer reality over the other. Hence Schmitt's earlier skepticism of Däubler's ability to formulate an articulate rational standpoint when he opposes a totalizing rationality with an equally totalized spirituality.

Recasting the arguments of *Political Romanticism*, Schmitt sets out in *Political Form* the typology of the "radical dualism" that governs "every sphere of the contemporary epoch":

> Its common ground is a concept of nature that has found its realization in a world transformed by technology and industry. Nature appears today as the polar antithesis of the mechanistic world of big cities whose stone, iron and glass structures lie on the face of the earth like colossal Cubist creations. The antithesis of this empire of technology is nature untouched by civilization, wild and barbarian – a reservation into which "man with his affliction does not set foot." (*RC*, 9–10)

Likewise, Lukács points out that "nature is a social category" (*HCC*, 130), reminding us that this untouched nature that supposedly exists outside the realm of modern rationalization is itself an ideological construct that conforms with rationalization. Schmitt indicates the many variations that the oppositions – of which technology/nature is just a single example – may take: classicism/romanticism, abstract/concrete, form/content, objective/subjective, rationality/irrationality, "mute practicality"/"rapturously overpowering music," and so on – "A whole assortment of antitheses with which to play!" (*RC*, 23).

In the preface to the second edition of *Political Romanticism*, published a year after *Political Form* in 1924, Schmitt again identifies this theoretical problem as "agreement in negation": "Negative commonalities of this sort lead to unexpected and absurd associations" (*PR*, 6). The one that Schmitt finds particularly irksome in both books is the romantic linking of Catholicism with nature, irrationality, and sentimentality. In *Political Romanticism*, he expresses discomfort with the fact that the major examples of romantics that he analyzes, such as Müller and Schlegel, all converted to Catholicism (*PR*, 32). He tries to dissociate romantics who merely "toyed" (*RC*, 9) with Catholicism from "active" Catholics like Bonald, Maistre, Donoso Cortés, and the closet Catholic, Burke (*PR*, 32).[68] He angrily rejects such a correlation (*PR*, 49) and points out how Catholicism and Protestantism can both be mistakenly identified as expressions of romanticism (*PR*, 12, 14).

The romantic attempt to associate the Roman Church with the latter sides of these oppositions, "to make the Church into the antagonistic pole of the mechanistic age," only serves to perpetuate the first sides of the antitheses and the whole of the mechanistic age itself (*RC*, 11). Like Däubler's poem, the church would be a mere "complement" to the age: "Were the Church to have rested content with being nothing more than the soulful polarity of soullessness it would have forgotten its true self; it would have become the desired complement to capitalism – a hygienic institution for enduring the rigors of competition, a Sunday outing or a summer sojourn of big-city dwellers" (*RC*, 11–12). In 1923, Catholicism serves as Schmitt's standpoint of critique precisely because it supposedly does not fall into one or the other sides of the modern dualism: "Such a dichotomy between a rationalistic-mechanistic world of human labor and a romantic-virginal state of nature is totally foreign to the Roman Catholic concept of nature" (*RC*, 10). For Schmitt, the manner in which Catholicism "represents" humanity and sustains it as something neither purely material nor wholly transcendent – neither matter nor spirit, machine nor ghost – grants the institution this place between these two poles. This notion of representation and its political implications will be taken up again in Chapter 4.

Lukács also sees economic-technical rationality and romantic intuitions as part of the same structure – misunderstood "antinomies of bourgeois thought" – but comes to this conclusion from a standpoint other than Roman Catholicism. Drawing on the origins of modern philosophical rationalism, much as Schmitt did in *Political Romanticism* and continues to do in *Political Form*, Lukács describes how Enlightenment philosophy from Descartes to Kant conceives of the world as the product of the knowing subject by means of mathematics and geometry that are derived from the

---

68 Schmitt goes so far as to suggest, in 1919, that the counterrevolutionaries were "real" Catholics, something he retracts in 1922, when he acknowledges the apostasy of their insistence on the evil of human nature; see *PT*, 57.

"formal presuppositions of objectivity in general" (*HCC*, 111–12). Unable to account for the thing-in-itself, Enlightenment philosophy turns increasingly "inward" to find the subject from which knowledge can be derived (*HCC*, 122). But Kantian rationality illustrates not only how "every rational system will strike a frontier or barrier of irrationality" but also, because of the penetration of abstract rationality into all aspects of society through the commodification of everything, why irrationality "erodes and dissolves the whole system" (*HCC*, 114). Concrete reality, imputed with irrationality by a rationality that must interact with these objects by manipulating them through technology, gains a revenge by disrupting the formally abstract nature of such rationality.

Lukács theorizes economic-technical rationality and romantic intuitions as part of the same structure through the analysis of the "fetish character of commodities" that takes on both "an objective form" and "a subjective stance" (*HCC*, 84). The two poles are "inextricably interwoven with each other. For here we can see that 'nature' has been heavily marked by the revolutionary struggle of the bourgeoisie: the 'ordered,' calculable, formal and abstract character [of nature, in addition to nature as] the repository of all the inner tendencies opposing the growth of mechanization, dehumanization and reification" (*HCC*, 136). The nonrational is set forth by the rational system itself: "For irrationality, the impossibility of reducing contents to their rational elements . . . can be seen at its crudest in the question of relating the sensuous content to the rational form" (*HCC*, 116).[69] Kantian rationality, rather than increasing rationalization, actually accentuates and encourages irrationality, because it cannot account for "the whole" – the source of the rational system in terms of the system itself and without reference to irrational reality; and moreover because it cannot *fully* abstract from the concreteness of its objects (*HCC*, 116). The thing-in-itself, which cannot be known within the Kantian system but whose existence is nevertheless affirmed by the latter, generates an indeterminacy that undermines the universal claims of the system's supposed totalizing rationality. Unrationalized nature is hence a source for a revival in "ecstasy," "resignation and despair," "irrational mystical experience" – "life" in the Nietzschean sense (*HCC*, 110). In other words, what is not rationalized is instead aestheticized. Lukács speaks of the resulting "ever-increasing importance of aesthetics" in this regard and how this new social development "conferred upon aesthetics and upon consciousness of art philosophical importance that art was unable to lay claim to in previous ages" (*HCC*, 137).

---

69 Cf. Pippin, *Kant's Theory of Form*, pp. 216–21.

Typically less economically focused than his Marxist alter ego, Schmitt attributes the relationship of the poles of the antinomies to more voluntaristic sources. For his part, several years later in a discussion of history in the "Neutralizations" essay, Schmitt describes how the nineteenth century was "characterized by the seemingly impossible combination of aesthetic-romantic and economic-technical tendencies," yet again demonstrates how the two tendencies are in fact interrelated. Romanticism, according to Schmitt, is

> only an intermediary step of the aesthetic situated in between the moralism of the eighteenth century and the economism of the nineteenth. It was only a transition which was affected easily and successfully by means of the aestheticization of all intellectual fields. For the path from metaphysics and morality to economics proceeds through the aesthetic. This path, traversing the most sublime state of aesthetic consumption and pleasure, is the safest and most comfortable path towards a general economization of the spiritual life and towards a state of mind which finds in production and consumption its central categories of human existence. (*ND*, 133)

The subjective morality of the eighteenth century, a subjectivity freed from the constraints of religion and dogma, gives way in the nineteenth to the subjective aesthetic appreciation of objects, again a realm once governed by traditional restraints. Capitalism and liberalism are hence allied with romanticism not opposed to it: "It is only in an individualistically disintegrated society that the aesthetically productive subject could shift the intellectual center to itself" thus causing alienation, anomie, passivity, and so on (*PR*, 19–20).

Romantics, as Schmitt had observed in *Political Romanticism*, seek out objects and situations as mere occasions for the expression of their subjective feelings. Lukács, following Marx, attributed this phenomenon to the use value of the commodity form, which is determined by the qualitatively specific and concrete modes of labor that produce it and, as such, invites an aesthetic absorption with the particular qualitative and concrete attributes of things – an arbitrarily subjective ascription of content to particular objects.[70] Schmitt recognizes, as do Marx and Lukács, that this aestheticization does not run in opposition to a simultaneous "economization" but is rather

---

70   Cf. Postone, *Time, Labor and Social Domination*, pp. 149–54, 168–70.

its "typical accompanying phenomenon" (*ND*, 133).[71] Capitalism is driven as much by the celebration of concrete reality, the sensual consumption of concrete objects, as by the abstract rationality that characterizes industrial production.

For Marx and Lukács, the latter conforms with the other moment of the commodity, its exchange value, which is reflective of the general or abstract labor that characterizes industrialized society as a whole. It is this side of modern society that is responsible for the total commensurability of commodities, the reduction of qualitatively different entities to quantitative equivalents, the rationality abstracted from material particularity, and the apparently resulting "valuelessness" of modernity. It is to this completely formal aspect of modern society that Schmitt refers when he remarks in *Political Form* that capitalism is utterly indifferent to the production of "a silk blouse or poison gas or anything whatsoever" (*RC*, 14–15). Nietzsche's complaint that since Plato "every concept arises from the equation of unequal things"[72] is embedded by Marx and Lukács within the practices of modern capitalism itself in a manner more historically specific and shown to be only a partially accurate account of modern phenomena.

Although Schmitt obviously would not concur with the Marxian claim that modernity is driven by the compulsion toward surplus value, the affinity I have highlighted helps demonstrate how Schmitt's account of modernity is free of some of the deficiencies that plague the thought of other major theorists from his intellectual milieu, particularly Weber but Nietzsche and Heidegger as well. Whereas these latter thinkers most often characterize modernity primarily in terms of its abstract, "valueless," formal and quantitative moment in their respective theories of "rationalization," "nihilism," or "enframing," Schmitt recognizes with Lukács and the tradition of critical theory that modernity also produces its own peculiar form of the concrete and the qualitative. Weber, Nietzsche, and Heidegger tend to view the concrete and qualitative as either remnants of the premodern past or something that must be "willed" into the modern present. As demonstrated,

71 In fact, years later Lukács cites this passage of Schmitt's with approval: Lukács remarks that Schmitt "was entirely in the right about liberal neo-Kantianism, as indeed he was in his sometimes ingenious polemic against liberal sociology. . . . He often saw clear through the unsubstantiated dogmatism masquerading as strict epistemology by which neo-Kantians converted justice into an autonomous, self-legitimizing area, on the pattern of its epistemology or aesthetics" (*The Destruction of Reason*, pp. 652–4).
72 Nietzsche, "On Truth and Lies in a Non-Moral Sense," in *Philosophy and Truth: Selections from Nietzsche's Notebooks of the Early 1870's*, trans. Daniel Breazeale (New Jersey: Humanities Press, 1990), p. 179.

Schmitt is more sensitive to the particular dualisms that make up modernity and modern thought and their interrelatedness: objective/subjective, form/content, abstract/concrete. How he attempts to resolve the dualisms will be a different story altogether.

Capitalism, Politics, or Class?

Thus Schmitt sees an unrestrained, irrational subjectivity as the "accompanying phenomenon" of a particularly restraining hyperrational objectivity in modernity. In portions added to *Political Romanticism* after *Political Form*, Schmitt describes the subjectivity thus: "In this society, it is left to the private individual to be his own priest. But not only that. Because of the central significance and consistency of the religious it is also left to him to be his own poet, his own philosopher, his own king, and his own master-builder in the Cathedral of his personality" (*PR*, 20). In other words, art, philosophy, politics, psychology, as well as religion become sites of subjective expression, of personal aestheticization. Anything, the revolution of 1789, or Catholicism itself, can become matter for aesthetic consumption (*RC*, 9, 12). The objects of aesthetic absorption differ as much as the innumerably variable possible aesthetic reactions to one particular object: "One romantic makes the Middle Ages into a paradise. Another . . . makes it into a gloomy vault where there is ghostlike moaning and groaning" (*PR*, 10). This analysis can even serve to criticize the kinds of positions we will find Schmitt taking vis-à-vis modernity in Chapter 2, positions that center on the figure of the Antichrist and the crucial friend/enemy thesis:

> Considered sociologically, the general process of aestheticizing serves only to privatize through the medium of the aesthetic the other domains of intellectual life as well. When the hierarchy of the intellectual sphere disintegrates, then everything can become the center of intellectual life. The nature of everything that is intellectual, including art itself, however is changed and falsified, when the aesthetic is absolutized and elevated to the focal point. Herein lies the first and most simple explanation of the plethora of romantic contradictions that seem to be so complicated. Religious, moral, political, and scientific matters appear in fantastical draperies and in strange colors and hues because, consciously or unconsciously, they are treated by the romantics as a theme for artistic and art-critical productivity. Neither religious, moral, or political decisions nor scientific concepts are possible in the domain of what is exclusively aesthetic. But it is certainly the case that all substantive oppositions and differences, good and evil, *friend and enemy, Christ and Antichrist,* can become aesthetic contrasts and means of intrigue in a novel, and they can be

aesthetically incorporated into the total effect of a work of art. In that case, the contradictions and complexities are profound and mysterious only as long as they are regarded with objective seriousness in the domain to which the romanticized object belongs; whereas we should allow them to have only an aesthetic effect on us. (*PR*, 16, emphasis added)

As Schmitt remarks in the 1919 text of *Political Romanticism,* there is nothing wrong with aesthetics qua aesthetics, provided it remains consigned to its appropriate fields. However, there are certain disquieting ramifications of the modern romantic tendency to aestheticize anything, indeed everything, and with this Lukács is in full agreement:

> [I]n the aesthetic mode, conceived as broadly as possible, [the contents of life] may be salvaged from the deadening effects of the mechanism of reification. But only in so far as these contents become aesthetic. That is to say, either the world must be aestheticized, which is an evasion of the real problem. . . . Or else, the aesthetic principle must be elevated into the principle by which objective reality is shaped: but that would be to *mythologize* the discovery of intuitive understanding. (*HCC*, 139–40, emphasis added)

In concurrence with the Schmitt of the passage above, according to Lukács, the romantic aestheticization of an object is an obfuscating move rather than a clarifying one, a move reminiscent of the Kantian rationality it seeks to escape: "[W]hat would seem to be the high-point of the interiorization of nature [characteristic of romanticism] really implies the abandonment of any true understanding of it. To make moods into the content presupposes the existence of unpenetrated and impenetrable objects (things-in-themselves) just as much as do the laws of nature" (*HCC*, 214). Agreeing with Schmitt, "irrational" aesthetic romanticism itself is a form of positivism – an unreflected and mechanical accepting of what is given – as much as economic-technical rationality, as stated previously, is a form of irrationality, an avoidance of a reality that must be taken into account in any serious theoretical endeavor.[73] Schmitt, for reasons I will discuss later in the chapter, does not, like Lukács, equate aestheticizing and mythologizing.

The failure of modern rationality to account for concrete reality – rationalization's reduction of it to quantitative measurements suitable for technological production and romanticism's attribution of qualities gener-

---

73   Theodor W. Adorno levels the same criticism against existentialism in *The Jargon of Authen-ticity* (1964), trans. K. Tarnowski and F. Will (Evanston, Ill.: Northwestern University Press, 1973), p. 43. See also Habermas, "Dogmatism, Reason and Decision: On Theory and Practice in Our Scientific Civilization" (1963), in *Theory and Practice.*

ated subjectively from the idiosyncrasies of the observer – has devastating ramifications for action in the world. The only possible resulting activity is technical manipulation, however impressively carried out by modern machinery, or detached observation, however intensely experienced by the individual subject. Like Schmitt, who asserted in *Political Romanticism,* that both the commercial activity of industrialism and the aesthetic activity of romanticism were inherently passive, Lukács also claims that the Cartesian-Kantian rationality that makes possible the mere manipulation of objects stripped of quality is contemplative activity not *practice* (*HCC,* 89). Because workers contribute nothing intelligent to the mode of production, their work is reactive and not creative, conforming only to preexisting forms, and hence is inherently passive (*HCC,* 89). The idea of qualitative reality being realized in the a priori Kantian forms is exposed here in the capitalist production process as a *pacifying* rather than a *realizing* process: "[T]he abstract, quantitative mode of calculability shows itself here in its purest form: the reified mind necessarily sees it as the form in which its own authentic immediacy becomes manifest and – as reified consciousness – does not even attempt to transcend it" (*HCC,* 93).

Weber's "iron cage" is hence a misrecognition of the role of production in modernity. The predictability of the rationalization process narrows human activity to what is already preordained, blinding it to the fact that it could in fact actively change the process itself.[74] The Kantian dilemma of a rationality that ultimately divorces ethics from the rationalized world, as elucidated by Schmitt and Lukács, thus becomes played out in Weberian practice. Lukács writes, "The reified world appears henceforth quite definitively . . . as the only possible world, the only conceptually accessible, comprehensible world vouchsafed to us humans. Whether this gives rise to ecstasy, resignation or despair, whether we search for a path leading to 'life' via irrational mystical experience, this will do absolutely nothing to modify the situation as it is in fact" (*HCC,* 110). Unlike Weber, Lukács does not designate the irrational as an emotional or psychological response to rationalization but rather as a different component of the modern mode of production that itself is misrecognized as having *only* a rationalizing effect by Weberian categories: The celebration of the concrete qualitative elements of modernity by romanticism are engendered by the use value moment of commodification that, veiled by the quantifying moment of exchange value, emerges inevitably in a nonrational as opposed to rationally mediated manner. However, irrationality's basis in a particular historical

74   Cf. Feenberg, *Lukács, Marx, and the Sources of Critical Theory,* pp. 95, 104–5.

practice implies that it can be overcome by a change in that practice as opposed to being simply willed away by Weber's attempt to ridicule and suppress the romantic or "mystical" impulse in others and force it to conform with the objective reality of the times, by encouraging only appropriately "responsible" subjective stances toward it. This ridicule, suppression, and compulsion reveal the "rationality" of Weber to be itself latently irrational.

According to Lukács, the fear of what cannot be apprehended through scientific means in the Weberian paradigm is sublimated into an increased reification of those means, which consequently ascertain less and less, further intensifying the original fear, and demand more conformity with objective reality (*HCC*, 128). Schmitt and Lukács would certainly have most readily recognized this disposition in Weber. In fact, the "Vocation" lectures make a perfect case study for this kind of dynamic: The more Weber champions the "objectivity" of his scientific method in the "Science" lecture, the more he must necessarily point up the drawbacks inherent in it. As a result, as his lecture continues, the scientific method is defended less as a rational procedure than as an existential stance. Consequently, his attacks on those he considers irrational become more personally polemical and themselves irrational; he says, for example, "it is *weakness* not to be able to countenance the stern seriousness of our fateful times."[75] The result in the "Politics" lecture, the solution to a disenchanted, value-free world is the "responsible" but still only subjectively justified, resolute, personal stand.[76] The ethics of responsibility supposedly entails more appreciation of objective reality than the ethics of conviction, but again Weber gives no evidence of how this slips any less precipitously into a warring-gods position. Hence, Weber's attempt to purify his methodological standpoint (value neutrality) serves to intensify the potential irrationality of his own political positions (value stances). But this necessarily raises the question of the practical consequences of Schmitt's and Lukács's own methodological-cum-political critiques of Weber's position.

History as Secularized Protestantism, Political Catholicism, or Messianic Socialism

Just a few pages before embarking on "The Standpoint of the Proletariat" section of *History and Class Consciousness,* Lukács states that "in the case of

---

75   Weber, "Science as a Vocation," p. 149, emphasis added.
76   Weber, "Politics as a Vocation," pp. 127–8.

almost every insoluble problem we perceive that the search for a solution leads us to history" (*HCC*, 143). According to Lukács, history points the way to the overcoming of form and content, sheer rationality, and aestheticized whim. In the next chapter, I show more elaborately that Schmitt, too, turns explicitly to history as an answer to the entrenched dualisms of modernity. But some remarks can be made here that bring together what I have discussed in this chapter and that establish some themes that I treat in subsequent ones.

In *Political Romanticism,* Schmitt identifies two different kinds of politically romantic conceptions of history that emerged in the nineteenth century. The first is the revolutionary version that views history as the irresistible universalizing of Enlightenment principles:

> [For the Left] the unlimited community is essentially a revolutionary god that eliminates all social and political barriers and proclaims the general brotherhood of humanity as a whole. If the removal of all limits and the need for totality were sufficient in itself to define the romantic, then there would be no finer example of a romantic politics than the resolution of the National Convention decreeing aid and fraternity to all peoples who request liberties. Such a *politique sansculotte* abolishes all national boundaries and overwhelms the *politique blanches,* the international policy of the Holy Alliance and the legitimist status quo. (*PR,* 61, translation amended)

The second is represented by the counterrevolutionaries whose conservative notion of history as an organic development of a people served as an attempted "corrective to revolutionary license":

> [History] is the conservative god who restores what the other has revolutionized. It constitutes the general human community as the historically concretized people, which becomes a sociological and historical reality by means of this delimitation and acquires a capacity to produce a particular law and a particular language as the expression of its individual national spirit. Therefore, what a people is "organically" and what the *Volksgeist* signifies can be ascertained only historically. In addition, here the people is not its own master, as in Rousseau, but rather the result of historical development. The idea of an arbitrary power over history is the real revolutionary idea. . . . [In comparison,] the unrestrained fanaticism of the Jacobin was "unhistorical" thought. (*PR,* 62)

Schmitt's new conservatism – as we will see, his own brand of fascism – is to conjoin what is most radical from both the leftwing and rightwing nineteenth-century notions of history. Combining rather than overcoming

Weber's contradiction of responsibly willed action versus structural irresistibility, Schmitt adopts the radically leftist notion of intervention into, and control over, history, by elites in the service of an ostensibly traditionalist but in reality thoroughly modern, concretist, *Schicksalgemeinschaft* notion of a *particular* "people." Sometimes Schmitt identifies this entity as "Europe," "Central Europe," or "Germany." Rather than rely on traditional continuity as an imperative to which one appeals in this debate over history, as did traditional conservatives, he will adopt the leftist strategy of appeal to the technoeconomic forces of history that "self-evidently" justify his particular reactionary solution. In this way, the threat of leftist universalism can be met with an aggressive strategy of conflict rather than the defensive nineteenth-century strategy of a Metternich-legitimist or Holy Alliance policy of containment that buckled in 1848 and ultimately collapsed in 1917. This is why the more intense of the counterrevolutionaries, such as Donoso Cortés, become his primary spiritual inspiration, instead of say, Burke. Moreover, despite the appeal to technoeconomic imperatives, Schmitt will continue to treat technology quite ambiguously, as we will see, for reasons inherent in his own theoretical critique of it (Chapter 2), and his fear that a modern sociopolitical strategy that emphasizes technology will eventually only put it in the hands that will use it in an extortionist ploy against an otherwise powerful, supposedly neutral state (Chapter 6).

For Lukács, the proletariat is the agent of this similarly conceived historical process that will transcend the object/subject dualism of modernity. Schmitt's agent of history, however, is not the industrial proletariat but the European intellectual elite. Lukács sought such a grounding in the trans-historical primacy of labor and the revolutionary conclusions that would follow from that, including class conflict. Schmitt privileges his own individually appointed object for the subjective ascription of meaning as the source of a generalizable objective reality: cultural conflict with Soviet Russia. Both eventually aestheticize conflict, Schmitt culturally centered, Lukács class-centered; Schmitt anti-Russia, Lukács pro-Russia. Lukács wishes to appropriate the leadership of *society* through *class conflict;* Schmitt, the leadership of the *state* with churchly authority, initially, and, as will be explained, *nationalist conflict,* ultimately. In a preliminary manner, it can be asked here: How is the *reactionary* action of the Church and the *revolutionary* action of the proletariat to be facilitated?

History for Lukács displays the impasse between ethics and social reality that can be overcome by a revolution from the standpoint of the worker, who is the qualitative essence oppressed by the quantifying production process. History tells Schmitt that the age of formal rationality is over, not, as in Weber's analysis, permanent. For Schmitt the meaninglessness of the secularized Protestantism of liberalism has prepared the West for the reassertion of Roman Catholicism, the institution that transcends the form/content oppositions of modernity and itself is perfectly willing to provide the rules "for the normative guidance for human life" (*RC*, 12) that make life meaningful, especially rules about the choice between friends and enemies. Catholicism, which in Schmitt's estimation in *Political Form* is a perfect marriage of form and content – a "complex of opposites" – by its nature makes frequent alliances with the most varied political entities (*RC*, 7). But knowing who to make one's friend entails knowing who to make one's enemy, the former category having no meaning in Schmitt's worldview without the latter.

Weber, as is well known, suggested that meaning was derived only through conflict, ultimately violent conflict;[77] less widely discussed is his fairly serious obsession with Russia.[78] But Schmitt intimates that Weber's imperialist liberalism, so tied to Protestantism, capitalism, and functional-formalism, could never lay the grounds for a truly "political" theory, its separation of subjective morality from the objectively rational world precludes meaningful action, such as great politics. In *Political Form,* Schmitt begins to blueprint such a truly political theory himself by promoting Catholicism as friend and Russia as enemy. He asserts that the essence of Catholicism is hence inherently political. It makes alliances and declares enemies. The title of the work highlights the difference between Catholicism and Protestantism, according to Schmitt: *Protestant* ethic and the spirit of *capitalism,* and *Roman Catholicism* and *political* form. Whereas the sociological manifestation of Protestantism is economics, that of Catholicism is politics. Economic and technical thinking is for Schmitt value-neutral and ultimately contentless and can neither ally with nor oppose something. For Schmitt, already prefiguring his "concept of the political" thesis of 1927, politics is the manufacture of meaning by identifying concrete friends and enemies.

Both Schmitt and Lukács thus perceive a dramatic structural transformation in European society in the early twenties that most liberals – to some extent, Weber included[79] – sought to ignore. It is this transformation that

---

77 *ES,* 1399; and "Religious Rejections of the World and Their Directions," p. 335.
78 See Weber's *Biography,* pp. 327, 636; Weber frequently attacked "Bakuninism" (*ES,* 988) and apparently often invoked the image of the Grand Inquisitor ("Politics as a Vocation," p. 122).
79 See Herbert Marcuse, "Industrialization and Capitalism" in *Max Weber and Sociology Today.*

makes possible their political strategies. Recognizing that abstract and formal theories of society and politics were relatively obsolete in the contemporary incipient welfare-state fusing of state and society,[80] Lukács and Schmitt
sought to formulate theories that let concrete manifestations of social
existence – substances whose actualities were occluded by the generalized
categories of the nineteenth century – exert themselves in the context of the
emerging primacy of the political. Schmitt's solution is a top-down lending
of substance to the previously "neutral" state – be it through clerical sanction or, eventually, nationalist fervor. Lukács's solution is bottom-up, "truly"
delivering to the proletariat – the content that transcends form and content
oppositions – the whole of society. Irrespective of the direction of the impetus, the place for such elites as Lukács and Schmitt themselves is essential to
these scenarios. Shut out by the laissez-faire and self-regulating ideologies of
the nineteenth century, a prominent place is now assured for intellectual-
political elites to facilitate the aforementioned transformation: one a fascist
fantasy, the other a communist one.

Thus, history is the facilitator of Schmitt's superpolitical theory and
Lukács's supersocial theory, although they understand history somewhat
differently. Lukács views this historical process as authored by humans but
without their awareness. Again, as we will see in Chapter 2, Schmitt more
and more supplants Weber's account of rationalization as a spillover of
Protestant anxiety with one that deems it the product of the conscious
choice of elites.[81] Recall from *Political Romanticism* that Schmitt attributes
the development of the dualities of modernity to the efforts of Copernicus,
Descartes, and Kant; Lukács treats them as subtle reflections of a socioeconomic structure. For Schmitt modernity is the product of conscious decision on the part of elites who sought to free themselves from the sanction of
traditional authority. Having rendered themselves superfluous in the self-
regulating society of the nineteenth century that they themselves helped
construct, they now have the opportunity to intervene – again, consciously
and decisively – to reassert their role. Lukács understands history as labor
coming to realize itself as the primary human condition soon to be consum-
mated. But the process of reification that makes all qualitative entities appear as quantitative ones blinds the proletariat to its own proximity to this
qualitatively preeminent activity, hence necessitating a vanguard party to

---

80   See Cohen and Arato, *Civil Society and Political Theory,* especially chap. 5, for an account of
      this transformation.
81   Cf. *ND,* 132–9.

spark their awareness.[82] In Schmitt's theory, at first religious and then secular, it is the elites who formulate the rules and then dictate them to society. This difference may account for the greater extent of Schmitt's complicity with National Socialism a decade later than Lukács's with Lenin and then Stalin: Lukács's task was merely to encourage the process of class consciousness – no doubt with the indispensable help of the Communist party – whereas Schmitt's was to aid in a total elite-driven reconfiguration of state and society. It is the difference between awakening a will and generating it oneself.[83]

As we will see in the next chapter, the more Schmitt radicalizes his critique of technology and the more he seeks to resolve the problematic associated with it in the realm of starkly defined political action – action in the sense of the counterrevolution and not the supposed passivity of the romantics – the more he appears like the romantics he criticizes. In *Political Romanticism,* he declares that one of the chief characteristics of the romantic is a rebellion against the law of cause and effect and a concomitant aestheticizing of the "opportune and the accidental"; a valorizing of *occasio* over *causa* (16–17, 82–3). But, as we will see in Chapter 3, in his promotion of the exception as a central category of political theory, a miracle-like monkey wrench to be thrown into the works of the liberal-positivist machine, that observation is an apt description of Schmitt himself. Schmitt also accuses the romantics of intellectual sloth, as a result of their complacency in letting the dualisms they recognize stand as theoretical categories: "Every clear antithesis exercises a dangerous power of attraction over other distinctions that are not as clear" (*PR,* 26). But Schmitt himself may settle for the convenience of easily defined oppositions in place of the theoretical tracing of them to their historical sociostructural sources that his theory pretends to promise. The extremity of his thought may in fact be generated by precisely the frustration that ensues from the intuition that he ought to move further but cannot in fact do so – his own failures to work through and ground the

---

82 Lukács's party elitism is expressed more explicitly in *Tactics and Ethics* (1919–21), trans. M. McColgan, ed. R. Livingstone (New York: Harper & Row, 1972); and *Lenin: A Study of the Unity of His Thought* (1924), trans. N. Jacobs (Cambridge, Mass.: MIT Press, 1971).

83 For an account of Lukács's Communist career, his fall from favor soon after the publication of *History and Class Consciousness,* and his continued faithfulness to the party, see Kadarkay, *Georg Lukács: Life, Thought and Politics.* On Schmitt's Weimar support for right wing authoritarians, his enrollment in the National Socialist Party when it came to power in 1933, and his own fall from grace in 1936, consult Bernd Rüthers, *Carl Schmitt im Dritten Reich: Wissenschaft als Zeitgeist-Verstärkung?* (Munich: C. H. Beck, 1989).

oppositions he perceives are inevitably followed by aesthetic eruptions in his writings. His own theoretical detrumescence, exposed here in such works as *Political Romanticism* and *Political Form,* hides behind the political-theoretical bravado of *Political Theology* and *Parlamentarismus,* as we will see.

Weber, Romanticism, Authoritarianism

In the interest of fairness, it is appropriate to ask the question: Ultimately, to what extent is Weber culpable in the behavior of his protégés by most clearly setting out the categories that they sought to overcome but perhaps only radicalized? Despite the long history of debates over this issue, it is still unclear whether Weber's irrational tendencies can be identified as the source of the persistence of myth, explicit and implicit, in his students' thought. As early as *Political Romanticism,* Schmitt reveals his proclivity toward myth by his exclusion of it from the structure of the dualisms he elucidates. Myth, according to Schmitt, is not an example of the random, passive aestheticization characteristic of romanticism but is in fact a legitimate component of political action: Romantic passive action "is not the irrationality of myth. That is because the creation of a political or historical myth arises from political activity, and the fabric of reasons, which myth cannot forgo either, is the emanation of political energy. A myth arises only in the real war" (*PR,* 160).[84] Moreover, even the most sympathetic commentators note the latent attraction to mythology that remained in Lukács's thought even after his turn to Hegelianism.[85] Lukács's fascination with the "miracle," the "accident," the "marvel" that disrupts the order of everyday life, exhibited as far back as *Soul and Form,* was not sufficiently purged from his theory.[86] The activity of Don Quixote, so important to both of their early accounts of modernity, is hopelessly tragic within a Kantian-Weberian framework in which the objective world could not be changed by a subjective stance. Quixotic activity is, however, rendered potentially destructive in a radical manner within the new paradigms of the authors when it appears that such change is in fact possible.

As Schmitt becomes more existentially myth-promoting in Weimar, he simultaneously radicalizes rather than deconstructs Weber's categories. For instance, as we will see, he takes far too literally Weber's claim that politics involves the subjectively personal choice between God and the devil, as well

---

84 On Schmitt's use of myth, see the last chapter of *Parlamentarismus* and Chapters 2 and 6 of the present volume.

85 Cf. Arato and Breines, *The Young Lukács,* pp. 121, 143.

86 Lukács, *Soul and Form,* e.g., pp. 71, 153.

as the likelihood that one will "contract with diabolical powers."[87] I conclude in Chapter 2 that Schmitt's theory both demonstrates the capacity to critique the language of the "satanic" that so pervasively accompanies the relationship between politics and technology in Weimar, and itself lapses into the abuse of that kind of language.

Schmitt and Lukács, for their part, were not willing to absolve their teacher of responsibility for generating the modern irrationality that they themselves would put into practice. Long after his Weimar career, his subsequent affiliation with National Socialism, and toward the end of his lifelong banishment from the academy in the Federal Republic of Germany, Schmitt would offer a critique of the irrationalism that, according to him, necessarily erupts within Weber's rationalization thesis:

> [T]he individual avoids the absolute value-freedom of scientific positivism and opposes it with his free, that is subjective world-view. The purely subjective freedom of value-determination leads, however, to an eternal struggle of values and world-views, to a war of all against all, an eternal *bellum omnium contra omnes* which is truly idyllic in comparison with the old *bellum omnium contra omnes* and even the lethal state of nature of Thomas Hobbes's state theory. The old gods rise from their graves and fight their old battles once again, but now disenchanted and now, as should be added, with new means of struggle which are no longer mere weapons but terrifying means of annihilation and extermination – dreadful products of value-free science and the industrialism and technology that it serves. What is for one the devil is for the other the god. . . . With such penetrating observations as Weber's one is aware of many sides. It is always values that precipitate the conflict and sustain enmity. That the old gods have become disenchanted and become merely accepted values makes the conflict specter-like and the antagonists hopelessly polemical. This is the nightmare Max Weber's depiction presents to us.[88]

After World War II, Lukács, remaining behind the Iron Curtain, would also criticize his former mentor, who, in struggling against irrationalism, only "provided a bridge to a higher stage of it":

> Max Weber banished irrationalism from his methodology and analysis of isolated facts only in order to introduce it as the philosophical basis of his world-

---

87 See Weber, "Science as a Vocation," p. 148; and "Politics as a Vocation," p. 126. On the full theoretical force of "demonic" and "diabolical" metaphors in Weber, see Harvey Goldman, *Politics, Death and the Devil: Self and Power in Max Weber and Thomas Mann* (Berkeley: University of California Press, 1992).

88 Schmitt, "Die Tyrannei der Werte," in *Der Tyrannei der Werte*, ed. Carl Schmitt et al. (Hamburg: Lutherisches Verlagshaus, 1979), p. 35.

view with a firmness hitherto unknown in Germany. Granted, even this elimination of irrationalism from the methodology was not total. Just as Weber
relativized everything in sociology into rational types, so likewise his type of
non-hereditary leader who attains office as a result of "charisma" was purely
irrationalistic. That aside, however, imperialist neo-Kantianism really crossed
the bridge into irrationalist existentialism for the first time in [the "Vocation"
lectures].[89]

Schmitt and Lukács had indeed effectively shown how Weber's stand of
"ethical responsibility" was untenable in the face of his own rationalization
thesis. It is still an open question whether this gives them license to tacitly
attribute to the "sins of the father" their own contributions to the "night-
mare" of "irrationalist existentialism" that was twentieth-century totalitarianism, and in so doing forsake their own responsibility for such
contributions.

Liberalism, Romanticism, and the Persistence of the Antinomies

Contemporary liberalism in even its most articulate expressions maintains
the dichotomy of the subjectively romantic and the objectively rational that
Schmitt and Lukács sought to overcome. Presently influential is a brand of
"political liberalism" formulated such that the more-or-less formally rational
public boundaries of liberal politics maintain within their confines the possibility of private subjective or even expressly romantic sensibilities.[90] Such a
suspension of these poles that are presented by this kind of liberalism as
normatively incommensurable and descriptively incommensuralizable is
made possible by a rather static conception of history that postulates increasing rationalization or differentiation – that is, more of the present

89 Lukács, *The Destruction of Reason,* pp. 614, 619.
90 This would include the recent reformulations of John Rawls's liberalism in his own *Political Liberalism* and, relatedly, the efforts of Charles Larmore, the latter being particularly
illustrative, because they specifically address the contemporary persistence of romanticism. In *The Morals of Modernity* (Cambridge: Cambridge University Press, 1996), Larmore
withdraws from the political domain what he calls the "aesthetic aspect of modernity" (pp.
2, 13, 131–3), which as history and the next chapter of this book show, can itself serve as a
domain of political contestation during political crises – often, in fact, the source of
reactionary politics. It is the failure to resolve this opposition between the objective and
the subjective in a substantively rational manner that rendered Weber's worldview and the
historical reality to which it corresponded unstable and also rendered Schmitt's and
Lukács's attempts at resolution and the political experiments with which they aligned
themselves disastrous.

instead of its radical change. However, this "balance" proves potentially unstable and dangerous at moments of transformation, when romantic sensibilities often become, à la Weber, Lukács, and Schmitt, suprarational political stands.[91] One need not necessarily draw exclusively or even extensively on the Frankfurt School critique of the aestheticization of politics, as I do throughout this book, to raise such a claim.[92] There is certainly a risk of philosophical/political excess associated with Hegelian theoretical perspectives,[93] a risk borne out by the fact that two adherents of such a perspective, Schmitt and Lukács, became spokesmen and agents of the very forces of social and political disorder that they accused liberalism of unwittingly fostering. But it is some sensitivity to the dynamics of social change within modernity expressed by varying types of Hegelian theoretical orientations that helps to expose the potential inadequacy of the postulation of an abstract, liberal, public form within which can be sustained concrete, private, romantic content. Such a balance could not be maintained in Weimar, and a similar one seems to suffer the threat of disruption in the historically transforming reality of the present.

Again, the controversy over the relationship between Weber's neo-Kantian methodology and the existentialist leanings of some of his political positions toward the close of his life raises the question of the adequacy of such methodological and political approaches for moments of crisis and change like Weimar.[94] Certainly the more radical alternatives for which Weber's students opted in their attempt to transcend Weber's approach may encourage many to judge that the disease was unequivocally better than the attempted cures. Whatever the epistemological and methodological sources of the later Weber's preferences for charismatic authority, which I will discuss in Chapter 4, the critical theorists cum political existentialists who stand in self-understood opposition to a Kantian standpoint, as in the case of Lukács and Schmitt, sense the relative obsolescence of abstract categories, encourage their evaporation, and promote the new, concretely

---

91 See Breuer, "The Illusion of Politics." Larmore, for instance, fails to ultimately determine – except through appeals to the work of Karl-Heinz Bohrer (pp. 189–204) – what, during moments of change and crisis, would definitively distinguish the "romantic sensibility" that he defends from what, for instance, he terms the "notorious irrationalism" of Nietzsche (p. 7). As we observe in the next chapter, the romanticism left rationally unmediated by liberalism may serve as precisely the source of Nietzschean irrationality in certain contexts.

92 See, for instance, Stephen K. White, *Edmund Burke and the Dangers of Modernity: Modernity, Politics and Aesthetics* (London: Sage, 1994).

93 Cf. Pippin, *Hegel's Idealism*, pp. 17, 31, 37, 180, 254; and Habermas, *Theory and Practice*.

94 See Mommsen, *Max Weber and German Politics*.

grounded reality from which society can be restructured.[95] A contemporary critical theory hopes to avoid the excesses of its early-twentieth-century progenitors on the Left and the Right by, on the contrary, seeking new categories, in a manner that does not regressively choose between the abstract or concrete antinomies offered by the moment. It seeks new categories that reflect a privileging of neither subject nor object but an understanding of them in the moment and character of change.

This is not to say that theorists who have recently sought to ground in a more dialectical manner than liberal or conservative critics current cultural-intellectual trends within socioeconomic transformations have been undeniably successful in doing so.[96] Recent work of this kind has gone to great lengths to demonstrate the homologous relationship between, for instance, the rise of postmodernism, on the one hand, and the decline of the welfare state, on the other, but have been caught somewhat short in specifying the intrinsic links between the two phenomena. Although the desire to avoid resorting to the economic or political determinism that is characteristic of Lukács and Schmitt, respectively, is understandable, admirable, and necessary, a critical theory as practiced by such scholars must show in greater detail how "subjective" cultural entities are expressions of the "objective" transformations of history. As I hope this analysis of Schmitt and Lukács shows, the proper resolution of these intellectual poles, particularly at moments of transformation and crisis, is indispensable for finding progressive alternatives to either an apparently vulnerable, static liberalism or an activist left- or right-wing authoritarianism that seeks to overcome liberalism's intellectual dead ends and practical shortcomings.[97] Examples of how *not* to

---

95 Despite their self-understood progressive orientations, the feminism of a MacKinnon and the legal philosophy of an Unger are often criticized today for a tendency toward the expression of "will to power" dispositions. See Catherine MacKinnon, *Toward a Feminist Theory of the State* (Cambridge, Mass.: Harvard University Press, 1989); and Roberto Unger, *Law in Modern Society* (New York: Free Press, 1976).

96 See David Harvey, *The Condition of Postmodernity* (Oxford: Blackwell, 1989); Fredric Jameson, *Postmodernism, or, The Cultural Logic of Late Capitalism* (Durham, N.C.: Duke University Press, 1991); Craig Calhoun, "Postmodernism as Pseudohistory: The Trivialization of Epochal Change," in *Critical Social Theory: Culture, History and the Challenge of Difference* (Oxford: Blackwell, 1995); Krishnan Kumar, *From Post-Industrial to Post-Modern Society: New Theories of the Contemporary World* (Oxford: Blackwell, 1995); Terry Eagleton, *The Illusions of Postmodernism* (Oxford: Blackwell, 1996); and Moishe Postone, *Time, Labor and Social Domination.*

97 Recent political philosophy and social theory still contains residues of the notion of history that Schmitt and Lukács found inadequately theorized by Weber. In *The Morals of Modernity* and *Between Facts and Norms,* both Charles Larmore and Jürgen Habermas gesture toward Hegel to validate professed sensitivity to contemporary concrete reality (see,

conduct such a theoretical-political strategy will be the main theme of subsequent chapters on Schmitt. I will remark on the more positive possibilities of such a program in the conclusion of the book.

It is somewhat disquieting and certainly disappointing that two thinkers who so rigorously interrogated the rationality/irrationality predicament of modern thought – as expressed here, the technology/romanticism relationship – should themselves succumb to the aestheticization of violent conflict and totalitarian politics as the supposed transcendence of that opposition. From Schmitt's own analysis of the antinomies of economic-technical thought and the comparison of it with the attempt of Lukács, we know that modernity inspires an attempt to aestheticize particular objects and experiences in such a way as to serve as a complement to the abstract rationality of the age. Schmitt observed in *Political Romanticism* how history could be aestheticized, and Lukács in *History and Class Consciousness* demonstrates how the modern reemergence of myth is linked inextricably to romantic aestheticization. How could Schmitt and Lukács be so unaware that their own theories engaged in the blatant aestheticization cum mythification of history and the respective roles of specific political and economic actors within it?

In the passage from *Capital* cited at the close of my introduction, Marx associates money with the biblical beast from Revelation. Marx's use of the Antichrist is metaphoric; he satirizes the way that surface phenomena, such as money, arouse hysterical reactions that prevent observers from theoretically penetrating beyond surface forms to grasp an underlying social reality. This is not all that different from Schmitt's and Lukács's modes of procedure in the works just considered. However, after admitting the inadequacy of such an approach and attempting a more theoretically rigorous one that moves beneath the surface phenomena that appear as simply

---

respectively, *The Morals of Modernity,* pp. 2, 8; and *Between Facts and Norms: Contributions to a Discourse Theory of Law and Democracy* [Cambridge, Mass.: MIT Press, 1996], pp. 386–7). However, both rely too extensively on a Kantian methodology that results in an understanding of empirical reality and its changing nature in terms of systems differentiation and social complexity that replays much of the linear qualities of Weber's rationalization thesis. Larmore ultimately confesses greater partiality for conceptions of history that emphasize continuity over disrupture (p. 2), and ultimately for Kant over Hegel (pp. 14–15); Habermas forswears the excesses of a "philosophy of history" (p. 287) and establishes Kant as the central theoretical-intellectual figure of his work (chap. 1). The influence of such notions of change in both authors can be traced to their engagements with the work of systems theorist Niklas Luhmann: see Larmore, *Patterns of Moral Complexity;* and Habermas and Luhmann, *Theorie der Gesellschaft oder Sozialtechnologie* (Frankfurt a. M.: Suhrkamp, 1971).

demonic, Schmitt explicitly demonizes characteristic phenomena of modernity, such as economic or technical thinking, with the language of the Antichrist and projects it onto Soviet Russia. As we will see in the next chapter, this strategy becomes much more discernibly derivative of Nietzsche than of Marx and Hegel.

In closing, it is perhaps excessively easy to demonstrate what Schmitt has in common with the political romantics he so vigorously criticizes. But there is one point that is too ironic and too important to ignore – the denouncement of the political opportunism of the political romantics, such as Schlegel and Müller, by one of the twentieth century's most despicable examples of such opportunism:

> Their character also lay in a character that was not their own, and they too sought to acquire their productivity in this way. Lacking all social and intellectual stability, they succumbed to every power-complex in their vicinity that made a claim to be taken as true reality. Thus lacking all moral scruples and any sense of responsibility other than that of a zealous and servile functionary, they could allow themselves to be used by any political system. (*PR*, 106)

That both Schmitt and Lukács would misjudge the position and capabilities of the intellectual in a context like this demonstrates the dangerous game that is an attempt to overcome the technical/romantic categories of modernity by endorsing a particular social or political movement. In future chapters, I further trace out Schmitt's attempts at dissolving various incarnations of these categories, as well as his journey – in a profound sense bound with such attempts – toward his own disastrous political affiliation.

Therefore, having examined Schmitt's foray into dialectical analysis in this chapter, in the next, I demonstrate how "the political" takes on increasing importance in Schmitt's work, particularly with respect to issues mentioned earlier: history, elites, liberalism, and technology. In dealing with these topics, Schmitt no longer so deliberately or frequently employs the language of a critical rationality but reverts to the existential language of myth that is reminiscent of Nietzsche.

MYTH AS ANTIDOTE TO THE "AGE OF NEUTRALIZATIONS"

NIETZSCHE AND CULTURAL CONFLICT AS RESPONSE TO TECHNOLOGY

Martin Heidegger is the most famous philosophical critic of modern technology.[1] Indeed, his critique of technology as well as the influence of Friedrich Nietzsche on his thought has generated a vast literature.[2] Yet, as I demonstrated in the last chapter and as I would like to continue demonstrating in this chapter, it is actually Heidegger's fellow Weimar conservative and eventual National Socialist, Carl Schmitt, who in the twenties set out most explicitly a cultural-philosophical critique of technology.[3] This chapter examines the Nietzschean elements of Schmitt's Weimar critique of technology and explores the implications of Schmitt's strategy for dissolving the hold of technology on twentieth-century Europe: the promotion of mythic conflict versus Soviet Russia. The Nietzschean image of the Antichrist emerges as central to Schmitt's confrontation with, and proposed

---

1 See Martin Heidegger, *The Question Concerning Technology and Other Essays,* trans. William Lovitt (New York: Harper & Row, 1977).
2 Two noteworthy examples from the literature are Reiner Schürmann, *Heidegger on Being and Acting: From Principles to Anarchy* (Bloomington: Indiana University Press, 1987); and Michael E. Zimmerman, *Heidegger's Confrontation with Modernity: Technology, Politics, Art* (Bloomington: Indiana University Press, 1990).
3 On the subject of Heidegger's involvement with National Socialism, see Richard Wolin, ed., *The Heidegger Controversy* (Cambridge, Mass.: MIT Press, 1993). On Schmitt in the same regard, see Joseph Bendersky, *Carl Schmitt: Theorist for the Reich* (Princeton: Princeton University Press, 1983); and Bernd Rüthers, *Carl Schmitt im Dritten Reich: Wissenschaft als Zeitgeist-Verstärkung?* (Munich: C. H. Beck, 1989).

solution to, technology in three works spread out across his Weimar career: his 1916 book-length commentary on Theodor Däubler's epic poem "Northern Lights"; *Roman Catholicism and Political Form*, from 1923; and his influential lecture of 1929, "The Age of Neutralizations and Depoliticizations."[4] The critical-Hegelian moments of these works were discussed in Chapter 1; here I wish to draw out their more existential moments.

Curiously, Schmitt very rarely mentioned Nietzsche in his work, and little has been written on his debt to the philosopher.[5] This is perhaps due to the fact that the intellectual figure who most influenced Schmitt, Max Weber, is widely acknowledged to be a devotee of Nietzsche's,[6] and thus it is assumed that any trace of Nietzsche in Schmitt's thought was simply passed on to him from Weber.[7] As this chapter demonstrates, there is a more direct link

4 Schmitt, *Theodor Däublers "Nordlicht": Drei Studien über die Elemente, den Geist und die Aktualität des Werkes* (Berlin: Duncker & Humblot, 1991) is cited as *N*. Schmitt, *Roman Catholicism and Political Form* (1923), trans. G. L. Ulmen (Westport: Greenwood, 1996), hereafter referred to as *Political Form* and cited as *RC*. "Das Zeitalter der Neutralisierungen und Entpolitisierungen" appears in *Der Begriff des Politischen* (Berlin: Duncker & Humblot, 1963) and is cited as *ND;* the English quotations are from the translation by Matthias Konzett and John P. McCormick, "The Age of Neutralizations and Depoliticizations," *Telos* 96 (summer 1993). On the persistence of the theme of the satanic in Schmitt's thought, see Lutz Berthold, "Wer hält zur Zeit den Satan auf? – Zur Selbstglossierung Carl Schmitts," *Leviathan: Zeitschrift für Sozialwissenschaft* 21:2 (1993); Günter Meuter, *"Der Katechon": Zu Carl Schmitts fundamentalistischer Kritik der Zeit* (Berlin: Duncker & Humblot, 1994); and the review of the latter by Stefan Breuer, "Der letzte Ritter der heiligen Johanna. Ein Anti-Hobbes: Günter Meuter legt die Fundamente von Carl Schmitts Zeitkritik frei," *Frankfurter Allgemeine Zeitung* (Feb. 27, 1995).

5 The only notable exceptions are Karl Heinz Bohrer, *Die Ästhetik des Schreckens: Die Pessimistische Romantik und Ernst Jüngers Frühwerk* (Munich: Hanser, 1978); and Reinhard Mehring, *Carl Schmitt: Zur Einführung* (Hamburg: Junius, 1992). On Nietzsche's influence in Weimar more generally, see Steven E. Aschheim, *The Nietzsche Legacy in Germany* (Berkeley: University of California Press, 1992). The major work to consult on Nietzsche's thought as a whole is still Walter Kaufmann's *Nietzsche: Philosopher, Psychologist, Antichrist* (1950), (Princeton: Princeton University Press, 1974); although a more recent study that has gained a kind of interpretive hegemony is Alexander Nehamas, *Nietzsche: Life as Literature* (Cambridge, Mass.: Harvard University Press, 1985). Of particular interest to students of political and social theory are Tracy Strong, *Friedrich Nietzsche and the Politics of Transfiguration* (Berkeley: University of California Press, 1988); Mark Warren, *Nietzsche and Political Thought* (Cambridge, Mass.: MIT Press, 1990); and Leslie Paul Thiele, *Friedrich Nietzsche and the Politics of the Soul* (Princeton: Princeton University Press, 1990).

6 See Wolfgang Mommsen, "The Antinomian Structure of Max Weber's Thought," *Current Perspectives in Social Theory* 4 (1983).

7 Works by Weber dealt with in this chapter are "Science as a Vocation" and "Politics as a Vocation," both of which appear in *From Max Weber: Essays in Sociology*, ed. and trans. H. H. Gerth and C. Wright Mills (Oxford: Oxford University Press, 1958); *The Protestant Ethic and the Spirit of Capitalism* (1904–5), trans. Talcott Parsons, (New York: Scribner's, 1958); and *Economy and Society: An Outline of Interpretive Sociology* (1920), ed. Guenther Roth and Claus

between Nietzsche, the renowned, late-nineteenth-century *philosophical* existentialist, and Schmitt, the infamous, early-twentieth-century *political* existentialist. The issue at stake is ultimately not whether technology is correctly identified as demonic or divine, as it is by the authors under consideration, but whether this mythically anti-Christian or pseudo-Christian language that seems irresistibly generated by the question of technology is itself a normatively bankrupt and politically dangerous discourse.

Mastery, Meaninglessness, and the Antichrist

Nietzsche himself actually spoke very little about technology, as such, but more about science in his own specific sense of the word. As we know from the previous chapter, it was Weber who in fact reframed Nietzsche's critique of Enlightenment rationality into a critique of technical rationality for Schmitt's generation. In this spirit, Heidegger, during the twenties would identify "machine technology" with "the domination of nature . . . which rages around 'the world' today like an unchained beast."[8] And as early as 1916, Carl Schmitt had already accepted a description of modernity as an age in which "intellect frees itself from all chains and pursues its rationalism unrestrained; its goal is to apprehend and be master of the earth" (*N,* 66).[9]

But even before the intervention of Weber, such diagnoses of this crisis of mastery over meaning brought on by "technical" reason can already be found explicitly in Nietzsche. For Nietzsche, modern meaninglessness itself is brought on by a particular kind of faith, one not unlike the faith described in Weber's *Protestant Ethic:*

> [T]he faith with which so many materialistic natural scientists rest content nowadays, the faith in a world that is supposed to have its equivalent and its measure in human thought and human valuations – a "world of truth" that can be mastered completely and forever with the aid of our square little reason. What? Do we really want to permit existence to be degraded for us like this – reduced to a mere exercise for a calculator and an indoor diversion for

Wittich (Berkeley: University of California Press, 1978), hereafter *ES.*

8   Heidegger, *The Metaphysical Foundations of Logic* (1928), trans. Michael Heim (Bloomington: Indiana University Press, 1984), p. 215.

9   On Schmitt and Heidegger, see Christian Graf von Krockow, *Die Entscheidung: Eine Untersuchung über Ernst Jünger, Carl Schmitt, Martin Heidegger* (Frankfurt a. M.: Campus, 1990); Richard Wolin, *The Politics of Being: The Political Thought of Martin Heidegger* (New York: Columbia University Press, 1990); and Reinhard Mehring, "Der philosophische Führer und der Kronjurist: Praktisches Denken und geschichtliche Tat von Martin Heidegger und Carl Schmitt," *Deutsches Vierteljahrsschrift für Literaturwissenschaft und Geistesgeschichte* 68 (1994).

mathematicians? Above all, one should not wish to divest existence of its *rich ambiguity*. . . . That the only justifiable interpretation of the world should be one in which *you* are justified because one can continue to work and do research in *your* sense (you really mean, mechanistically?) – an interpretation that permits counting, calculating, weighing, seeing, and touching and nothing more – that is a crudity and naiveté, assuming that it is not a mental illness, an idiocy. . . . A "scientific" interpretation of the world, as you understand it, might therefore still be one of the *most stupid* of all possible interpretations of the world, implying that it would be one of the poorest in meaning. This thought is intended for the ears and consciences of our mechanists who nowadays like to pass as philosophers and insist that mechanics is the doctrine of the first and last laws on which all existence must be based as on a ground floor. But an essentially mechanical world would be an essentially *meaningless* world.[10]

For Schmitt this intrinsic relationship between a world that is viewed mechanistically and the dramatic loss of meaning for that world is key for his critique of technology. A meaninglessly mechanistic view of the world, such as the one Nietzsche derides, renders it, in Schmitt's words, nothing more than a "grinding machine" (*N*, 61). Nietzsche, as is well known, finds Christianity thoroughly complicitous with the rise of the mechanistic thinking described in this lengthy quote and the resulting relativism and nihilism that characterize modernity.[11] Christian moralism, for Nietzsche, is the source of the very spirit that in science "demonizes" nature, denigrates the world, and renders *life* worthless.[12] It is Christianity that is inextricably tied to the technological faith in the domination of nature: "Our whole attitude toward nature, the way we violate her with the aid of machines and the heedless inventiveness of our technicians and engineers, is *hubris;* our attitude toward God as some alleged spider of purpose and morality behind the great captious web of causality, is *hubris.*"[13] It is in opposition to such scientism and technicism that Nietzsche would take up in his writings the standpoint of the "Antichrist."[14] The early Schmitt, a devout Catholic until his

10 Nietzsche, *The Gay Science* (1882), trans. Walter Kaufmann (New York: Vintage, 1974), p. 335.
11 See Nietzsche, *Beyond Good and Evil* (1886) and, especially, *On The Genealogy of Morals* (1887), in *Basic Writings of Nietzsche*, ed. and trans. Walter Kaufmann (New York: Random House, 1968), pp. 462–4.
12 Nietzsche, *The Birth of Tragedy* (1872), in *Basic Writings*, p. 23; and *On The Genealogy of Morals*, p. 528.
13 Nietzsche, *On The Genealogy of Morals*, p. 549.
14 Friedrich Nietzsche, *The Antichrist* (1895), in *The Portable Nietzsche*, ed. and trans. Walter Kaufmann (New York: Viking Press, 1954).

break with the church in the mid twenties, deems the technological, on the contrary, *un*-Christian or at least anti-Catholic and, as we will see, deems *technology* the Antichrist. Although their respective uses of this demonic term seem at first glance diametrically at odds, ultimately there is a great concurrence between the two critics.

Recall that in *Roman Catholicism and Political Form*, from 1923, Schmitt claims that in the valueless rationality of economic-technical thought is found the "fundamental antithesis to the political idea of Catholicism" (*RC*, 13). Attempting to retain some semblance of the rationality that Nietzsche comes precariously close to jettisoning wholesale, Schmitt argues that because Catholicism is concerned with human beings *as such*, as opposed to as universally lifeless matter, it is *more* rational than economic-technical thinking: "Everything that to modern economics is synonymous with objectivity, honesty, and rationality is at variance with . . . the rationalism of the Catholic Church that embraces ethically the psychological and sociological nature of man" (*RC*, 13, translation amended). This rationalism is not indifferent to what persons are or what they do, as are the "laws" of the market and of science, according to Schmitt. Human activity, *life* in Nietzsche's sense, is its utmost concern: "Catholic argumentation is based on a particular mode of thinking whose method of proof is a specific juridical logic and whose substantive interest is *the normative guidance of human life*" (*RC*, 12, emphasis added). Foreshadowing the issue of intellectual elites that will be so important in his confrontation with technology, Schmitt asserts that Catholicism maintains strict rules as to what people should do, supposedly with an eye toward what is good. Economics and technology, according to Schmitt, obscure this distinction, are indifferent to "life," and thus arouse the "specific Catholic anxiety," spoken of in the last chapter, that there is no longer a distinction between "a silk blouse and poison gas" (*RC*, 14). It is this apparently autonomous, rationalized, inhuman, value-neutral phenomenon that Schmitt likens to the Antichrist: Indeed "the modern economic-technical apparatus arouses a similar fear and loathing" (*RC*, 15).

Yet Schmitt recognizes not only something to be feared in the image of the Antichrist; like Nietzsche, he acknowledges something that may in fact be used *against* the malignant rationality of technology: "The mythical power of this image is deeper and stronger than any economic calculation; its aftereffects long endure" (*RC*, 3). A mythic figure such as the Antichrist may be powerful enough to withstand and even triumph over economic-technical rationality. Throughout the three works under consideration here, Schmitt is not reluctant to resort to such mythic imagery himself. Even after he has officially given up Catholicism by the time he publishes the "Neutralizations" essay in 1929, Schmitt still employs negative theological imagery to describe what he would come to identify as "technicity," the animate spirit behind the inanimate instruments of technology: It is "evil," "demonic," "terrifying," "fantastic," "satanic" (*ND*, 140–1).[15]

Nietzsche denounces as "advocates of the devil" those who would make an "idol" out of the objective "fact," for a fact is "always stupid and has at all times resembled a calf more than a god."[16] The issue of false gods and positivism suggested by the images of idols, calves, and naked facts is crucial to Schmitt's association of the Antichrist with the religions of the "fact": economic-technical thinking, particularly as manifested in positivism.[17] In the 1916 work *"Northern Lights,"* Schmitt suggests that the present historical moment wherein all reality is merely matter to be manipulated signifies that the "prophecy" that was promulgated by "indescribable fear in the face of inescapable evil" has been fulfilled: The Antichrist has arrived. His power is to be feared more than that of any worldly tyrant, because it is not clear whether he is absolute good or absolute evil:

> He knows to imitate Christ and so makes himself resemble Christ, and thus tricks everyone out of their souls. He presents himself as friendly, correct, incorruptible and reasonable. All praise him as a blessing to mankind and say: what a great and righteous man! . . . His concealed power lies in his imitation of God. God created the world; the Antichrist renders it a forgery. . . . The uncanny enchanter recreates the world in order to change the face of the earth and make nature submissive. It serves him for whatever reason, for any satisfaction – artistic whim, luxury, comfort. Those who allow themselves to be deceived by him see only the fabulous effects. Nature appears overcome; the age of security begins; all are provided for. (*N*, 61–2)

The analogy is clear. Just as the Antichrist seems to deliver salvation and eternal peace, on the contrary, only to actually bring destruction and despair, technology and commercialism promise a heaven on earth but

---

15   On the ramifications of this distinction between "technicity" and "technology," see my "Introduction to Carl Schmitt's 'The Age of Neutralizations and Depoliticizations,'" *Telos* 96 (summer 1993).

16   Nietzsche, *On the Advantage and Disadvantage of History for Life* (1873), trans. Peter Preuss (Indianapolis: Hackett, 1980), p. 48.

17   In his constitutional work from this period, the legal positivism of Hans Kelsen is Schmitt's chief target: see as just two examples, Schmitt, *Political Theology: Four Chapters on the Concept of Sovereignty* (1922), trans. George Schwab (Cambridge, Mass.: MIT Press, 1985); and Schmitt, *Verfassungslehre* ([1928] Berlin: Duncker & Humblot, 1989). These works and Schmitt's critique of legal positivism are addressed in Part Two of this study.

bring only a worse form of impoverishment and devastation, which may not even be readily recognized as such. One of the characteristics of modern technology is that it can mechanically reproduce virtually anything. Schmitt plays on this theme of reproduction with the image of the Antichrist. If one cannot distinguish between God and Satan, then what *can* be distinguished? Everything becomes the same. Everything is neutralized. The Antichrist/technology is described as "uncanny [*unheimlich*]" because of the epistemological uncertainty involved in deciphering precisely what it is. It simulates the familiar and authentic, but is it? The very nature of what real *is*, is called into question in the age of technology. According to Schmitt, "The confusion becomes unspeakable"(*N*, 63).[18]

In this sense, technology and science obfuscate as much as they clarify. Just as Nietzsche pronounces that modern science with its evolutionary theory cannot distinguish a human being from the "living slime" that resides at the "bottom of the ocean,"[19] Schmitt argues that it cannot tell the difference between a man and an ape (*N*, 63). It even confuses the resurrection of the body with the invention of the airplane: "The crowning work of the magnificent technology – man can fly, corporeal flight" (*N*, 63).

Pathologies of Myth and Technology

What Schmitt calls "the unspeakable confusion" (*N*, 61) posed by the Antichrist and technology is directly related to the issue of myth. According to theorists who studied the subject in response to its violent expressions in this century, in the dynamic of mythologizing, one *names* what one does not understand in order to exert some control over it and thereby alleviate one's own fear, one's own confusion. Ernst Cassirer explains in terms reminiscent of my discussion of Nietzsche and Schmitt:

> Myth has always a dramatic character. It conceives the world as a great drama – as a struggle between divine and demonic forces, between light and darkness, between the good and the evil. There is always a negative and a positive pole in mythical thought and imagination. Even the political myths were incomplete so long as they had not introduced demonic power. The process of deification

18 On the psychological implications of the epistemologically uncertain, see Freud's classic piece, "The Uncanny" (1919), in *The Complete Psychological Works of Sigmund Freud*, vol. 22, ed. and trans. James Strachey (London: Hogarth Press, 1963). Heinrich Meier picks up on this aspect of the Antichrist and its place in Schmitt's work in *Carl Schmitt and Leo Strauss: The Hidden Dialogue*, trans. J. Harvey Lomax (Chicago: University of Chicago Press, 1995), p. 48.

19 Nietzsche, *On the Advantage and Disadvantage of History for Life*, p. 48.

had to be completed by a process that we may describe as "devilization." . . . In the mythical pandemonium we always find maleficent spirits that are opposed to the beneficent spirits. There is always a secret or open revolt of Satan against God.[20]

Max Horkheimer and T. W. Adorno directly address the question of why mythic fear still grips so firmly in the age of "reason" and technology. As Enlightenment rationality has come to focus more and more on the surface reality of nature through positivism, naked empiricism, economic thinking, and the scientific method, it becomes more and more subconsciously afraid of the part of nature that it ignores and for which it cannot account. Consequently, Enlightenment itself becomes "paralyzed by fear of the truth" and fixates increasingly on what it *can* control – that which is in the domain of its empirical methods – and thus becomes "mythic fear turned radical." Positivism is "the myth of things as they are," and technology, "the essence of this knowledge."[21]

Nietzsche, whom Horkheimer and Adorno explicitly acknowledge as a source of their thesis,[22] directly identifies science and technology as myth. "To make existence appear comprehensible and thus justified" is the purpose of science and indeed myth as well.[23] To think in terms of cause and effect, to think mechanically, according to Nietzsche, is also to think mythologically.[24] He even asserts that the origin of science is *fear*. Science and technology must provide psychoemotional support by demonstrating the "eternal consistency, omnipresence, and infallibility of the laws of nature": it must be shown that "so far as we can penetrate here – from the telescopic heights to the microscopic depths – everything is secure, complete, infinite, regular and without any gaps."[25] Science is thus an electric security blanket.

20   Ernst Cassirer, *Symbol, Myth and Culture: Essays and Lectures, 1935–1945*, ed. Donald Philip Verene (New Haven: Yale University Press, 1979), p. 238.
21   Max Horkheimer and T. W. Adorno, *Dialectic of Enlightenment* (1944), trans. John Cummings (New York: Continuum, 1989), pages xiii, 16, x, 4, respectively. See Jürgen Habermas's reworking of this thesis in "Dogmatism, Reason and Decision: On Theory and Practice in Our Scientific Civilization" (1963), in *Theory and Practice,* trans. John Viertel (Boston: Beacon Press, 1973). See also Hans Blumenberg, *Work On Myth* (1979), trans. Robert Wallace (Cambridge, Mass.: MIT Press, 1989).
22   Horkheimer and Adorno, *Dialectic of Enlightenment,* p. 44.
23   Nietzsche, *The Birth of Tragedy,* p. 96.
24   Nietzsche, *Beyond Good and Evil* , p. 218.
25   Nietzsche, "On Truth and Lies in Their Nonmoral Sense" (1873), in *Philosophy and Truth: Selections from Nietzsche's Notebooks of the Early 1870's,* trans. Daniel Breazeale (New Jersey: Humanities Press, 1990), p. 87.

But Nietzsche's main focus is on scientific rationality as *murderer* of myths and on the pressing necessity of creating new, non–rationally-scientific, ones. This is most explicit in his first book, *The Birth of Tragedy:* "[M]yth was annihilated [by] the progressing spirit of science" (106); "The un-Dionysian . . . seeks to dissolve myth, it substitutes for a metaphysical comfort an earthly consonance, in fact a *deus ex machina* of its own, the god of machines and crucibles" (109); "[m]yth, the necessary prerequisite of every religion, is paralyzed everywhere" (111).

The "Dionysian," which Nietzsche identified retrospectively as the Antichrist,[26] offers – at least in this early work – the promise of a nature undominated and a humanity not dehumanized by science: "[N]ot only is the union between man and man reaffirmed, but nature which has become alienated, hostile, or subjugated, celebrates once more her reconciliation with her lost son, man."[27]

In Nietzschean terms, then, technology is a myth that inspires countermyth. Nietzsche identifies the myth of science with Christianity and resorts to the myth of the Antichrist in response. Schmitt calls the myth of technology itself the Antichrist and resorts, at least provisionally, to Roman Catholicism as a response. Horkheimer and Adorno, for their part, note that Enlightenment rationality itself is myth. Alternatively, Cassirer addresses the fact that myth is deployed rationally in the age of Enlightenment. These are important insights regarding both Nietzsche and Schmitt, for there are certain implications in employing myth so consciously and strategically in the "age of reason." Cassirer, although a renowned Kantian, comes very close to the "dialectic of Enlightenment" thesis when he examines the relationship of technology and twentieth-century political myth. Myth is no longer a spontaneous and noncognitive outgrowth of culture but rather, with modern totalitarian movements in mind, a strategically employed technology:

> Myth has always been described as the result of an unconscious activity and as a free product of imagination. But [in the twentieth century,] we find myth made according to plan. The new political myths do not grow up freely; they

---

26 Nietzsche, "An Attempt at Self-Criticism," written fifteen years after *The Birth of Tragedy* and added to subsequent editions of it, p. 24. Here Nietzsche identifies his Zarathustra as a "Dionysian monster." Because of the complexity – and perplexity – of Nietzsche's most important work, *Thus Spoke Zarathustra* (1883–85), I have chosen not to deal with it here, despite the fact that the work is filled with Christ/Antichrist images and allusions. But again it is obviously not my goal here to provide anything close to a comprehensive account of Nietzsche's thought.

27 Nietzsche, *The Birth of Tragedy*, p. 37.

are not wild fruits of an exuberant imagination. They are artificial things fabricated by very skillful artisans. It has been reserved for the twentieth century, our own technical age, to develop a new technique of myth. Henceforth myths can be manufactured in the same sense and according to the same methods as any other modern weapon – as machine guns or airplanes. That is a new thing – and a thing of crucial importance.[28]

Yet the work of Horkheimer and Adorno and the insight of Cassirer undeniably reveal something fundamental about the way that both Nietzsche and Schmitt are caught in the thrall of the technical rationality they seek to escape. By deploying myth in such a strategic manner, they necessarily succumb to the very instrumental rationality they wish to overcome.[29] I return to this later.

Technology and the Political

In 1927 Schmitt develops the thesis most readily associated with his name, "the concept of the political."[30] However, there are clear traces of the famous friend/enemy distinction in his work as early as 1923, particularly in *Roman Catholicism and Political Form*. It is the proper identification of, and energetic mobilization against, an "enemy" that emerges as Schmitt's antidote to technology.

In *Political Form*, Schmitt makes the observation that Catholicism is no longer confronted by world-historical enemies in Western Europe. The enmity generated by the nineteenth-century conflicts between the Catholic Church and the states of Germany and France is "harmless by comparison with Cromwell's demonic rage. Since the eighteenth century the argumentation has become evermore rationalistic or humanitarian, utilitarian and shallow" (*RC*, 3). Catholicism once waged mythic battles with radical Protestantism and later with the bourgeois, liberal intellectuals of the Enlightenment. Confirming Weber's characterization of the "heroism" of the early-modern bourgeoisie, Schmitt remarks, "The fire and flame of this opponent

28 Ernst Cassirer, *The Myth of the State* (New Haven: Yale University Press, 1946), p. 282.
29 Manfred Frank examines the relationship of "the death of God" to pagan mythologizing in Nietzsche; see *Der kommende Gott: Vorlesungen über die neue Mythologie* (Frankfurt a. M.: Suhrkamp, 1982). Reinhard Mehring argues that Schmitt's Weimar mythologizing is a Nietzschean response to his own ultimately godless universe; see *Carl Schmitt: Zur Einführung*, pp. 49–50.
30 Schmitt, *The Concept of the Political*, trans. George Schwab (New Brunswick: Rutgers University Press, 1976); this English edition is a translation of the full-length German version of *Der Begriff des Politischen*, published in 1932.

was [sic] especially noble" (*RC,* 33).[31] As Nietzsche declares, although "there are no worse and no more thorough injurers of freedom than liberal institutions," once they have been established, "these same institutions produce quite different effects while still being fought for; then they really promote freedom in a powerful way. On closer inspection, it is war that promotes these effects, the war for liberal institutions, which as war permits illiberal instincts to continue."[32] Schmitt, too, is impressed with the fact that the Enlightenment literati were bold enough to "war" against Catholicism's substantive notion of humanity with a notion of humanity all their own. Hence, the confrontation between the two had real meaning. However, Schmitt laments, "The Catholic Church in Europe today has no adversary that so openly and vigorously challenges it as an enemy as did this spirit of the eighteenth century" (*RC,* 35). Without an adversary, presumably, the institution itself has no value, or perhaps becomes self-destructive. As Nietzsche asserts, without external enemies, the human animal becomes an enemy of itself.[33]

Contemporary Catholicism, according to Schmitt, is undecided on the question of just who is the present enemy, and precisely how he casts this dilemma explicitly recalls the question of the Antichrist: Catholics like Alexis de Tocqueville, Marc René Montalembert, and Jean Baptiste Lacordaire took liberal stands "at a time when many of their fellow Catholics still saw in Liberalism the Antichrist or at least its forerunner. . . . Some Catholics are tactically aligned with a socialism that others believe to be in league with the devil" (*RC,* 4). One of the main thrusts of the book is to clarify for such Catholic intellectual elites exactly who the enemy *is,* who *really* represents an opponent of the stature of the Antichrist.

Schmitt finds the mythic enemy of Catholicism to the east of Europe in Russia: "Only with an adherent of Russian orthodoxy, with Dostoyevsky in his portrayal of the Grand Inquisitor, does the anti-Roman dread appear once again in secular force" (*RC,* 3). Schmitt asserts that Dostoyevsky manifests a particularly Russian antipathy to form and authority of any kind and consequently sees in Roman Catholicism (as a source of an impressive

---

31 Weber, *The Protestant Ethic,* p. 37; Weber also foreshadows the Schmittian thesis that "Catholicism has to the present day looked upon Calvinism as its real opponent," p. 87.

32 Nietzsche, *Twilight of the Idols* (1889), in *The Portable Nietzsche,* p. 541. The "injuries" that Nietzsche claims liberalism causes to freedom are ones that Schmitt would similarly criticize: "[T]hey make men small, cowardly, hedonistic . . . Liberalism: in other words, herd animalization." Kaufmann's cautionary remarks against making too much of Nietzsche's "celebration" of war, however, should be taken seriously; see *Nietzsche,* pp. 386–90.

33 Nietzsche, *On The Genealogy of Morals,* p. 521.

authority), "the devil triumphant": "With the Grand Inquisitor Dostoyevsky strongly projected his own, latent atheism into the Roman Church. Every power was something evil and inhuman to his fundamentally anarchistic (and that always means atheistic) instinct" (*RC,* 32). Dostoyevsky portrays the priest in the tale as one who has "consciously succumb[ed] to the wiles of Satan," because Dostoyevsky can do nothing but see in any office and in any *intellectual leader* an embodiment of evil (*RC,* 32). Schmitt acknowledges the eternal presence of a "temptation to evil" in the maintenance and administration of any secular power, no matter what may be the good intentions of the officer. But echoing Weber's admonishment, in the "Politics" lecture, of those who think they can overcome power itself, Schmitt remarks, "the desire to escape this conflict by rejecting every earthly power would lead to the worst inhumanity" (*RC,* 32).[34] The rebellion against order, against form per se, could only lead to the greatest abuses of order. Later, in the "Neutralizations" essay, Schmitt notes the irony that, despite the rhetoric of anarchism and "state-withering-away" Marxism, in Russia "a state comes into being that is more and more intensively statist than had ever been any state of the absolute princes, Philip II, Louis XIV, or Frederick the Great" (*ND,* 131).

Thus, for Schmitt, Russia is the seat of an economic-technical *rationality* in communism as well as an *irrational* counterforce to order of any kind in anarchism. The Russian anarchist Bakunin, that "naive beserker," waged battles against metaphysics, religion, politics, jurisprudence, and the phenomenon of "the idea" as such (*RC,* 36). In this Schmitt claims that the spirit of the Soviet Union is actually in opposition to that of its ideological fathers, Marx and Engels, who were ultimately *Europeans* and *intellectuals* with faith in moral *authority,* who consequently despised the likes of Bakunin, and were despised by him:

[T]heir hatred of the Russian arose from their most deeply-rooted instincts and manifested itself in the struggle within the First International. Conversely everything in the Russian anarchist rose in revolt against the "German Jew" (born in Trier) and against Engels. What continually provoked the anarchist was their intellectualism. They had too much of "the idea"; too much "gray matter." Bakunin can only utter the word "*cervelle*" with sibilant fury. Behind this word he rightly suspected the claim to authority, discipline and hierarchy. To him every type of cerebralism is hostile to life. . . . When Marx and Engels

34   Weber, "Politics as a Vocation," pp. 122–8. Weber also draws on Dostoyevsky and the Grand Inquisitor.

are at pains to distinguish their true proletariat from the "rotten" rabble they betray how strongly they are still influenced by traditional moral and West European conceptions of education. They want to imbue their proletariat with a social value. This is only possible with moral concepts. But here Bakunin had the incredible courage to see the *Lumpenproletariat* as the harbinger of the future and to appeal to the *canaille*. (*RC*, 36–7)

Schmitt claims that the antagonism between Marx and Engels, on the one hand, and Bakunin, on the other, "sets the stage whereon the essence of the present situation is clearly recognizable and Catholicism stands as a political force" (*RC*, 38). Because of this division, Catholicism can make its political choice regarding an enemy. Russia is so extreme in its contentlessness, in its embrace of the technical, and so radical in its rebellion against form of any kind, in its embrace of spiritual anarchy, that it is actually a form/content counterforce worthy of Catholicism, the historical institution that for Schmitt marries human substance with political or representative form. Technology is the only standard that Russia can uphold, according to Schmitt; it is the authorityless authority – "the machine has no tradition" (*RC*, 22). The "paradoxical situation" has arisen that in Russia economic-technical thinking has been taken up as a standard by "fanatics" who do not believe in standards at all (*RC*, 27). "The fact that they met on Russian soil, in the Russian Soviet Republic, has a profound justification in the history of ideas. . . . [T]he alliance is no accident of world history" (*RC*, 38). According to Schmitt, despite Catholicism's past and present difficulties with liberalism or Western socialism, the Church must ally with them against the Soviets. It must stand "on the side of the *idea* and West European civilization" and against "the atheistic socialism of the Russian anarchist" (*RC*, 39, emphasis added).

Once Schmitt fully develops his "concept of the political" and stops speaking in terms of political Catholicism, four years later in 1929, he is in a better position to explain why the meeting of economic-technical rationality and fanatical anarchism in Russia is "no accident of world history" and why European intellectuals, not just Catholic ones, need to be aware of this fact. Six years later, in even more extreme Nietzschean language, he does so in "The Age of Neutralizations and Depoliticizations."

History, Elites, and Technology

In the first paragraph of the "Neutralizations" essay, Schmitt makes a puzzling observation about the Russians: "[T]heir strength in orthodoxy with regard to *good and evil* is overwhelming" (*ND*, 130, emphasis added). And it is interesting that in a work entitled *Beyond Good and Evil,* Nietzsche anticipates much of Schmitt's claims about Russia: its strength of will, this threat to Europe, the uncertainty as to the exact nature of its threat, the necessity of a new European elite to unite the continent in opposition to it, impending global conflict, and, explicitly, the return of politics, the return of what Schmitt calls "the political":

> The strength to will . . . is strongest and most amazing by far in that enormous empire . . . in Russia. There the strength to will has long been accumulated and stored up, there the will – uncertain whether as a will to negate or a will to affirm – is waiting menacingly to be discharged. . . . It may take more than Indian wars and complications in Asia to rid Europe of its greatest danger. . . . I do not say this because I want it to happen: the opposite would rather be more after my own heart – I mean such an increase in the menace of Russia that Europe would have to resolve to become menacing, too, namely to acquire one will by means of a new caste able to cast its goals millennia hence – so the long-drawn-out comedy of its many splinter states as well as its dynastic and democratic splinter wills would come to an end. The time for petty politics is over: the very next century will bring the fight for dominion of the earth – the compulsion to large-scale politics.[35]

Schmitt announces that this prophecy is soon to be fulfilled.

The "political" intent of the "Neutralizations" piece is expressed in no uncertain terms in its very first sentence: "We in Central Europe live under the eyes of the Russians" (*ND*, 130). The point of the essay is to convince its European audience, particularly, as this sentence indicates, a German-speaking European audience, that the Soviet Union is the enemy and must be recognized as such. The grounds for this "political" position vis-à-vis the Russians rest again with the issue of technology: "Their vitality is strong enough to seize both our knowledge and technology as weapons" (*ND*, 130). More urgently Schmitt adds, "on Russian soil the antireligion of technicity is put into practice" (*ND*, 131). Through his application of such terms as "antireligion" and "technicity" to Russia, Schmitt is raising the specter of the Soviet Union as the embodiment of the Antichrist even more strongly than he does at the conclusion of *Political Form.* Technicity, we must remember, is for Schmitt that "demonic" and "satanic" force driving technology that fosters "the mass belief of an anti-religious this-worldly activism" (*ND*,

35 Nietzsche, *Beyond Good and Evil,* p. 321.

141).[36] Why the Soviet Union and its orientation toward technology poses a threat to Germany, and equally important, why Germany must be actively reminded of this fact by Schmitt himself is the result of particular historical circumstances.

Just as in the nineteenth century, Europe reacted to the turbulence of the French Revolution and Napoleonic Wars with exhaustion, according to Schmitt Europe in the twenties is predisposed toward the status quo in the wake of the Great War of 1914. Yet while Europe remains fixated on things as they are, according to Schmitt, Russia recognizes the changes that underlie historical circumstances and seeks to appropriate the moment: "[T]he acquiescence of the restoration mood serves a rapid and undisturbed development of new things and new circumstances whose sense and direction remain hidden beneath the restored facades. When the decisive moment arrives, the legitimating foreground vanishes like an empty phantom" (*ND*, 131). Just as the Soviets stunned the European order with the Revolution of 1917, Schmitt intimates that they are again poised to shatter the veneer of neutrality in League of Nations Europe in 1929. As Schmitt remarks, the impending confrontation between West and East is "the consequence of European development over the last centuries"(*ND*, 131). Schmitt follows with his theory of history in which technology plays a climactic role.

According to Schmitt, the dynamic of modern Western history is driven by the search for a neutral sphere completely free from conflict and contestation. In response to the strife of the religious civil wars, Europe since the sixteenth century has sought in each successive century a different fundamental organizing principle – a central sphere [*Zentralgebiet*] – that might serve as the source of peace and agreement. Thus the controversial central sphere of the sixteenth century, theology, was abandoned in the

36 Thus Schmitt is in agreement with Heidegger's later and more famous argument that the "essence" of technology "is itself nothing technological," because it is not exclusively concerned with machines and the concretely material manifestations of mechanical processes as such ("The Question Concerning Technology" [1954], in *The Question Concerning Technology and Other Essays*, p. 20). However, unlike Heidegger, and Nietzsche for that matter, Schmitt does *not* trace the origins of the technicistic spirit back to ancient Greece: Heidegger claims that "the limitless domination of modern technology in every corner of this planet is only the late consequence of a very old technical interpretation of the world, an interpretation usually called metaphysics." See 1941/42 lecture, quoted in Zimmerman, *Heidegger's Confrontation with Modernity*, p. 166. Cf. Heidegger's tracing of *Gestell* back to classical antiquity in "The Question Concerning Technology." For Schmitt, the technology Heidegger describes is part of the thoroughly modern phenomenon of "neutralization," without roots in a premodern past that happens to bear artificial fleurs du mal in modernity.

seventeenth for the more "neutral" sphere of metaphysics, which was itself superseded in the eighteenth century by humanitarian ethics and morality. According to Schmitt, the sphere of economics dominated the nineteenth century, and as of 1929, at least provisionally, technology governs the twentieth century. The European spirit [*Geist*] could not remain perpetually in any one of these neutral spheres, because the repressed human inclination toward conflict – the political – inevitably returns to render the supposedly objective sphere again controversial:

> [I]t belongs to the dialectic of such a development that one creates a new conflict area through the very shift of a central area. In this new area first considered to be a neutral area the opposition of men and interests unfolds itself immediately with new intensity. . . . European humanity always wanders out of one conflict area into a neutral one, and the neutral area always becomes immediately a conflict area again and it becomes necessary to search for a new neutral sphere. (*ND*, 138)

Although he explicitly criticizes Marxism, in the "Neutralizations" essay, for being outdated and appropriate only to the nineteenth century's economic mode of thought, Schmitt credits it for at least recognizing within the nineteenth century's central sphere the genesis of that of the twentieth century: Marxism "already sees in the core of the economic the technical" (*ND*, 134). In the twentieth century, another neutral area is sought in the technical but, as we will see, Schmitt claims that the technical instead becomes a new and definitive source of conflict. Schmitt's goal is to make this case to a generation of German intellectuals who, as far as he is concerned, have been too long under the spell of the cultural and technological pessimism of such figures as Weber, Spengler, Troeltsch, and Rathenau (but not Nietzsche!), who have unintentionally fostered a spirit of passivity that contributes to the "exhaustion" of the age (*ND*, 140). His point is to warn this generation that the "technicity" behind "technology" may indeed not be benign, but it is not "lifeless," "soulless," "dead," or "spiritless," as the German romantic tradition, in many of its forms, had led it to believe.[37] It is Schmitt's task to convince the central European intellectual elite that this "satanic" spirit has moved in right next door: "The [opening] remark about the Russians was meant to remind us of this" (*ND*, 131).

---

37 Recall from Chapter 1 that Schmitt's first critique of romanticism, *Politische Romantik*, was published in 1919; see *Political Romanticism*, trans. Guy Oakes (Cambridge, Mass.: MIT Press, 1985); hereafter *PR*.

Although Weber sought desperately to inspire a class of elites to guide Germany in the new century, in "Politics as a Vocation,"[38] according to Schmitt – and Lukács, it will be remembered – his forecast of more profound meaninglessness fostered by increasing rationalization, bureaucratic domination, and creeping technicism stymies that possibility.[39] Elites are even more crucial to Schmitt's concerns, because he attributes modernity's movement from one central sphere to another sphere of neutrality to the conscious activity of European intellectuals whom he calls "clerics."[40] These clerics guided Europe in four centuries from theology finally to technology, which is "seemingly . . . the absolute and final neutral ground" (*ND*, 138). But Schmitt cautions, "this is only a tentative characterization of the whole situation," for there are at least two problems with technology as a source of neutrality.

The first problem lies with the "great masses" of the West, for whom technology could never be truly neutral. The very success and efficiency of technology, the almost supernatural way it transforms nature, inspire the masses to infuse it with theological meaning. "According to this religion all problems resolve themselves through technical progress" (*ND*, 135). From this arises the religion/antireligion of technicity described earlier. As Walter Benjamin observed, technology does not increase the rationalization of the general population, but further inclines them toward the theological, toward myth.[41] There are dire implications of this: What was abandoned as a central sphere at the outset of modernity – the theology of the sixteenth century – thus returns within the twentieth century's central area. Intensifying the problem, according to Schmitt, is the fact that unlike the clerics, "the great masses of the industrialized countries" were themselves never fully secularized. The elites detheologized themselves as they moved from one century, one central sphere, to another; the masses, on the other hand, jumped directly from traditional religion to technical religion:

38 Weber, "Politics as a Vocation," in *From Max Weber*, p. 95.

39 See Walter Struve, *Elites Against Democracy: Leadership Ideals in Bourgeois Political Thought in Germany, 1890–1933* (Princeton: Princeton University Press, 1973) for an account of German elites in the early decades of the twentieth century.

40 Schmitt may have appropriated the term *clercs* and at least some of the theoretical meaning associated with it from Julien Benda's work from 1927, *La trahison des clercs* (Paris: Grasset, 1981), a work widely popular in intellectual circles at the time.

41 "Only a thoughtless observer would deny that there are correspondences between the world of modern technology and the archaic symbol-world of mythology." Benjamin, "Konvolut N [Re the Theory of Knowledge, Theory of Progress]," in *Benjamin: Philosophy, Aesthetics, History*, ed. Gary Smith (Chicago: University of Chicago Press, 1989), p. 49.

They skipped all intermediary stages, which are characteristic of the thought of the leading elites, and in their case a religion of miraculous and other-worldly belief without intermediary turns into a religion of technical miracles, human achievement and of the domination of nature. A magical religiosity transforms into a likewise magical technicity. Thus the twentieth century appears at its beginning as the age not only of technology, but also of a religious belief in technology. (*ND*, 134)

With the return of theology in technicity, Schmitt implies that controversy and conflict not unlike that which surrounded the theology of the sixteenth century is destined to return, in other words, wars of religion.[42]

---

42   Contemporary liberals, such as Stephen Holmes, Charles Larmore, and even John Rawls, seem to subscribe to a grand narrative of modernity quite similar to that set forward by Schmitt in the "Neutralizations" essay. This is especially true with respect to the notions of modernity's genesis in the religious civil wars and political liberalism as the immediate solution to that particular crisis. See Rawls, *Political Liberalism* (New York: Columbia University Press, 1993); Holmes, *The Anatomy of Antiliberalism* (Cambridge, Mass.: Harvard University Press, 1993); Holmes, *Passions and Constraint: On the Theory of Liberal Democracy* (Chicago: University of Chicago Press, 1995); and, more particularly, Larmore, *The Morals of Modernity* (Cambridge: Cambridge University Press, 1996), pp. 12, 122, 143–4, 212–13. Schmitt, the chauvinistic Catholic, does not, as do these liberal theorists, rely so exclusively on the St. Bartholomew's Day massacre as the preferred example of religious fanaticism, at least not until the Third Reich when he needed to distance himself from his earlier political Catholicism; see Schmitt, "The Plight of European Jurisprudence" (1944), trans. G. L. Ulmen, *Telos* 83 (spring 1990), p. 66. The problem with such metanarratives in their liberal form is that they reinforce unhelpful ideological stereotypes with respect to contemporary forms of political regression as the return or revival of older forms of authoritarianism. In so doing, they invite an understanding of political crisis as a replay of previous forms of pluralist confessional conflicts, for which similar or identical remedies are suitable contemporary applications. Moreover, the manner in which heroes and villains, or rather friends and enemies, are depicted in such narratives may serve to confirm suspicions – either harbored by the likes of Schmitt or, for example, contemporary poststructuralists – that the Enlightenment was not the victory of universal principles but rather of particular cultural interests, namely, those of white, Anglo-Saxon, Protestant males. The main difference between the Schmittian and the liberal versions of this narrative, besides obviously contradictory evaluations of its historical success, resides in the fact that Schmitt conceived this course of history as entailing the possibility of radical breaks or even of the process itself coming to a close. Liberals of either an optimistic Whiggish or a negative or agnostic Weberian stripe quite often conceive of this course of history in terms of a rationalization process that proceeds linearly into the indefinite future. A tension in liberalism, especially in the authors mentioned here, is whether contemporary conflicts of incommensurable worldviews reflect, in this vein, an increasing sociological likelihood as the result of ever-greater societal subsystem complexity and differentiation, or rather a transhistorical "fact" of modernity. See Holmes, "Differenzierung und Arbeitsteilung im Denken des Liberalismus," in *Soziale Differenzierung: Zur Geschichte einer Idee*, ed., Niklas Luhmann (Opladen: Westdeutscher, 1985); and Larmore, *Patterns of Moral Complexity* (Cambridge: Cambridge University Press, 1987). As we will see in subsequent chapters,

For his part, Nietzsche admires wars of religion, because they demonstrate that the general population has beliefs: "Religious war has signified the greatest progress of the masses hitherto; for it proves that the mass has begun to treat concepts with respect. Religious wars start only after the more refined quarrels between sects have refined reason in general to the point where even the mob becomes subtle and takes trifles seriously."[43] In the same work, he predicts and welcomes the coming of another such warlike age.[44]

If the first problem with technology as a neutral sphere, according to Schmitt, lies with the masses, the second one lies with the clerics themselves, or more precisely the particular lack of clerics in the age of technology. There can be no intellectual elite in a society governed by the technical (*ND*, 139).[45] The clerics thought they had good reason to push society toward the technical, "for apparently there is nothing more neutral than technology" (*ND*, 138). The "refreshingly factual" quality of technology, the way it seemingly appeals in the same way to all people objectively, made it appear to be "a sphere of peace, of understanding and of reconciliation" (*ND*, 138). But the clerics encouraged their own extinction, because the utter universality of technology requires no true intellectual elites or clerics to guide its use. The early centuries of modernity opened up new possibilities for the "active elite" (*ND*, 132) of Europe who were no longer bound by traditional sanction. They were able to interpret the central spheres for the masses – they were able to create values for them, in the Nietzschean sense – and as a result control them. But technology, according

there is also a tension in Schmitt's thought between historicist inclinations that are attuned to dramatic historical change within modernity and a transhistorical privileging of the purportedly eternal human propensity toward conflict. Chapter 6, in fact, demonstrates more specifically how Schmitt came to view the crisis situation of Weimar in terms of the religious civil wars of the sixteenth century and sought redress for the former in a restructuring of the foundation of the political philosophy of Thomas Hobbes. Unlike Holmes, Larmore, and Rawls, his solution is not to revive or recast liberal solutions formulated during these crises but to devise an alternative that would preclude liberal remedies.

43 Nietzsche, *The Gay Science*, pp. 192–3.
44 Ibid., p. 228.
45 In his emphasis on the importance of elites, Schmitt has much in common with the turn-of-the-century Italian theorists of "elitism," Gaetano Mosca and Vilfredo Pareto. Unlike them, however, Schmitt is not sure whether "the class-conscious proletariat of the big cities and the Russian masses estranged from Europe" (*RC*, 64) can actually be tamed by elites. See Mosca, *The Ruling Class* (1896), trans. A. Livingston (New York: McGraw-Hill, 1939); and Pareto, *The Mind and Society* (1916), trans. A Livingston and A. Bongioro (New York: Harcourt, Brace & Jovanovich, 1935). Weber was of course also concerned with the relationship of elites and the masses; see "Science as a Vocation," p. 395.

to Schmitt, is contentless, and nothing truly important can be derived from it as a central area, "neither a concept of cultural progress, nor the type of cleric or intellectual leader, nor a specific political system" (*ND*, 139). Technology is so devoid of content that not everyone will in fact see in it the very same thing and use it in the very same way, rendering it a source of universal commonality. Rather, everyone will see in it something subjectively different to be employed in a different way, and it will become instead the ultimate means of conflict: "[E]very strong politics will make use of it" (*ND*, 141).

Relatedly, there are two ramifications of Schmitt's distinction between the phenomena of technicity and technology in the "Neutralizations" essay: one for the Soviet Union and one for German intellectuals, the first corresponding to technicity, the second to technology. As Heidegger observes, the purely instrumental attitude that accompanies technology fosters an *anxiety* regarding mastery: "So long as we represent technology as an instrument, we remain transfixed in the will to master it."[46] According to Schmitt, a comparable anxiety manifests itself in the attitude of both the industrialized masses, generally, and the Soviet Union, specifically, who, possessed by the spirit of technicity, seek mastery for mastery's sake. Bewitched by an "activist metaphysics," they desire to drive the will to mastery as far as it will go.[47] "They hope to become masters of these fearful weapons [of technology] and claim the monstrous power with which they are bound" (*ND*, 141).

The anxiety regarding mastery manifests itself in the opposite way for the German intellectual elite who resign themselves to the apparent fact that technology *cannot* be mastered. Schmitt attributes the widely noted malaise of the intellectuals of his generation to the indecision of would-be clerics over the use of technology: Their "fear was ultimately nothing other than doubt over their own power to put into service the great instruments of the new technology waiting only to be used" (*ND*, 140). As early as *"Northern*

---

46 Heidegger, "The Question Concerning Technology," p. 32.

47 Weber speaks of how the socialist intelligentsia was able to raise "the eschatological expectations of the masses," who seek support "in prophecies rather than postulates" (*ES* 873–4). The bourgeois intellectuals, on the other hand, have no such power. See Weber's criticisms of his demagogically inclined academic colleagues who inspire their students toward flights of mysticism instead of responsible action, in the "Science" lectures (pp. 137, 140–3). Schmitt himself describes elsewhere the mindset of bourgeois intellectuals in the era of the First World War: "German bourgeois culture persisted in having no interest in developing a state theory. In one sense, it was an unpolitical, technical, bureaucratic culture; in another sense, it was just a nonpolitical, private culture essentially concerned with the aesthetic consumption of shadowy literary images." Schmitt, *Hugo Preuß: Sein Staatsbegriff und seine Stellung in der deutschen Staatslehre* (Tübingen: J. C. B. Mohr [Paul Siebeck], 1930), p. 16.

Lights" in 1916, Schmitt notes the peculiar effect that the emergence of technology has on Western intellectuals. Will it augment their power or restrain it? Ultimately, what is it? Schmitt describes "the mood" that has "taken control" of many of "the best minds of the day": a "distrust of the world and every man"; a "feeling of eternal deception"; a doubt not unlike that of "whether Christ and the Antichrist are distinguishable" (*N,* 70). In the face of such indeterminacy, some aestheticize their incapacity to act; in effect, they wallow in it: "[T]heir particular sickness is interesting to them. . . . They want to see themselves described and want to hear themselves speaking about their doubt and to continue doubting because at bottom they love their condition and give themselves to it in a resigned manner in order not to be obliged to a deed. They do not want to use power" (*N,* 70–1). Other intellectuals simply confuse the power of their rhetoric with power itself: "It is a typical mistake of intellects of lesser rank to infer from the violence of their affectivity the aesthetic and historical importance of its expression" (*N,* 66). They consider it indicative of their "ambition," "power," "libido," and "potency" (*N,* 66).

In the "Neutralizations" piece thirteen years later, Schmitt retains this attitude of disapproval toward the intellectuals who aestheticize their own passivity or overestimate the potency of their "great words" (*ND,* 130). It is to this effect that he starkly contrasts the technicity of the Soviet Union and the neutrality of the European clerics who have abdicated their rightful position of leadership because of a particular view of technology. Germany's intellectual elite laments the utter contentlessness of technology and recognizes that the culture of technology needs no elite to guide it. As a result, instead of seeing the technicity of the Soviet Union for what it is, a demonic opponent that must be confronted, they have collapsed into despair and paralysis: "a German generation that complains about a soulless age of technology in which the soul is helpless and unconscious," and the elite thinks itself "powerless" (*ND,* 140). It is Schmitt's task to inform this generation that the age of neutralization that fosters their romantic pessimism "has been carried to an end" (*ND,* 140). As the apparently self-anointed *cleric* of postneutralization Europe, Schmitt seeks to make them aware of what technicity actually is and where it resides and prod them into taking a thoroughly "political" stance toward it.

In *Political Form,* Schmitt bristles at the suggestion by one of his intellectual heroes, Georges Sorel, that Catholicism no longer has the capacity to sustain such myths as the Antichrist (*RC,* 15). By the time of the "Neutralizations" piece, Schmitt may have come to see Sorel as correct, for he has turned to more secularly mythic means to overcome the age of technology.[48] Indeed, Sorel is a kind of model for the type of cleric who can lead Europe out of its exhaustion: "Sorel did not remain an engineer, but rather became a cleric" (*ND*, 139). Yet Schmitt sees a generation of German intellectuals who feel supplanted by engineers and technicians who know nothing of culture, politics, and myth. The battle between *Naturwissenschaft* and *Geisteswissenschaft* has been won by the former in the eyes of this generation, which is content to retire and complain.

Nietzsche was most specific about the passivity encouraged by natural science and mechanistic thinking. In one place he writes, "knowledge kills action; action requires the veils of illusion," and he later identifies Socrates as "the demonic power" that is the source of this kind of knowledge.[49] As a result of Platonic rationality, Nietzsche claims elsewhere, man "now places his behavior under the control of abstractions."[50] He often laments that knowledge "enfeebles activity" and encourages the "avoiding of life and action."[51] In *The Gay Science*, he poses the question, even though science has shown that it can "annihilate" goals of action, will it perhaps someday provide them?[52] The literature and scholarship of the late nineteenth and early twentieth century are filled with examples of this kind of anxiety over the possibility of action. Despite the obvious "action" that science and technology make possible against nature, it is not construed by intellectuals as *meaningful* action. On the contrary, as we observed in the first section, it is action that deprives the world of meaning. Nietzsche, Schmitt, Lukács, and Heidegger perceive this type of activity as a kind of passivity.[53]

The intrinsic relationship between the passivity, or exhaustion, that Europe was experiencing and the process of neutralization that Schmitt describes were already perceived before the war by Nietzsche, who defined this exhaustion thus:

48   Sorel is central for Schmitt's treatment of "political myth" in *The Crisis of Parliamentary Democracy* (1923), trans. Ellen Kennedy (Cambridge, Mass.: MIT Press, 1985); and "Die politische Theorie des Mythos"(1923) in *Positionen und Begriffe im Kampf mit Weimar – Genf – Versailles: 1923–1939* (Hamburg: Hanseatische Verlagsanstalt, 1940), discussed in the next chapter.

49   Nietzsche, *The Birth of Tragedy*, pp. 60, 82.

50   Nietzsche, "Truth and Lies," p. 84.

51   Nietzsche, *On the Advantage and Disadvantage of History for Life*, p. 1.

52   Nietzsche, *The Gay Science*, p. 82.

53   For a comparison of the fear of passivity in Schmitt and Heidegger, see Mehring, "Der philosophische Führer und der Kronjurist." In response to the supposed passive nihilism of romanticism, Mehring describes how Schmitt and Heidegger take up an active nihilism that is obsessed with the political leadership of intellectual elites.

[T]he esteem for war and the pleasure in war diminish, while the comforts of
life are now desired just as ardently as warlike and athletic honors were formerly. But what is generally overlooked is that the ancient national energy and
national passion that became gloriously visible in war and warlike games have
now been transmuted into countless private passions and have merely become
less visible. Indeed, in times of "corruption" the power and force of the national energies that are expended are probably greater than ever and the
individual squanders them as lavishly as he could not have formerly when he
simply was not yet rich enough.[54]

In *Political Form,* Schmitt attributes this kind of corruption to the Protestant
privatization of religion (*RC,* 28–9), and in *Political Romanticism,* he attributes it to the romantic subjective aestheticization of morality (*PR,* 16).
Both are symptoms of the neutralization of values and the suppression of
the political, which is poised to return triumphant. The age is thus torn
between resignation in the face of nihilism or neutralization, on the one
hand, and, on the other, anticipation that these processes have come to
their ends and new opportunities for elites have emerged. This can be seen
at times in Nietzsche, who promotes emerging alternatives to the age of
total equalization:

> We have a different faith; to us the democratic movement is not only a form of
> the decay of political organization but a form of the decay, namely the diminu-
> tion, of man, making him mediocre and lowering his value. Where, then, must
> *we* reach with our hopes?
>   *Toward new philosophers;* there is no choice; toward spirits strong and origi-
> nal enough to provide the stimuli for opposite valuations and to revalue and
> invert "eternal values"; toward forerunners, toward men of the future who in
> the present tie the knot and constraint that forces the will of millennia upon
> *new* tracks.[55]

But for Nietzsche it is (intentionally?) unclear how these intellectual elites
should lead. Schmitt, however, is more specific.[56]

---

54 Nietzsche, *The Gay Science,* p. 96.
55 Nietzsche, *Beyond Good and Evil,* p. 307.
56 Siegfried Kracauer analyzes how the intellectual circle that surrounded the journal *Die
    Tat,* with which Schmitt was affiliated, was obsessed with being "concretely aware of the
    concrete situation"; with the question of whether their intellectual positions were irra-
    tional or beyond rationality; with a conception of *Volk* that transcends notions of both
    Western individualism and Eastern holism. They were conscious of using the Soviet Union

Asceticism and the Antichrist

Schmitt's identification of the Soviet Union as the enemy, at the outset of the "Neutralizations" essay, can now be understood more fully. The distinction between technicity and technology helps clarify why he sees the Soviets as so dangerous and why the central European intellectuals need to be alerted to this. As foreshadowed in *Political Form,* he claims that the Russians are courageous "in rationalism and its opposite" and have "realized the union of Socialism and Slavism" (*ND,* 130). In other words, the Soviet Union embodies not only economic rationality, socialism, but also what Schmitt identifies earlier in *Political Form* as "anarchism," the irrational revolt against all form and order that manifests itself in an ecstatic nationalism, Slavism. Were Russia wholly motivated by the former element, it would be a formal, mechanical, lifeless *technological* state. But Schmitt emphasizes the expressly lifelike, spiritual, willful, even satanic quality of the *technicistic* Soviet state. In *Political Form,* he maintains that a politics built purely on technology would not last a day, but, combined with the spirit exhibited by Dostoyevsky and Bakunin, it poses a considerable threat to Europe (*RC,* 17).

Schmitt is appalled that the intellectuals of his generation do not recognize the Soviet Union as the home of a very much alive and very dangerous anti-Western spirit. Their self-absorption and resignation in the face of a supposedly soulless, lifeless, and mechanical technology hinder their ability to behave "politically" when confronted by a vigorous enemy. Such thinking has "only the value of a romantic elegy" (*ND,* 142). And it is indeed significant that Schmitt again raises the issue of romanticism, "the essence of which is," we will recall he remarks in *Political Romanticism,* "passivity" (*PR,* 115). Like the romantics, whom Schmitt so thoroughly reviled, but whom he ultimately resembles in so many respects, German intellectuals ascribe subjective aesthetic value to a particular object, even though in the case of technology it is a negative aesthetic value. This is of course ludicrous for Schmitt, because the German intelligentsia ascribe content to the very object they themselves assert can have no inherent objective content: technology. They claim that it is soulless and lifeless, yet they remain aesthetically preoccupied with it. This preoccupation prevents them from seeing the lively, satanic technicity that drives the material, lifeless technology.

as a negative model from which to forge their own conception of central Europe. See Kracauer, "The Revolt of The Middle Classes" (1931), in *The Mass Ornament: Weimar Essays,* ed., T. Levin (Cambridge, Mass.: Harvard University Press, 1995), pp. 107–9, 115.

In the ecstatic closing paragraph of "Neutralizations," Schmitt accuses his fellows and colleagues of being the ones who are beholden to technology, despite their criticisms of it, because those who maintain the "comfortable antithesis of organic and mechanistic" are themselves thinking in a "rawly mechanical" manner (*ND*, 142). Such thinking is in fact "a renunciation of the struggle" (*ND*, 142). According to Schmitt, "the right to dominate" rests on "a correct assessment of the whole historical situation" and *knowing* one's own "temporal and cultural predicament" (*ND*, 130). The Russians have made such an assessment – they "know" and the Germans do not. The Soviets have "seen through our great words"; that is, they see through the superficial neutrality of the day. They recognize "the core of modern European history" and have "drawn the ultimate consequences" from it: The age of neutralization is over; conflict has returned (*ND*, 130). Europe obsesses over the status quo politically and technology intellectually, and thus misrecognizes the historical moment "and thereby renounces its claim to dominate" (*ND*, 141). As a result, Schmitt intimates, it necessarily invites domination.

The "Neutralizations" essay is filled with calls for "conscious self-assessment" and a coming to terms with present historical reality. Schmitt remarks that Europe "lives under the gaze of the more radical brother who compels one to drive practical conclusions to the end" (*ND*, 131). The Soviets have defined themselves in relation to technology and technicity, socialism and Slavism. Again appropriating Weber's *Protestant Ethic* thesis for his own purposes, Schmitt identifies them as the new "ascetics," who are willing to forgo the "comfort" of the present for control of the future (*ND*, 141). They will dominate their own nature for the sake of dominating external nature and the nature in others (*ND*, 141).

Nietzsche generally associates the ascetic ideal with science and thereby denounces it as an enemy of life.[57] But he also recognizes the tremendous source of power offered by the ascetic ideal, particularly in regard to the domination of the masses *by* themselves and *of* others: "Asceticism and puritanism are almost indispensable means for educating and ennobling a race that wishes to become master over its origins among the rabble and that works its way toward rule."[58] As such, asceticism is not *death*-driven, as it first appears, but rather *life*-affirming: "[L]ife wrestles in it and through it with death and *against* death; the ascetic ideal is an artifice for the *preservation* of

---

57 See, e.g., Nietzsche, *On The Genealogy of Morals*, p. 589.
58 Nietzsche, *Beyond Good and Evil*, p. 263.

life."[59] Schmitt accuses his Western colleagues of renouncing life, for anyone who sees "in his enemy no more than empty mechanics is closer to
death than to life" (*ND*, 142). Schmitt finds the European intellectuals
indulgent in their passively aesthetic enrapture with the present and with
the status quo, in contrast to the Soviets who seek to ascetically overcome
the present and seize the future. Echoing Nietzsche, Schmitt declares, "All
new and great impulses, every revolution and every reformation, every new
elite comes out of asceticism and voluntary or involuntary poverty, whereby
poverty means above all renunciation of the status quo" (*ND*, 141).

The European intellectuals, however, see in such behavior a "nullity," a
"void," "nothingness," a will to "death" and not to life. But this is a potentially fatal misrecognition. Soviet power, generated by technicity, Slavism,
anarchism, and asceticism, "grows silently and in the dark." It is alive and
should not be understood as "only a return to nothingness" (*ND*, 141). As
Nietzsche observed explicitly in a discussion of passivity, "the Russians . . .
have an advantage over us Westerners in dealing with life."[60] Schmitt fears
that what is an advantage will become domination.

In the spirit of the closing paragraphs of Weber's "Politics as a Vocation"
essay, Schmitt challenges the German intellectual elite to forsake the comfort of their organic/mechanical, life/death dichotomies and their self-
indulgent obsession with the status quo and to instead define the West
culturally and politically in opposition to this satanic force that resides to
the east. If they choose to sit idly by and view Russia as a lifeless nothingness,
they will succumb to the identical fate of all previous ruling orders who
refused to see in burgeoning self-abnegating movements their own future
rulers. Like those who initially ridiculed and denounced the early Christians
or the radical Protestants, only to be swept away in the wave of their eventual
triumph, the German intellectual elite faces the prospect of being held
under the sway of the "this-worldly activism" (*ND*, 140) that grows more
powerful in Russia everyday. They would confirm Weber's great fear that
Germany would become a nation "without the opportunity of counting in
the arena of world politics – and also without the moral right to do so" (*ES*,
1462; translation amended).[61]

---

59   Nietzsche, *On The Genealogy of Morals*, p. 556.
60   Ibid., p. 519.
61   One of the central themes that Siegfried Kracauer discerns in the fascist writings of the *Tat*
     circle, with which Schmitt was affiliated, is a fetishization of territorial space: space where
     the *Volk* presents itself, space from which the state emerges, and space over which the
     Soviet Union is a rival. See Kracauer, "The Revolt of the Middle Classes," pp. 109–10, 116.
     It is worth noting that under present conditions of global transformation, space as a social

Aestheticism and the Antichrist

Schmitt's portrait of the German intellectuals of his day, in the "Neutralizations" piece, in fact tells us much about Schmitt himself; it is Schmitt's
criticism of others that provides the grounds for a critique of him. In the
"Neutralizations" essay, he defines the dominant mood of the intellectuals
of his age as exhaustion and despair. In *Political Romanticism,* he invites us to
"see the despair that lies behind the romantic movement – regardless of
whether this despair becomes lyrically enraptured with God and the world
on a sweet, moonlit night, utters a lament at the world-weariness and the
sickness of the century, pessimistically lacerates itself, or frenetically plunges
into the abyss of instinct and life" (*PR,* 20). For once Schmitt explicitly
names Nietzsche as one of the "high priests" of this kind of despair. Yet as we
have seen, Schmitt has more than a little in common with Nietzsche on
many grounds, and so we must ask what kind of a high priest Schmitt is and
what the source and consequence of his own "despair" are.

From the theorists of myth prevously discussed, such as Cassirer,
Horkheimer, and Adorno, we learn that myth is inspired by fear. Out of the
fear of the unknown or the obscure, a hasty identification or "naming" in
the stark terms of good and evil, divine and demonic, is performed so as to
alleviate the anxiety aroused by this condition of epistemological uncertainty. Because the identification may not be accurate in any realistic sense –
because it is merely a mythic construct and not a fully theoretical

theoretical category is again becoming an object of intense theoretical inquiry; see Neil
Brenner, "State Territorial Restructuring and the Production of Spatial Scale: Urban and
Regional Planning in the Federal Republic of Germany, 1960–1990," *Political Geography*
15:1 (1996). Space is also becoming the subject of even more intense geopolitical con-
flict; see Stephen J. Del Rosso, Jr., "The Insecure State: Reflections on 'the State' and
'Security' in a Changing World," *Daedalus* 124:2 (spring 1995). Although the primacy of
political space is clearly presupposed in the "Neutralizations" essay, it is not until World
War II and the postwar years that Schmitt begins to theorize "territoriality," as such. See
his formulation of the Third Reich's "Monroe Doctrine" for Europe, his *Grossraum* thesis:
"Grossraum gegen Universalismus" (1939), in *Positionen und Begriffe im Kampf mit Weimar –
Genf – Versailles: 1923–1939.* See also his postwar ruminations on land appropriation, as
elaborated in *Der Nomos der Erde im Völkerrecht des Jus Publicum Europaeum* ([1950] Berlin:
Duncker & Humblot, 1974), part of which appears in English as "Appropriation/
Distribution/Production: Toward a Proper Formulation of the Basic Questions of any
Social and Economic Order," trans. G. L. Ulmen, *Telos* 95 (spring 1993). For an analysis of
the relationship of Schmitt's theory of "space" with that of Hannah Arendt, on the one
hand, and contemporary poststructuralism and Marxist geography, on the other, see John
Ely, "The Polis and 'The Political': Civic and Territorial Views of Association," *Thesis Eleven*
46 (August 1996).

apprehension – fear persists, with specific consequences for political domination in modernity.[62]

Schmitt is quick to point out the fear that motivates others: In all three works under consideration, *"Northern Lights,"Political Form,* and the "Neutralizations" piece, fear is associated with the "unspeakable confusion" or the "anxiety" generated by technology in early-twentieth-century intellectuals. In response to the apparent meaninglessness of the age of technology and the confusion regarding what is real, however, meaning and reality can be discerned only with great care. In his promotion of geopolitical conflict, Schmitt obviously believes that the human propensity toward conflict – the political – is a transhistorically valid, objectively firm foundation on which to build meaning in an age stripped of it by the neutralizing force of technology. Like Heidegger, Schmitt is a master at exposing the ungrounded, subjective, aesthetic ascriptions performed by others (e. g., the random "occasionalism" of romantics, or the empty aesthetic enrapture of Weimar intellectuals with technology). How can he not recognize the potential arbitrariness of his own ultimately aesthetic elevation of such phenomena as human conflict or, more specifically, intercontinental conflict?[63]

What makes these theoretical-political moves any less random aesthetic "occasions" for Schmitt's own romantic "despair" than the passive and pessimistic enrapture of Weimar intellectuals with technology? The fact that Schmitt so often explicitly acknowledges the myth-making quality of his endeavor reveals the theoretical deficiency that defeats the promise of his critique of technology. As we will see, a mythic response to the "unspeakable confusion" of a "concrete historical circumstance" can be neither theoretically adequate nor politically emancipatory – and as such can never really alleviate fear.

In a discourse regarding "the value of having enemies," Nietzsche reveals just what is at stake in creating meaning through friend/enemy distinctions:

> [I]t means acting and thinking in the opposite way from that which has been the rule. The church always wanted the destruction of its enemies; we, we immoralists and Antichristians, find our advantage in this, that the church

---

62   In Chapter 6, I will explore Schmitt's own Weimar attempt to revive Hobbesian "fear" in an authoritarian theoretical-political attempt to fortify the German state. In terms of the present discussion of fear, see the classic essay, "Anxiety and Politics," of Schmitt's former student and subsequently strident critic, Franz Neumann , included in Herbert Marcuse, ed., *The Democratic and the Authoritarian State: Essays in Political and Legal Theory* (New York: Free Press, 1957).

63   For a comparison of the *aporiai* of Schmitt's "myth of the soil" and Heidegger's "mysticism of Being," see Mehring, "Der philosophische Führer und der Kronjurist," p. 362.

exists. . . . Almost every party understands how it is in the interest of its own self-preservation that the opposition should not lose all its strength; the same is true of power politics. A new creation in particular – the new *Reich,* for example – needs enemies more than friends: in opposition alone does it *feel* itself necessary, in opposition alone does it *become* necessary.[64]

Of course the language of the Antichrist – so central to this chapter, and to which I will return shortly – is still apparent. The more immediate point is that, if one can only find the necessity of one's own existence in the opposition to another, one can function by definition only as a *negation,* as a part of an already-existing structure. In the terms developed in Chapter 1, if one resolves the concrete situation of one's historical moment solely in terms of cultural conflict, how can one be sure that one is not merely accelerating one's "historical plight" as a mere negative moment *within* the concrete situation, rather than sufficiently apprehending it theoretically and hence actually transforming it?

In his account of his fellow intellectuals, Schmitt is obviously anxious to make sure that *his* response to his own fear of technology is not the same as that of his colleagues, namely, reversion to passivity. And accordingly, already in 1923, and certainly by 1929, political action takes precedence over theoretical rigor in his thinking. Because such action cannot be technological action, which is necessarily devoid of meaning, it becomes *mythic* action – action that creates meaning, action against a world-historical opponent. Nietzsche maintains that only myths unify a culture,[65] and he observes that, at the end of the nineteenth century, *"Europe wants to become one."*[66] Schmitt supplies such a supposedly culture-unifying myth in the form of an anti-European Russia.

Schmitt remarks, "Where political activity begins, political romanticism ends" (*PR,* 160). This implies of course that a political decision and the resulting action is the *transcendence* of the duality of the age of technology that Schmitt identifies in *Political Form:* subjectively random valorization of the concrete, a "completely irrational consumption," on the one hand; and objectively abstract rationality, a "totally rationalized production," on the other (*RC,* 14). But this is obviously not the case. Political activity in the Schmittian sense does not escape the confinement of *either* moment of the dichotomy. Characteristic of romanticism, as Schmitt himself describes it,

64 Nietzsche, *Twilight of the Idols,* p. 488. Nietzsche celebrates the opposition of friends and enemies in many places; see for example, *The Gay Science,* pp. 57–8, 107.
65 Nietzsche, *The Birth of Tragedy,* p. 135.
66 Nietzsche, *Beyond Good and Evil,* p. 386.

his notion of the political subject as embodied in clerics or elites and the political enemy as manifested by Soviet Russia – indeed, the very notion of "the political" itself – are all ungrounded occasions for Schmitt's own subjective aesthetic consumption. His narrative concerning the elite- and neutrality-driven course of modern European history, however fascinating and ingenious, is ultimately no more compelling than the nineteenth-century philosophies of history from which he explicitly attempts to distance it (*ND*, 132).

Likewise, characteristic of economic-technical thought, as Schmitt theorizes it, "the political" is itself devoid of any substantive content. The meaning generated by conflict in "political activity" varies according to the changing configuration of the particular combatants. In a Schmittian sense, therefore, political activity is *precisely* political romanticism. And despite the fact that Schmitt may be more sensitive to the antinomies of modernity than are the romantics and the neoromantics he criticizes, his own romanticism would have far more lethal consequences than theirs, in large part as a result of the centrality of the myth of the Antichrist to his approach.

Schmitt writes of Däubler's "Northern Lights": "[I]t contains elements of such a strong apocalyptic mood that it could probably call forth a religious epidemic" (*N*, 65). The same could easily be said of large portions of Schmitt's own work, which, as we have seen, are often infused with a language reminiscent of theology.[67] Even in much of Schmitt's post–World War II writings, he is preoccupied with the notion of the *Katechon,* a medieval concept of the force, embodied either in an institution or a person, that can hold off the coming of the Antichrist.[68] Schmitt considers the tradition of European jurisprudence and even himself in his "defense" of it against positivist law as examples of a *Katechon.*[69]

As is apparent in every passage I have quoted from Nietzsche, he also extensively employs the language of the sacred and the profane, frequently centering on the notion of the Antichrist. However, Nietzsche often interchanges what is at one juncture sacred with what is at another profane in his work. As we have seen, Nietzsche can identify his opponents as "advocates of the devil," or as a "demonic force," and then describe himself in those very terms. In his last days, as whatever was left of his sanity and his life slipped away, he randomly identifies himself in his letters with Christ or the Anti-

---

67 See Schmitt, *Political Theology,* as well as *Politische Theologie II. Die Legende von der Erledigung jeder politischen Theologie* (Berlin: Duncker & Humblot, 1970).

68 See Schmitt, *Der Nomos der Erde.*

69 See Schmitt, *Ex Captivitate Salus: Erfahrungen der Zeit 1945/47* (Cologne: Greven, 1950), p. 31.

christ.[70] The distinction had either lost its meaning for Nietzsche, or the blurring of the distinction was indeed his purpose.

In terms of the analysis of myth just discussed, there are potentially discomforting ramifications of this readiness to so quickly "name" one or another historico-social phenomenon as demonic or divine. In the three works by Schmitt I have examined in this chapter, he describes technology or technicity in terms of the Antichrist or the satanic. But he also recognizes that technology is a source of "unspeakable confusion": science and technology equate entities that ought not be equated, and technological reproducibility raises the question of whether there is anything that is in fact authentic. Particularly relevant here is Adorno's critique of existentialists who utter "words that are sacred without sacred content";[71] a critique that reflects traditional Judaism's reluctance to represent the divine, lest the profane be falsely worshipped:

> In Jewish religion, in which the idea of the patriarchate culminates in the destruction of myth, the bond between name and being is still recognized in the ban on pronouncing the name of God. . . . Jewish religion allows no word that would alleviate the despair of all that is mortal. It associates hope only with the prohibition against calling on what is false as God, against invoking the finite as infinite, mendacity as truth.[72]

That Nietzsche and Schmitt so enthusiastically invoke the profane displays how "Christian" they are in the most vulgar sense, whatever their respective qualifications and equivocations of the issue.[73] Moreover, the attempt to preserve or restore some premodern religiosity in the "age of reason" through the use of sacred language clearly only further profanes it. Indeed, the attempt to create a *new* religiosity by such means is itself profanity. Weber's advice to those who were so inclined – go back to the traditional religions – should have been heeded by his own student.[74] Schmitt's return to more orthodox religiosity after the war was unfortunately too little, too

---

70 See *Selected Letters of Friedrich Nietzsche*, ed. and trans. Christopher Middleton (Chicago: University of Chicago Press, 1969), e.g., pp. 344–5.

71 Theodor W. Adorno, *The Jargon of Authenticity* (1964), trans. K. Tarnowski and F. Will (Evanston, Ill.: Northwestern University Press, 1973), p. 9.

72 Horkheimer and Adorno, *Dialectic of Enlightenment*, p. 23; translation amended. See Richard Wolin, "Reflections on Jewish Secular Messianism," in *Labyrinths: Explorations in the Critical History of Ideas* (Amherst: University of Massachusetts Press, 1995), p. 54.

73 See Schmitt, *Der Nomos der Erde*, pp. 96, 131; and *Ex Captivitate Salus*, p. 75. Nietzsche's attitude toward Christianity is of course more or less explicit.

74 Weber, "Science as a Vocation," p. 155.

late to keep him out of the despicable mischief that his faux religiosity facilitated in the early thirties.[75]

As Ernst Fraenkel observed regarding Schmitt: "[W]hile writing still in the name of political Catholicism [he] described the incongruity between functional and substantial rationality with . . . acuteness and lucidity."[76] Fraenkel proceeds to quote the passage from *Political Form* cited earlier, where Schmitt describes the "specific Catholic anxiety" over economic-technical rationality's indifference to the production of "a silk blouse or poison gas." Fraenkel then remarks on Schmitt's conversion from theologically based yet still rational interrogation to the theoretically ungrounded exaltation of myth:

> As long as Carl Schmitt believed that Roman Catholicism would eventually be triumphant . . . he was profoundly disturbed by this incongruity. . . . After he had turned his back on the Catholic Church, Schmitt lost his 'specific Catholic anxiety' as well as the realization that the only essential rationality is the rationality of ends. He sought security instead in Sorel's theory of myth.[77]

This is not to imply that the only legitimate way to come to terms with the deformations of modernity is through the intellectual means of traditional religion. On the contrary, as expressed at the conclusion of the last chapter, the theoretical approach of a broadly defined "critical theory" practiced by other authors whom I draw on to criticize Schmitt (e. g., Adorno, Benjamin, Horkheimer, Fraenkel, Neumann) certainly offers a more adequate methodology.[78] The more pressing point is, however, if one wishes to confront

---

75   For accounts of Schmitt's influence on theology, before and after the war, see the collection edited by Bernd Wacker, *Die eigentlich katholische Verschärfung . . . : Konfession, Theologie und Politik im Werk Carl Schmitts* (Munich: Wilhelm Fink, 1994). Two studies that perhaps too heavily emphasize Schmitt's faith, are Meier, *Carl Schmitt and Leo Strauss;* and Andreas Koenen, *Der Fall Carl Schmitt: Sein Aufstieg zum "Kronjuristen des Dritten Reiches"* (Darmstadt: Wissenschaftlichen Buchgesellschaft, 1995). See Joseph Bendersky, "Review: Andreas Koenen, *Der Fall Carl Schmitt: Sein Aufstieg zum 'Kronjuristen des Dritten Reiches,'* and Heinrich Meier, *Carl Schmitt, and Leo Strauss: The Hidden Dialogue," Journal of Modern History* (1997). Meier, for instance, lumps together all of Schmitt's theological references from across his career with no account of Schmitt's relationship to Catholicism at any particular time, especially during his excommunication. See Meier, *Carl Schmitt and Leo Strauss,* e.g., pp. 19–20, 48, 68.

76   Ernst Fraenkel, *The Dual State: A Contribution to the Theory of Dictatorship* (1941), trans. by E. A. Shils (New York: Octagon Books, 1969), p. 207.

77   Ibid., translation amended.

78   On the prospects for a critical social theory deriving from the efforts of some of these authors, especially Adorno, see Axel Honneth, *The Critique of Power: Reflective Stages in a Critical Social Theory,* trans. Kenneth Baynes (Cambridge, Mass.: MIT Press, 1991), particularly the preface to the most recent edition.

the problem of the meaninglessness of modern science and technology but *not* from the standpoint of the traditional religions of substantive meaning, one ought not, as does Schmitt, resort to a "new" religiosity that seeks to make meaning through the manufacture of myth. The very language one must resort to in describing this Nietzschean or Sorelian strategy reveals its limitations: "make," "manufacture," "strategy." As Cassirer explained, the new religion or mythology that seeks to conquer technology necessarily succumbs to it.[79] As Adorno remarks so aptly, "Those who have run out of holy spirit speak with mechanical tongues."[80]

Heidegger, who cannot be completely excluded from this discussion, wrote in 1959 regarding technology, "It would be shortsighted to condemn it as the work of the devil."[81] Yet is this not tantamount to what he does when he exclaims in the face of "global technology" that "only a God can save us?"[82] Certainly if he, too, were not caught up in the enterprise of divinizing and demonizing, he would not have made the mistake of originally seeing in National Socialism the "countermovement" to "global technology," only to "realize" later that it was in fact the *culmination* of the age of technology.[83] The latent technicity in the strategy of reviving myth makes such misrecognitions, such "mistakes," possible.[84]

The fact that Schmitt made the same "mistake" as Heidegger regarding National Socialism, combined with the fact that the Nazis were able to so abuse and distort Nietzsche's philosophy, only emphasizes the question of whether such "mistakes" are inherent to the language of the Antichrist. The ancient Jewish prohibition on naming mentioned by Adorno discourages the intense aestheticization of either the sacred or the profane that has emerged so frequently in this chapter. It insures that such "mistakes" are not made. At such a level of aestheticization, it is impossible to ground a moral-

79 Cassirer, *The Myth of the State*, p. 282.

80 Adorno, *The Jargon of Authenticity*, p. 10.

81 Heidegger, *Discourse on Thinking* (1959), trans. J. M. Anderson and E. H. Freund (New York: Harper & Row, 1966), p. 53.

82 See "'Only a God Can Save Us': *Der Spiegel's* Interview with Martin Heidegger" in Wolin, *The Heidegger Controversy*, p. 107.

83 Quoted in Wolin, *The Politics of Being*, pp. 98–103.

84 See Habermas's discussion of Heidegger's mythologizing in his accounts of the philosopher in *Philosophical-Political Profiles*, trans. F. Lawrence (Cambridge, Mass.: MIT Press, 1983); and *The New Conservatism: Cultural Criticism and the Historians' Debate*, trans. Shierry Weber Nicholsen (Cambridge, Mass.: MIT Press, 1989). However, Robert Pippin cautions, "While it is always roughly accurate to say that Heidegger wants to revive attention to the mythic or archaic, his own re-writings of *archai* and *mythos* are so extensive as to make the characterization misleading." Pippin, *Modernism as a Philosophical Problem: On the Dissatisfactions of European High Culture* (Oxford: Basil Blackwell, 1991), p. 195, n. 79.

ity; one is necessarily *beyond* good and evil, or worse, one can no longer tell the two apart. There is a danger that by demonizing something, something else that is completely unworthy of such reverence may be necessarily sacralized in response. The language of the Antichrist that is supposed to dissolve the spirit of technology, on the contrary, further engenders that same "unspeakable confusion" fostered by what Schmitt calls economic-technical thought. His evoking the language of the Antichrist helped ensure that he would not be remembered as the *Katechon* of the twentieth century, as he would have liked, but rather as the Mephistopheles of Weimar Germany.[85]

When the philosophical existentialism of Nietzsche is transposed into the political existentialism of Sorel or Schmitt, the normative *end* of addressing the latent (and often not-so-latent) moments of domination concomitant with modern, technical rationality becomes itself subsumed by the mythological, hence necessarily aesthetic, *means* of doing so. As Fraenkel puts it:

> Sorel stripped the class struggle of its visionary goal and approved it as a movement for its own sake. He transformed it into a myth because to him the movement was everything and the goal was nothing. Thus Sorel became the prophet of politics without ultimate goal – the advocate of action for the sake of action. . . . Whoever believes that political action is nothing more than acquiesence in the laws of social development will share the fate of Sorel. Like Sorel he will pass from Syndicalism to *l'Action Française;* like Mussolini, a disciple of Sorel, he will shift from Socialism to Fascism; like Carl Schmitt, the admirer of Sorel, he will desert political Catholicism for National Socialism, as soon as he is convinced that integral nationalism is the order of the day.[86]

85   Karl Loewenstein, quoted in Ulmen, *Politischer Mehrwert,* p. 26.
86   Fraenkel, *The Dual State,* p. 130. Fraenkel remarks on Schmitt's confession that his endorsement of National Socialism was prompted by the diagnosis that "We are witnessing today the bankruptcy of *idées génerales*": "The fact that the most brilliant political theorist of [inter]war Germany adheres to a political movement, not because of its ideas, but because of its lack of ideas is a symptom of the degree of development of that political estheticism [sic] that worships violence for its own sake" (ibid., p. 131). Like Franz Neumann and Otto Kirchheimer, Fraenkel was a young, Jewish legal scholar of the Left who had learned much from Schmitt during the Weimar Republic. These scholars harbored no illusions about Schmitt's conservatism but nevertheless felt stunned and betrayed by his endorsement of a regime that would threaten their very existence and force their emigration. On Schmitt and Fraenkel, see Pasquale Pasquino, "Politische Einheit, Demokratie und Pluralismus: Bemerkungen zu Carl Schmitt, Hermann Heller und Ernst Fraenkel," in *Der Soziale Rechtsstaat,* ed. C. Müller and I. Staff (Baden-Baden: Nomos, 1984). A recent work on the legal figures in the tradition of critical theory is William E. Scheuerman's *Between the Norm and the Exception: The Frankfurt School and the Rule of Law* (Cambridge, Mass.: MIT Press, 1994).

Once Schmitt had come to the conclusion that the age of neutralizations had reached its end, instead of theorizing whether myth was the most efficacious way of confronting technology, he fabricated in the language of the Antichrist the quasi-Nietzschean myth of a European elite forging meaning through cultural-political combat with Soviet Russia. He subsequently offered his services to a regime that also valorized elites and demonized the Soviet Union but that could not itself distinguish between "a silk blouse and poison gas."

Prefatory Remarks on Part Two

Having emphasized in Part One the role of technology in Schmitt's Weimar cultural-political writings, I turn in Part Two to its significance in Schmitt's constitutional and institutional writings. Chapter 3 focuses on emergency powers and serves as an overview of Schmitt's Weimar oeuvre, because it deals with political works from throughout the republic. Techniques of managing the ever-immanent political exception that itself defies the age of technology emerge as Schmitt's foremost theoretical-practical concern, the very heart of his critique of liberalism, and the genesis of his intensifying fascism.

II

LIBERALISM AS TECHNOLOGY'S
INFILTRATION OF POLITICS

3

EMERGENCY POWERS

The first line of Schmitt's *Political Theology* is perhaps the most famous sentence, certainly one of the most infamous, in German political theory: "Sovereign is he who decides on the exception" [*Souverän ist, wer über den Ausnahmezustand entscheidet*].[1] And yet the full significance of this famous sentence is often underestimated. In this chapter, I focus on (1) its significance in the overall trajectory of Schmitt's Weimar work, and (2) its significance for constitutional theories of emergency powers in general.

I will examine Schmitt's first major theoretical engagement with the issue of emergency powers, in *Die Diktatur* from 1921,[2] and explain how his position, or at the very least his mode of presentation, changes in his second effort on this subject, *Political Theology*, published only a year later. In the earlier work, Schmitt describes the classical Roman institution of dictatorship as a theoretical-historical standard for emergency measures that preserve a constitutional order in a time of dire crisis and also explicitly as the appropriate conjunction of *Technik* and *Politik*. In classical dictatorship, political technology is consigned only to the temporary exceptional mo-

---

1 Schmitt, *Political Theology: Four Chapters on the Theory of Sovereignty* (1922), trans. George Schwab (Cambridge, Mass.: MIT Press, 1986), p. 5; hereafter *PT*. German references to the work come from *Politische Theologie: Vier Kapitel zur Lehre von der Souveränität* (Munich: Duncker & Humblot, 1934), here, p. 11.
2 Schmitt, *Die Diktatur: Von den Anfängen des modernen Souveränitätsgedankens bis zum proletarischen Klassenkampf* (Berlin: Duncker & Humblot, 1989), hereafter *D*.

ment, and in this scheme the normal and rule-bound regular order is considered substantively correct by Schmitt and worthy of restoration. However, in the latter work, *Political Theology,* the exceptional situation is that which calls for the emergence of a potentially all-powerful sovereign who must not only rescue a constitutional order from a particular political crisis but also charismatically deliver it from its own constitutional procedures, procedures that Schmitt pejoratively deems technical and mechanical. The question I want to pose and answer is, why does Schmitt in the span of a year change his position in one work, in which a temporary dictatorship is presented as an appropriate use of functional rationality and a rule-bound constitutional order is presented as something worth defending and restoring, to the position in the second work, in which an unlimitedly powerful sovereign is one who in a time of crisis restores existential substance to constitutional orders that of necessity grow "torpid" through "mechanical repetition?"[3] Just as in Chapters 1 and 2 we observed Schmitt's transition from a merely conservative cultural-political critic of technical rationality and romantic irrationality to a more engaged radically reactionary one, in this chapter we will begin to see the constitutional and institutional manifestations of this latter orientation. The subject of emergency powers provides a promising thread with which to trace Schmitt's overall intellectual trajectory in Weimar, because it is a central concern throughout his writings of the period.

Dictatorship as Technology

Schmitt takes up *Die Diktatur* (*Dictatorship*) in the context of the extensive use of emergency powers by the Weimar Republic's first president, Friedrich Ebert, under Article 48 of the Weimar constitution. Ebert used such measures against the forces that were besieging the republic on all sides in its early years: right-wing and communist rebellion, as well as an overwhelming economic crisis.[4]

---

3   Schmitt, *Politische Theologie,* p. 22.
4   See Frederick Mundell Watkins, *The Failure of Constitutional Emergency Powers under the German Republic* (Cambridge, Mass.: Harvard University Press, 1939), chaps. 2 and 3, for an account of Ebert's use of Article 48 against the authoritarian Kapp putsch of 1920, against the Hitlerian Beer Hall putsch of 1923, as well as against the many communist insurrections between 1919 and 1923. On Ebert's use of the article in the economic sphere, see Clinton Rossiter, *Constitutional Dictatorship: Crisis Government in Modern Democracies* (Princeton: Princeton University Press, 1948), pp. 41–3. See also Hans Boldt, "Article 48 of the Weimar Constitution, Its Historical and Political Implications," in *German Democracy and the*

Thus Schmitt engages in a historical-theoretical study of the institution of dictatorship to confront a contemporary crisis, yet he travels very far from contemporary conditions. In *Die Diktatur*, he extols the classical Roman institution of dictatorship precisely because of its purely technical characteristics. Why is Schmitt here appreciative of something politically technical when we have seen that such phenomena generally elicit a thoroughly negative response from the theorist? He writes favorably of the limited sphere of classical dictatorship and the limited employment of what he calls in the work "technicity [*Technizität*]," or the "objectively-" or "factually-technical [*sachtechnische*]" aspect of dictatorship.

The Roman dictator was appointed in a time of dire emergency to address the concrete specifications of that emergency and no other. The Roman Senate proclaimed an emergency: usually a foreign invasion, an insurrection, a plague, or a famine. It then asked the consuls to appoint a dictator, who could in fact be one of the consuls themselves. The dictator had unlimited power in his task, acting unrestrained by norm or law, while being severely limited beyond the specific task in that he could not change or perpetually suspend the regular order. Instead, he was compelled to

---

Triumph of Hitler, ed. Anthony Nicholls and Erich Matthias, (London: Unwin & Allen, 1971). On the context of the book, *Die Diktatur*, more specifically, see Joseph Bendersky, *Carl Schmitt: Theorist for the Reich* (Princeton: Princeton University Press, 1983), pp. 30–1.

Under the rather broad powers provided for by Article 48, the directly elected *Reichspräsident* could compel, with armed force if required, an individual state or *Land* to comply with federal law (par. 1); and could take "necessary measures" to restore or protect "public order and safety" by suspending constitutional rights and by recourse to armed force when it was "disturbed or endangered" (par. 2). The limits to the president's emergency powers as enumerated within the article itself include the immediate informing of the general parliamentary body, the *Reichstag*, of any emergency action, the *Reichstag's* right to revoke such action (both par. 3), and a called-for statute to prescribe the exact details of the president's authority (par. 5); from without the article itself, the countersignature of the chancellor of the parliamentary government was required for all presidential measures including those issued under Article 48 (Art. 50), and there existed a constitutional provision for impeachment (Art. 43). The President could bypass such restrictions by dissolving the *Reichstag* (Art. 28) or by colluding with the chancellor (and, as an aside, the statute to circumscribe presidential emergency powers was never brought into being). Social Democrat Ebert did not abuse the constitution in any of these ways during the Republic's early period of crisis, as did conservative Paul von Hindenburg, in machination with successive right-wing chancellors (Brüning, von Papen, and von Schleicher), during the second and final period of crisis between 1929 and 1933 (see Karl Dietrich Bracher, *Die Auflösung der Weimarer Republik: Eine Studie zum Problem des Machtverfalls in der Demokratie* [Düsseldorf: Droste, 1984], and Detlev Peukert, *The Weimar Republic: The Crisis of Classical Modernity* [New York: Hill & Wang, 1987]). I will deal with Schmitt's writings on presidential emergency powers and complicity with the right-wing constitutional usurpers during this period in later sections of this chapter.

return to it through the functional nature of his activity and the time limit placed on him. However, in the performance of his duty, the dictator knew no right or wrong but only expedience: According to Schmitt, for the dictator, "a procedure can be either false or true, in that this determination is self-contained by the fact that the measure taken is in a factually-technical [*sachtechnische*] sense right, that is expedient" (*D*, 11). Normative or ethical notions of wrong and right, legal and illegal, are not brought to bear in dictatorship, only what is "in the factually-technical [*sachtechnische*] sense harmful [to the regime], and thus false" (*D*, 12). The "peculiarity" of dictatorship, according to Schmitt, lies in the fact that "everything is justified that appears to be necessary for a concretely gained success" (*D*, xviii). The particular "concrete situation [*Lage der Sache*]" calls for the particular kinds of "tasks, powers, evaluations, empowerments, commissions and authorities" to be taken up by the dictator (*D*, xviii). The specifics of a crisis – an immediate end – generate the specific "means [*Mittels*]" to be employed by the dictator, whereas the ultimate end is understood, a situation of status quo ante:

> A dictatorship therefore that does not have the purpose of making itself superfluous is a random despotism. Achieving a concrete success however means intervening in the causal path of events with means whose correctness lies solely in their purposefulness and is exclusively dependent on a factual connection to the causal event itself. Dictatorship hence suspends that by which it is justified, the state of law, and imposes instead the rule of procedure interested exclusively in bringing about a concrete success. . . . [a return to] the state of law. (*D*, xvi)

It is important to note that this purely technical aspect of dictatorship is at the very heart of the concept and the institution for Schmitt and that it had much to do in his mind with the contemporary use, disuse, and abuse of the concept in the early twentieth century. According to Schmitt, the "bourgeois political literature" either ignores the concept altogether or treats it as a kind of slogan to be used against its opponents (*D*, xi–xii). Schmitt is alarmed that the concept seems to be taken seriously only by the Communists with their doctrine of the "dictatorship of the proletariat" (*D*, xiii). The Communists have the concept partially right, according to Schmitt, for they recognize its purely technical and temporary characteristics: "The dictatorship of the proletariat is the technical means for the implementation of the transition to the Communists' final goal" (*D*, xiv). The "centralizing machine" and "domination-apparatus" of the state seized by the proletariat is not, according to their ideology, "definitive" for the Communists, but rather "transitional" (*D,* xiv).

Schmitt notes that one might then see the communist theory of dictatorship as simply a modern incarnation of the classical institution: a negation of parliamentary democracy without formal democratic justification (because the Communists are often a minority) and a replacement of the personal dictator with a collective one (the party) (*D,* xiii). But this obscures the truly fundamental transformation of the essence of the classical concept: The communist institution employs technical means to create a new situation; the classical institution employed them to restore a previously existing one. This difference has important ramifications for the question of just how limited a dictatorship can be if it is legitimated and bound by a future situation as opposed to being legitimated by a previously existing one.[5] This difference also lays the groundwork for the theoretical-historical distinction that governs the whole of *Die Diktatur:* the one between the traditional concept of "commissarial dictatorship," which is bound by allotted time, specified task, and the fact that it must restore a previously standing order; and "sovereign dictatorship," which is unlimited in any way and may proceed to establish a completely new order.[6] I will return to these issues in greater detail in subsequent sections.

So, if the Communists partially understand the essence of dictatorship, liberals, to the extent that they pay any attention to the concept at all, completely misapprehend it, according to Schmitt.[7] Liberals have com-

---

5 Schmitt's one-time student, Otto Kirchheimer, criticizes the way socialists wrongly define dictatorship and cites, problematically, *Die Diktatur* and *Politische Theologie* as equivalents; see "The Socialist and Bolshevik Theory of the State" (1928), in *Politics, Law and Social Change: Selected Essays of Otto Kirchheimer,* ed. F. S. Burin and K. L. Shell (New York: Columbia University Press, 1969), p. 6. He goes on to paraphrase Schmitt on the apparently commissarial yet actually sovereign nature of Bolshevik dictatorship (p. 15). As faithful as Schmitt's leftist students often were to Schmitt's theory of dictatorship, their frequent equating of the arguments of *Die Diktatur* and *Politische Theologie* have done as much to obfuscate as to clarify the crucial issues involved (Kirchheimer repeats this equation in his essay from 1944, "In Quest of Sovereignty," in the same volume, p. 191). On the specifics of Schmitt's intellectual relationship to such leftist legal scholars as Kirchheimer and Franz Neumann, see William E. Scheuerman, *Between the Norm and the Exception: The Frankfurt School and the Rule of Law* (Cambridge, Mass.: MIT Press, 1994); as well as Scheuerman, ed., *The Rule of Law Under Siege: Selected Essays of Franz L. Neumann and Otto Kirchheimer* (Berkeley: University of California Press, 1996).
6 On Schmitt's appropriation of the etymological-theoretical distinction from Jean Bodin, and a general discussion of the thesis, see George Schwab, *The Challenge of the Exception: An Introduction to the Political Ideas of Carl Schmitt between 1921 and 1936* (Westport: Greenwood, 1989), pp. 30–1.
7 Interestingly, Schmitt's complaint from the twenties is still relevant today, as the "bourgeois

pletely forgotten its classical meaning and associate the idea and institution solely with the kind described by Schmitt as "sovereign" dictatorship: "[A] distinction is no longer maintained between dictatorship and Caesarism, and the essential determination of the concept is marginalized . . . the commissarial character of dictatorship" (*D*, xiii). Liberals deem a dictator to be any single, individual ruling through a centralized administration with little political constraint, often democratically acclaimed, and they equate it unreflectively with authoritarianism, Caesarism, Bonapartism, military government, and even the papacy (*D*, xiii).[8]

But by corrupting the notion of this important technique for dealing with emergencies and subsequently banishing it from constitutional concerns, liberal constitutionalism leaves itself especially susceptible to emergencies. Its blind faith in the technical apparatus of its standing constitutions and the scientistic view of the regularity of nature encourages liberalism to believe that it needs no technique for the extraordinary occurrence, be-

---

political literature" in English on dictatorship and emergency powers is paltry and out-dated: Besides the classics by Watkins (*The Failure of Constitutional Emergency Powers under the German Republic*) and Rossiter (*Constitutional Dictatorship*), see most recently John E. Finn, *Constitutions in Crisis: Political Violence and the Rule of Law* (Oxford: Oxford University Press, 1991); and Jules LoBel, "Emergency Powers and the Decline of Liberalism," *Yale Law Review* 98 (1989). The most attention paid to constitutional dictatorship in the traditional literature is by Schmitt's own former student, C. J. Friedrich; see "Dictatorship in Germany," *Foreign Affairs* 9:1 (1930); "The Development of Executive Power in Germany," *American Political Science Review* 27 (1933); and *Constitutional Reason of State: The Survival of the Constitutional Order* (Providence: Brown University Press, 1957). On Friedrich's intellectual debt to Schmitt, see George Schwab, "Carl Schmitt: Through a Glass Darkly," *Schmittiana – Eclectica* 71–2 (1988): 72–4. It is still the Left that exhibits more interest in the concept of dictatorship: Two post-Marxists influenced by Schmitt who have written extensively on the subject are Paul Hirst and Norberto Bobbio. See Hirst: "Carl Schmitt's Decisionism," *Telos* 72 (summer 1987); *The Pluralist Theory of the State* (London: Routledge, 1989); *Representative Democracy and Its Limits* (Cambridge: Polity Press, 1990); "The State, Civil Society and the Collapse of Soviet Communism," *Economy and Society* 20:2 (May 1991). See Bobbio, *Which Socialism? Marxism, Socialism and Democracy* (1976), trans. Roger Griffin (Minneapolis: University of Minnesota Press, 1987); *The Future of Democracy: A Defense of the Rules of the Game* (1984), trans. Roger Griffin (Minneapolis: University of Minnesota Press, 1987); *Democracy and Dictatorship: The Nature and the Limits of State Power* (1985), trans. Peter Kenealy (Minneapolis: University of Minnesota Press, 1987).

8 Schmitt's one-time student, leftist lawyer Franz Neumann, remarked in the fifties, "Strange though it may seem, we do not possess any systematic study of dictatorship." He cites Schmitt's *Die Diktatur* but declares with no explanation that "his analysis is not acceptable." See "Notes on the Theory of Dictatorship" (1954), in *The Democratic and the Authoritarian State: Essays in Political and Legal Theory*, ed. Herbert Marcuse (New York: Free Press, 1957), pp. 233, 254, n. 1. As I will argue, this conclusion can be drawn only by conflating too dramatically the respective analyses of *Die Diktatur* with *Political Theology*.

cause the regular constitutional techniques are assumed to be appropriate to a nature free of the extraordinary. Classical dictatorship is a wholly technical phenomenon that restores what is not wholly technical, the normal legally legitimated order. Liberal constitutionalism is an order become increasingly technical through its formulation of a conception of normalcy that excludes the extraordinary. Unlike the separation of powers that, according to Schmitt, despite its fixation on equilibrium, ironically, cannot ensure stability, or despite legal positivism that, due to its mechanical nature, cannot distinguish between right and wrong and hence legality and legitimacy, dictatorship has an end that is not simply the perpetual means to another end. The classical dictatorship emphasizes the importance of the regular order – something that eludes the liberal positivism of Hans Kelsen, "for whom the problem of dictatorship has as much to do with a legal problem, as a brain operation has to do with a logical problem. This is a result of a relativistic formalism that misunderstands that dictatorship deals with something else entirely, namely, that the authority of the state cannot be separated from its value" (*D*, xix). Dictatorship emphasizes the importance of the regular order through the imperative to bring it to restoration. For Schmitt, the separation of powers and legal positivism defile it through the emphasis on uninterrupted processes and not what is substantively important about a regime.

According to Schmitt, there is a dialectical relationship between the exceptional situation (and consequently, the dictatorship appropriate to it) and the normal one, a relationship that is ruptured by the liberal denial of the exception and the Communist temporal perpetuation of it. Liberalism does not consider the possibility of an exceptional situation and hence necessarily misconceives the nature of dictatorship. For a liberal constitutional order in all of its historical manifestations (rule of law, rights-granting, and mass-democratic), "what has validity as a norm can be determined positively through a standing constitution or also through a political ideal. From this a state of siege is called a dictatorship because of the suspension of positive constitutional designation" (*D*, xiv).[9] If liberalism

9 Schmitt distinguishes between dictatorship and a state of siege, in "Diktatur und Belagerungszustand: Eine staatsrechtliche Studie," *Zeitschrift für die gesamte Strafrechtswissenschaft* 38 (1917). For an extensive discussion of the essay that may, however, too baldly read back Schmitt's later more extreme authoritarianism into this early work, see Peter C. Caldwell, *Popular Sovereignty and the Crisis of German Constitutional Law: The Theory and Practice of Weimar Constitutionalism* (Durham, N. C.: Duke University Press, 1997).

would recognize the possibility of exceptions, it would be more open to the idea of exceptional measures to address them, such as dictatorship – purely technical ones that have as their goal the restoration of a liberal order. This denial, however, encourages a further technicization of the normal order in an attempt to dominate political nature in the same way that technology dominates material nature. What should be more than mere machine, the constitutional order, is made increasingly so in avoiding the appropriate use of political technology, the dictatorship.

In *Die Diktatur,* Schmitt gives no indication that this need *necessarily* continue to be the case for a liberal regime or a *Rechtsstaat*. The communist doctrine of dictatorship, on the other hand, completely changes the relationship of normal and exceptional situation, and hence Communism inevitably and irreversibly transforms the nature of dictatorship. "From a revolutionary standpoint the whole [bourgeois] standing order is designated a dictatorship" and the Communists free themselves from the constraints of the rule of law associated with that standing order, as well as implicit in the classical constitutional notion of dictatorship, because their norm is no longer "positive-constitutional" but rather "historical-political"; that is, dictatorship is now dependent on a yet-to-be-realized telos rather than a previously established constitutional order (*D,* xv). The Communists are "entitled" to overthrow the liberal state, because the conditions are "ripe," but they do not give up their own dictatorship, because conditions are not yet "ripe" (*D,* xv). The communist dictatorship is defined as the temporary negation not of the past or the present but of what is to come: present, absolute statism versus future, absolute statelessness. Unlike classical dictatorship, however, communist dictatorship, Schmitt predicts, will not perform the ultimate task with which it is charged, its self-negation, that is, relinquishing the state.

The communist dictatorship represents, for Schmitt, the culmination of the modern, historical trend toward totally unrestrained political action. In contrast to the literally conservative orientation of traditional politics, wherein political activity is sanctioned by a previously existing good, according to Schmitt, the radical orientation of modern politics is driven by a fervor to bring about some future good, whose qualities are so vague as to justify unbounded means in the achievement of the end. For Schmitt, this is generated by the merging of the wholly technical activity of dictatorial action with a politics of normalcy in modern political theory and practice. Both the liberal and the communist responses to dictatorship are hence different manifestations of the modern technicization of politics. In *Die Diktatur,* Schmitt traces the origin of this development back to Niccolò

Machiavelli, the modern writer who perhaps took the classical theory of dictatorship most seriously.[10]

Machiavelli, Technicity, and the State

Schmitt notes that Machiavelli correctly emphasizes the purely technical character of dictatorship, and Schmitt himself adopts Machiavelli's formulation of the theory in the *Discorsi:*

> Dictatorship was a wise invention of the Roman Republic. The dictator was an extraordinary Roman magistrate, who was introduced after the expulsion of the kings, so that a strong power would be available in time of peril. His power could not be curtailed by the authority of the consuls, the principle of collegiality, the veto of the people's Tribune, or the provocation of the people. The dictator, who was appointed on petition of the Senate by the consuls, had the task of eliminating the perilous crisis, which is the reason for his appointment, such as the direction of a war effort or the suppression of a rebellion. . . . The dictator was appointed for six months, although it was customary for him to step down before the full duration of his tenure if he successfully executed his assigned commission. He was not bound by law and acted as a kind of king with unlimited authority over life and death. (*D*, 1–2)

Unlike the "sovereign" dictatorships of Caesar and Sulla, who used the office to change the constitutional order so as to further their own grasping at unlimited power, the classical notion was wholly commissarial (*D*, 3).

Schmitt observes how Machiavelli's *Discorsi* has been maligned as a "cheap imitation" of Aristotle, Polybius, and especially Livy, whose history serves as the ostensible occasion for Machiavelli's reflections (*D*, 6). However, Machiavelli's remarks on dictatorship are "independently interesting and decidedly influential" (*D*, 6). More clearly than most, Machiavelli recognizes that the collegiality of republican government prevents such a re-

---

10 Schmitt's affinity with Machiavelli transcends the realm of the purely intellectual or academic. Schmitt's biographer describes how Schmitt compared his post–World War II banishment from the German university to the fate of the great Florentine, "who had to endure similar ostracism despite . . . significant intellectual contributions. Schmitt even referred to his house as San Casciano, the place where Machiavelli lived while in exile after losing favor with the Medici family." See Bendersky, *Carl Schmitt: Theorist for the Reich*, p. 287. On the commonality between Schmitt and Machiavelli, and their respective receptions, see Paul Hirst, "Carl Schmitt – Decisionism and Politics," *Economy and Society* 17:2 (May 1988); Dolf Sternberger, "Machiavelli's *Principe* und der Begriff des Politischen," in *Schriften*, vol. 3 (Frankfurt: Fischer, 1980); and Heinrich Meier, "The Philosopher as Enemy: On Carl Schmitt's *Glossarium*," *Graduate Faculty Philosophy Journal* 17:1–2 (1994).

gime from making quick decisions, and he also recognizes that exceptional circumstances require exceptional measures (*D, 6*). For Machiavelli, "the dictator is not a tyrant, and dictatorship is not some form of absolute domination but rather a republican constitution's proper means of protecting liberty" (*D, 6*).

Schmitt suggests that Machiavelli inverts Aristotle's notion of normalcy in formulating a concept of dictatorship: For Aristotle, the normal political situation requires separating those who deliberate on the law from those who execute it; for Machiavelli, the dictator is the one who both deliberates on a measure and executes it (*D, 7*). But this collapsing of deliberation and action does not render the dictator completely unlimited: "The dictator cannot alter standing law, nor cancel it, nor make new law. The ordinary authority obtains for Machiavelli as a kind of control on the dictator" (*D, 7*). As such, dictatorship was a "constitutional institution" of the republic until, by Machiavelli's account, the decemvirate endangered the republic by using dictatorship to effect changes in the constitution (*D, 7*).

Thus, a dictator is not the equivalent of a prince in Machiavelli's theory, according to Schmitt, but rather its opposite: The former uses unlimited power in extraordinary circumstances to bring about the termination of his power, whereas the latter uses unlimited power throughout an indefinite duration of time to perpetuate this power (*D, 7*). Yet in the state-building literature of the sixteenth and seventeenth centuries, the distinction between the two is increasingly obscured (*D, 7*). But the comparison of a prince and a dictator does raise the issue of what Schmitt calls, "the puzzle of *The Prince*": How could Machiavelli author the liberty-espousing *Discorsi* as well as the tyrant-advising *Il Principe* (*D, 7*)? The solution to the puzzle, for Schmitt, lies not with claims, still put forth today, that the latter book is a "veiled attack on tyranny" or a manifestation of Machiavelli's "despaired nationalism" but rather with the issue of "technicity [*Technizität*]": Machiavelli, like many Renaissance authors, was driven by "purely technical interests"; his dominant problems were "technical problems" (*D, 7–8*). This is borne out by the fact that "Machiavelli himself was most occupied by the purely technical problems of military science" (*D, 8*). Thus, *Il Principe* is the technical handbook of principalities, the *Discorsi*, of republicanism (*D, 8*). Schmitt describes this Machiavellian spirit of technicity in a way that recalls his critique of functional rationality from his cultural-political writings:

> Out of this absolute technicity develops the indifference towards any further political purpose in the same manner as an engineer can have a technical interest in the production of a thing, without being the least interested in the

purpose that the product serves. Any political result – be it absolute domination by an individual or a democratic republic, the power of a prince or the
political liberty of a people – is performed as a mere task. The political power
organization and the technique [*Technik*] of their maintenance and expansion differ according to the various types of government, but always as something that can be brought about in a factually-technical [*sachtechnische*] manner, in the way an artist fashions a work of art according to a rationalist
orientation. (*D*, 8–9)

Even people are viewed as "raw material" by this worldview, according to
Schmitt, foreshadowing the criticisms he would level against "economic-
technical" thought, in *Roman Catholicism and Political Form*, two years later:
"In *Il Principe* they [people] are not treated with an eye toward moral or
juridical establishment, but rather for the rational technology of political
absolutism" (*D*, 9). Various human material is appropriate for various regime types and must be calculated as such through "technical procedure"
(*D*, 9–10).

As a result, according to Schmitt, dictatorship is one technique among
many in a Machiavellian scheme dominated by technicity, and hence it loses
its essential extraordinary characteristic. Machiavelli's technicity regarding
political practice and his agnosticism regarding the substantive worth of
different regimes subvert the notion of dictatorship as a technical exception
of a nontechnical politics of normalcy and reduce all of politics to technology.[11] Thus, despite the fact that Machiavelli "never laid out a state theory,"
he is responsible for modern state theory's development out of the theory of
dictatorship (*D*, 6):

> The three aspects of rationalism, technicity, and executive, oriented in dic-
> tatorship (in the sense that the word implies a kind of order that is not subject,
> in principle, to the agreement or acknowledgment of the addressee[s] and
> that need not wait for their consent), engender the origin of the modern state.
> The modern state develops historically out of a politically technical matter
> [*politischen Sachtechnik*]. With it begins, as its theoretical reflection, the theory
> of the reason of state, which is a sociological maxim gained solely out of the
> necessity of the domination and expansion of political power elevated beyond
> the opposition of right and wrong. (*D*, 13)

11 For an alternative to Schmitt's account of Machiavelli's conception of exceptional circum-
    stances and the institutional means with which to deal with them, see my "Addressing the
    Political Exception: Machiavelli's 'Accidents' and the Mixed Regime," *American Political
    Science Review* 87:4 (December 1993).

As the practical task of early modern state builders becomes the expansion of political power by prosecuting boundary-defining external war and suppressing internal, religious civil war, the normatively unencumbered and technically disposed executive becomes the model of political practice, a model that still has contemporary ramifications as far as Schmitt is concerned:

> Principally now an exclusive technical interest exists in state and political matters such that legal considerations are in the same way inappropriate and contradictory to the matter at hand. The absolutist-technical state conception. . . . has no interest in the law but rather only in the expediency of state functioning, specifically, the single executive who requires no legal norm to proceed. (*D*, 12)

All of politics becomes technical and dictatorial politics; correspondingly, both elements themselves change through the transformation: In a traditional framework, the technical was a means to a prior-sanctioned good, but in modernity it becomes an end in itself; dictatorship changes from a "commissarial" phenomenon to a "sovereign" one. Civil war and foreign war, traditionally considered exceptional circumstances that might occasionally call for a dictator, become something else in the writings of such state theorists as Thomas Hobbes and Jean Bodin. In line with these historical transformations, Hobbes, who will become Schmitt's intellectual hero, further inverts the relationship of a normal political situation and an exceptional one with his concept of the "natural condition" or the "state of nature."[12] For Hobbes, the present manifestation of "Warre" is an exceptional circumstance that in the past, or more accurately beneath the veneer of the present, is actually a normal state of affairs, the "natural condition" or "state of nature." Thus, the exceptional circumstance is viewed actually as a return to normalcy and the regular order as a kind of exceptional situation – the distinction becomes deliberately blurred. Hobbes's "sovereign" and state are hence a kind of dictatorship that has as its sole task guarding over the ever-present exception and, as such, is no longer commissarial but appropriate to its own name, sovereign. In this way is "the technical concep-

---

12   On Schmitt's appropriation of Hobbes, see Herfried Münkler, "Carl Schmitt und Thomas Hobbes," *Neue Politische Literatur* 29 (1984); David Dyzenhaus, "'Now the Machine Runs Itself': Carl Schmitt on Hobbes and Kelsen," *Cardozo Law Review* 16:1 (August 1994); and my "Fear, Technology and the State: Carl Schmitt, Leo Strauss and the Revival of Hobbes in Weimar and National-Socialist Germany," *Political Theory* 22:4 (November 1994).

tion of the origin of the modern state directly related to the problem of dictatorship" (*D*, 10).[13]

According to Schmitt, this process is radicalized as sovereignty becomes increasingly defined as *popular* sovereignty, as authority derives not from a specific and definite individual person, like an absolute monarch, but rather from an amorphous and differentiated populace. As a result, emergency action becomes more extreme, because it is soon carried out by an elite whose actions are supposedly sanctioned by such "popular" sovereignty. Concomitantly, there is a historical justification for the violent destruction of an old order and the creation of a new one out of nothing. Sovereign dictatorship becomes the power to perpetually suspend and change political order in the name of an inaccessible "people" and an eschatological notion of history. Schmitt's chief examples of this development are the writings of the French revolutionary theorists, such as Mably (*D*, 115–16) and especially Sieyés (*D*, 143–5) and more immediately the Bolsheviks.

Theologizing the Exception

I will return to the issues of the state, sovereignty, and technology in the thought of Hobbes, and Schmitt's later interpretation of them, in Chapter 6. What is important to notice here is that, in *Die Diktatur*, Schmitt treats these elements very differently than he does in his very next book that deals with similar concerns, *Political Theology*. The point is that in *Die Diktatur* he describes the rise of the modern state as a colonizing of one aspect of politics by a technical influence more appropriately left to an isolated realm, and the classical form of dictatorship as superior on many levels to what he describes as the sovereign dictatorship at the heart of the modern state.

Yet from the first sentence of *Political Theology*, written only a year later, it is clear that Schmitt has come to endorse something much closer to this latter kind of dictatorship: "Sovereign is he who decides on the exception" (*PT*, 5). He seems to celebrate the very merging of the normal and exceptional moments that in *Die Diktatur* he analyzed as politically pathological. He even encourages it with the ambiguous use of the preposition "on [*über*]," which belies the distinction he himself acknowledges in the earlier

---

13 For a recent interpretation of the early-modern reason of state literature, see Maurizio Viroli, *From Politics to Reason of State: The Acquisition and Transformation of the Language of Politics, 1250–1600* (Cambridge: Cambridge University Press, 1992).

book between, on the one hand, the body that *decides* that an exceptional situation exists – in the Roman case, the Senate through the consuls – and, on the other, the person who is appointed by them to *decide* what to do in the concrete particulars of the emergency, the dictator himself or herself. The two separate decisions, one taking place in the moment of normalcy, the other in the moment of exception, are lumped together and yet hidden behind the ostensible directness of Schmitt's opening statement in *Political Theology*. Indeed, further on in the work Schmitt explicitly and deliberately conflates the two decisions: The sovereign "decides whether there is an extreme emergency *as well as* what must be done to eliminate it" (*PT,* 7, emphasis added).

There is also no attempt in *Political Theology* at prescribing what a priori time- or task-related limits might be imposed on a sovereign's action in the exceptional situation; Schmitt suggests in fact that this is potentially impossible:

> The exception, which is not codified in the existing legal order, can at best be characterized as a case of extreme peril, a danger to the existence of the state, or the like. But it cannot be circumscribed factually and made to conform to a preformed law.
>
> It is precisely the exception that makes relevant the subject of sovereignty, that is, the whole question of sovereignty. The precise details of an emergency cannot be anticipated, nor can one spell out what may take place in such a case, especially when it is truly a matter of an extreme emergency and how it is to be eliminated. The preconditions as well as the content of a jurisdictional competence in such a case must necessarily be unlimited. (*PT,* 6–7).

According to the commissarial notion of dictatorship, the dictator was free to do whatever was necessary in the particular exceptional moment to address a crisis that is identified by another institution and that may never have been foreseen in codified law. And the dictator was bound as a "precondition" to return the government to that law. Schmitt occludes this crucial distinction in the second, more famous work and expands the unlimitedness of dictatorship by renouncing the very characteristics of the classical model he only recently admired *as well as* those of the liberal constitutionalism he consistently derides: "If measures undertaken in an exception could be circumscribed by mutual control, by imposing a time limit, or finally, as in the liberal constitutional procedure governing a state of siege, by enumerating extraordinary powers, the question of sovereignty would then be considered less significant" (*PT,* 12). Indeed, his use of the term "sovereign" implies some kind of lawmaking or lawgiving power that could change the previous order or even create a new one.

Schmitt's attitude, however, toward the normal order itself changes from *Die Diktatur* to *Political Theology*. Even though in *Die Diktatur* he chides the liberal political order for its infiltration by natural-scientific thinking, and its consequent blindness to both the possibility of the exception and to the potential necessity of resorting to the institution of the dictator on such an occasion, he never suggests that it would be impossible for that order to become aware in such a way. In fact, one of the upshots of the bulk of the book is precisely such an effort: a subtle call for the revival of the institution of a commissarial dictatorship to preserve a republican, if not specifically liberal, political order to which Schmitt does not seem at all opposed. But in *Political Theology*, the normal, liberal political order is presented as being so corrupted by science and technology that it is actually *redeemed* by the exception and the sovereign dictatorial action it calls for: "In the exception, the power of real life breaks through the crust of a mechanism that has become torpid by repetition" (*PT*, 15). In *Die Diktatur*, sovereignty is the bearer of the dangerous technicity and protoauthoritarianism that culminates with the Jacobins and the Communists and endangers any substantively worthy constitutional order; in *Political Theology*, sovereignty is that which is illegitimately suppressed by the mechanisms of constitutional orders, such as the separation of powers: "[T]he development and practice of the liberal constitutional state . . . attempts [*sic*] to repress the question of sovereignty by a division and mutual control of competences" (*PT*, 11).

What accounts for the shift in Schmitt's position? One explanation may concern his reception of Max Weber's theory of charisma. In the book originally dedicated to Weber, *Political Theology*, does he make a theoretical-political move reminiscent of the great sociologist? Weber shifted from a detached, wary, and yet somewhat condescending analysis of charisma, at the turn of the century, to an endorsement of it as a solution to the mechanization brought on by bureaucratic politics. In parallel fashion, Schmitt moves from a cautious analysis of the rise of the concept of sovereignty in the reason of state literature, in *Die Diktatur*, to an endorsement of it as a solution to the Weimar predicament, in *Political Theology*. The exception changes from a purely functional-political problem for a regime to a kind of moment of divine intervention likened to a miracle (*PT*, 36); Schmitt remarks with satisfaction that "the exception confounds the unity and order of the rationalist scheme" (*PT*, 14).

Weber's definition of charisma at least remained consistent while his own orientation toward it changed; Schmitt, however, sees sovereignty as tied to

the increasing technicization of politics, in *Die Diktatur,* whereas he promotes it as the very solution to such technicization, in *Political Theology.*
Weber's category of charisma may hold the key to Schmitt, because it is only
as a charismatically imbued figure that the sovereign dictator can possibly
be seen to deliver a constitutional regime from the danger of technicity.[14]
In *Die Diktatur,* Schmitt remarks that the concept of the political exception
has not been "systematically" treated and that he will do so himself elsewhere (*D,* xvii). In *Political Theology,* he offers not the promised systematic
treatment of the concept but rather the mythologizing of it.

The difference between the two works – the puzzle of *Political Theology,* as
it were – is perhaps better explained by the following chart:

	Die Diktatur (1921)	*Political Theology (1922)*
exception	dangerous, not good; must be met with technical ex- actitude and temporal fini- tude by a dictator.	dangerous but good be- cause an occasion for re- vivification; must be met by ambiguously defined quasi- charismatic sovereign.
normal order	rule of law; normatively val- ued; worth restoring.	formally scientistic legality; abstract and lifeless; worth restoring but in need of re- enlivening.

The conclusion one is compelled to draw from Schmitt's analysis in
Political Theology is that a regime with institutional diversity, a constitutionally
enumerated "division and mutual control of competences" (*PT,* 11), or
what is more generally known as separation of powers, is merely an overly-
mechanical construction that inevitably paralyzes a state in the face of an
exception, because it obscures who is sovereign, who must decide and act at
that moment: "If such action is not subject to controls, if it is not hampered
in some way by checks and balances, as is the case in a liberal constitution,

14 A discussion of Schmitt and Weber that deals specifically with the relationship between
dictatorship and charisma is G. L. Ulmen, *Politische Mehrwert: Eine Studie über Max Weber und
Carl Schmitt* (Weinheim: VCH Acta humaniora, 1991), pp. 390–400. Ulmen correctly
points out that Weber, unlike Schmitt, *always* associates dictatorship with charisma and
hence as a kind of Caesarism, whereas Schmitt, at least in *Die Diktatur,* recognizes and
emphasizes the purely functional nature of the classical notion of commissarial dictatorship. But as George Schwab observes, and as I will demonstrate more specifically in
subsequent sections, Schmitt moves increasingly toward the sovereign type of dictator
after the publication of the work; see Schwab, *The Challenge of The Exception,* pp. 40, 44.

then it is clear who the sovereign is. . . . All tendencies of modern constitutional development point towards the eliminating of the sovereign in this sense" (*PT,* 7). Fixation on the letter of the constitutional law to discern "competence" will either create a vacuum if no relevant competence is enumerated, or conflict should it not be clear.[15] Neither is of course a desirable state of affairs in the face of an emergency: "Who assumes authority concerning those matters for which there are no positive stipulations . . . ? In other words, Who is responsible for that for which competence has not been anticipated?" (*PT,* 11). According to Schmitt's formulation, in all cases of emergency, it would seem necessary to have recourse to a unitary institution with a monopoly on decisions, so that no such confusion or conflict occurs. Because the likelihood of such an occurrence is great (especially in the Weimar context), and because the same figure who acts on the exception must first declare that it exists, it would seemingly be best to have such a person vigilant even during normal times. Thus, in violation of the main principles of classical dictatorship, normalcy and exception are collapsed, and ordinary rule of law is dangerously encroached on by exceptional absolutism.

The second possible explanation for Schmitt's transformation may be offered by the overall thrust of *Die Diktatur* itself. Schmitt is distrustful of the general historical trend wherein the concepts of sovereignty – increasingly popular sovereignty – and emergency action are merged. Again, for Schmitt this culminates in the theorists of the French Revolution, such as Mably and Sieyés. In Schmitt's view, they advocate a sovereign dictatorship that destroys an old order and creates a new one *not* on the authority of a specific constitutional document or legal charge but as the agent of such a vague entity as the "people": "While the commissarial dictatorship is authorized by a constituted organ and maintains a title in the standing constitution, the sovereign dictator is derived only *quoad execitium* and directly out of the formless *pouvoir constituant*" (*D,* 145).

In the conclusion of *Die Diktatur,* Schmitt returns to the issue of the communist use of the term dictatorship, for he clearly sees the Communists as the heirs of the French Revolution: a radical elite that will use violent means in step with supposedly world-historical processes according to the sanction of an anointed populace to which it can never really be held accountable.

---

15 Later in *Verfassungslehre,* Schmitt discusses in great detail the dangers of literal constitutional interpretation: *Verfassungslehre* (1928) (Berlin: Duncker & Humblot, 1989), pp. 26–7, 56, 110, 125, 146, 200.

The concept of dictatorship . . . as taken up in the presentations of Marx and Engels was realized at first as only a generally requisite political slogan. . . . But the succeeding tradition . . . infused a clear conception of 1793 into the year 1848, and indeed not only as the sum of political experience and methods. As the concept developed in systematic relationship to the philosophy of the nineteenth century and in political relationship with the experience of world war a particular impression must remain. . . . Viewed from a general state theory, dictatorship by a proletariat identified with the people as the overcoming of an economic condition, in which the state "dies out," presupposes a sovereign dictatorship, as it underlies the theory and practice of the National Convention. Engels, in his speech to the Communist Union in March 1850 demanded that its practice be the same as that of "France 1793." That is also valid for the theory of the state which posits the transition to statelessness. (*D*, 205)

In other words, the dangerous spirit of France in 1793 – a spirit of sovereign dictatorship in the name of a newly sovereign people, a spirit that culminates for Schmitt only in domestic terror and continental war – was radicalized in the revolutions of 1848 and is now embodied by the Soviet power to Germany's east and by the German revolutionary organizations that, at the very moment that Schmitt wrote *Die Diktatur*, were attempting to seize the German state.

Why does Schmitt conclude the book with this specter? Why does his historical account of dictatorship offer such a situation? The tone of the conclusion differs significantly enough from that of the preface and the body of the work such that we can detect a subtle yet distinct change in strategy. The preface seems to suggest that his goal is (1) to make up for the scholarly deficiency in the "bourgeois literature" on the subject of dictatorship, (2) to make it possible to deem the communist use of the term dictatorship "sovereign" in essence and hence somehow illegitimate, and furthermore (3) to offer a more legitimate, constitutional, "commissarial" alternative with which the new republic might tackle the barrage of emergencies it was assaulted with. But Schmitt intimates, toward the close of *Die Diktatur*, that perhaps what should confront the sovereign notion of dictatorship touted by domestic and foreign revolutionaries is not a notion of commissarial dictatorship at all but perhaps a countertheory of sovereign dictatorship. Because both absolutism and mass democracy arise out of the same historical movement, Schmitt suggests, gently and furtively, that perhaps a radicalized notion of sovereignty derived from absolute monarchy should meet the radicalized notion of sovereignty derived from the French Revolution:

[A]t least for the continental constitutional liberalism of the eighteenth and nineteenth centuries the historical value of absolute monarchy lies in the annihilation of the feudal and estatist powers and that through that it created a sovereignty in the modern sense of state unity. So is this realized unity the foundational presupposition of the revolutionary literature of the eighteenth century? The tendency to isolate the individual and to abolish each social group within the state and with that set the individual and the state directly across from one another was emphasized in both the depiction of the theory of legal despotism and that of the social contract. . . . [According to Condorcet,] we live today no more in a time, in which there are within the state powerful groups and classes; the *puissante* associations have vanished. . . . In the years 1832 and 1848 – important dates for the development of the state of siege into a significant legal institution – the question was asked whether the political organization of the proletariat and their counter-effect did not in fact create a whole new political situation and with that create new state and legal concepts. (*D,* 203–4)

There are several possible conclusions to be drawn from this rather murky paragraph: Because of the trajectory of history, perhaps the conjunction of emergency powers and mass sociopolitical movements as embodied in the revolutionary/counterrevolutionary moments of 1832 and 1848 ought not to be severed, as a revival of the notion of commissarial emergency powers would entail. Perhaps the return of powerful social groups threatening the state in the form of working-class movements ought to be met by a political response new and yet akin to the way that the absolute monarchs had earlier neutralized or destroyed aristocratic and religious groups. Perhaps the populist Soviet state, which can be directed to do almost anything by an all-powerful, unaccountable, historically legitimated elite, should be engaged by a similarly defined German state directed by a charismatically legitimated president. These are conclusions implicitly suggested, not explicitly argued, by the closing pages of *Die Diktatur.* Yet these pages serve as a signpost for his subsequent book, *Political Theology,* and the rest of his Weimar work. Gone from Schmitt's writings after *Die Diktatur* are the neo-Kantian attempts to keep his authoritarian tendencies within a rule-of-law framework that characterizes his earlier writings and governs the moderating impulses of most of that book.

In *Political Theology,* as described earlier, Schmitt espouses a neo-sovereignty embodied in the *Reichspräsident,* encumbered not by constitutional restraints but only by the demands of the political exception. The president, as the personal embodiment of the popular will that cannot be procedurally ascertained in a time of crisis, has the authority to act –

unconstitutionally or even anticonstitutionally – with all the force and legit-imacy of that originary popular will.[16] Schmitt champions the very fusing of popular sovereignty and emergency powers that he showed to be potentially abusive in *Die Diktatur.* Subsequently, as it will be recalled from the previous chapter, in *Roman Catholicism and Political Form,* from 1923, Schmitt calls for a mythologically united Europe to confront the satanically described Soviet Union. In the next chapter, we will observe how in his book *Parlamentarismus* from the same year, after theoretically undressing the chief institutional rival to the *Reichspräsident,* the *Reichstag,* he suggests that the only myth to counterbalance the Soviet's myth of a worldwide stateless and classless so-ciety is the myth of the nation.[17] And Schmitt spends much of his *Ver-fassungslehre,* from 1928, building just such a conception of the nation into constitutional law and providing the preeminent place within it for the *Reichspräsident.* Perhaps most dramatically, recall Schmitt's remarks on the Soviets in the essay appended to his notorious *Concept of the Political,* in 1932: "We in Central Europe live under the eyes of the Russians. . . . Their psycho-logical gaze sees through our great words and our institutions. Their vi-tality. . . . their prowess in rationalism and its opposite . . . is overwhelm-ing."[18] The strategy of formulating a neoabsolutist presidency that can fortify Germany in withstanding the Soviet threat becomes central to his Weimar work.[19]

16   On the relationship between the French Revolutionary theory of sovereignty and Schmitt's own, see Stefan Breuer, "Nationalstaat und pouvoir constituant bei Sieyés und Carl Schmitt," *Archiv für Rechts- und Sozialphilosophie* 70 (1984); and Pasquale Pasquino, "Die Lehre vom pouvoir constituant bei Abbe Sieyés und Carl Schmitt: Ein Beitrag zur Untersuchung der Grundlagen der modernen Demokratietheorie," in *Complexio Op-positorum: Ueber Carl Schmitt,* ed. Helmut Quaritsch (Berlin: Duncker & Humblot, 1988). On the contemporary ramifications of this conception of sovereignty, see Ulrich K. Preuß, "The Politics of Constitution Making: Transforming Politics into Constitutions," *Law & Policy* 13:2 (April 1991); "Constitutional Powermaking for the New Polity: Some Delibera-tions on the Relations between Constituent Power and the Constitution," *Cardozo Law Review* 14:3–4 (January 1993): 651–2; as well as the essays included in *Revolution, For-tschritt und Verfassung* (Frankfurt a. M.: Fischer, 1994).

17   See Schmitt, *Roman Catholicism and Political Form,* trans. G. L. Ulmen (Westport: Green-wood, 1996); and *The Crisis of Parliamentary Democracy,* trans. Ellen Kennedy (Cambridge, Mass.: MIT Press, 1985).

18   Schmitt, "The Age of Neutralizations and Depoliticizations" (1929), trans. M. Konzett and J. P. McCormick, *Telos* 96 (summer 1993): 130.

19   On Schmitt's attempt to formulate a radical answer to the external threat of the Soviet Union and the internal one of working-class parties, see Reinhard Mehring, *Pathetisches Denken. Carl Schmitts Denkweg am Leitfaden Hegels: Katholische Grundstellung und antimarx-istische Hegelstrategie* (Berlin: Duncker & Humblot, 1989).

Schmitt would also continue to deal with emergency powers in Weimar. And although he had substantively abandoned the powerful notion of commissarial dictatorship that he revived in *Die Diktatur,* as we will see, he still tried to maintain the appearance of it in his writings.

Guardian or Usurper of the Constitution?

In the practical-political treatises that deal with emergency powers, written after *Political Theology* – "The Dictatorship of the *Reichspräsident* According to Article 48 of the Weimar Constitution" (1924), *Der Hüter der Verfassung* (1931), and *Legalität und Legitimität* (1932) – Schmitt continues to argue that only the *Reichspräsident* can defend the Weimar constitutional regime in a crisis.[20] However, it is not at first glance clear whether the powers Schmitt wishes to confer on the president are, according to the terms he developed in 1921, commissarial or sovereign. But the introduction of the issues of charisma and sovereignty to his discussion strongly suggests the latter.

The "Article 48" piece has made an accurate assessment of Schmitt's theory of emergency powers difficult, because it was included in later editions of *Die Diktatur,* thus coloring the pre–*Political Theology* work with a post–*Political Theology* perspective. Many commentators have thus concluded that Schmitt had unqualifiedly implied a sovereign type of dictatorship for the president's emergency powers from the start.[21] Yet even the essay written later is not so obviously an endorsement of sovereign dictator-

20 Schmitt, "Die Diktatur des Reichspräsident nach Art. 48 der Weimarer Verfassung" (1924), appended to subsequent editions of *Die Diktatur,* and thus hereafter *D2; Der Hüter der Verfassung* (Tübingen: J. C. B. Mohr [Paul Siebeck], 1931), hereafter *HV;* and *Legalität und Legitimität* (Munich: Duncker & Humblot, 1932), hereafter *LL,* from the reprint in *Verfassungsrechtliche Aufsätze aus den Jahren 1924–1954: Materialien zu einer Verfassungslehre* (Berlin: Duncker & Humblot, 1958).

21 Ernst Fraenkel, for instance, describes the whole book as an attempt to "exploit" Article 48; see *The Dual State: A Contribution to the Theory of Dictatorship* (1941), trans. E. A. Shils (New York: Octagon Books, 1969), p. 213, n. 17. This does not prevent him from explicitly appropriating Schmitt's distinction between commissarial and sovereign dictatorship (p. 213, n. 4). To his credit though, Fraenkel is more sensitive than Schmitt *ever* was to the fact that an emergency can very easily be used as an occasion for a coup (p. 10). Another of Schmitt's Leftist "students," Otto Kirchheimer, reminds us that modern emergency powers are used more often than not to reintegrate the proletariat into the state order; see "Weimar – and What Then?" (1930), in *Politics, Law and Social Change,* p. 42. There is indeed vast historical precedence for this, as it should be pointed out that despite the positive light in which I have presented the Roman institution of dictatorship, it was quite often used as a tool by the Roman Senate to keep the plebeians at bay.

ship.[22] Schmitt declares that, according to Article 48, "dictatorial authority" is only "lended" to the president (*D2, 255*), and he argues for the scope of that authority to remain seemingly within a commissarial rubric:

> The typical image of a rule-of-law regulation of the exceptional situation . . . presumes that the extraordinary authority as well as the content of that author-ity is circumscribed and delimited, as well as that a special control be estab-lished. Nevertheless with that a certain latitude [*Spielraum*] must remain to make possible the very purpose of the institution – energetic engagement – and to prevent the state and constitution from perishing in "legality." (*D2, 255*)

Certainly the Roman dictatorship as Schmitt describes it in *Die Diktatur* fits just this description: legally prescribed time and task yet wide room for play within those established limits. And the dictatorship's very reason to be was in fact to suspend the legal constitution so as to restore it, rather than blindly maintain it and allow for its destruction. But somewhat less in the spirit of republican dictatorship, Schmitt does not want *too* extensive a limitation on the emergency powers of the president, because a constitution "is the organization of the state; and it decides what order is – what normal order is – and provides for the unity and security of the state. It is a dangerous abuse to use the constitution to delineate all possible affairs of the heart [*Herzensangelegenheiten*] as basic law and quasi-basic law" (*D2, 243*). Moreover, Schmitt's descriptions of the source of the president's legitimacy in preserving the constitution in "Article 48" increasingly sound as though they were mandated *not* by the constitutional order itself but by something like a sovereign will that is itself *prior* to that order: "The dictatorship of the *Reichspräsident* . . . is necessarily commissarial as a result of specific circum-stances. . . . In as much as it is allowed to act so broadly, it operates – in fact, not in its legal establishment – as the residue of the sovereign dictatorship of the National Assembly" (*D2, 241*).

At the conclusion of the essay, Schmitt recalls the framing of Article 48 at the Republic's constitutional founding: "In the Summer of 1919 when Arti-

22   There is little scholarly consensus on the exact moment of Schmitt's conversion to sov-ereign dictatorship. Renato Cristi, for instance, locates it already in the 1921 main text of *Die Diktatur,* whereas Stanley L. Paulson dates it even after the 1924 "Article 48" essay: Cristi, "Carl Schmitt on Sovereignty and Constituent Power," *Canadian Journal of Law and Jurisprudence* 10:1 (1997); Paulson, "The Reich President and Weimar Constitutional Politics: Aspects of the Schmitt-Kelsen Dispute on the 'Guardian of the Constitution' " (paper presented at the annual meeting of the American Political Science Association, Chicago, August 31–September 3, 1995).

cle 48 came to be, one thing was clear: Germany found itself in a wholly abnormal crisis and therefore for the moment a one-time authority was necessary which made possible decisive action" (*D2, 258–9*). Schmitt calls for similar "abnormal" and "decisive" action but attempts to allay the fears of those who might be concerned with the constitutional status of such action with his final sentence: "That would be no constitutional alteration" (*D2, 259*). In other words, he is not calling for constitutionally abrogating action characteristic of sovereign dictatorship on the part of the president, but rather commissarial, constitution-preserving action. But of course his harkening back to the *crisis* in which the constitution was founded and to the preconstitutional constituting *decision* and not to the body of the constitution itself implies a repetition of a sovereign act of founding to save the constitution – in which the constitution may in fact be changed as long as the preconstitutional will is not. This strategy of justifying presidential dictatorial action on the basis of the preconstitutional sovereign will of the people and not the principles embodied within the constitution itself becomes more pronounced after Schmitt formulates his constitutional theory in the 1928 book of that name, *Verfassungslehre*, along precisely these lines, and as he seeks a solution to the Weimar republic's most severe crisis, in his books published in the wake of devastating economic depression and widespread political unrest in the early thirties, *Der Hüter der Verfassung* and *Legalität und Legitimität*.

Schmitt begins *Der Hüter der Verfassung* (*Guardian of the Constitution*) in much the same way that he began his book on dictatorship exactly ten years earlier. He blames nineteenth-century liberalism for bringing a crucial constitutional institution into ill repute, and he draws on examples from classical Sparta and Rome to demonstrate the historical legitimacy of such a concept and authority. But, whereas in *Die Diktatur* the example Schmitt is attempting to revive is commissarial dictatorship, in *Guardian* it is the notion of a defender of the constitution (*HV, 7–9*), and indeed the merging of the two phenomena – emergency powers and the question of what charismatic institution sovereignty lies in – is again just his strategy.[23]

By consistently appealing to emergency circumstances, Schmitt is able to sufficiently discredit the Weimar judiciary to keep it from any potential role in "guarding" the constitution: The judiciary presupposes norms, and a guardian of the constitution may need to act beyond norms (*HV, 19*), and,

---

23 For a detailed account of this strategy, see Ingeborg Maus, *Bürgerliche Rechtstheorie und Faschismus: Zur sozialen Funktion und aktuellen Wirkung der Theorie Carl Schmitts* (Munich: C. H. Beck, 1980), pp. 127–31.

moreover, because the judiciary acts *post factum*, it is always, "politically speaking, too late" (*HV*, 32–3). Schmitt does not fully engage the important question of whether in normal times the judiciary could be a guardian of the constitution through a practice of judicial review; he absolves himself from doing so by appealing to "the abnormal contemporary situation of Germany . . . of neither economic prosperity nor internal security" (*HV*, 13) – a claim repeated throughout the book to forswear the theoretical responsibility of confronting logical arguments that would weaken his position.

When raising the question of whether the requisite executive attention to the contemporary crisis is "dictatorial" (*HV*, 117), Schmitt still writes superficially as though it could in fact be performed according to commissarial principles: "[S]trong attempts at remedy and counter-movement can only be undertaken *constitutionally* and *legally* through the *Reichspräsident*" (*HV*, 131). But the substance, limits, and justification of such remedies smack of what Schmitt had previously defined as constitutionally dangerous sovereign action. As I explain in far more detail in subsequent chapters, according to Schmitt, the socioeconomic fracturing of society caused by an uncontrolled pluralism has rendered parliament superfluous and threaten the very existence of the state: "The development toward an economic state was encountered by a simultaneous development of parliament into a stage [*Schauplatz*] for the pluralist system and thus in that lies the cause of the constitutional entanglement as well as the necessity for establishing a remedy and countermovement" (*HV*, 117). However, this particular situation that the president must address necessarily calls for activity that is substantially beyond commissarial action and restitution; it entails the wholesale redirecting of structural historical transformation on a macroeconomic, social, and political scale;[24] a redirecting that could never be met in the time- and task-bound fashion of commissarial dictatorship but must be met by the constitution amending of sovereign dictatorship. Does Schmitt expect that he can address the wholesale reconstruction of the state/society relationship that he describes in *Guardian* and not be perceived as simultaneously calling for the wholesale reconstruction of the Weimar constitution?[25] As Hans Kelsen points out in his response to the book, Schmitt reduces the whole constitution to the emergency powers of Article 48.[26] This fact, in combination with Schmitt's besmirching of the prestige of the

24   On the radically dynamic as opposed to statically conservative character of Schmitt's socioeconomic proposals, see Maus, Ibid., pp. 109, 126.
25   On Schmitt and this subject, see Jean Cohen and Andrew Arato, *Civil Society and Political Theory* (Cambridge, Mass.: MIT Press, 1992), pp. 231–41.
26   Kelsen, "Wer soll der Hüter der Verfassung sein?" *Die Justiz* 6 (1930/31).

other branches of government – judiciary and legislative – means that he can effectively ignore the constitution without literally destroying it. As such, he can claim ingenuously to promote a commissarial dictatorship of the president.

Moreover, in marginalizing the other branches of government, in *Guardian,* Schmitt cleverly removes any checks that could give the president's dictatorial actions any semblance of a commissarial character: He admits that a working *Reichstag* would be an appropriate check on presidential emergency powers (*HV*, 130–1). But because such a situation does not obtain, he makes no effort to search for an alternative check. In fact, precisely because the president is plebiscitarily elected by the people, there is no need for checks, because the unity of the people's sovereign will is charismatically embodied within him and his emergency action is thus necessarily legitimate (*HV*, 116, 156–7).

Thus, in *Guardian,* Schmitt is a kind of prisoner of the very theoretical paradigm that he himself set out a decade earlier in *Die Diktatur.* He feels the need to at least attempt to cloak his sovereign dictatorship in the garb of the commissarial one he described in the earlier work, a work that he suspiciously never mentions. There is no reference to the first edition of *Die Diktatur,* despite the fact that he cites the post–*Political Theology* essay from 1924 on Article 48 that is included as an appendix in the second edition (*HV*, 130–1). He does not, however, neglect to recapitulate the key sentence of *Political Theology:* "The exceptional situation . . . unveils the core of the state in its concrete singularity" (*HV*, 131). Accordingly, he has continued the equation of sovereignty and emergency powers.

Despite the avoidance of *Die Diktatur,* however, his post–*Political Theology* merging of the concept of sovereignty with emergency powers is, as stated before, a response to the conclusions worked out in that book about the historical trajectory of popular sovereignty and state power. By the conclusion of *Guardian,* Schmitt has formulated a popularly legitimated sovereign dictatorship of the nation in the person of a charismatic German president that in essence mirrors the popularly legitimated sovereign dictatorship of the proletariat in the body of the Soviet Communist party. Presumably, it is against this external enemy and its domestic partisans that Schmitt's nation is ready to take "action": The Weimar Constitution, concludes Schmitt,

presupposes the entire German people as a unity which is immediately ready for action and not first mediated through social-group organization. It can express its will and at the decisive moment find its way back to unity and bring its influence to bear over and beyond pluralistic divisions. The constitution seeks especially to give the authority of the *Reichspräsident* the possibility of binding itself immediately with the political total will of the German people and precisely thereby to act as guardian and protector of the unity and totality of the German people. (*HV,* 159)

In his book-length essay from the following year, *Legalität und Legitimität* (*Legality and Legitimacy*), Schmitt would continue this line of thought such that it is almost impossible to recognize when he is talking about normal constitutional operations and when he is talking about emergency ones; all of the former have been subsumed in the latter. The oft-asserted existence of a tension within the Weimar constitution that serves as the source for the title of the book – "plebiscitary legitimacy" versus "statutory legality" (*LL,* 312) – is to be resolved in favor of the former. The grounds for this lie in the historical necessity of a mass-democratic moment, what Schmitt calls "the plebiscitary immediacy of the deciding people as legislator" (*LL,* 314). And he cites the intellectual originator of this historical moment, Rousseau and his "argument for immediate, plebiscitary, non-representative democracy" (*LL,* 314). The president, as vessel for such "immediacy," takes on authority similar to that of the traditional "extra-ordinary legislator," who may act "against the law" (*LL,* 320). As we will see, John Locke's notion of executive prerogative allows for political action that works explicitly against the law and yet is still true to the constitutional order; but a legislator such as the one Schmitt draws from Rousseau, as Schmitt himself explains in *Die Diktatur,* acts against the constitution and may in fact found a new one.

According to Schmitt, in the person of the president,

> the simple jurisprudential truth breaks through all normative fictions and obscurities: norms are only valid for normal situations and the presupposed normalcy of the situation is a legal positivist component of its "validity." But the legislator of the normal situation is something different than the Action-Commissar of the abnormal crisis who restores the normal situation of "security and order." If one views him as a "legislator" and his measures as "statutes" then despite all such equalizations of differences the "legislative measures" of the Action-Commissar – as a direct result of their equalization with "statutes" – destroy the system of legality of the parliamentary statutory state. (*LL,* 321)[27]

---

27 "Action-Commissar (*Aktionskommissar*)" is an allusion to the *Reichskommissar* who was the agent of the federal government, appointed in exceptional circumstances to govern over a particular territoriality within Germany, in place of the local authorities, and who was answerable only to the *Reichspräsident.* Schmitt uses the term here because it evokes

Schmitt appears concerned that the distinction might be lost between law made under normal legislative circumstances and measures issued by executive decree during emergency ones. His emphasis on the distinction might allay the fears of those who worry about the latter alternative becoming permanent. But his categories would make it impossible to remove such a regime once in place by appeals to "normalcy." Thus it is *Schmitt's* equalization of the normal and the exceptional that would intentionally "destroy" the parliamentary state.

In a 1958 introduction to *Legalität und Legitimität,* Schmitt claimed that he had always – and particularly in that work – argued for commissarial dictatorial authority for the president, because that is all that was granted to him by the Weimar constitution.[28] As we can see, by 1932 Schmitt had moved so far away from this position that the distinction between sovereign and commissarial dictatorship no longer had any meaning. In *Die Diktatur,* he criticizes the Communists for underestimating and disparaging the importance of the normal political order at the expense of the exceptional one: "Whoever sees in the core of all law only [the possibility of its suspension] is not quite able himself to find an adequate concept of dictatorship because for him every legal order is only latent or intermittent dictatorship" (*D,* xvii). He thus aptly describes the Carl Schmitt of *Political Theology* and after, the one who would attain such infamy for his subsequent Weimar and post-Weimar career.[29] But is there anything to be culled from Schmitt's Weimar work on emergency powers that can help inform contemporary reflections on the subject?

Constitutional Emergency Powers

I have demonstrated how Schmitt's book on emergency powers, *Die Diktatur,* is not simply the unqualified apology for executive absolutism that most interpreters have deemed it. For the most part, this book differs significantly

---

"commissarial" emergency action *in name* when *in fact* it was becoming increasingly deployed as a tool for the right-wing government's "sovereign" emergency action in the early thirties.

28   Schmitt, *Verfassungsrechtliche Aufsätze aus den Jahren 1924–1954,* pp. 260–1.
29   In the autumn of that very year, Schmitt had a chance to put his theory of presidential dictatorship into practice before the High Court by defending the German state's "emergency" seizure of Prussia's government earlier in July. For an excellent account of the historical events leading up to the state's coup and the theoretical-political stakes involved in the subsequent court hearing, see David Ludovic Dyzenhaus, *Truth's Revenge: Carl Schmitt, Hans Kelsen and Hermann Heller in Weimar* (Oxford: Oxford University Press, 1997).

from the works that would follow it – especially Schmitt's next effort, *Political Theology* – even if within *Die Diktatur* is found the germ of his subsequent transformation. Through this we can observe perhaps more clearly than before where, how, and even why a particularly brilliant Weimar conservative in fact became a Weimar fascist: To confront the malignant development of popular sovereignty as revolutionary dictatorship in Soviet Russia and state-threatening internal revolutionary groups, Schmitt resorts to a no-less-malignant definition of sovereignty as expressed in a nationalist presidential dictatorship. His role in undermining the Weimar constitution and his subsequent political affiliation need no comment at this particular juncture.[30]

This is more or less consequential from the standpoint of the history of political thought, but one might still ask what can this authoritarian beserker – to employ the term with which Schmitt would often refer to fanatics on the Left – offer anyone remotely interested in constitutional democracy? There are several important points to be drawn from Schmitt's Weimar work on emergency powers, particularly as they relate to the distinction between commissarial and sovereign dictatorships and to the infamous first sentence of *Political Theology* that explodes that very distinction:

a. liberal constitutionalism has been insufficiently attentive to the idea of political exceptions;
b. the notion of sovereignty should be uncoupled from the institution of emergency powers in constitutions that have them; and
c. there ought to be a constitutional distinction between who decides and who acts in emergency situations.

(a) Liberalism and the Decline of the Exception. According to Schmitt's account, as Enlightenment political thought falls increasingly under the thrall of modern natural science, it comes to regard nature, and hence political nature, as more of a regular phenomenon. Consequently, there is deemed less need for the discretionary and prudential powers, long conferred on judges and executives by traditional political theories, including Aristotelianism and Scholasticism – discretion and prudence that found their extreme example in the case of classical dictatorship. As the functional necessity of such discretion apparently subsides in the Enlightenment, the normative assessment of it becomes increasingly negative, and

---

30 On the subject of Schmitt's involvement with National Socialism, see Bernd Rüthers, *Carl Schmitt im Dritten Reich: Wissenschaft als Zeitgeist-Verstärkung?* (Munich: C. H. Beck Verlag, 1989); and my own remarks on the subject in Chapter 6 of this book.

such prudence becomes associated with arbitrariness and abuse of state power.[31]

However, Schmitt accuses liberalism of abandoning exceptional prudence far earlier than is actually the case. In *Political Theology*, he remarks that the exception was "incommensurable" with John Locke's theory of constitutionalism (*PT*, 13). Yet Locke's famous "prerogative" power is actually the "last hurrah" of the notion of political prudence within liberalism:

> 'tis fit that the Laws themselves should in some Cases give way to the Executive Power . . . that as much as may be, all the Members of the Society are to be preserved . . . since many accidents may happen, wherein a strict and rigid observation of the law may do harm. . . . [I]t is impossible to foresee, and so by laws provide for, all Accidents and Necessities, that may concern the publick . . . therefore there is a latitude left to the Executive power, to do many things of choice, which the laws do not prescribe.[32]

In refutation of Schmitt's interpretation, Locke does have a notion of acting above or against the law in times of unforeseen occurrences, a notion that is compatible with – nay, is embedded within – his constitutionalism.

Although it has become a kind of ritual for liberals to wave their copies of the *Second Treatise* (open to the passages on prerogative) in response to the criticism that they have an inadequate notion of exceptional circumstances and emergency powers, Schmitt's criticisms of liberalism after Locke are in fact quite legitimate. And his focus on the subsequent theory of the separation of powers, particularly in the form that Montesquieu made so influential, as somehow culpable in the mechanistic de-discretionizing of politics is on the mark.[33] The simple fact that the supposed pinnacle of Enlighten-

---

31 Another of Schmitt's students, historian Reinhart Koselleck, traces the historical decline of attention to the "contingent" in the Enlightenment, in *Futures Past: On the Semantics of Historical Time* (1979), trans. Keith Tribe (Cambridge, Mass.: MIT Press, 1985), pp. 119–25.

32 John Locke, "The Second Treatise on Government," XIV, 159, 15–19, in *Two Treatises on Government*, ed. Peter Laslett (Cambridge: Cambridge University Press, 1988), p. 375. Or, as he defines it more succinctly later in the text: "Prerogative being nothing, but a Power in the hands of the Prince to provide for the publick good, in such Cases, which depending upon unforeseen and uncertain Occurrences, certain and unalterable Laws could not safely direct, whatsoever shall be done manifestly for the good of the people" (XIII, 158, 15–20; p. 373).

33 See Baron de Charles de Secondat Montesquieu, *The Spirit of the Laws*, ed. and trans. A. M. Cohler, B. C. Miller, and H. S. Stone (Cambridge: Cambridge University Press, 1989), xi, 6. As Bernard Manin observes, "One of Montesquieu's most important innovations was precisely to do away with any notion of a discretionary power in his definition of the three governmental functions." See "Checks, Balances, and Boundaries: The Separation of Powers in the Constitutional Debate of 1787," in *The Invention of the Modern Republic*, ed. Biancamaria Fontana (Cambridge: Cambridge University Press, 1994), p. 41, n. 51.

ment constitutional engineering, the United States Constitution, does not have a clearly enumerated provision for emergency situations is a powerful testament to liberalism's neglect of the political exception. It is this liberalism, particularly in its post-Kantian form, that Schmitt was most concerned to criticize for attempting to systematize all political phenomena.[34] As Schmitt remarks rather chillingly about modern liberal politics: "The machine now runs by itself" (*PT,* 48).[35]

Schmitt compares the exception in constitutional theory to the miracle in theology; the latter is God's direct intervention into the normal course of nature's activity, and the former is the occasion for the sovereign's intervention into the normal legal order (*PT,* 36–7). But the "rationalism of the Enlightenment rejected the exception in every form" (*PT,* 37). Deism, with its watchmaker God, who never interacts with the world after its creation, "banished" the miracle from religious thought; and liberalism, with its strict enumeration of governmental powers, "rejected" any political possibilities outside of those set forth within the parameters of its constitutions (*PT,* 37). Again, Schmitt may certainly be correct in detecting a certain narrowing of the conception of natural irregularity in the Enlightenment. As Hans Blumenberg describes it in his analysis of *Political Theology:* "For the Enlightenment, the repudiation of the 'exceptional situation' was primarily related to the laws of nature, which, no longer conceived as legislation imposed upon nature but rather as the necessity issuing from the nature of things, could not allow any exception, any intervention of omnipotence to con-

---

34 After all, the framers of the United States Constitution of 1787 are perhaps the most famous practitioners of separation of powers and of checks and balances. In the essays defending the Constitution, collected as *The Federalist Papers* (New York: Mentor, 1961), it is interesting to observe the contrast between the papers written by James Madison, the liberal technician who seeks to account for all possibilities by enumerating them or building them into the constitutional mechanism, and those by Alexander Hamilton, the proponent of political prerogative who seeks to keep open the possibility of exceptional circumstances. In his study of parliamentarism, Schmitt, not surprisingly, criticizes the Madisonian *Federalist Papers* and praises the Hamiltonian ones (*P,* 40, 45).

35 Koselleck demonstrates how this trend was expressed in eighteenth-century historiography, particularly in the work of von Archenholtz and Montesquieu. The power and presence of *Zufall* – the chance or accidental occurrence – was increasingly subordinated in favor of "general causes." Consistent with Schmitt's thesis, this process was completed in the nineteenth century when "chance, or the accidental, was completely done away with" as a legitimate factor to be considered in the writing of history; see *Futures Past,* pp. 119–25. As we observed in Chapters 1 and 2, however, the fascination with the accidental or the contingent did not disappear in modernity but became the preoccupation of many kinds of romantics.

tinue to be possible."[36] If scientific laws, which no exception could resist, governed the natural world, then so too, it was presumed, could these rules regulate the political and social world. Consequently, any concern for the exception was discarded.

Liberalism's denial of the exception and avoidance of the discretionary activity that was traditionally sanctioned to deal with it, not only makes liberal regimes susceptible to emergencies but also leaves them vulnerable to alternatives like the one eventually put forth by Schmitt. As Bernard Manin describes it, "Once the notion of prerogative power was abandoned, no possibility of legitimately acting beside or against the law was left."[37] The only apparent recourse available in this milieu to political actors confronted with a political exception is to act *illegitimately* and hope to pass off such action as legitimate.[38] Lack of constitutionally facilitated emergency pre-

---

36 Blumenberg, *The Legitimacy of the Modern Age,* trans. Robert Wallace (Cambridge, Mass.: MIT Press, 1985), p. 92. Schmitt's "secularization" thesis that modern political concepts are detheologized premodern ones has generated quite a literature; see Karl Löwith, *Meaning in History* (Chicago: University of Chicago Press, 1949); and Schmitt's response to Blumenberg, in *Politische Theologie II. Die Legende von der Erledigung jeder politischen Theologie* (Berlin: Duncker & Humblot, 1970).

37 Manin, "Checks, Balances, and Boundaries," p. 41. Albert Dicey even went as far as to define the rule of law exclusively as the opposite not only of "arbitrariness" but also "of prerogative, or even of wide discretionary authority on the part of the government." A. C. Dicey, *Introduction to the Study of the Law of the Constitution* ([1915] Indianapolis: Liberty Classics, 1982), p. 120. A somewhat more nuanced definition of the rule of law is offered by Gerald F. Gaus, "Public Reason and the Rule of Law," in *The Rule of Law,* ed. Ian Shapiro (*Nomos* 36) (New York: New York University Press, 1994).

38 Without recourse to specifically enumerated, constitutionally legitimated emergency provisions to address a large-scale political rebellion in the American Civil War, Abraham Lincoln was forced to stretch the traditional means of suspending habeas corpus far beyond reasonable limits, putting himself in the position of being called a tyrant, in his sincere attempt to preserve the republic. Constitutional enabling provisions would prevent a legitimately acting executor from running the risk of compromising his or her legitimacy at a time when it is most important. On these issues, see R. J. Sharpe, *The Law of Habeas Corpus* (Oxford: Oxford University Press, 1991); and Mark E. Neely, Jr., *The Fate of Liberty: Abraham Lincoln and Civil Liberties* (Oxford: Oxford University Press, 1991).
    Another case in point from the American context is Franklin Roosevelt's well-known and perhaps over-extended appeal to the "general welfare" clause of the preamble of the U. S. Constitution as justification in dealing with the economic emergency of the Great Depression. A far-fetched justification for emergency measures may in some respect compromise a constitution at the very moment when it is most threatened, should the appeal be successfully challenged as illegal and in fact illegitimate. The respective "successes" of the two emergency actors in these two examples should not be taken at face value as proof of the efficacy of *not* having constitutional emergency provisions; the political proficiency of the respective political leaders and the "prudence" that is allegedly characteristic of the American populace surely cannot be counted on in all circumstances of crisis. Blind faith in the inevitable emergence of true "statesmen," and the acquiescence

rogative may then provide the opportunity to those like Schmitt who would use this particular liberal deficiency as a ruse to scrap the whole legal order. In this sense, Schmitt's deciding sovereign can be seen as the violent return of the prerogative repressed by scientistic liberalism.[39]

(b) Disengaging Sovereignty from Emergency Powers. Put most crudely, sovereignty concerns self-defined political entities that, through noncoercive procedures, such as constitutional conventions, transfer a political will into a constitution that allows for further expression of that will through formally correct laws, and even change of that will through emendations to the constitution itself. Constitutional mechanisms, such as parliamentary procedure and separation of powers, are not meant to thwart, stymie, or retard the political will of a populace but rather to ensure that this will does not behave self-destructively through rash demands and abuse of numerical minorities.[40] An emergency provision should be seen as one such mechanism among many constitutional provisions. It therefore has no privileged link, neither direct nor exclusive, with the "original" political will, a link that Schmitt so dramatically asserts in *Political Theology.* Furthermore, in a constitution with a proper scheme for separating powers, no branch, whether explicitly responsible for emergency activity or not, has an independent claim on sovereignty. As we will see in later chapters, the separation of powers as well as parliamentary deliberation and judicial review are precisely the kinds of liberal principles that Schmitt works so hard to discredit and destroy, in his political theory after 1921. Using Schmitt against himself, the refreshingly technical quality of classical dictatorship should be brought to bear in considerations on modern emergency powers and not the substantively existential quality of sovereign dictatorship. As Schmitt demonstrates in *Die Diktatur,* the Roman Republic was not reduced to a mere technocracy

to them by an understanding "people" in times of crisis is as unreasonable and naive as is the complete trust in purely constitutional means of addressing political emergencies consistently and rightfully derided by *Realpolitikers.*

39   Indeed, the devious acumen of Schmitt's Weimar political strategy lies in the fact that he points out liberalism's theoretical deficiencies vis-à-vis the "exception" at the very historical moment when liberalism is grappling with the sociopolitical reality of the exceptional or situation-specific measures implemented by the twentieth-century welfare state in the German context. Schmitt intimates that his authoritarian interventionism is more appropriate to the historical reality of such exceptionalism than anything liberalism could ever offer. On Schmitt and the exceptionalism of welfare-state law, see Scheuerman, *Between the Norm and the Exception.*

40   For a more fully elaborated argument of how such constitutional procedures do not hinder democratic expression but render it more articulate, see Stephen Holmes, "Precommitment and the Paradox of Democracy," in *Constitutionalism and Democracy,* ed. Jon Elster and Rune Slagstad (Cambridge: Cambridge University Press, 1988).

by the highly "technical" deployment of emergency powers; nor would a modern liberal democracy be so reduced by uncoupling the notion of democratic "substance" from executive emergency action.[41]

In short, therefore, Schmitt's exclamation in *Political Theology* that "It is precisely the exception that makes relevant the subject of sovereignty, that is, the whole question of sovereignty" (*PT,* 6) is a patently false and, as he himself suggested in his previous book, a dangerous position. The exception does not reveal anything, except perhaps that eighteenth- and nineteenth-century liberals were politically naive about constitutional emergencies; and perhaps that constitutions and their framers are not omniscient. It offers no more existentially profound truth than that. If the constitution's primary purpose is to establish an institution, such as a presidency, to exclusively embody the preconstitutional sovereign will in a time of crisis, then the constitution is inviting its own disposability. The ultimate purpose of emergency powers, as Schmitt knew quite well, is a goal diametrically opposed to this one, that is, the prolonged endurance of a constitution.

(c) Who Decides on the Exception? Who Acts on It? Besides the sovereignty/exception dichotomy, there is another distinction that is deliberately obfuscated by the first sentence of *Political Theology:* the previously mentioned

41 The U. S. Constitution seemingly identifies the document itself, and thereby the sovereign popular will manifested within it, with the institution of the president. In a way that it does not for any other representative of any other governmental branch, the Constitution dictates the inaugural oath for the president and concludes it with the declaration that he or she will "preserve, protect and defend the Constitution of the United States" (Art. II, sec. 1, par. 8). But this is certainly an added precautionary measure against the branch that is the most likely institutional threat to the Constitution rather than any substantively existential equating of the document to the office itself. Ironically, the Weimar constitution contained an oath for the *Reichspräsident* that less explicitly identified the institution as a "guardian" of the constitution in the existential Schmittian sense than does the U. S. Constitution's oath (Weimar Article 42 requires only "observance" of the constitution by the president). The Basic Law of the German Federal Republic also enumerates an oath for its president (Art. 56), whose role is, however, more ceremonial than that of the U. S. or the Weimar president.
    The French constitution of 1958 is perhaps a more problematic example of the relative identity of the executive to constitutionally expressed popular sovereignty because its definition of the presidency was clearly framed with the charismatic Charles DeGaulle in mind. Article 5 declares that the president "shall see that the constitution is observed, . . . shall ensure the proper functioning" of the government and "the continuity of the state," as well as serve as, among other things, the "guarantor of national independence." But surely these clauses can be interpreted as statements regarding the *functional efficacy* of the president's performance of these duties rather than as pronouncements of his or her *personal identification* with the constitution, the government, the state, and the nation.

ambiguity over the theoretical-political implications of the preposition "on [*über*]." The genius of the classical notion of dictatorship that Schmitt reveals in 1921 and then conceals in 1922 is this: The normal institution that decides that an exceptional situation exists (for instance, the Roman Senate) itself chooses the one who acts to address that situation (for instance, the dictator through the consuls). This has the obvious practical advantage that a collegial body of numerous members, like the Senate, commissions a smaller body, such as the consuls, to appoint a single individual to more expediently deal with an emergency than could a multimembered body. But there are more subtle ramifications as well: For instance, the initiating institution cannot so readily declare an exception that it might in turn exploit into an occasion for the expansion of its own power, because emergency authority is placed in the hands of another institution. Moreover, given how jealous political actors are of the boundaries of their own authority, the fact that the normal institution decides to give up its own power in the first place will probably ensure that a real emergency exists. This technique also helps guarantee that an agent is chosen who is sufficiently trustworthy to relinquish power. This external authorization on the execution of emergency powers works simultaneously as a kind of check on, and compensation for, the relinquisher of power who declares an emergency, as well as a potentially astute selection device for the executor on the exception.[42] This technique, neglected by even the more sophisticated formulations of emergency provisions in modern constitutions, is worth reconsidering.[43]

---

42   I am indebted to Bernard Manin specifically for the use of the term and the conceptual ramifications of "external authorization."

43   Article 16 of the French constitution allows for the president's initiative in emergency circumstances after he or she first "officially consults" with representatives of the other governmental branches. The postwar German constitution – which does not have a specific article that deals with emergencies but rather disperses such provisions throughout the constitution (no doubt in reaction to the "fate" of the singular Article 48 in Weimar) – generally gives emergency initiative to the "federal government" or cabinet (and hence de facto to the chancellor, whose office and person is seldom mentioned explicitly in these provisions) provided that there is either consultation with the *Bundestag* or the *Bundesrat*, or a power of revocation residing with either of those bodies (e. g., Art. 35: natural disasters – revocation by *Bundesrat;* Art. 37: federal coercion of individual *Länder* to comply with federal law – consent of *Bundesrat;* Art. 81, pars. 1 and 2; the so-called legislative emergency, in which the government in conjunction with the *Bundesrat* overrules the *Bundestag* on a law; Art. 87a, par. 4: use of armed forces against insurgents – revocation of *Bundestag* and *Bundesrat;* Art. 91, par. 2: appropriation of local police forces by the federal government – rescinding by *Bundesrat*. Only the complicated Art. 115a employs a clear-cut authorization: The "state of defense" is requested by the chancellor and then determined by *Bundestag* and *Bundesrat*). The general point is whether the determinate quality of an act of authorization by one body over another is superior to the

None of the preceding is meant to suggest that constitutional emergency provisions will necessarily prevent the collapse of regimes in crisis. Indeed we know from both the contemporary context of certain Latin American regimes and Schmitt's own context of Weimar Germany that emergency provisions can themselves serve on occasion as the pretense for coups. In societies that do not have firm civilian control of the military, constitutional emergency provisions may hence often do more harm than good. Nor is this presentation intended to imply that the institution of classical commissarial dictatorship ought to be revived and applied wholesale to contemporary constitutional concerns. Clearly, although the classical institution of dictatorship suspended the rule of law in a relatively unproblematic fashion, it did not have the now-indispensable notion of rights to grapple with. Although the formula of suspending law only to reinstate it shortly more or less makes sense, it finds no corollary with the element of rights; it is far less convincing to argue that it is necessary to suspend or violate rights in order ultimately to uphold them. This is the kind of logic that is all too characteristic of the many modern "sovereign" dictatorships that effectively eclipse the classical notion.

But certainly Schmitt's exposure of liberalism's metaphysical bias against constitutional contingency at least suggests a reconsideration of the relative prudence of constitutional emergency provisions in contemporary, liberal, democratic regimes. Moreover, the potential abuse of the merging of emergency powers and popular sovereignty as both forewarned against, and perpetrated by, Schmitt deserves serious attention. Finally, the precise mechanisms for better identifying and addressing an emergency situation are a necessity of contemporary constitution making, particularly in places like the former communist regimes of Eastern Europe.[44]

Emergency Powers and Authoritarianism

Schmitt argues that one could define the essence of a particular regime by specifically discerning what its emergency provisions negated: If the classical dictatorship negated the rule of law, then that was the essence of classical Roman politics. One might not wish to vouch for the analytical or metaphys-

---

vagueness inherent in a "consultation" between them. Moreover, it may be arguably more legitimate for one body to revoke the action of another body if that first body commissioned or authorized the action rather than was merely a "consultant" in the emergency initiative.

44 See my "The Dilemmas of Dictatorship: Carl Schmitt and Constitutional Emergency Powers," *Canadian Journal of Law and Jurisprudence* 10:1 (January 1997).

ical efficacy of this theoretical method in general. But I do think that by considering what Schmitt himself negates with the opening sentence of *Political Theology* and observing how that work repudiates much of what is valuable in the book published before it, we may learn something about the history, the potential necessity, and the better deployment of constitutional emergency powers.

As stated earlier, the contents of Schmitt's first book on emergency powers, *Die Diktatur,* are often conflated with those of an essay appended to it in 1924 as well as with the arguments of the more famous and more extremist treatise of 1922, *Political Theology.* I have demonstrated how the intuitive thrusts of *Die Diktatur* are in fact quite different from what has often been presented by commentators. I say "intuitive thrust" because *Die Diktatur* is not necessarily a book of arguments but rather one of historical musings and suggestive moments. It is by no means an explicit argument for, or straightforward endorsement of, a liberalesque rule-of-law approach to emergency powers. But it is precisely the unargued explication of the history of emergency powers, in *Die Diktatur,* that allows certain potentially nonauthoritarian facets of that tradition to emerge, even if Schmitt himself violently repudiates those instances in his very next book. In the course of the chapter, I have suggested that this transition from *Die Diktatur* to *Political Theology* indicates a shift from conservatism to fascism in Schmitt's theory. As he starts to sense the irresistibility and intensity of the leftist mass-democratic movements he describes in *Die Diktatur,* he begins to formulate a rightist mass-democratic conception in *Political Theology.* Wary of the revolutionary fusing of popular sovereignty and emergency provisions in *Die Diktatur,* Schmitt begins to endorse a reactionary fusing of the two in *Political Theology,* an endorsement announced by its dramatic first line.

In the next chapter, I examine how Schmitt's authoritarianism manifests itself in his writings on representation and parliamentary government. After explaining how political representation has degenerated into technocracy in twentieth-century mass democracies, Schmitt suggests that the mass democratic moment can be redeemed from its technified malaise through the mythic politics of aggressive nationalism and plebiscitary dictatorship.

4

REPRESENTATION

In Part One, I established more firmly Schmitt's notion of technology, its relationship to "economic-technical thought," and the broader significance it has within his work as a whole and even within twentieth-century German intellectual history in general. In this chapter, I concentrate on the way Schmitt understands technology functioning within and through the liberal political institution of the Western European parliament.

We know from Part One how an often-neglected work of 1923, *Roman Catholicism and Political Form,*[1] serves as the center of Schmitt's early theory of technology, as well as the soil from which his more famous "concept of the political" would later develop. In the present chapter, I show how, in *Political Form,* Schmitt lays out his theory of representation, a theory that he would bring to bear on his critique of the liberal theory and practice of representation in his more widely influential book *The Intellectual and Historical Plight of Contemporary Parliamentarism,* published later that same year.[2] The "personalist" ideal of representation set forth against "technological" and "economic thought" in the first work is the tacit criterion employed to criticize the

---

1 Schmitt, *Roman Catholicism and Political Form* (1923), trans. G. L. Ulmen (Westport: Greenwood, 1996), hereafter referred to as *Political Form* and cited as *RC*.
2 Schmitt, *Die geistesgeschichtliche Lage des heutigen Parlamentarismus* ([1923] Berlin: Duncker & Humblot, 1969); translated by Ellen Kennedy as *The Crisis of Parliamentary Democracy* (Cambridge, Mass.: MIT Press, 1985). References are to this edition, cited hereafter as *Parlamentarismus* or *P.*

modern institution of representation, parliament, in the second work. According to Schmitt, the representation entailed by the presently dominant process of technological reproducibility – the mass replication of material objects – has infiltrated *political* representation, which originally meant literally the re-presentation of substantive ideals. By comparing the two modes of representation, Schmitt reveals the modern parliamentary scheme to be a degeneration into positivist functionality. However, his own alternative to technologically corrupted parliamentary representation is not the neo-medieval, *ständische* conception of representation that his critique might suggest but a more radically modern one: executive-centered, plebiscitary democracy. Drawing on the reflections of Walter Benjamin and Jürgen Habermas, I suggest that pressing twentieth-century sociopolitical reality, as much as Schmitt's theological-cultural background, makes relevant and plausible his comparison between medieval practices of representation and those that were emerging in the mass-democratic party state in the Weimar Republic.[3]

Economic-Technical Thought and Representation

Political Form begins as an apparent explanation or justification for the "limitless opportunism" of the Roman Catholic Church (*RC,* 4): Why has it allied itself at various times and places, or even simultaneously, with feudal, absolutist, antimonarchist, democratic, or reactionary political powers (*RC,* 6)? This opportunism is responsible for "the lingering fear of the incomprehensible political power of Roman Catholicism" (*RC,* 3). Schmitt is initially rather cavalier in his explanation of the Church's behavior: "From the

3   I will draw on Benjamin's "Artwork in the Age of Its Technological Reproducibility" (1936), translated by Harry Zohn as "The Work of Art in the Age of Mechanical Reproduction," in *Illuminations,* ed. Hannah Arendt (New York: Schocken, 1968); and Habermas's *Structural Transformation of the Public Sphere* (1962), trans. Thomas Burger with Frederick Lawrence (Cambridge, Mass.: MIT Press, 1989); hereafter *STPS.* On the controversial intellectual relationship of these theorists and Schmitt, see Ellen Kennedy, "Carl Schmitt and the Frankfurt School," *Telos* 71 (spring 1987); Norbert Bolz, "Charism and Souveränität: Carl Schmitt und Walter Benjamim im Schatten Max Webers," in *Der Fürst dieser Welt: Carl Schmitt und die Folgen,* ed. Jacob Taubes (Munich: Wilhelm Fink, 1983); and Samuel Weber, "Taking Exception to Decision: Walter Benjamin and Carl Schmitt," *Diacritics* 22:3–4 (fall/winter 1992). Another important work that draws extensively on *Parlamentarismus* is Reinhart Koselleck's *Critique and Crisis: Enlightenment and the Pathogenesis of Modern Society* ([1959] Cambridge, Mass.: MIT Press, 1988). On many of these issues and intellectual cross-comparisons, see Jean Cohen and Andrew Arato, "The Historicist Critique: Carl Schmitt, Reinhart Koselleck and Jürgen Habermas," in *Civil Society and Political Theory* (Cambridge, Mass.: MIT Press, 1992).

standpoint of a comprehensive world-view all political forms and possibilities become nothing more than a tool for the realization of an idea. . . .
To every worldly empire belongs a certain relativism with respect to the
motley of possible views, ruthless disregard of local peculiarities as well as
opportunistic tolerance for things of no central importance" (*RC,* 5–6).

It sounds as though Roman Catholicism is guilty of precisely those of-
fenses for which we observed Schmitt condemn economic-technical
thought in the first chapter: an instrumental attitude toward the world; and
the eradication of all concrete particularity for the sake of an imperializing
universalism. But Schmitt is concerned to show that the relationship between universal form and concrete content is qualitatively different in Roman Catholicism than in economic-technical thinking because of the former's capacity to *represent:*

> From the standpoint of the political idea of Catholicism the essence of the
> Roman-Catholic *complexio oppositorum* lies in a specific, formal superiority over
> the matter of human life in a way no other imperium has ever known. It has
> succeeded in constituting a sustaining configuration of historical and social
> reality that, despite its formal character, retains its concrete existence at once
> vital and yet rational to the nth degree. This formal character of Roman
> Catholicism is based on the strict realization of the principle of representa-
> tion. In its particularity this becomes most clear in its antithesis to the
> economic-technical thinking dominant today. (*RC,* 8)

Roman Catholic form somehow preserves the content of worldly reality
through the process of representation, whereas economic-technical
thought eradicates it. Catholicism is not like the homogenizing/colonizing
force of Baconian technoscience, whose explicit intention is to crush the
concrete particularity of what it conquers and reduce all qualitative
difference to quantitative identity.[4] Economic-technical thought, we may
recall from previous chapters, makes no distinction between "a silk blouse
and poison gas" (*RC,* 14); all material reality is commensurable in its worldview. It cannot recognize, let alone preserve, the individuality of particularity in the march of its abstractly totalitarian formalism. As Schmitt endeavors to explain, Catholic representation preserves what is essential but
not readily apparent in the original and makes it apparent and real through
the practices of representing. Technological representation merely replicates the quantitative reality of an original, thus negating its originality and
particularity.

4 Cf. Andrew Feenberg, *Critical Theory of Technology* (Oxford: Oxford University Press, 1991).

As a result of this somewhat elusive quality of "representation," according to Schmitt, Roman Catholicism maintains a balance between the purely formalistic rationalism of a liberalism influenced by economic-technical thought and the irrational content worship of the many strands of romanticism. Catholicism is above such oppositions, because it is a *complexio oppositorum* – a complex of opposites – which knows "no antithesis of empty form and formless matter" (*RC*, 11) but holds both within itself.

Thus, the apparent political opportunism of Roman Catholicism is only the result of the Church's capacity for representation, according to Schmitt; a capacity that distinguishes it from most contemporary social and political formations, which themselves become increasingly dominated by the economic and the technical and which hence lack any substantively representative power. As a complex of opposites, Catholicism is utterly versatile in its political manifestations, standing above, as it does for Schmitt, the various antitheses of modern political thinking. According to Schmitt, the Church is simultaneously pagan and monotheistic (with its reverence for a communion of saints alongside its worship of one God); both patriarchal and matriarchal (with its primacy of priests yet devotion to Mary); and although it certainly accentuates the existence of sin, it does not set forth as doctrine the utter worthlessness of humanity (*RC*, 8).[5]

Moreover, by *embodying* all political forms, the Church can find grounds to *ally* with all political forms. The Church functions simultaneously as a monarchy (in the person of the pope), an aristocracy (in the institution of the College of Cardinals), and as a democracy (in its practice of equal opportunity for entry into the ranks of the religious) (*RC*, 7). Schmitt, if not accurately then certainly shrewdly, given the nature of his apologia, describes Roman Catholic institutions in terms of the classical republican model for mixed government or the liberal model of the moderate regime, in an attempt to subvert the general view that Catholicism is inherently authoritarian and allies itself with other political entities only in the pursuit of gaining political advantage. On the contrary, Schmitt argues, the Church allies itself with these other entities because it is just as natural to do so with them as it is to ally itself with an authoritarian regime. He cites various nineteenth- and twentieth-century nationalist and democratic movements in which the Catholic Church played a role, dwelling primarily on the Irish and the Polish cases. But the practical-political justification for the political

---

5   Schmitt cites the Council of Trent's pronouncement that "man" is not evil to this effect here and also in *Political Theology: Four Chapters on the Theory of Sovereignty* (1922), trans. George Schwab (Cambridge, Mass.: MIT Press, 1985), p. 57; hereafter *PT*.

policies of the Roman Church is not nearly as interesting, nor as important for his analysis of parliamentarism, as is his account of the Roman Catholic notion of "representation," which requires further inquiry.

For Schmitt, Roman Catholicism's form is particularly sensitive to its content, unlike economic-technical thinking, which "knows only one type of form, namely technical precision," a characteristic that could not be "further from the idea of representation" (*RC*, 20). Schmitt tells us that the "association of the economic with the technical . . . requires the actual presence of things" (*RC*, 20) and hence is concerned only with positive reality. "Actual presence" in a technological sense is concerned solely with the "material" of something *qua* material, its "immediate" appearance. But the only value economic thought recognizes is that of efficiency or technical precision – the effective manipulation of that material matter – a value unconcerned with qualitative reality, particularly the reality of humanity, which Schmitt claims is the central concern of Roman Catholicism.

For Schmitt, the idea of representing natural resources, machinery, or commodities through production, and, as we will soon see, even people through an electoral process, is a contradiction in terms. (Schmitt points with satisfaction to the fact that the Soviets could not use the machine as their "badge of rule" but had to resort instead to the more traditional hammer and sickle as a symbol, because the technological image could not represent anything as substantive as political power.) Representation, as practiced in the Middle Ages and still practiced by the Catholic Church, according to Schmitt, does not entail making present again what is already physically present. It indeed means making present something real or "actual" but something that is only given material presence precisely through the representation process. The idea of an "actual presence" in a medieval sense, for Schmitt, is concerned in the utmost with the "essence" of something. Put conversely, the given material reality of something does not reflect what it really is. Thus, in "true" representation an essential material presence is achieved *through* the representative process; it is not physically present a priori. The theological residues of this notion are still apparent when Schmitt argues in a more secular manner five years later, in his *Verfassungslehre*, that,

> To represent means to make visible and present an invisible entity through an entity which is publicly present. The dialectic of the concept lies in the fact that the invisible is assumed to be absent but simultaneously made present. This is not possible with any arbitrary entity, since a particular kind of being is assumed. Something dead, something that is of little value or indeed is value-

less, something trivial, cannot be represented. Some such thing lacks the intensified kind of being capable of such an existence – of elevation into public being. Words such as greatness, nobility, majesty, glory, worthiness and honor come close to capturing the special nature of an intensified being that is capable of being represented.[6]

This notion of prior-ity, the idea that something is made present *through* representation, is not merely neo-Scholastic gibberish for Schmitt but something that sets "substantive" representation apart from what he regards as its modern vulgarizations. As we know from Chapter 1, Schmitt interprets Russian radicalism as a revolt against form in the highest sense – a revolt against the very notion of an "Idea." This has ramifications for the Soviets' conception of representation that seeks to eliminate the "idea" lurking within traditional substantive theories:

> In the springtide of socialism young Bolsheviks turned the struggle for economic-technical thinking into a struggle against the idea, even against every idea. So long as even the ghost of an idea exists so also does the notion that something preceded the given reality of material things – that there is something transcendent – and this always means an authority "from above." To a type of thinking which derives its norms from the economic-technical sphere this appears as an outside interference, a disturbance of the self-propelling machine. (*RC*, 27)

The Soviets' positivistic fear that material reality may be more than just material reality is aroused by a Catholicism, according to Schmitt, that is the only institution left that maintains the position *within a rational scheme* that there is more to material reality than what is positively apparent. For Schmitt, Catholic representation is able to maintain the claim that material reality, especially as manifested in human life, is more than quantitatively apprehended material, without at the same time slipping into the romantic and irrationalist random ascription of transcendent meaning to particular objects discussed earlier. He criticizes what Max Weber calls "disenchantment" without immediately elevating a notion of "enchantment": Through a "juridical" or "institutional" rationality, the Church asserts that life is *not* mere matter, while at the same time "knowingly and magnificently succeeding in overcoming Dionysian cults, ecstasies, [etc.]" (*RC*, 23). This "juridical" rationality that navigates between positivism and irrationality is exemplified by the Catholic institution of offices:

6   Schmitt, *Verfassungslehre* ([1928] Berlin: Duncker & Humblot, 1989), p. 209; hereafter *V.*

The Pope is not the Prophet but the Vicar of Christ. Such a ceremonial function precludes all the fanatical excesses of an unbridled prophetism. The fact that the office is made independent of charisma signifies that the priest upholds a position which appears to be completely apart from his concrete personality. Nevertheless he is not the functionary and commissar of republican thinking. (*RC,* 14)

Weber had recognized that the offices of the Catholic Church were not sources of what Schmitt calls "the fanatical excess" associated with charisma: "[T]he bishop, the priest and the preacher are in fact no longer, as in early Christian times, carriers of a purely personal charisma, which offers otherworldly sacred values under the personal mandate of a master."[7] But Weber proceeds to suggest that "they have become officials in the service of a functional purpose, a purpose which in the present day 'church' appears at once impersonalized and ideologically sanctified" (*ES,* 959). In response, Schmitt wishes to maintain that the Catholic "juridical" theory of offices falls between the poles of irrational devotion to the *concrete personality* of the priest, on the one hand, and the recognition of the purely *formal function* of the office, on the other. Such an office is not impersonalized in the hyperrational way that Weber claims, nor is it yet an expression of romantic irrationality.[8] Priestly office is *not* purely formal or functional because of its connection to what might be seen, at least by Schmitt while still a Catholic, as a reason that human life can never be deemed "mere matter": "God become man in historical reality" (*RC,* 19). As Schmitt writes, "In contradistinction to the modern official [the priest's] position is not impersonal because his office is part of an unbroken chain linked with the personal mandate and concrete person of Christ" (*RC,* 14).[9] Jesus Christ is the symbol of the divinity within humanity, the "dignity" that transcends sheer biology.

7 Max Weber, *Economy and Society: An Outline of Interpretive Sociology* (1920), ed. Guenther Roth and Claus Wittich (Berkeley: University of California Press, 1978), p. 959; cf. p. 1141; hereafter *ES.*
8 Schmitt does not consider whether Weber's other categories, such as "traditional authority" or the "routinization of charisma," would be appropriate for what Schmitt describes as the "juridical" quality of Catholic representation; see *ES,* 226–40, 246–54.
9 Hanna Pitkin describes the medieval concept of representation in similar terms: "[I]ts real expansion begins in the thirteenth and early fourteenth centuries, when the Pope and the cardinals are often said to represent the persons of Christ and the Apostles. The connotation is still neither of delegation nor of agency; the church leaders are seen as the embodiment and image of Christ and the Apostles, and occupy their place *per successionem.*" *The Concept of Representation* (Berkeley: University of California Press, 1967), pp. 241–2.

Schmitt asserts that the juridical, the essence of law, lies not in probability, as it does in the Weberian definition (*ES*, 32) – a prediction about the
causal functioning of government action – but rather in the maintenance of
something superior to mere precision.[10] As such, "the Church is the consummate bearer of the juridical spirit and the true heir of Roman jurisprudence" (*RC*, 18). In Catholic judicial thinking, there must be an inherent
dignity in the process of governance that for Schmitt is absent in modern
politics. Because the human being is the most important example of the
transcendence of materiality, anything of worth must be represented "personally" by a human being:

> The idea of representation is so completely governed by conceptions of per-
> sonal authority that the representative as well as the person represented must
> maintain a personal dignity – it is not a materialist concept. To represent in an
> eminent sense can only be done by a person, i. e., not simply a "deputy" but an
> authoritative person or an idea which, if represented, also becomes person-
> ified. God or "the people" in democratic ideology or abstract ideas like free-
> dom and equality can all conceivably constitute a representation. But this is
> not true of production and consumption. Representation invests the repre-
> sentative person with a special dignity because the representative of a noble
> value cannot be without value. (*RC*, 21)

Economic or technological rationality is responsible for sapping all *social*
relationships of any humanity through its impersonality (*RC*, 18), whereas
Catholicism continues to be the only institution that fully and "personally"
embodies the nonpositivist representation of humanity. A business corpora-
tion or a "joint-stock company" can never truly represent, because it is
merely a "system of accountancy," a glorified adding machine whose raison
d'être is only the quantities it calculates not the qualities it affects. Something so devoid of worth and personality, in the truest sense of the word, is
incapable of representation, according to Schmitt.

In *The Structural Transformation of the Public Sphere*, Jürgen Habermas attempts to clarify Schmitt's argument. In the Middle Ages, "representation
pretended to make something invisible visible through the public presence
of the lord. . . . He displayed himself, presented himself as an embodiment
of some sort of 'higher' power. . . . The nobleman was authority inasmuch
as he made it present. He displayed it, embodied it in his cultivated personality" (*STPS*, 7, 13). Habermas describes how the noble could represent

---

10 I will deal with Schmitt's critique of Weber's sociological jurisprudence in greater detail in
    Chapter 5.

abstract concepts such as "authority," and indeed Schmitt does not suggest that only conservative "ideas" like this one are capable of being truly represented: "God or 'the people' in democratic ideology or abstract ideas like freedom and equality can all conceivably constitute a representation"; only "production and consumption" are excluded from the theory (*RC*, 21).

If one grants to Schmitt the point that multinational corporations as the representatives of economic forces have less "dignity" than the Catholic Church as the representative of Jesus Christ and the whole of humanity, he still seems to glide over a major important difference between modern and medieval concepts of representation. One does not need Habermas to point out that medieval representation is more elitist, and perhaps even *less* substantive in some sense, because it takes place "not *for* but '*before*' the people."[11] It is a public representation *to* them: "Representation in the sense in which the members of a national assembly represent a nation or a lawyer represents his clients had nothing to do with this publicity of representation" (*STPS*, 7). But Schmitt maintains that the people are not any less important nor in any way demeaned by the medieval scheme of representation: "Not only do the representative [i.e., the Church] and the person represented [i.e., Christ, "authority," or humanity] require a personal value, so also does the third party whom they address [i.e., the people]. One cannot represent oneself to automatons and machines anymore than they can represent or be represented" (*RC*, 21). The third party and its importance are indispensable to medieval representation, because without them there would be no "publicity of representation" as Habermas puts it. According to the medieval scheme, a noble or the Church without the public to acknowledge and recognize it does not exist; it is not real. For Schmitt, this form of publicity is as important to representation as is the human substance of both what is being represented and its personal embodiment in a worthy representative. Schmitt would later confirm, in *Verfassungslehre* how important this notion of publicity is to his theory of representation:

11   Ibid., p. 8, emphasis added. Although Pitkin attempts to treat medieval representation with objectivity, she is at a loss for any adjective to describe it except "mystical." To emphasize the point, she quotes Maude V. Clarke, who remarks that medieval representation "resists analysis." See *The Concept of Representation*, p. 295. Weber, typically, cuts through the metaphysical fog, suggesting that the mystique surrounding medieval representation results from the concern with unanimity in medieval political and clerical appointments, elections, and acclamations. Because the choice for such offices was supposedly sanctioned by God, this needed to be reflected in the selection procedure by ensuring unanimity to prevent theologically embarrassing dissension. This was achieved by deciding the officeholder in advance and merely cloaking this fact afterward in charismatically imbued language and ritual (*ES*, 1126).

> The people is a concept that only exists in the public sphere. The people
> appears only in a public, indeed, it first produces the public. The people and a
> public are established together; there is no people without a public and vice
> versa. It is especially through its presence that the people produces the public.
> Only the present people actually assembled is a people that establishes a
> public. (*V*, 243)
> Representation can only proceed in the public sphere. There is no representa-
> tion which takes place in secret or *in camera*. . . . A Parliament only has a
> representative character as long as it is believed that its proper activity is a
> public affair. Secret sessions, secret agreements and consultations of some
> committee or other can be very significant and important, but they can never
> have a representative character. (*V*, 208)

This contrast between public and private, the floor and the committees
in Parliament, will return in *Parlamentarismus,* but it has broader ramifications for Schmitt in *Political Form.* The form of publicity just described is
endangered with the transformation of the medieval conception of publicity into the liberal economic one: "The tendency of the economic to
perpetuate civil law means in effect a limitation of juridical form. Public life
is expected to govern itself. It should be governed by public opinion, the
opinion of private individuals. Public opinion in turn should be governed by
a privately owned free press. Nothing in this system is representative; everything is a private matter" (*RC,* 28). In what was earlier identified as a
consciously Catholic reply to Weber's "Protestant Ethic" thesis, then,
Schmitt asserts that it is Protestantism that privatizes politics and hence
extracts the representative element from politics:

> Historically considered "privatization" has its origin in religion. The first right
> of the individual in the sense of the bourgeois social order was freedom of
> religion. In the historical evolution of the catalogue of liberties – freedom of
> belief and conscience, freedom of association and assembly, freedom of trade
> and commerce – it is the fountainhead and first principle. But whatever place
> is assigned to religion it always and everywhere manifests its capacity to absorb
> and absolutize. If religion is a private matter it also follows that privacy is
> revered. The two are inseparable. Private property is thus revered precisely
> because it is a private matter. (*RC,* 28)

The sacralization of privacy inhibits the practice of displaying publicly
what is important and depreciates the public sphere that was once an arena
for the re-presentation of what is important. The modern public sphere is a
collection of private property owners vying to promote their own material
interests. Thus, these participants are no longer representatives in any real

sense. The result is a society devoid of fully substantive figures; roles become economic-technical functions.[12] As their moral conflict with the ancien régime fades, figures like the intellectual and the merchant become formally empty, as they more and more assume the role of caretakers of the "iron cage":

> In order to obtain a clear picture of the extent to which the representative capacity has disappeared we have only to consider the attempt to rival the Catholic Church with an enterprise drawn from the modern scientific spirit. Auguste Comte wanted to found a "positivistic" church. The result of his effort was an embarrassingly telling imitation. . . . [He] discerned the representative types of the Middle Ages – the cleric and the knight – and compared them with the representative types of modern society – the savant and the merchant. But it was an error to hold up the modern savant and the modern merchant as representative types. The savant was only representative in the transitional period of struggle with the Church; the merchant, only as a Puritan individualist. Once the wheels of modern industry began to turn both became increasingly servants of the great machine. It is difficult to say what they truly represent. (*RC*, 19)

What then is the status of the modern institution that is charged with the responsibility of representing, parliament, if "the Catholic Church is the sole surviving contemporary example of the medieval capacity to create representative figures" (*RC*, 19)? In *Political Form*, Schmitt does not totally ignore or even explicitly denounce parliament. Indeed, he admits that even though "one can observe how the understanding of every type of representation disappears with the spread of economic thinking," with respect to parliament's "hypothetical and theoretical basis," the contemporary parliamentary system "at least includes the idea of representation" (*RC*, 25). But as he explains what the parliamentary system's ideal is, it becomes clear that Schmitt still has in mind something closer to the medieval model and not what today would be considered representation.

12 Of course this is precisely the somewhat distorted image of the nineteenth-century bourgeois public sphere that Habermas attempts to rehabilitate in *Structural Transformation*, although, as we will see in the discussion of *Parlamentarismus*, he agrees with Schmitt's assessment of what became of that public sphere in the twentieth century. For criticisms of Habermas's reconstruction of the reality of the public sphere, see Oskar Negt and Alexander Kluge, *Public Sphere and Experience: Toward an Analysis of the Bourgeois and Proletarian Public Sphere* (1972), trans. P. Labanyi, J. O. Daniel and A. Oksiloff (Minneapolis: Minnesota University Press, 1993), as well as the numerous excellent contributions to *Habermas and the Public Sphere,* ed. Craig Calhoun (Cambridge, Mass.: MIT Press, 1992).

When parliament "personifies" the nation, when it represents the nation before another representative, such as a king, it satisfies its representational role (*RC*, 25). But when representation "signifies only a representation of the electorate," that is, as the result of the mere tallying up of votes, then representation "does not connote anything distinctive" (*RC*, 25). Schmitt points to the classic conflict between a representative elected by individual electors with specific interests and the role he or she is supposed to play as representative of the nation at large. The former kind of representation has the air of the modern, merely positivistic or quantitative way of thought; the latter preserves some substance of the medieval concept of representation. With the marriage of the two in modern representational theory, the influence of the former denigrates the importance of the latter. Schmitt describes how one degenerates into the other, using the Soviets as the foil to the quasi-medieval notion:

> The simple meaning of the principle of representation is that the members of parliament are representatives of the whole people and thus have an independent authority vis-à-vis the voters. Instead of deriving their authority from the individual voter they continue to derive it from the people. "The member of parliament is not bound by instructions and commands and is answerable to his conscience alone." This means that the personification of the people and the unity of parliament as their representative at least implies the idea of a *complexio oppositorum*, i. e., the unity of the plurality of interests and parties. It is conceived in representative rather than economic terms. The proletarian system of soviets therefore seeks to eliminate this remnant of an age devoid of economic thinking and emphasizes that parliamentary delegates are only emissaries and agents, deputies of the producers, with a "*mandat impèratif*" (liable to be recalled at any time), administrative servants in the process of production. The "whole" of the people is only an idea; the whole of the economic process a material reality. (*RC*, 26–7)

This analysis will be crucial for Schmitt's arguments in *Parlamentarismus*, where he applies what he says here about the Soviets to the European parliamentary scheme: As representatives in parliament come to re-present party dogma, material interest, and a quantified electorate, parliament is sovietized and technified.

But already in *Political Form*, Schmitt presents the logic of representation in the European parliament as somewhat askew. Parliamentary representation does not exalt what it represents but, on the contrary, diminishes its authority: A "secondary organ" (parliament) represents a "primary organ" (the people) that in effect has no will apart from that of the secondary organ. The organ of secondary importance is not even accountable to the primary organ on a day-to-day basis but only at the moment of election. A third body, the cabinet government, is more accountable to the second, parliament, than parliament is to the people. The people seem to be made less important through this representative process (*RC*, 26), and thus, in medieval terms, the principle of the dignity of the represented is violated. Without the reference to the Middle Ages, this argument is actually reiterated in *Parlamentarismus* (*P*, 34).

In *Political Form,* Schmitt clearly attempts to distinguish a traditional notion of representation from a modern one that entails the mere multiple reproduction of material objects, either an electorate defined numerically or plural economic interests. He attempts to distinguish representation from reproduction. In this sense, his arguments foreshadow the observations that Walter Benjamin was to make regarding the implications of technological reproduction – mechanical re-presentation – for art:

> That which withers in the age of mechanical reproduction is the aura of the work of art. This is a symptomatic process whose significance points beyond the realm of art. One might generalize by saying: the technique of reproduction detaches the reproduced object from the domain of tradition. By making many reproductions it substitutes a plurality of copies for a unique existence. . . . From a photographic negative, for example, one can make any number of prints; to ask for the "authentic" print makes no sense.[13]

Schmitt clearly champions an auratic conception of political representation rather than a mechanistic-positivistic one. Traditional representation sanctions a particular object or, more important, a person to stand for a transcendent reality that cannot be accessed through merely quantitative means. Modern representation is purely material: One silk blouse is equal to another, or perhaps to eight ounces of poison gas. One congressman is equal to 19,995 popular votes, or to 1 party vote on the floor, or to fifty thousand dollars' worth of influence from the tobacco lobby. It is a quantity that is represented, not a quality that may be greater than the particular sum of its parts. A medieval official *represents* the people in their essence; a modern member of parliament *reproduces* the political "weight" of his or her constituency, numerically defined. The aura of the representation process has withered.[14]

---

13 Benjamin, "The Artwork in the Age of Its Technological Reproducibility," pp. 221, 224.
14 Habermas, too, emphasizes a growing quantification of representation in the transition

Benjamin, however, unlike his associate on the Right, was pleased by the modern disintegration of the aura, because he saw in it a source of egalitarian emancipation. The previously distant and removed auratic object of art is brought to "the beholder or listener in his own particular situation."[15] Schmitt dismisses the numerous parallel bases for defending the modern political practice of representation as more egalitarian: the benefits of interest aggregation, and governmental accountability, to name only two. But it would be plethoric and uninteresting to simply suggest that Schmitt is, in this or other respects, "conservative"; how *radical* he is in his conservatism is a more important issue and one that becomes more apparent in the following sections.

Parliament is not the main object of concern for Schmitt in *Political Form.* As we have seen in both this chapter and previous ones, in this work he targets modern economic-technical thought in general. I now turn to *Parlamentarismus* and show how Schmitt traces the effects of technological-economic thought on the institution of parliament, and how he tacitly compares the reality of modern representative government with the medieval Catholic ideal of representation. The practical solution suggested by his critique, however, is not the revival of a traditional scheme of political authority but something much closer to the other target of Benjamin's thesis, the modern fascist aestheticization of politics.

Parlamentarismus: The 1926 Preface

Schmitt's *Parlamentarismus* is generally viewed as one of the most devastating critiques of twentieth-century representative government.[16] Its impact is

from nineteenth- to twentieth-century parliamentarism: "To the extent that social reproduction still depends on consumption decisions and the exercise of political power on voting decisions made by private citizens there exists an interest in influencing them – in the case of the former, with the aim of increasing sales; in the case of the latter, of increasing formally this or that party's share of voters or, informally, to give greater weight to the pressure of specific organizations" (*STPS*, 176). However, as I will discuss later, Habermas links this growing quantification to a process of neofeudal group representation under mass democracy and does not contrast the two as Schmitt does here.

15   Benjamin, "The Artwork," p. 221.
16   Since its original publication, the book has been particularly popular among leftist scholars. It has a singularly prominent place in the writings of Franz Neumann, a student of Schmitt who attended Schmitt's seminars in 1931, and Otto Kirchheimer, for whom Schmitt served as dissertation director; see the essays collected in *Social Democracy and the Rule of Law: Otto Kirchheimer and Franz Neumann*, ed. Keith Tribe (London: Allen & Unwin, 1987). It has not lost its influence in the present wave of "Left-Schmittianism"; see Chantal Mouffe, *The Return of the Political* (London: Verso, 1993); Richard Bellamy and

reinforced by the high degree of subtlety employed in the delivery of the argument, if not always in the argument's accuracy. Schmitt wavers deftly in his presentation between criticism and assault. He claims that parliamentary government's theoretical foundations have not proven themselves immune to the corrosive influence of economic-technological thought. Whether this rot was present from the outset or developed only later is not immediately clear, according to Schmitt's account. At times liberal parliamentarism is criticized for being "antiquated" (*P,* 7): It no longer satisfies the ends for which it was constructed, although at one time it did. On the other hand, Schmitt also attacks, implicitly and explicitly, parliamentarism and the whole *Rechtsstaat* tradition with which it is bound, as naive, delinquent, and ill fated from the start. I explicate these two lines of argument and show how Schmitt shifts from the former, less controversial position to the latter, more radical one, all the while demonstrating that his criticisms are derived from the critique of the economic and the technical and their implications for representation, in *Political Form.*[17]

Schmitt's strongest statements along reformist lines come mostly in the "Preface to the Second Edition," published in 1926. The main body of the text, published in 1923, the same year as *Political Form,* is more wholeheartedly antiparliamentarist.[18] Responding primarily to constitutional theorist Richard Thoma's commentary on the first edition of 1923, in the second edition's preface, Schmitt presents himself as a friend of government-by-discussion who bemoans this parliamentary principle's demise: "[P]arliament today has for a long time stood on a completely different foundation [than openness and discussion]. That belief in openness and discussion appears today as outmoded is . . . my fear" (*P,* 2).

Peter Baehr, "Carl Schmitt and the Contradictions of Liberal Democracy," *European Journal of Political Research* 23 (February 1993); Bernard Manin, "The Metamorphoses of Representative Government," *Economy and Society* 23:2 (May 1994); and Bill Scheuerman, "Is Parliamentarism in Crisis?: A Response to Carl Schmitt," *Theory and Society* 24:1 (February 1995). The originality of Schmitt's treatise is sometimes exaggerated, as it is clear that he derived significant portions of his thesis from the classic volume by Mosei Ostrogoski, *Democracy and the Organization of Political Parties* ([1902] New York: Haskell, 1970).

17   It is somewhat surprising that perhaps the foremost contemporary Schmitt scholar in Germany and even the world, Reinhard Mehring, misses Schmitt's "foundational" critique and focuses exclusively on the "anachronistic" critique in *Parlamentarismus;* see Mehring, "Liberalism as a 'Metaphysical System': The Methodological Structure of Carl Schmitt's Critique of Political Rationalism," *Canadian Journal of Law and Jurisprudence* 10:1 (January 1997).

18   For reasons that will become apparent, I choose to deal with the work's specific sections in the order in which they appear in the most common edition, and not in the chronological order in which they were written.

Emphasizing the principle of publicity that in *Political Form* Schmitt establishes as crucial for any mode of representation, he claims that he is critical of parliament presently only because its theoretical justifications are no longer valid: "Parliament is only 'true' as long as *public* discussion is taken seriously and implemented" (*P,* 4, emphasis added). When public discussion did not simply mean "negotiation" (*P,* 5), when it had the substantive quality of pursuing truth and basing legislation on that truth, then parliament was worth defending. Schmitt describes how parliamentary discussion *should* lead to legislation and, presumably, once did: "Laws arise out of a conflict of opinions (not out of a struggle of interests). To discussion belong shared convictions as premises, the willingness to be persuaded, independence of party ties, freedom from selfish interests" (*P,* 5). But parliamentary discussion no longer concerns itself with truth; its aim is now to foster deal making and vote counting: "[T]oday . . . it is no longer a question of persuading one's opponent of the truth or justice of an opinion but rather of winning a majority in order to govern with it" (*P,* 7).[19]

Schmitt's language reminds us of many of the arguments put forth in *Political Form*, such as the one criticizing the inability of economics to distinguish the substantively "good" or the "true" from the merely "efficient," and the argument that decries interpretations of the world that sacrifice quality to quantity: "The question of equality is precisely not one of abstract, logical-arithmetical games. It is about the substance of equality" (*P,* 9). The similarities between the two works are especially apparent when Schmitt expresses his disdain for the aspects of parliamentary representation that deal with what is "electoral" over what is "representational" in a substantive sense. The type of representation in which "every member of parliament is the representative, not of a party, but of a whole people and is no way bound by instruction" is contrasted positively with "conduct that is

---

19 Schmitt is not particularly accurate in his assessment of parliamentary theory and its relationship with truth, especially as it is expressed in the work of the very authors he cites: Burke, Bentham, Guizot, and Mill (*P,* 2). Bernard Manin shows that Schmitt has misconstrued or distorted the intellectual-historical facts. All of these advocates of parliamentarism as well as most other founders of modern representative theory made room quite early on for such elements as interest, negotiation, and even party. See Manin, *Principles of Representative Government* (Cambridge: Cambridge University Press, 1996). On Schmitt's misreading/misrepresentation of Guizot, see Charles Larmore, *The Morals of Modernity* (Cambridge: Cambridge University Press, 1996), pp. 184–6. As for the nineteenth-century historical reality that Schmitt idealizes, see Scheuerman, "Is Parliamentarism in Crisis?" For an account of some of Schmitt's other distortions of liberalism in *Parlamentarismus* and elsewhere, see Stephen Holmes, "Schmitt: The Debility of Liberalism," in *The Anatomy of Antiliberalism* (Cambridge, Mass.: Harvard University Press, 1993), pp. 57–60.

not concerned with discovering what is rationally correct, but with calculating particular interests and the chances of winning and with carrying these through according to one's own interest" (*P*, 5–6).

Schmitt employs the argument that parliamentary government has become an exercise in mere *form* at the expense of crucial *content,* in the same way that he criticized economics, technology, and positivism, in *Political Form:*

> The situation of parliamentarism is critical today because the development of modern mass democracy has made argumentative public discussion an empty formality. Many norms of contemporary parliamentary law, above all provisions concerning the independence of representatives and the openness of sessions, function as a result like a superfluous decoration, useless and even embarrassing, as though someone had painted the radiator of a modern central heating system with red flames in order to give the appearance of a blazing fire. (*P*, 6)

An institution that is supported by merely "social-technical justifications" (*P,* 8) becomes subject to the whims of the latest empirical research that declares what is efficient. Like economics, it is consequently empty of any normative content and is inherently ephemeral: "If parliament should change from an institution of evident truth into a simply practical-technical means, then it only has to be shown *via facta* . . . that things could be otherwise and parliament is then finished" (*P,* 8). If an institution has no moral justification for its existence and is supported solely on the grounds of efficiency, as soon as something more efficient comes along the original institution is by definition defunct. As we will see, Schmitt may be willing to provide a more moral as well as more efficient alternative himself.

In general, Schmitt seeks to keep the level of analysis above that of mere *functionality* and more attuned to matters of *principle:*

> Just as everything else that exists and functions tolerably, [parliamentarism] is useful – no more and no less. It counts for a great deal that even today it functions better than other untried methods, and that a minimum of order that is today actually at hand would be endangered by frivolous experiments. Every reasonable person would concede such arguments. But they do not carry weight in an argument about principles. (*P,* 3)

The fact is, however, as we will see, Schmitt will argue against parliamentarism on the grounds of principle *and* efficiency; ultimately parliament does *not* run "reasonably well" (*P,* 4).

Again, Schmitt is careful to give his critique a specific time frame in the second edition's preface. For instance, he assures us that it has only been since the nineteenth century that "every single vote was registered and an arithmetical majority was calculated." As a result, "quite elementary truths have thus been lost and are apparently unknown in contemporary political theory" (*P*, 16). But why does Schmitt feel the need to assert time and again in the preface that he is not inherently antagonistic to parliamentarism generally, and government by open discussion specifically? Why does he repeatedly emphasize that it is the perverted, social-technical, overly quantitative form of parliamentarism and the tainted, negotiation-soiled form of discussion that have accompanied the rise of mass parties that he actually abhors and wishes to abandon?

Perhaps a passage from Thoma's commentary on the first edition that surmises Schmitt's unstated political preferences holds the key: "I would hazard to guess, but not assert, that behind these ultimately rather sinister observations there stands the unexpressed personal conviction of the author that an alliance between a nationalistic dictator and the Catholic Church could be the real solution and achieve a definitive restoration of order, discipline, and hierarchy."[20] Given the admiration that Schmitt expresses for Roman Catholicism politically in the work discussed earlier,[21] combined with his political affiliations before, during, and after the collapse of the republic, Thoma's is far from an unfeasible suggestion. Either Schmitt felt that Thoma had hit too close to the mark and had exposed Schmitt's antiparliamentary inclinations, or Schmitt felt he had to defend his true beliefs. We will decide which possibility is most likely when we examine the main body of the text, in the next sections. However, in the preface itself, Schmitt makes only one direct response to Thoma's claim: "The utterly fantastic political aims that Thoma imputes to me at the end of his review I may surely be allowed to pass over in silence" (*P*, 1).

In any case, after legitimately or fraudulently displaying his intellectual-political pedigree as a good classical parliamentarian throughout most of the second edition's preface, Schmitt closes his preface with a passage that brings together most of the themes discussed so far: his disdain for the quantitative and the technical; his desire for a truer, or what he now calls more "vital" form of representation; his abandonment of a parliamentarism

---

20 Thoma, "On the Ideology of Parliamentarism" (1925), translated by Ellen Kennedy and included as an appendix to her edition of *Parlamentarismus* (*P*, 82).

21 Although, as I pointed out, Schmitt goes to great lengths to show that some form of authoritarianism need not be the only, or even most likely, political ally for the Catholic Church.

that has supposedly only recently been corrupted; and one theme that has yet to be fully discussed, but is raised by the Thoma quote – Schmitt's flirtation with dictatorial or plebiscitary democracy:

> The will of the people can be expressed just as well and perhaps better through *acclamation,* through something taken for granted, an obvious and unchallenged presence, than through the *statistical apparatus* that has been constructed with such meticulousness in *the last fifty years.* The stronger the power of democratic feeling, the more certain is the awareness that democracy is something other than a *registration system for secret ballots.* Compared to a democracy that is direct, not only in the *technical sense* but also in the *vital sense,* parliament appears [to be] an *artificial machinery,* produced by liberal reasoning, while dictatorial and Caesaristic methods not only can produce the acclamation of the people but can also be a direct expression of democratic *substance* and *power. (P,* 16–17, emphases added)

The criteria by which he evaluates parliamentary representation are principles we recognize as derivative of the Catholic theory of representation discussed earlier; but the practical alternative to parliamentary representation, intimated by Schmitt, is the quite modern theory of plebiscitary representation or government by acclamation. It is not merely hypocrisy that allows Schmitt to shift from the former, in his role of theoretical inquisitor, to the latter, in his role of practical sponsor, but also sociology.

Excursus: Weber on Parliament, Bureaucracy, and Caesarism

It is well known that Weber had come to expound views similar to those just expressed regarding Caesarism, in the years following the First World War. As with so many issues in Schmitt's thought, Weber is the one to establish the terms of the argument on the question of plebiscitary democracy and twentieth-century parliamentarism. But a perennially controversial question is how legitimate an heir of Weber is Schmitt on this question? Before embarking on an analysis of the main text of *Parlamentarismus,* a brief discussion of Weber's work on parliamentarism and plebiscitary democracy is in order. Only after such a discussion can we accurately gauge the intensity of Schmitt's critique of liberal parliamentarism and the extremity of his proposed solution to its early-twentieth-century dilemmas.

In his scholarly writings on European parliamentarism, bureaucracy, and charisma, Weber describes the paradoxes of this constellation of issues with Olympian objectivity; he offers no potential solutions to the recently emerging problems, because the evidence does not suggest any. Democracy and bureaucratization emerge together historically (*ES*, 983) and become un-happily bound at the level of party organization and state administration. In terms that Schmitt would later use disparagingly, Weber describes how the increasing quantification of democracy encourages party bureaucratization: "Every advance of simple election techniques based on numbers alone as, for instance, the system of proportional representation, means a strict and inter-local bureaucratic organization of the parties and therewith an in-creasing domination of party bureaucracy and discipline" (*ES*, 984). In-creasingly, it becomes the parties who dictate politics to the people not vice versa, thus thwarting democratic impulses. By presenting "candidates and programs to the politically passive citizens," party bureaucratization acceler-ates "the general tendency to impersonality," and "the obligation to con-form to abstract norms" in "modern parliamentary representation" (*ES*, 294). Governmental bureaucracy also frustrates the democratic tide with which it emerges, according to Weber. The demand for "substantive justice" on the part of democracy "will unavoidably collide with the formalism and the rule-bound and cool 'matter of factness' of bureaucratic administration" (*ES*, 980). Bureaucratic imperatives, such as the maintenance "of a closed status group of officials" and the expansion of the "authority" of experts, confront the democratic demand for publicity and accessibility (*ES*, 285).

However, Weber suggests no alternative to this quandary: Democratic "reforms" tend to increase party power by decreasing the autonomy of the representative (*ES*, 1128), and charisma does not as yet present itself as a viable way out. In several places, Weber associates charisma *with* party poli-tics[22] and indeed asserts that charisma may foster rationalization as easily as it may serve as an antithesis to it (*ES*, 269).

Yet after the war, given the not-very-promising political state of affairs in Germany as well as the fact that he was no longer writing for an exclusively academic audience, Weber's remarks become more engaged and more polemical. In the collection of essays gathered under the title of "Parlia-ment and Government in a Reconstructed Germany," Weber asks the ques-tion, is democracy compatible with bureaucracy? His answer is a qualified yes, but there is a tension between the two kinds of democracy that he offers to stand its ground against bureaucracy. One is centered on the parliament: a class of parliamentary leaders whose personal conviction and popular authority can hold the technocrats and the bureaucracy accountable. The

---

22 *ES*, 1128–30; even as late as the "Politics as a Vocation" lecture, Weber associates charisma with and not against the party "machine"; see *From Max Weber: Essays in Sociology*, ed. H. H. Gerth and C. Wright Mills (New York: Oxford University Press, 1958), pp. 103, 105–6.

second is centered on the executive: a plebiscitarily elected, charismatic president can tame both the administrative machinery of bureaucracy and the bureaucratized parliament. Both "solutions" hinge on the question of leadership, for it is leadership that is most endangered by "the present condition of uncontrolled bureaucratic domination" (*ES,* 1419).

In the "Politics as a Vocation" lecture, Weber voiced the fear that at the center of German government would be "an unpolitical Parliament in which genuine leadership finds no place."[23] One would assume that this is the actual state of affairs from Weber's description in the "Parliament and Government" piece. Representatives are compelled, on the one hand, to become technocrats – civil servants without conviction and ingenuity (*ES,* 1412,1418) – or, on the other, to become mere party hacks.[24] Foreshadowing Schmitt's critique of government by discussion, Weber describes how parliamentary speeches are no longer concerned with addressing vital issues or persuading others but instead take the appearance of a bad stage play:

> The speeches of the deputies today are no longer personal professions, still less attempts to win over opponents. They are official statements addressed to the country. . . . After representatives of all parties have spoken once or twice in turn, the *Reichstag* debate is closed. The speeches are submitted beforehand to a party caucus, or at least agreed upon in all essentials. The caucus also determines who will speak for the party. The parties have experts for every issue, just like the bureaucracy. (*ES,* 1412)

Party bureaucracy infantilizes representatives through this enforced role playing and ill prepares them for the pressing task of checking the administrative bureaucracy. Clerks who possess no convictions, who are committed to impartiality, and who adhere to general rules have been a total failure in the management of politics, which should be left to those who have a calling, are engaged, and are sensitive to the specificities of concrete cases. Weber is adamant: "Parliament's first task is the supervision of these policymakers. . . . Politicians must be the countervailing force against bureaucratic domination" (*ES,* 1417). This clearly assumes that parliament has not been completely technified by bureaucratization and can live up to the task demanded by all of Weber's writings from this period – the training of leaders in parliament.

The other alternative suggested in the "Parliament and Government" essay and fully endorsed by Weber elsewhere reveals a lack of faith on

23 Weber, "Politics as a Vocation," p. 114.
24 Ibid., pp. 106–7.

Weber's part with this likelihood.[25] Weber recognized the drawbacks in-volved with a plebiscitarily elected president – the most competent person is most often *not* selected for the office, for instance – but compared to rule by bureaucrats, he deemed it a far more "responsible" mode of government (*ES*, 1415). Although he understood that "pure" Caesarist democracy was ideally incompatible with parliamentarism (*ES*, 1452), Weber did not pro-pose it as a substitution for parliament: "Whether we hate or love parliamen-tary politics – we cannot eliminate it" (*ES*, 1408). Its functions in maintain-ing order during intervals of presidential succession (*ES*, 1457), training potential leaders (*ES*, 1417), supervising budgetary matters (*ES*, 1454), and attempting to keep the "authoritarian" bureaucracy at bay (*ES*, 1453) are too valuable to abandon even within a presidential system, according to Weber. Schmitt, however, would later criticize such justifications for parlia-ment as rather slim (*V*, 341) and suggest that plebiscitarianism itself rules out the necessity of parliament-trained leadership:

> The idea of the selection of political leadership justifies no parliament consist-ing of several hundred party functionaries, but leads rather to the desire for political leadership based directly on the confidence of the masses. If such leadership is successfully found, then a new, powerful *representation* emerges. But it is a representation against parliament, whose inherited presumption of being a representation is thereby eliminated. (*V*, 314)

Weber's turn toward a plebiscitary theory was not exclusively motivated by the need to have a substantive, charismatic, value-embodied entity opposite the bureaucracy. His definition of presidential democracy was perhaps much more narrow than that. A conversation between Weber and General Ludendorff, relayed in Weber's biography, is potentially quite revealing:

WEBER: In a democracy the people choose a leader whom they trust. Then the chosen man says, "Now shut your mouths and obey me. The people and the parties are no longer free to interfere in the leader's business." LUDENDORFF: I could like such a "democracy!"[26]

There are certainly Schmittian-authoritarian overtones to some of We-ber's justification for a strong presidency: Foreshadowing Schmitt's associa-

25 See Mommsen, *Max Weber and German Politics*, pp. 332–89, for a full account of Weber's views.
26 Marianne Weber, *Max Weber: A Biography*, trans. Harry Zohn (New York: Wiley, 1975), p. 653.

tion of presidential authority with exceptional crises, as discussed in the previous chapter, Weber remarks in more qualified terms: "[L]et us ensure that he is only permitted to intervene in the machinery of the *Reich* during temporary, irresolvable crises."[27] Although in Chapters 5 and 6 I will explain how Schmitt endorses a president who can transcend the pluralistic and antagonistic actors of society, Weber had already exclaimed that "particularism cries out for a bearer of the principle of the unity of the *Reich*."[28] However, he declares in unmitigated terms what Schmitt would never bring himself to recommend: "Let us ensure that the *Reichspräsident* sees the prospect of the gallows as the reward awaiting any attempt to interfere with the laws or to govern autocratically."[29]

Therefore, whatever Weber's failings in advocating a Caesarist presidency, whatever his skepticism regarding democracy, he never advocated eradicating parliament and in fact could not imagine that anyone might possibly do so in good faith: "The complete abolition of the parliaments has yet to be demanded seriously by any democrat, no matter how much he is opposed to their present form" (*ES*, 1454). We will see to what extent Weber's student, that peculiar "democrat" Carl Schmitt, would make such a demand.

Parlamentarismus: The 1923 Edition

No matter how shocked readers might be by the possible implications regarding plebiscitary democracy suggested in the conclusion to Schmitt's preface, they might at least take solace in the fact that the author proclaims himself to be a one-time supporter of parliamentarism who has reevaluated the institution and its principles in light of changing times. One might even take the arguments more seriously precisely as a result of such a claim; after all, Weber himself had made somewhat similar arguments. As readers moved on to the body of the main text of *Parlamentarismus,* which was written before the preface, they would not immediately find the argument any different: Schmitt does not early on declare parliamentarism to be "rotten at the core" but rather gradually shifts from the moderate position just outlined to this more stark position.

In the introduction to the first edition of *Parlamentarismus,* Schmitt at first speaks of parliament in a way consistent with the second edition's

---

27   Weber, "The President of the Reich" (1919), in *Weber: Political Writings,* ed. Peter Lassman and Ronald Speirs (Cambridge: Cambridge University Press, 1994), p. 307.

28   Ibid.

29   Ibid., p. 305.

preface: "[T]he institution itself has lost its moral and intellectual foundation and only remains standing through sheer mechanical perseverance as
an empty apparatus" (P, 21). Parliament is indeed spoken of as having been
infected by a technological influence and as being a substanceless form, but,
in declaring that parliament has lost its moral and theoretical foundation,
Schmitt obviously implies that it indeed had one at some point. He embarks
on a mission to recover this moral-intellectual foundation. By shifting away
from the "tactical" and the "technical" (P, 27), he hopes "to find the ultimate core of the institution of modern parliament" (P, 20). But when he
does indeed find this foundation, he does not necessarily vindicate a vir-
tuous parliament of the past; nor is he as neutral as he claims to be when he
states that his aim is neither to "confirm nor refute" the intellectual foundations of parliamentarism. Schmitt's mission is neither of the rescue nor of
the reconnaissance sort; it is a mission, so to speak, to search and destroy.

Schmitt argues that a transformation has taken place that threatens the
efficacy and legitimacy of parliamentary government: "[T]he form and content of authority, publicity, and representation are [now] essentially
different" (P, 25). The question is whether the transformation that Schmitt
is ultimately concerned to criticize is the one from nineteenth-century
laissez-faire liberalism to twentieth-century mass-party, state-interventionist
liberalism or, in light of *Political Form,* the transformation from more traditional politics of "authority, publicity and representation," pure and simple,
to *any* kind of progressive Enlightenment political model.

In chapter 2 of *Parlamentarismus,* Schmitt again locates the foundation of
the parliamentary system in the principle of government by discussion, but
he does not employ friendly rhetoric toward it, as he does in the 1926
preface and in the introduction to the first edition. Parliament, writes
Schmitt, is based on

> a process of confrontation of differences and opinions, from which the real
> political will results. The essence of parliament is therefore public delibera-
> tion of argument and counterargument, public debate and public discus-
> sion. . . . Parliament is accordingly the place in which particles of reason that
> are strewn unequally among human beings gather themselves and bring pub-
> lic power under their control. (P, 34–5)

But, invoking von Mohl, Schmitt asserts that the system collapses if such
"particles of reason" do not in fact collect in parliament. If the discussion
taking place in parliament is insufficiently informed, then any outcome of
this discussion would be incomplete, faulty, and not "truthful."

Schmitt proceeds to link government by discussion, *in principle,* to economic-technical thought:

> Normally one only discusses the economic line of reasoning that social harmony and the maximization of wealth follow from the free economic competition of individuals, from freedom of contract, freedom of trade, free enterprise. But all this is only an application of a general liberal principle. It is exactly the same: that the truth can be found through an unrestrained clash of opinion and that competition will produce harmony. (*P,* 35)

Like the market, like supply and demand, which cannot produce a normative outcome, discussion cannot produce truth; it can only generate more discussion: Truth "becomes a mere function of the eternal competition of opinions" (*P,* 35). In spite of his earlier expressions of admiration for parliamentarism's pursuit of truth, Schmitt here demonstrates his belief that truth and discussion have nothing at all to do with each other. How can an "unending conversation" (*P,* 36) generate the truth? "In contrast to the truth, [government by discussion] means renouncing a definite result" (*P,* 35). Previously in the work, Schmitt implied that parliamentary discussion can produce only a defective outcome; here he declares that it generates no outcome at all. Moreover, he does not claim here that this is a late development of parliamentarism, as he does in the 1926 preface and the 1923 introduction; here the defect is an original element of the very theory itself. A year earlier, in *Political Theology,* Schmitt described what his intellectual heroes thought about government by discussion: "Catholic political philosophers such as Maistre, Bonald, and Donoso-Cortès . . . would have considered everlasting conversation a product of a gruesomely comic fantasy, for what characterized their counterrevolutionary political philosophy was the recognition that their times needed a decision" (*PT,* 53). The opposition between discussion and decision will prove crucial to Schmitt's conclusion in *Parlamentarismus.*

In his return to the theoretical foundations of parliamentarism, Schmitt finds not only an ultimately vapid normative justification for government by discussion (the futile pursuit of truth) but an inherently technical justification as well (discussion as "technique"). He is again able to argue on two levels: (1) the techniques developed through the parliamentary system (namely, government by discussion, as well as publicity, and division of powers) no longer properly perform their allotted tasks; and (2) such techniques were destined to fail since their inception – they could *never* perform the tasks assigned.

Government by open discussion was not only supposed to promote truth, it was also intended as an antidote to the *arcana rei publicae* tradition, the tradition of "state secrets" (*P,* 37): "Openness be[came] an absolute value, although at first it was only a practical means to combat the bureaucratic, specialist-technical secret politics of absolutism" (*P,* 38). The advocates of openness and discussion sought to utilize these elements to shatter the *Staatsraison,* the *ratio status* theory associated with Machiavelli that "treats state politics only as a technique for the assertion of power and its expansion" (*P,* 37, translation amended). Interestingly, it is the raison d'état tradition with which Schmitt himself is most often associated – often self-admittedly – that he describes here in purely technocratic terms, and it is liberalism that appears to be the politics of moral substance through its answering "the power ideal of political technique [*Technik*] with the concept of law and justice" (*P,* 37). Ultimately, as we will see, Schmitt contrasts the theory and practice of early liberalism with the "political-technical secrets" of absolutism only to emphasize how contemporary liberalism itself has succumbed to such amoral cum immoral *technische* practices.

In *Political Form,* Schmitt expressed his disdain for political solutions that resort to value-neutral and merely technical means. In *Parlamentarismus,* he is barely able to restrain his feelings of contempt for the naïveté of the proponents of liberal publicity and political discussion: "The elimination of secret politics and secret diplomacy becomes a wonder cure for every kind of political disease and corruption, and public opinion becomes a totally effective controlling force. . . . [W]here there is freedom of the press, the misuse of power is unthinkable; a single free newspaper would destroy the most powerful tyrant" (*P,* 38). These Pollyannaish sentiments are contrasted in Schmitt's text with the theories of Mill and Tocqueville: liberals who saw that the very institutions that were designed to protect against coercive government – freedom of the press, open debate, public discussion, public opinion, and so on – could become forces of coercion themselves (*P,* 39).[30] The optimistic sentiments of the early proponents of openness are also presumably contrasted by Schmitt with his own contemporary political reality. In Weimar, those institutions became the means to paralyze the workings of parliament not to promote them.

So far, Schmitt has described the openness of parliamentary politics as an ineffectual and ultimately dangerous technique, devoid of any moral content; he has also depicted the principle of government by discussion as a ridiculous, "unending conversation" that never had the remotest chance of

---

30   Cf. Habermas, *STPS,* 133, 137.

attaining a glimmer of the truth. He proceeds to argue that the principle of division or separation of powers (which he claims is "bound" to openness and government by discussion) (*P,* 39) was also promoted technically and normatively but, like the others, failed on both counts, because of the enslavement of normativism to technicism.

According to Schmitt, "the division or balance of different state activities and institutions" was derived from the same reasoning that advocated government by discussion, and capitalist economics for that matter, namely, the idea that from "competition . . . the truth will emerge" (*P,* 39).[31] But as with discussion, neither truth nor anything so value-laden could survive the multiplicitous technical apparatus that is constructed to produce it. According to Schmitt, the "mechanical conception" of division of powers within the state perpetuates itself to the point of absurdity. Political structure becomes an infinite regression of division:

> One has become accustomed to seeing parliament as only a part of the state's functions, one part that is set against the others (executive and courts). Nevertheless, parliament should not be just a part of this balance, but precisely because it is the legislative, parliament should itself be balanced. This depends on a way of thinking that creates multiplicity everywhere so that an equilibrium created from the imminent dynamics of a system of negotiations replaces absolute unity. First through this process can the legislative itself be balanced and mediated either in a bicameral system or through federalism; but even within a single chamber the balancing of outlooks and opinions functions as a consequence of this special kind of rationalism. (*P,* 40–1)

This phenomenon of political subsystem differentiation, as Schmitt describes it here, obviously draws on Weber's rationalization thesis and looks ahead to the systems theory of Luhmann.[32] This "special kind of rationalism" is of course akin to the "fantastically warped" rationality that Schmitt denounces, in *Political Form,* as being overly enamored with form at the expense of substance, and more concerned with material manipulation

---

31 Schmitt never actually demonstrates the philosophical links among government by discussion, publicity, and separation of powers. The fact is that they probably developed much more independently of each other than Schmitt would have it. For a summary of the theoretical pitfalls involved in equating liberal political practices and those of the market, see Bernard Manin, "On Legitimacy and Political Deliberation," *Political Theory* 15:3 (August 1987).

32 On Schmitt as an unacknowledged conduit from Weber to Luhmann, see Cohen and Arato, *Civil Society and Political Theory,* pp. 323–5. For a Luhmannian critique of Schmitt, see Thomas Vesting, *Politische Einheitsbildung und technische Realisation: Ueber die Expansion der Technik und die Grenzen der Demokratie* (Baden-Baden: Nomos, 1990).

than with human needs. The technique of separating powers is carried through to such an extent that its substance or purpose – providing citizens with a strong and stable government – is lost in the process. Schmitt, always quick to point out possible contradictions or hypocrisies, reveals the tension within liberal constitutionalism between the supposed primacy of the parliamentary body and the fact that in every modern person's mind "a constitution is identical with division of power" (*P*, 41). Liberal parliamentarism is hypocritical for championing both.

Indeed, the contradictions within parliamentarism are such that Schmitt speaks of parliamentarism as betraying its purpose. In both the medieval and liberal conceptions of representation, what is public is of the utmost importance. In both schemes, although in different ways, the public is represented in the act of representing. In one, public values are represented publicly; in the other, private values are represented publicly. In the medieval conception, without a public before which what is to be represented can be made present, representation cannot be made real. In the liberal parliamentary scheme, a public is necessary to make demands on, serve as watchdog for, and verify the actions of the parliament, ensuring that it does not infringe on private rights, thus rendering it legitimate. This is why parliamentary discussion is to remain open. But as Schmitt describes it, "As things stand today, it is of course practically impossible not to work with committees, and increasingly smaller committees; in this way the parliamentary plenum gradually drifts away from its purpose (that is, from its public), and as a result it necessarily becomes a mere facade" (*P*, 49). Not only has parliament become a mere form, not only is it a failure technically and morally, but it has become exactly like what it was designed to combat: a government of *arcana rei publicae*. Clearly inspired by Weber's analysis of the necessary "bureaucratization" an oppositional movement must undergo when challenging bureaucratic rule (*ES*, 224), Schmitt describes how government by parliament has become government by "antechamber" (*P*, 7) and, as such, is no better than the absolutist-bureaucratic regimes it supplanted:

> The idea of modern parliamentarism, the demand for checks, and the belief in openness and publicity were born in the struggle against the secret politics of absolute princes. The popular sense of freedom and justice was outraged by arcane practices that decided the fate of nations in secret resolutions. But how harmless and idyllic are the objects of cabinet politics in the seventeenth and eighteenth centuries compared with the fate that is at stake today and which is the subject of all manner of secrets. (*P*, 50)

Schmitt has again reverted to speaking about the principles that parliament has "lost," but he has said enough about these principles throughout most of the 1923 text to let the reader know what he thinks about those principles even before the time when they were in fact "lost."[33]

What about the obvious flaws in Schmitt's argument? Besides his distortion of the intellectual origins of parliamentarism's principles, what about such claims that parliamentary discussion degenerates into "endless discussion?" Surely Schmitt knows that nearly every modern parliament has instituted, and every theoretical advocate of parliamentarism has justified, devices that bring discussion to a necessary conclusion. Schmitt invites retorts like this so that he can further illustrate the contradictions within liberal parliamentarism. For instance, he describes how parliament is founded on the *Rechtsstaat* tradition, which promotes the primacy of "law which is general and already promulgated, universally binding without exception, and valid in principle for all times" over "personal order which varies case to case according to particular concrete circumstances" (*P,* 42). He implies that any encroachment on the flow of discussion is, according to parliamentarism's own theory, an invasion on the pursuit of truth by naked power – a hypocritical act and a reversion to what Locke called, "the way of beasts" (*P,* 49). In order to interrupt parliamentary procedure, an arbitrary force is required – exactly what parliamentary procedure is established against. For Schmitt, liberal parliamentarism on its own terms cannot render truth when it allows discussion to perpetuate, nor can truth be guaranteed when discussion is arbitrarily brought to a close.

This emphasis on impersonal law over personal authority is another

33 Providing the sociological verification of Schmitt's descriptive, if not his prescriptive, thesis after the fact, Habermas describes how the merging of state and society necessitated extraparliamentary bargaining and the subsequent parliamentary display of its results: "Although agreements here were pursued and concluded outside the parliament, that is, by circumventing the state's institutionalized public sphere, both sides nevertheless prepared them noisily and accompanied them glaringly by so-called publicity work. To the extent that state and society penetrated each other, the public sphere (and along with it the parliament, i.e., the public sphere established as an organ of the state) lost a number of its bridging functions. A continuous process of integration was accomplished in a different fashion. Correlative to a weakening of the position of the parliament was a strengthening of the transformers through which the state was infused into society (bureaucracy) and, in the opposite direction, through which society was infused into the state (special-interest associations and political parties). The publicity effort, however, a carefully managed display of public relations, showed that the public sphere (deprived, for the most part, of its original functions) under the patronage of administrations, special-interest associations, and parties was now made to contribute in a different fashion to the process of integrating state and society" (*STPS,* 197).

feature that separates modern from medieval or Catholic representation. No doubt Schmitt saw *Rechtsstaat* theorists such as Junius Brutus, who "wanted to advance 'mathematical ethics' and replace the concrete person of the King with an impersonal *authority* and a universal *reason*" (*P*, 42), as accomplices in the ascendance of an ultimately amoral, positivistic network of rules that now govern modern life. As Schmitt explained in *Political Form*, an ideal must be embodied in a *person* in order for it to be made real, for it to have any connection to what is human, for it to have any normative substance.

In the Middle Ages, according to Schmitt, the noble embodied authority, the priest embodied the higher authority of Christ, and so on (*RC*, 19). It is a form of the "standing for" representation, not the "acting for" type. Parliamentary representatives, on the other hand, do not embody the people or any subset thereof; they are merely deputized by a specific geographically determined number of them, nor, on the other side of the process, do they represent the law *to* the people; representatives simply help make it for them. The difference between the priest and the member of parliament, for Schmitt, is similar to Habermas's distinction between the nobleman and the bourgeois: "The nobleman was what he represented; the bourgeois, what he produced" (*STPS*, 13). And because the parliamentary representatives could not produce law by themselves before the public, as the noble could represent authority, parliamentary representatives cannot embody the law. Along these lines, just as the infiltration of openness and discussion by the technical robbed representation of its necessary *public* aspect; the infiltration of *Rechtsstaat* by the formal, the mathematical – what Schmitt would call "the economic-technical" – robbed representation of its equally necessary *personal* aspect. For Schmitt, as expressed in *Political Form*, "the economic-technical" is completely antithetical to what is representational (*RC*, 13). Schmitt then demonstrates, in *Parlamentarismus*, that this is what plagues liberal parliamentarism.[34]

The difference between the primacy of the public versus the primacy of the private – which Schmitt dwells on at length in *Political Form* – has implica-

---

34   Peter Carl Caldwell astutely points out how Schmitt uses bureaucratic words like *Beauftragte* to describe parliamentary representation, in *Verfassungslehre*, so as to implicitly distinguish it from more substantive notions of the concept; see *Popular Sovereignty and the Crisis of German Constitutional Law: The Theory and Practice of Weimar Constitutionalism* (Durham, N. C.: Duke University Press, 1997). Larmore detects Schmitt's juxtaposition of notions of *Identifizierung* (identification) and *Identität* (identity) in *Parlamentarismus* that emphasizes the lack of substance in liberal parliamentary representation; see *The Morals of Modernity*, pp. 178–9.

tions for the relationship between liberalism and democracy in *Parlamentarismus*. For Schmitt, *the* modern political principle is democracy. The main thrust of *Parlamentarismus* is that liberalism is not the best realization of this principle; on the contrary, it is the very violation of it. Because of the practical and theoretical failures mentioned earlier and also, as per *Political Form*, because of the inherent link among liberalism, the privileging of privacy, and the economization of politics, liberalism is incompatible with the realization of democracy: "[A] political form of organization ceases to be political if it is, like the modern economy, based on private law. . . . [I]t stands to reason that one cannot give democracy content by means of a transfer into the economic sphere" (*P*, 25). Privacy and economic rationality violate the essence of democracy which is in various ways the identity of ruler and ruled:

> [A]ll democratic arguments rest logically on a series of identities. In this series belong the identity of governed and governing, sovereign and subject, the identity of the subject and the object of state authority, the identity of the people with their representatives in parliament, the identity of the state and the current voting population, the identity of state and the law, and finally an identity of the quantitative (the numerical majority or unanimity) with the qualitative (the justice of the laws). (*P*, 26)

Schmitt would develop this line of thought even further in *Verfassungslehre*:

> Something that serves only private concerns and interests can indeed be tended to; it can find its agents, advocates and exponents, but is not represented in the special sense of the term. It is already either actually present or it is brought to attention by commissars, delegates or agents. In representation by contract, a higher mode of being becomes concrete. The idea of representation lies in the fact that as a political unit, an existing people has a higher and more intensified kind of being as opposed to the natural presence of groups of individuals who just happen to live together. When the meaning of this special nature of political existence lapses and people give priority to other kinds of being, then also lapses the comprehension of a concept such as representation. (*V*, 210)[35]

---

35   In *Verfassungslehre*, Schmitt defines democratic identity, or "homogeneity," thus: "Democratic homogeneity is a substantive homogeneity because all citizens partake of this substance, are treated equally, have the same voting rights and so forth. The substance of homogeneity, however, can differ over time, depending on the democracy in question" (*V*, 228). The content of homogeneity for Schmitt can be religion or class, and now it is nationality.

The chief rival of liberalism, according to Schmitt, is the "educational democracy" of Jacobin and Bolshevik stripes that "suspends democracy in the name of a true democracy that is still to be created" (*P*, 28). Like liberalism, this form of democracy clearly denigrates the entity being identified: in twentieth-century liberalism, the populace is betrayed by party-bound delegates cutting deals in smoke-filled antechambers; in Jacobinism, a public identification that does not necessarily exist is asserted between ruler and ruled by a clique.

Yet "the people" must be represented in some way on both pragmatic and ethical grounds: The populace as a collectivity cannot efficiently govern themselves in any institutional sense, and the concept of "the people" does not manifest itself in the physical populace – in the realm of positive materiality. "The people" is constituted by more than such quantitative notions as the counting of persons within the populace: "Identities are not palpable reality, but rest on a recognition of the identity. It is not a matter of something actually equal legally, politically, or sociologically, but rather of identification" (*P*, 26–7). Thus, for the practice of representation to be true to democracy, for Schmitt, it must avoid the artificiality and disingenuousness of both the liberal and Jacobin models in making identity *real*:

> The various nations or social and economic groups who organize themselves "democratically" have the same subject, "the people," only in the abstract. *In concreto* the masses are sociologically and psychologically heterogeneous. A democracy can be militarist or pacifist, absolutist or liberal, centralized or decentralized, progressive or reactionary, and again different at different times without ceasing to be a democracy. . . . [And] they can never reach an absolute, direct, identity that is actually present at every moment. A distance always remains between real equality and the results of identification. The will of the people is of course always identical with the will of the people, whether the decision comes from the yes or no of millions of voting papers, or from a single individual who has the will of the people even without a ballot, or from the people acclaiming in some way. Everything depends on how the will of the people is formed. (*P*, 25–7)

Does the inevitable "distance" between the people and the representative mean that democracy will necessarily be betrayed? Schmitt's answer is seemingly pessimistic: "Democracy seems fated then to destroy itself in the problem of the formulation of the will" (*P*, 28). However, the references to the "yes and no of millions of people," the "single individual who has the will of the people," and the notion of acclaiming foreshadow Schmitt's actual response. He asks the alarming question that, read in light of the book as a whole, rings out as an affirmative declaration: Might not a Caesarist dictatorship be more *technically* efficient *and* more *substantively* democratic than parliamentarism?

> [I]n spite of all its coincidence with democratic ideas and all the connections it has to them, parliamentarism is not democracy any more than it is realized in the practical perspective of expediency. If for practical and technical reasons the representatives of the people can decide instead of the people themselves, then certainly a single trusted representative could also decide in the name of the same people. Without ceasing to be democratic, the argument would justify an antiparliamentary Caesarism. (*P*, 34)

In *Parlamentarismus*, Schmitt identifies parliamentarism as the quintessential "rationalist" political project (*P*, 34). If this has proved to be a total failure, according to Schmitt, would a postrationalist plebiscitary democracy take its place? The last two chapters of the work answer this question.

The Politics of Rationality and Irrationality

We know from Chapter 2 that Schmitt concludes *Political Form* with an exhortation to the forces of the West – liberal, socialist, Protestant, and Jew – to combine under the banner of Roman Catholicism and confront the Russian enemy that marries rationality and irrationality, technology and myth, an exhortation that is repeated without Catholic trappings or such explicit inclusiveness in "The Age of Neutralizations and Depoliticizations," in 1929. What is startling is that Schmitt devotes the final two chapters of *Parlamentarismus*, ostensibly a more historically accurate and theoretically rigorous treatise than *Political Form* and one intended for a wider audience, to similar themes. These chapters confirm the fact that Schmitt's intent was to abandon parliamentary liberalism and not hold out even a "modest hope" for the possibility of its continuation.[36]

The penultimate chapter of *Parlamentarismus*, "Dictatorship in Marxist Thought," describes how the path to post-Enlightenment irrational politics was paved by Marxist theory, although Marx himself remained ultimately within a rational framework. The final chapter, "Irrationalist Theories of the

---

36 Ellen Kennedy, "Introduction: Carl Schmitt's *Parlamentarismus* in Its Historical Context" (*P*, xxxviii).

Direct Use of Force," demonstrates how the revolutionary generation that succeeded Marx had stepped over fully into the realm of the irrational, and intimates that this is where the Western democracies must follow if they are to survive.

In the chapter on Marxism, Schmitt declares that, despite the stereotypes that abound pertaining to Marxist theory, it is *not* just deterministically scientific, *neither* is it concerned with "absolute technocracy,"[37] *nor* is it intended to "produce a politics of mathematical and physical exactness" (*P*, 54). Perhaps thinking of the kind of Left-Hegelian critique that Lukács directs at Weber's technologically determinist liberalism, Schmitt remarks that unlike "the abstract rationalism of the Enlightenment. . . . Marxist science does not want to attribute to coming events the mechanical certainty of a mechanically calculated and mechanically constructed triumph; rather, this is left to the flow of time and the concrete reality of historical events" (*P*, 55). According to Schmitt, this "concrete reality" entails suprarational action and the identification of a world-historical enemy.

What is interesting about the *Communist Manifesto,* according to Schmitt, is not the theory of history as class conflict, for the bourgeoisie had already argued this. It is rather the call for the "single, final struggle of human history" (*P*, 54) in the confrontation with an enemy, the bourgeoisie, who were "not to be educated but eliminated" (*P*, 64). In Marx, the Enlightenment produces a "new rationalism [that] destroys itself dialectically," because "the real and bloody struggle that arises here requires a different chain of thought" from the traditional Hegelian one "whose core always remained contemplative" (*P*, 64). Despite the "demonically possessed" character of Marx's inquiry into the essence of capitalism (*P*, 62, translation amended), he and Hegel remain Western European "schoolmasters" (*P*, 70). In the hands of Lenin and Trotsky, however, revolutionary theory becomes

> no longer a rationalist impulse. . . . the governance of the unconscious by the conscious, of instinct by reason had been shaken to their very core. A new theory of the direct use of force arose in opposition to the absolute rationalism of an educational dictatorship and to the relative rationalism of the division of

37 Kennedy renders the word *Technizität* here as "technocracy." I think that this is appropriate in this context, because Schmitt had yet to distinguish between *Technik* (technology) and *Technizität* (technicity) in *Parlamentarismus,* as he later would in "Das Zeitalter der Neutralisierungen und Entpolitisierungen" (1929), in which "technicity" is more or less the opposite of "technocracy." See Chapters 1 and 2 of the present volume for a discussion of "technicity" and "technology."

powers. Against the belief in discussion there appeared a theory of direct action. (*P*, 64)

The Enlightenment's emancipatory politics of rationality had regressively progressed into myth. Myth, so central to the works discussed in Chapters 1 and 2, becomes the dominant theme of the conclusion of *Parlamentarismus*.

Schmitt reiterates the claim made in *Political Form* and repeated in the "Neutralizations" essay that Soviet Russia is not just a technocracy, not just a formally rational economic state; it is rather a marriage of this and a new form of *ir*rationality, "a new belief in instinct and intuition" (*P*, 66). Combined with an emphasis on technology as a means of emancipation and a necessarily positive attitude to technical rationality is a contradictory spirit, typified by Bakunin, that rebels against any formal rationality, any "systemic unity," especially that of science: "Even science does not have the right to rule. It is not life, it creates nothing, it constructs and receives, but it understands only the general and the abstract and sacrifices the individual fullness of life on the altar of its abstraction" (*P*, 67). It is this volatile combination that makes Russia so dangerous.

If Bakunin is the main exemplar of neoirrationality, in *Political Form*, in *Parlamentarismus* Schmitt devotes most of his attention to Georges Sorel. It is Sorel who most explicitly confronts the "mechanistic scheme" of liberal rationality "with a theory of unmediated real life" centered on "the use of force" (*P*, 67). Against the liberal notions of "balancing, public discussion and parliamentarism," Schmitt describes how Sorel invokes "the power of myth":

> Out of the depths of a genuine life instinct, not out of reason or pragmatism, springs the great enthusiasm, the great moral decision and the great myth. . . . From the perspective of this philosophy, the bourgeois ideal of peaceful agreement, an ongoing and prosperous business that has advantages for everyone, becomes the monstrosity of cowardly intellectualism. Discussing, bargaining, parliamentary proceedings, appear a betrayal of myth and the enormous enthusiasm on which everything depends. Against the mercantilist image of balance there appears another vision, the warlike image of a bloody, definitive, destructive, decisive battle. . . . [T]here is no greater danger than professional politics and participation in parliamentary business. These wear down great enthusiasm into chatter and intrigue and kill the genuine instincts and intuitions that produce a moral decision. . . . Every rationalist interpretation falsifies the immediacy of life. . . . In contrast, the revolutionary use of force by the masses is an expression of the immediate life, often wild and barbaric, but never systematically horrible or inhuman. . . . [I]n the place of

the mechanically concentrated power of the bourgeois state there appears a
creative proletarian force – "violence" appears in place of power. (*P,* 68–72)

Although Schmitt indicates that Sorel was correct in announcing that the
rational politics of liberalism had been supplanted by the irrationalist politics of myth, he identifies a shortcoming in Sorel's prophecy. Sorel adhered
to a transnational notion of myth: the working class as the agent of violent
revolution. But the mythic politics that succeeded in the early twentieth
century were predominantly nationalist. As the myth of the direct use of
force "migrated from west to the east" it accumulated "strong nationalist
elements," such that the ultimate impetus of the Bolshevik revolution was
the fact that "Russia again could be Russian, Moscow again the capital, and
the Europeanized upper classes who held their own land in contempt could
be exterminated. Proletarian use of force had made Russia Muscovite again.
In the mouth of an international Marxist [like Lenin] that is remarkable
praise, for it shows that the energy of nationalism is greater than the myth of
class conflict" (*P,* 75). The victory of Italian fascism only confirms for
Schmitt that the myth of the nation is stronger than the myth of the working
class (*P,* 75).

What is Schmitt's own view of the politics of myth he describes? In these
passages, it is hard to tell whether he speaks with his own voice or is simply
summarizing the arguments of these radical theorists. Is his silence regarding the validity of the attacks on liberalism to be construed as his purely
analytical summation of a particular state of affairs or as an expression of
affirmation or approval? Although it cannot be said definitively whether
Schmitt approves of the depiction of liberalism offered by the mythologists
of anarchism or socialism – Proudhon, Bakunin, Sorel, Lenin – it is difficult
to imagine that he did not recount their opinions with a certain satisfaction.
Indeed, Schmitt wittingly or unwittingly implicates himself in these expressions by introducing into the discussion of the mythic "opposition to parliamentary constitutionalism" the figure of Juan Donoso Cortés, who Schmitt
admits was a powerful influence on his own thought.[38] There are two kinds
of contemporary political mythologies, according to Schmitt:

> the side of tradition in a conservative sense, represented by a Catholic Span-
> iard, Donoso-Cortés, and a radical anarcho-syndicalism [represented by]
> Proudhon. . . . In the eyes of Donoso-Cortés, this socialist anarchist was an evil
> demon, a devil, and for Proudhon the Catholic was a fanatical Grand Inquisi-

38   See Schmitt, *Donoso-Cortés in gesamteuropäischer Interpretation: Vier Aufsätze* (Cologne:
Greven, 1950).

tor, whom he attempted to laugh off. Today it is easy to see that both were their own real opponents and that everything else was only a provisional half-measure. (*P*, 69–70)

Donoso-Cortés had the same view of liberalism as his opponents on the Left; indeed, Schmitt suggests that the radical conservative's views "might have come word for word from Sorel" (*P*, 70). He also had an equally mythic conflict-and-action-oriented response to liberalism, albeit a reactionary state-centered one as opposed to a mass-movement-centered one. Is Schmitt not implicitly offering a choice between the two myths as the only possible options for the future? Are not the "real opponents" for Schmitt still the mythic radical anarchosocialism that resides in Russia, on the one hand, a myth of tradition, authority, "the idea" in the West, on the other, and in the middle, liberalism, the "provisional half-measure?"

All the Spaniard's thoughts were focused on the great battle, the terrible catastrophe that lay ahead, which only the metaphysical cowardice of discursive liberalism could deny was coming. . . . For Donoso-Cortés radical socialism was something enormous, greater than liberal moderation, because it went back to ultimate problems and gave a decisive answer to radical questions – because it had a theology. (*P*, 69–70)

On the basis of what we know from Chapter 2 regarding his attitude toward the Soviet Union in *Political Form* and the "Neutralizations" essay, these exact same words can be applied to Schmitt.

Another important question pertaining to the final two chapters of *Parlamentarismus* is, what is the significance of Schmitt's distinction between class-based myth and nationalist myth for his own theoretical purposes? Why is there a discussion of myth at all in a book on parliamentarism? Schmitt has undressed the European parliament as a normative and technical failure and intimated a possible alternative political solution, plebiscitary democracy. It might be said that the second manifestation of the politics of myth – the myth of the nation – dovetails nicely with Schmitt's practical intimation.

In this regard, it is interesting to note how Schmitt speaks of Mussolini's victory in Italy: "The meaning in intellectual history of this example is especially great because national enthusiasm on Italian soil has until now been based on a democratic and constitutional parliamentary tradition and has appeared to be completely dominated by the ideology of Anglo-Saxon liberalism" (*P*, 76). The politics of Weimar Germany was often said to have been dominated by "Anglo-Saxon liberalism," and the "national enthusiasm" for "constitutional parliamentarism" could have been said to be weaker at this point in Germany than had been the case in Italy. Logically, might not Germany be on the verge of a transition from Anglo-Saxon–style constitutional parliamentarism to nationalist dictatorship as well?

Schmitt protests that the ramifications of such a mythic politics may be "dangerous": "Of course the abstract danger this kind of irrationalism poses is great. The last remnants of solidarity and feeling of belonging together will be destroyed in the pluralism of an unforeseeable number of myths" (*P*, 76). However, a mythmaker who emphasizes the "identity," or later the "unity," of a nation might be able to prevent the "pluralism" of myth and ensure the cohesion of a national state – the "solidarity and feeling of belonging together" – under a popularly acclaimed executive:

> [A] man who unites the confidence of the entire people beyond the limits and the framework of party organizations and party bureaucracies, not as a party man but a man with the full confidence of all the people. A Reich presidential election that genuinely takes account of this meaning . . . would be more important than any of the frequent elections that take place in a democratic state. It would be a splendid proclamation by the German people and would have the irresistibility that is associated with such acclamations. (*V*, 350)

And on the same subject in 1931,

> The whole German people is presupposed as a unity, that is ready for action spontaneously, not first inhibited by social group organizations. It can express its will at a crucial moment over and above pluralistic divisions, returning to unity and exerting itself. The constitution looks to provide the President, in particular, the authority to bind himself immediately with this whole political will of the German people, and thereby act as guardian and defender of constitutional unity and the wholeness of the German people.[39]

A nationalistically legitimated, plebiscitarily elected executive can solve both the sociological problem of an increasingly complex and differentiating world and the ideological problem of a multitude of myths or demons. It can overcome these two manifestations of pluralism so as to confront the technologically obsessed, fanatically driven threat that grows on Germany's and Europe's eastern frontier.

39 Schmitt, *Der Hüter der Verfassung* (Tübingen: J. C. B. Mohr [Paul Siebeck], 1931), p. 159; hereafter cited as *HV*.

Feudalism, Fascism, and Fordism

As noted above, in his famous "Artwork" essay, Benjamin celebrated the disintegration of the "aura" initially brought on by the age of technological reproducibility: "[T]he technique of reproduction detaches the reproduced object from the domain of tradition,"[40] and from a "parisitical" relationship with "ritual."[41] Liberating art from the quasi-naturalized rituals of tradition is concomitant with liberating humanity from unquestioned traditional domination as well. However, the danger suggested by Benjamin's essay is that aesthetics, once strictly defined and bounded by tradition, would now spill over into every sphere; everything would potentially become aestheticized, including politics. Fascism, for Benjamin, is the consummate aestheticization of politics and a form of domination more violent than the traditional forms of authority long since overcome.[42]

In *Political Form,* Schmitt revives a very traditional form of political authority, the medieval notion of representation, which might call to mind such adjectives as Aristotelian, Thomistic, and Scholastic. Schmitt holds this theory out against *both* hyperrational, technocratic-positivist political theory and the irrational, romantic aestheticization of politics. However, consistent with the presentation of Schmitt in Part One, he characteristically provides the best resources from which to criticize his own positions. In *Parlamentarismus,* particularly in the concluding chapters, Schmitt clearly engages in an aestheticization of executive-centered, irrationally nationalist politics, a politics liberated from the very traditional constraints he avows in *Political Form.* What is the difference between Schmitt, the proponent of neo-medieval substantive representation, in *Political Form,* and Schmitt the sly promoter of myth-intoxicated democratic-nationalist dictatorship, in *Parlamentarismus?* More important, what are the ideological-structural possibilities of Schmitt's historical moment that make such a comparison/contrast between the two types of representation even remotely appropri-

40 Benjamin, "The Artwork," p. 221.
41 Ibid., p. 224.
42 On the relationship of Benjamin's aesthetic theory to his brilliant, if tragically only preliminary, critique of fascism, see Susan Buck-Morss, *The Origin of Negative Dialectics: Theodor W. Adorno, Walter Benjamin, and the Frankfurt Institute* (New York: Free Press, 1977); Buck-Morss, "Aesthetics and Anaesthetics: Walter Benjamin's Artwork Essay Reconsidered," *October* 62 (fall 1992); and Richard Wolin, *Walter Benjamin: An Aesthetic of Redemption* (Berkeley: University of California Press, 1994). On the Jewish theological influences on Benjamin's theory of representation, see Gillian Rose, "Walter Benjamin: Out of the Sources of Modern Judaism" in *Judaism and Modernity: Philosophical Essays* (Oxford: Blackwell, 1993).

ate? It is not inconsequential that Benjamin, Schmitt, and Habermas would all begin their reflections on twentieth-century practices of representation with reflections on the "archaic," in the case of Benjamin, and the "feudal," in the case of Schmitt and Habermas. The sociostructural evidence suggests not only that this reflection is motivated to contrast mass-party representation with medieval methods but that something reminiscent of the latter is now strangely characteristic of the former. In other words, there are characteristics that appear ostensibly "feudal" about the emerging welfare-state socioeconomic reality, despite its exclusively modern, implicitly plebiscitary nature, as detected by Weber, Schmitt, Benjamin, and, most extensively, Habermas.[43]

In the opening pages of *The Structural Transformation of the Public Sphere*, Habermas extensively cites Schmitt's *Political Form* on medieval representation and attributes the Benjaminian notion of "aura" to it, for example, the aura that "surrounded and endowed" the noble's public authority (*STPS*, 6–7). Reiterating Schmitt's account, the concrete domination of feudal rule was legitimated by public "display" in the Middle Ages *before* not *for* the people: The virtues that subdued warrior codes under Christian norms, for instance, "had to be capable of public representation. . . . The aura of feudal authority . . . indicated social status" (*STPS*, 8). Even as political representation moved with the decline of feudalism and rise of absolutism from the various manors of particular lords to the court of the national prince, "Representation was still dependent on the presence of people before whom it was displayed" (*STPS*, 9–10). But in the ensuing historical rivalry between the publicity of absolutist authority and the general public that had grown increasingly independent of it ("state *publicum*" vs. "the public sphere of civil society"), the former assumes an increasingly technocratic role of maintaining order, while the latter becomes the realm that is to be "represented" as the bourgeois public sphere: "[T]he sphere of private people come together as a public . . . privatized but publicly relevant sphere of commodity exchange and social labor" (*STPS*, 23, 27). The notion of representation is changed, as Schmitt had described in *Political Form*, for publicity becomes the expression of private interests expressed publicly and not the public display of substantive values. Echoing Benjamin, Habermas describes how the traditional aura of representation is thereby lost:

43   Regarding the many influences on Habermas's *Structural Transformation* work, few commentators have detected Benjamin's; a notable exception is Richard Wolin, *Labyrinths: Explorations in the Critical History of Ideas* (Amherst: University of Massachusetts Press, 1995), pp. 17–18.

To the degree to which philosophical and literary works and works of art in general were produced for the market and distributed through it, these cultural products became . . . commodities [and] in principle generally accessible. They no longer remained components of the Church's and the court's publicity of representation; that is precisely what was meant by the *loss of their aura* of extraordinariness and by the profaning of their once sacramental character. The private people for whom the cultural product became available as a commodity profaned it inasmuch as they had to determine its meaning on their own (by way of rational communication with one another), verbalize it, and thus state explicitly what precisely in its implicitness for so long could assert its authority. (*STPS*, 36–7, emphasis added)

Capitalist commodification made culture itself an object of not consumption initially but rational discussion. What is accepted as quasi-natural in the medieval or absolutist scheme is now open to rational criticism in the eighteenth and nineteenth centuries. The loss of the aura and the fact that "within a public everyone was entitled to judge" (*STPS*, 40), is hence initially democratizing, according to both Benjamin and Habermas, not just a degeneration into either masturbatory romanticism or economic-technical rationality, as we have seen Schmitt claim repeatedly.

Even granted the extensive inequalities of class, race, and gender ignored by the early Habermas's idealization of the bourgeois public sphere,[44] the main thesis of the work is to demonstrate the foreclosing of its progressive possibilities in the transition to the welfare state of the late nineteenth, early twentieth century – a transition Habermas identifies as a "refeudalization" of society and its methods of representation (*STPS*, 141). What Habermas describes as mutual "societalization" of the state and "stateification" of society (*STPS*, 142) destroys the public sphere's condition of possibility, the separation of state and society:

[S]ocietal organizations. . . . by means of the collective representation of their interests in the public sphere have to obtain and defend a private status granted to them by social legislation. In other words they have to obtain and defend private autonomy by means of political autonomy. Together with the politically influential representatives of cultural and religious forces this competition of organized private interests in the face of the "neomercantilism" of an interventionist administration leads to a refeudalization of society insofar as, with the linking of public and private realms, not only certain functions in the sphere of commerce and social labor are taken over by political authorities

44   Cf. Negt and Kluge, *Public Sphere and Experience,* as well as the contributions to *Habermas and the Public Sphere.*

but conversely political functions are taken over by societal powers. (*STPS*, 231)

In place of the parliament that transferred and maintained the rational discussion generated by the populace over the deployment of authority, this role is now assumed by, and conducted among, private bureaucracies, special-interest groups, political parties, and the bureaucracy (*STPS*, 176). Inasmuch as popular sanction is necessitated to maintain legitimacy, these entities make a show of themselves and their "products" to the general public through "publicity work": "In the measure that it is shaped by public relations, the public sphere of civil society again takes on feudal features. The 'suppliers' display a showy pomp before customers ready to follow. Publicity imitates the kind of aura proper to the personal prestige and supernatural authority once bestowed by the kind of publicity involved in representation" (*STPS*, 195).

Politics, that which ideally serves all, becomes an object of cultural consumption instead of a subject of rational discussion. In Benjaminian-Marxian terms, the exchange value of commodification that neutralized the aura of traditional art and politics under laissez-faire capitalism, has been superseded by the use value of that process that once again emphasizes the sensual – visual, aural, psychological – consumption of politics and not rational participation in it: "Organizations and functionaries display representation. . . . The aura of personally represented authority returns as an aspect of publicity; to this extent modern publicity has affinity with feudal publicity. . . . The public sphere becomes the court *before* whose public prestige can be displayed – rather than *in* which public critical debate is carried on" (*STPS*, 200–1). However, unlike the naturalized domination of feudal authority in which the aura is an intrinsic aspect of legitimation, inherent to a person by birth or office, the modern aura must be manufactured, that is, produced through mass media. Hence, there emerges once again the perplexing problematic of the modern entwinement of the rational and irrational, of technology and myth, discussed in Part One. A technologically embedded media facilitates the mythic assent of the general populace to the outcomes agreed on by the state and social organizations mentioned earlier. According to Habermas, these organizations

> must obtain from a mediatized public an acclamatory consent, or at least
> benevolent passivity of a sort that entails no specific obligations, for a process
> of compromise formation that is largely a matter of organization-internal
> maneuvering but that requires public credit – whether to transform such

consent into political pressure or, on the basis of this toleration, to neutralize political counterpressure. . . . Today occasions for identification have to be created – the public sphere has to be "made," it is not "there" anymore. . . . The immediate effect of publicity is not exhausted by the decommercialized wooing effect of an aura of good will that produces a readiness to assent. Beyond influencing consumer decisions this publicity is now also useful for exerting political pressure because it mobilizes a potential of inarticulate readiness to assent that, if need be, can be translated into a plebiscitarily defined acclamation. (*STPS*, 200–1)

The phrase with which Habermas concludes this quote bespeaks the high stakes involved in the refeudalization of society, a characterization that is in fact ultimately metaphorical. The regressive result of a politics in which the population is conditioned in advance to "plebiscitarily acclaim" previously arranged policy decisions is as characteristic of the regime that obtained in Germany between the Weimar and Bonn republics as of those two regimes themselves. When refeudalization is distinguished by the policy outputs of large-scale, semipublicized private industry and semiprivatized bureaucracy, under the direction of competing mass-media-deploying parties, the regime may be classified as Fordist; when it is directed by a centralized, unaccountable state with a monopoly on mass media the regime is fascist. The latter type of regime is barely mentioned by name in *Structural Transformation,* although the affinities between it and the socioeconomic arrangements in the Federal Republic are more than implied by the narrative ellipsis between accounts of Weimar and the BRD.[45] Moreover, the book that is generally recognized as the most perceptive diagnosis of the ills of Fordist "neofeudalism" and the most insidious prescription for a fascist solution, *Parlamentarismus,* is cited only once (*STPS*, 204).[46]

45 Although such affinities are often loudly proclaimed today as the welfare state suffers what may be a terminal crisis, one should not underestimate the radically provocative nature of Habermas's intimations – set forth in a slightly circumspect manner – during the glory days of the *Sozialstaat* in the Federal Republic of Germany. On the other hand, Margaret Somers interrogates some of the more conventional presuppositions of Habermas's thesis in her two-part article, "What's Political or Cultural about Political Culture and the Public Sphere? Toward an Historical Sociology of Concept Formation," *Sociological Theory* 13:2 (1995); and "Narrating and Naturalizing Anglo-American Citizenship Theory: The Place of Political Culture and the Public Sphere," *Sociological Theory* 13:3 (1996).

46 This absence that suggests a presence has perhaps as much to do with Habermas's critique of the Federal Republic as it does with any attempt to disguise his intellectual debt to Schmitt. On the latter charge, see Kennedy, "Carl Schmitt and the Frankfurt School"; and the response by Ulrich K. Preuß, "The Critique of German Liberalism," *Telos* 71 (spring 1987).

Thus, there are sociostructural similarities inherent to the Fordist welfare state and the fascist warfare state that become salient on reflection over Schmitt's treatment of representation in *Political Form* and *Parlamentarismus*, Habermas's *Structural Transformation*, and Benjamin's "Artwork" essay. As Habermas describes it, the emergence of state capitalism in either its liberal or fascist form encourages the supplanting of a public with a mass: "[T]he social-psychological criterion of a culture of consumers, namely, non-cumulative experience, goes together with the sociological criterion of a destruction of the public sphere" (*STPS*, 167). Lack of rationally received continuity on the part of the public encourages case-to-case unmediated experience or consumption of, rather than reflection on, public issues. Display of interests takes the place of discussion of them; ephemeral compromise or arbitrary imposition replaces rational agreement (*STPS*, 179). Although the press once transmitted and clarified the terms of public debate, its twentieth-century technologically proliferated incarnation "shapes" the terms of debate in advance (*STPS*, 188). In election campaigns, parliamentary sessions, and public forums, "arguments are transmuted into symbols to which one can not respond by arguing but only by identifying with them" (*STPS*, 206).[47] Schmitt's pronouncement for a definition of democracy that emphasizes the "identity" of ruler and ruled is made feasible by a mass-party system in which the respective parties reflected in a historically unprecedented way a cultural and social isomorphism with their constituents.[48] Schmitt's intervention, his active reassertion of his role as an intellectual-political elite, was to facilitate a unitary/unified identification of rulers and ruled: the whole nation over a particular party. Schmitt would eventually endorse one party that he assumed could unite the nation according to his vision.

The alienation engendered by the public rituals of the mass-party state – fascist or Fordist – is more pronounced than that experienced under feudal domination, because mass democracy promises the possibility of rationally determined social change but reinforces only an unreflectively consumed status quo. As Benjamin observed,

47   On the specificities of the transitions from nineteenth-century laissez-faire to twentieth-century mass-party to contemporary postparty modes of parliamentarism, see Manin, "The Metamorphoses of Representative Government." His study also indicates how representative government is presently undergoing a second transformation with the decline of the mass parties, the prominence of the candidate's personality, party-independent media apparatuses, and the change of primary issues from election to election (pp. 157–60).

48   Ibid., p. 135.

Fascism attempts to organize the newly created proletarian masses without affecting the property structure which the masses strive to eliminate. Fascism sees its salvation in giving these masses not their right, but instead a chance to express themselves. The masses have a right to change property relations; Fascism seeks to give them an expression while preserving property. The logical result of Fascism is the introduction of aesthetics into political life. The violation of the masses, whom Fascism, with its *Führer* cult, forces to its knees, has its counterpart in the violation of an apparatus which is pressed into the production of ritual values.[49]

Thus, the immanent possibility of, and implicit call for, plebiscitarianism suggested by Schmitt's account in *Parlamentarismus* is not necessarily altogether incompatible in a sociostructural manner with the kind of medieval practices of representation elucidated in *Political Form*. Although Schmitt may apparently lament the demise of representation by estates, he is clearly not a Catholic "natural law" or *ständische* theorist like, for instance, Otto von Gierke, who might see in twentieth-century pluralism a positively valued neofeudalism.[50] As I discuss more extensively in Chapters 5 and 6, Schmitt abhors pluralism.[51] He even explicitly equates pluralism and feudalism, denouncing both socioeconomic arrangements: "In conjunction with the pluralist system, the polyacracy of the general economy would become increasingly splintered and recreate the situation of the medieval estate system, within which the German state had already once disappeared" (*HV*, 110). He claimed that Weimar's proportional voting arrangement engen-

49 Benjamin, "The Artwork," p. 241.
50 See the translations of portions of von Gierke's mammoth work *Das deutsche Gen-ossenschaftsrecht* (1881): *Political Theories of the Middle Ages*, trans. F. W. Maitland (Boston: Beacon Press, 1958), and *Community in Historical Perspective*, ed. Antony Black and trans. Mary Fischer (Cambridge: Cambridge University Press, 1990). Schmitt was also far too serious a student of Weber not to be familiar with Weber's claim that a modern substitution of representation by estates for representation by party would only serve to further, not limit, the bureaucratization and economization of parliament (*ES*, 1396). Moreover, one cannot attribute to Schmitt a political Aristotelianism of whatever stripe. He later admitted that *Political Form* was *not* a work of Scholastic thinking; see *Politische Theologie II. Die Legende von der Erledigung jeder politischen Theologie* (Berlin: Duncker & Humblot, 1970), p. 27. Schmitt had dabbled with Scholasticism earlier in his career; see "Die Sichtbarkeit der Kirche: Eine Scholastische Erwägung," *Summa: Eine Vierteljahresschrift* (1917); translated by G. L. Ulmen as "The Visibility of the Church: A Scholastic Consideration," and appended to *Political Form*.
51 See, e.g., Schmitt, "Staatsethik und pluralischer Staat" (1930), in *Positionen und Begriffe im Kampf mit Weimar – Genf – Versailles: 1923–1939* (Hamburg: Hanseatische Verlagsanstalt, 1940).

dered a "new feudalism" that represented entrenched estates and parties (*HV* 82–5).

Indeed, within the vast majority of his writings, Schmitt displays far more admiration for early-modern absolutism than for medieval feudalism. The practice of "identity" representation that he recommends in *Parlamentarismus* is effectively much closer to a Hobbesian/Rousseauian "substitution" for, or "absorption" of, the ruled by the ruler than a re-presentation of them by it in either the medieval metaphysical or democratic interest-aggregating sense.[52] Any gestures by Schmitt toward a corporatist notion of politics that draws on the kind of representation for which Schmitt professes admiration in *Political Form* are clearly attempts to appropriate the neofeudal trappings of his times in the service of his neoabsolutist, executive-centered agenda. Even before the formulation of his famous "concrete orders" theory under National Socialism, Schmitt had mused over the possibility of an institutional body that could represent various concrete social associations of Weimar society, such as industrial, agricultural, professional, and vocational groups.[53] However, particularist social groups and associations, or what he would later call "indirect powers," were always conceived as more of a problem than anything else in Schmitt's *Staatslehre*, as we will see definitively in Chapter 6.

The shift from a theory of representation in which political "essence" is embodied personally in king, aristocrat, pope, clergy, and parliament, and in which power is contested and often balanced among them, to a theory in which democratic "essence" and identity are embodied personally in a single, unchallenged sovereign is perhaps a historico-theoretically bogus shift for Schmitt to make. But it is one not necessarily unafforded by the sociostructural transformation of his historical moment. The final supercession of the medieval concept of representation was completed in 1933, when Schmitt would speak of democratic identity in the following terms: The *Führer*

52   On Hobbesian-absolutist representation as "substitution," see Manin, "The Metamorphoses of Representative Government," pp. 142–3; on such representation as "absorption," see Ulrich K. Preuß, "Problems of a Concept of European Citizenship," *European Law Journal* 1:3 (November 1995): 277.

53   See *V*, 170–4, as well as "Freiheitsrechte und institutionelle Garantien der Reichsverfassung" (1931), in *Verfassungsrechtliche Aufsätze aus den Jahren 1924–1954: Materialien zu einer Verfassungslehre* (Berlin: Duncker & Humblot, 1958). On "concrete orders thinking," see *Ueber der drei Arten des Rechtswissenschaftlichen Denkens* (Hamburg: Hanseatische Verlagsanstalt, 1934).

is a concept of the immediate present and actual presence. For this reason it entails also as a positive stipulation, an unconditional identity between the leader and the led. Both the continual and inviolable contact between leader and led and the mutual trust lie in identity. Only identity prevents the Führer's power from being tyrannical or capricious.[54]

The Structural Transformation of Representation

To sum up the comparison of *Political Form* and *Parlamentarismus,* when Schmitt resorts to terms like "apparatus," "empty form," "positivistic," "tactical," "technical" to describe parliamentary government, in *Parlamentarismus,* we know from *Political Form* that he is contrasting these with the terms he there ascribes to medieval representative forms, such as "essential," "vital," "true," "higher," "substantial," and, most important, "human." The three principles of parliamentary government have been rendered bankrupt by the influence of the villain of *Political Form,* technological-economic thought. According to Schmitt, technical concerns have either only recently turned discussion into a mere formal exercise that has no chance of reaching truth, or they had infected the principle from the start, rendering it inherently corrupt. The compulsion for the technical has trapped the principle of division of powers into a *reductio ad absurdum,* in which political institutions are compelled to divide continually and perpetually, like malignantly mutating cells. Publicity has become the very coercive technique it was designed to combat. In all three cases, any normative or ethical concerns that might have been set as goals have been suffocated by the insidious and ever-expanding power of technological and economic thought. Any remnants of the medieval form of representation that parliament may have desired to retain, either the "personal" or the "public" aspects of representation, have been supplanted by private or economic aspects that neither "embody" the nation nor "display" the nation unto itself in a meaningful sense.

Because Enlightenment thought is depicted as so thoroughly corrupt in *Political Form,* greater weight should be given to the argument in *Parlamentarismus,* as Schmitt's more deeply sustained opinion, that the modern parliamentary system, inasmuch as it is a product of modern thought, is also vile to its very core. That the strongest of Schmitt's "reformist" remarks appear only in a portion of the work that was added later, and that responds to a

---

54 Schmitt, *Staat, Bewegung, Volk: Die Dreiliederung der politischen Einheit* (Hamburg: Hanseatische Verlagsanstalt, 1934), p. 42.

review charging that Schmitt favored a dictatorship, further bears this out. I suggest that once Schmitt was confronted with an articulate response to the extremist implications of his critique, he, to some extent, simply backed off from his original assertions.[55] Certainly, after the economic and political stabilization of Weimar in 1924, Schmitt may simply have become more optimistic about the prospects of parliamentary government in Germany, and this might be reflected in the 1926 preface. But Schmitt himself makes no reference to any change in historical conditions in the 1926 edition that would have persuaded him to change his mind or temper his tone. On the contrary, he seems singularly occupied with Thoma's assertions.

More to the point, however, the contrast between medieval Catholic representation and liberal parliamentary representation proves to be something of a false opposition. The technocratic deficiencies that he accentuates in the latter actually produce sociopolitical results reminiscent of the kind of "publicity of display" that is characteristic of the former. It is the appropriation of the multiplicitous "feudal" aspects of the mass-party welfare state and the unification and centralization of them under the banner of nationally legitimated executive authority that become Schmitt's goal. The personally displayed quality of medieval representation embedded in the naturalized authority of ecclesiastical, manorial, civic, and courtly institutions dispersed among prenational provinces is something qualitatively different from the re-presentation that must be technologically reproduced within a unitary presidential regime that manufactures a nation ready for confrontation with other similarly constructed nations.[56]

Schmitt, therefore, ought not to be understood as an ordinary conservative. He is not fundamentally backward-looking in his orientation, despite his vast knowledge and deft manipulation of history. He is, rather, driven principally by the political present and is in fact an avowed historicist.[57] But his authoritarian strategy should attune the contemporary reader to the fact that regressive movements that would only bring about new and worse forms of oppression will cloak themselves in the less offensive garb of "tradi-

55   Therefore, Paul Gottfried's suggestion that Schmitt "was entirely open about discussing the defects of [Weimar] parliamentary government and about why he thought it was doomed" is somewhat misleading; see his *Carl Schmitt: Politics and Theory* (Westport: Greenwood, 1990), p. 58.

56   See Benedict Anderson, *Imagined Communities: Reflections on the Origins and Spread of Nationalism* (London: Verso, 1983); and Eric J. Hobsbawm, *Nations and Nationalism since 1780: Programme, Myth, Reality* (Cambridge: Cambridge University Press, 1995).

57   Schmitt was apparently fond of saying, "An historical truth is true only once"; see George Schwab, *The Challenge of the Exception: An Introduction to the Political Ideas of Carl Schmitt between 1921 and 1936* (Westport: Greenwood, 1989), p. 27.

tional conservatism." Although it has served the legitimation schemes of both liberalism and fascism to cast modern authoritarianism as remnants of a premodern past – respectively as backwardness or tradition – Schmitt's mode of operation demonstrates the inherently modern character of such phenomena. Liberals may defend the Enlightenment by portraying its critics as nostalgic seekers of aristocratic virtues and religioethical homogeneity,[58] and antiliberals may seek transhistorical legitimacy in precisely such values, but both misrecognize the historico-structural specificity of fascism and modern authoritarianism by focusing on its trappings and not its sources.[59]

As we will see in the next chapter, on Schmitt's legal theory, Schmitt again does not endorse the wholesale revival of premodern forms of domination to replace the liberal rule of law. On the contrary, it is the historical situation of the rule of law under the mass-party welfare state as described earlier that provides the starting point for Schmitt's fascist agenda. Just as the medieval notion of representation serves as the ideological red herring in his critique of parliamentary representation, the nineteenth-century abstract, formal rule of law becomes the strategic note to be played and played again. We have seen Schmitt criticize parliamentarism for failing to live up to an older type of representation that it in fact imitates in certain aspects, aspects that Schmitt can then manipulate into a fascist attempt to undermine parliament. In the next chapter, we will see Schmitt continually rail against an abstract rule of law that he himself admits at various junctures no longer obtains in practice in the twenties. However, his critique serves to reorient into an authoritarian constitutional alternative the factual jurisprudential reality to which twentieth-century liberalism corresponds.

58 See Holmes, *The Anatomy of Antiliberalism.*
59 On this important question, see Geoff Eley, "What Produces Fascism: Preindustrial Traditions or a Crisis of Capitalism?" *Politics and Society* 12:1 (1983). See also Eley, ed., *Society, Culture, and the State in Germany, 1870–1930* (Ann Arbor: University of Michigan Press, 1996).

5

LAW

According to Schmitt, the institution of parliament and the theory of representation are not the only facets of liberalism to have become ill affected by
the technical. Modern jurisprudence – liberalism's theory of law, especially
as expressed in legal positivism – has also degenerated into what he calls
mere technicism. If substantive representation is the foil with which Schmitt
negatively contrasts parliamentary representation, in *Political Form* and *Parlamentarismus,* then, as suggested in my earlier analysis of emergency
powers, Schmitt's appropriation and reconstruction of the early-modern
concept of sovereignty is the standard by which he criticizes liberal jurisprudence most forcefully in *Political Theology*[1] and his subsequent Weimar constitutional writings.[2]

In the first sections of this chapter, I discuss how Schmitt's critique of
positivist jurisprudence arises out of a particular interpretation of Max We-

---

1 Schmitt, *Political Theology: Four Chapters on the Concept of Sovereignty* (1922), trans. George
  Schwab (Cambridge, Mass.: MIT Press, 1985); English renderings are from this edition,
  which will be cited as *PT.* Any German references are to *Politische Theologie: Vier Kapitel zur
  Lehre von der Souveränität* (Munich: Duncker & Humblot, 1934), the second edition of the
  work, and the one on which the English translation is based.
2 Of these I will specifically deal with *Verfassungslehre* ([1928] Berlin: Duncker & Humblot,
  1989), hereafter *V; Der Hüter der Verfassung* (Tübingen: J. C. B. Mohr [Paul Siebeck], 1931),
  hereafter *HV;* and *Legalität und Legitimität* (Munich: Duncker & Humblot, 1932), hereafter
  LL, from the reprint in *Verfassungsrechtliche Aufsätze aus den Jahren 1924–1954: Materialien zu
  einer Verfassungslehre* (Berlin: Duncker & Humblot, 1958).

ber's sociology of law and comes to focus on the legal theory of Hans Kelsen. According to Schmitt, liberal legal theory avoids the reality of jurisprudence by denying the existence of "gaps" within the law and consequently demotes judges to the status of mere vending machines that mechanically dispense the law, without intellectual reflection or active contribution. It also leaves the legal theorist inadequately equipped to analyze law at the level of application. On the constitutional level, this theoretical shortcoming on the part of liberal jurisprudence manifests itself in the avoidance of the phenomenon of "the exception" – as explained in Chapter 3, the political circumstance that cannot be foreseen in extant constitutional provisions. Just as judges must exercise prudence in adjudicating "gaps," a "sovereign" – a mutually identified people and executive – must be allowed the prudence to "decide" on the exception. After evaluating such assertions, in the later sections of the chapter, I examine and critically assess Schmitt's own Weimar attempt to formulate a more "substantive" notion of jurisprudential practice and constitutional democracy than that of the Kelsenian liberalism he criticizes. More specifically than I could in the chapter on emergency powers, I will attempt to confront the Schmittian constitutional democracy that he offers as an alternative to the so-called empty, mechanical formalism of the liberal variety. I will ask whether Schmitt assails the abstractness of positivist jurisprudence because it allows concrete political reality to elude theoretical analysis or because it acts as a normative obstruction to his designs for a new form of concrete domination adequate to the twentieth-century state/ society relationship.

Formalism, Personalism, and the Sociology of Law

Although Austrian jurist Hans Kelsen is Schmitt's frequently named or unnamed interlocutor on constitutional matters during Weimar, Schmitt's confrontation with legal positivism as technology is not initially motivated by Kelsen's work. Rather Schmitt's critique of formalist jurisprudence is generated by his engagement with Max Weber's sociology of law as it is eventually published in Weber's massive *Economy and Society*.[3] Of the work, Schmitt wrote, "the enormous sociological material for the conceptual development of jurisprudence in Max Weber's *magnum opus posthumum* has still to be tested"; of the man himself, Schmitt later remarked, he was "an historian engaged in political theology," because of his analysis of the phe-

---

3 Weber, *Economy and Society: An Outline of Interpretive Sociology* (1920), ed. Guenther Roth and Claus Wittich, 2 vols. (Berkeley: University of California Press, 1978); hereafter *ES*.

nomenon of charisma.[4] It is only fitting then that Schmitt himself attempts to "test" the implications of Weber's sociology of law in a work, entitled *Political Theology*, originally dedicated to the great social scientist.[5]

Weber described the increasing "systematization" of law that characterizes modernity as

> an integration of all analytically derived legal propositions in such a way that they constitute a logically clear, internally consistent, and, at least in theory, gapless system of rules, under which, it is implied, all conceivable fact situations must be capable of being logically subsumed lest their order lack an effective guaranty. (*ES*, 656)

This "juridical formalism" that necessarily subsumes all concrete facticity under abstract rules "enables the legal system to operate like a technically rational machine" (*ES*, 811). According to Weber, at least at first blush, this mechanization of law will continue to expand progressively into the indefinite future (*ES*, 895).

Weber distinguishes two kinds of formalism in his study of law: The first is substantively rational formalism in which the "decision of legal problems is influenced by norms different from those obtained through logical generalization of abstract interpretation of meaning," norms that are expressed in "the utterance of certain words, the execution of a signature, or the performance of a certain symbolic act" (*ES*, 657). In other words, the *act* of the official or the jurist contributes to the meaning of the law; the concrete activity – verbal or physical – of some ritual to some extent embodies a substantial meaning and imparts it to law. The second type is logically rational formalism in which "the legally relevant characteristics of the facts are disclosed through the logical analysis of meaning and where, accordingly, definitely fixed legal concepts in the form of highly abstract rules are formulated and applied" (*ES*, 657). In terms of ideal types, the former clearly corresponds with a premodern notion of the law and the latter with what Weber describes as the contemporary "systematization" of the law. Validity in the first type is enmeshed with substantive, doxic, religiocultural norms that a judge is to actively uphold in legal practice, whereas validity for the second type is derived logically from abstract forms. Weber then describes the two valences of modern validity that pertain to the second type of formalism, rational formalism, in terms that are necessarily devoid of

4   G. L. Ulmen, *Politische Mehrwert: Eine Studie über Max Weber und Carl Schmitt* (Weinheim: VCH Acta humaniora, 1991), pp. 178, 20–1.
5   See Schwab, introduction to *PT*, p. xv, n. 11.

"content": (1) Legal validity in the textual sense is the normative meaning attributed to a verbal pattern that has the form of a legal proposition with correct logic; (2) empirical validity is based on the probability that people will obey the law (*ES*, 311). Neither definition makes any judgments as to the relative ethical substance of the law because the sociological point of view requires only the perspective of "legal technology" (*ES*, 717). One claims that law is valid because it is semantically logical, the other because it is obeyed.[6]

In *Political Theology*, Schmitt's target is precisely this latter legal state of affairs described by Weber, one that is strictly "oriented toward calculability and governed by the ideal of frictionless functioning," or "utility" and "technicity" (*PT*, 28). Schmitt argues that every emphasis or concern with "form" as such in terms of jurisprudence is not particularly unhealthy (contents need forms to be realized). But the peculiar situation of modernity that encourages what he calls in *Political Form* "the antithesis of empty form and formless matter" results in a jurisprudence that has ultimately become form for form's sake.

As the distinction between technological rationality and the juristic, representational rationality of Catholicism in *Political Form* rests on the question of personal embodiment, so, too, does the opposition between positivist jurisprudence and what he calls "decisionism" (as well as his theories of sovereignty and democracy, as we will see). According to Schmitt's conception, only a person, not a system, as in the formalist scheme of jurisprudence whose "interest is essentially material and impersonal" (*PT*, 35), can decide how to enforce or realize the law. Purely formal jurisprudence endangers the "personality" of judges, their ability to engage in the concrete particularity of a given case by confining them to the mechanical application of a pregiven statute. For Schmitt, between the law and concrete reality, there will always be a gap that must be mediated by a judge.

Weber describes an attitude very close to that of Schmitt regarding the

---

6   On the implications of Weber's sociology of law for legal and political theory, see Johannes Winckelmann, *Legitimität und Legalität im Max Webers Herrschaftssoziologie* (Tübingen: J. C. B. Mohr [Paul Siebeck], 1952). The legacy of analyzing law exclusively in terms of social expediency is carried on in the German postwar context most notably by Niklas Luhmann; see *A Sociological Theory of Law* (London: Routledge & Kegan Paul, 1985). On the successive theoretical rebellions in Germany and the United States against formalist jurisprudence, see Christian Joerges, "On the Context of German-American Debates over Sociological Jurisprudence and Legal Criticism: A History of Transatlantic Misunderstandings and Missed Opportunities," in *European Yearbook in the Sociology of Law*, ed. A. Febbrajo and D. Nelken (Brussels: Giuffrè, 1993).

depersonalization of judging under modern, formally rationalist jurisprudence:

> The idea of a "law without gaps" is, of course, under vigorous attack. The conception of the modern judge as an automaton into which legal documents and fees are stuffed at the top in order that it may spill forth the verdict at the bottom along with the reasons, read mechanically from codified paragraphs – this conception is angrily rejected, perhaps because a certain approximation of this type would precisely be implied by a consistent bureaucratization of justice. (*ES*, 979)[7]

But Weber is ambivalent about the empirical reality of this conception of judging. In his renowned "Parliament and Government" essay, for instance, he presents that description as a factual state of affairs (*ES*, 1395). Elsewhere, however, he questions whether this subsumptive mode of adjudication obtains in reality:

> [T]he judge is doing more than merely placing his seal upon norms which would already have been binding by consensual understanding and agreement. His decision in individual cases always produces consequences which, acting beyond the scope of the case, influence the selection of those rules which are to survive as law. . . . [T]he sources of "judicial" decision are not at first constituted by general "norms of decision" that would simply be "applied" to concrete cases, except where the decision relates to certain formal questions preliminary to the decision of the case itself. The situation is the very opposite: in so far as the judge allows the coercive guaranty to enter in a particular case for ever so concrete reasons, he *creates*, at least under certain circumstances, the empirical validity of a general norm as "law," simply because his maxim acquires significance beyond the particular case. (*ES*, 758, emphasis added)

Yet Weber notes that judges themselves, in their own "subjective beliefs," refuse to see themselves as "creators" of the law, and in fact understand themselves only as "mouthpieces" for already-existing law (*ES*, 894). But in reality this "creation" of law becomes more prevalent under the conditions of an expanding welfare state in the early twentieth century (*ES*, 882–9). In the service of wide-scale state intervention into particular spheres of society, more discretion becomes exercised by bureaucratic administrators and judi-

---

7   The particular "attack" on, or "rejection" of, this position Weber is referring to is that of Hermann Kantorowicz (a. k. a., Gnaeus Flavius), *Der Kampf um die Rechtswissenschaft* (Heidelberg: Carl Winter, 1906).

cial officers in implementing broadly defined social policy.[8] The contradiction in the *ideology* of abstract formalism versus the *reality* of increased concrete specification becomes central to Schmitt's Weimar jurisprudence, as we will see. Why Schmitt feels compelled to plead a seemingly desperate case against the automatic adjudication of gapless law and the tyranny of the separation of powers at the very moment that they were being eclipsed by sociopolitical reality will be a crucial question.

In his earliest work on the law, Schmitt, in accord with the methodological mode of procedure I laid out in Part One, attempted to mediate between the Weberian categories of the judge as creator ex nihilo of the law, on the one hand, and as mere automaton, on the other. In much the same way that he attempts to show in *Political Form* that the Catholic conception of offices falls between Weber's classifications of functionality and charisma, in *Gesetz und Urteil* (*Law and Judgment*), of 1912, he attempts to show that "the judge is neither a legislator nor the mouthpiece of the law."[9] Weber declares that a pure fact-oriented, case-to-case, judge-as-law-creator mode of jurisprudence could never be rational (*ES*, 787), and in his early work Schmitt attempts to mediate between the irrational position of sheer judicial prerogative and the hyperrational position of legal formalism.

In a move reminiscent of many kinds of neo-Kantian reappraisals of the deficiencies inherent in the sharp subjective/objective distinction inherited from Kantian rationality, Schmitt adopts a reformed-subjectivist stance in his early work.[10] According to Schmitt, whatever a community of judges in a particular culture could be expected to agree on in a specific case ought to

8 An analysis of this problematic of "deformalized" welfare-state law that draws on Weber, Schmitt, and, most extensively, Franz Neumann and Otto Kirchheimer, is William E. Scheuerman, *Between the Norm and the Exception: The Frankfurt School and the Rule of Law* (Cambridge, Mass.: MIT Press, 1994). Despite his polemics against formalized law, even Roberto Unger recognizes the potential problems posed to democratic principles by arbitrarily *de*formalized law; see *Law in Modern Society* (New York: Free Press, 1976), pp. 193–200. On the problematic of the rule of law in the welfare state in the American context more specifically, see Cass R. Sunstein, *After the Rights Revolution: Reconceiving the Regulatory State* (Cambridge, Mass.: Harvard University Press, 1990).

9 Schmitt, *Gesetz und Urteil: Eine Untersuchung zum Problem der Rechtspraxis* ([1912] Munich: C. H. Beck, 1969), p. 86. Ulmen discusses the impact of Weber's thought on *Gesetz und Urteil* and on Schmitt's *Habilitationschrift* of 1914, *Der Wert des Staates und die Bedeutung des Einzelnen* (Tübingen: J. C. B. Mohr [Paul Siebeck]), in *Politische Mehrwert*, pp. 108–10.

10 See Thomas Willey, *Back to Kant: The Revival of Kantianism in German Social and Historical Thought, 1860–1914* (Detroit: Wayne State University Press, 1978). Peter C. Caldwell shows how Schmitt in fact began his scholarly career with legal positions almost identical to Kelsen's; see *Popular Sovereignty and the Crisis of German Constitutional Law: The Theory and Practice of Weimar Constitutionalism* (Durham, N. C.: Duke University Press, 1997).

be adopted as a guideline for a judge's particular opinion.[11] Hence, a jurisprudential objectivity, if only consensually constructed, is established that maintains standards of legal determinacy that are not "automatic" and yet do not lapse into individually subjective, irrational arbitrariness. Despite the conservatively elitist character of this solution that preserves the law as the exclusive realm of jurists, a character that certainly must have appealed to Schmitt, he abandons it as he sheds his neo-Kantian skin. Although he would not abandon his devotion to the mission of jurists and jurisprudence throughout his subsequent careers, Weimar and National Socialist, Schmitt grows impatient with the categorical impasses of Kantianism and the still-latent potential within it for either mechanical formalism or un-acknowledged decisionism. He is ultimately unable or unwilling to negoti-ate a neo-Kantian or reformed-positivist middle way and turns to a celebra-tion rather than a genuine theorization of the "gaps" in the law by which the judge potentially becomes lawgiver.[12] In Schmitt's mind, as opposed to neo-Kantian orientations toward the law, his is a jurisprudence that comes to profess its decisionism in good conscience.

In *Political Theology*, the stakes become much higher, as Schmitt trans-poses this logic from the microjuridical level of statutes, judges, cases, ver-dicts, and gaps to the macropolitical one of constitutions, sovereigns, emergencies, decisions, and exceptions. What is immediately clear, accord-ing to Schmitt's account, is that the rationalist jurisprudes like Kelsen, com-pletely in line with Weber's analysis, refuse to acknowledge anything but formally normative imperatives in adjudication and consequently suppress the factual realities that highlight gaps in the law and demote judges ideo-logically to the status of mere automatons. Schmitt argues that Kelsen re-presses the irrationality of reality, but we will have to see whether Schmitt himself only exalts it.

Without naming him in *Der Hüter der Verfassung*, Schmitt derides Kelsen by referring to the "Austrian solution" to the role of the judiciary in a constitutional crisis (*HV,* 6) and also to those whose jurisprudence would

---

11   Schmitt, *Gesetz und Urteil,* pp. 71–9.
12   There is evidence of German jurists before Schmitt aestheticizing legal "gaps" in explicitly Nietzschean fashion; see Otto Behrends, "Von der Freirechtsschule zum konkreten Ordnungsdenken," in *Recht und Justiz im "Dritten Reich,"* ed. R. Dreier and W. Sellert (Frankfurt a. M.: Suhrkamp, 1989). See also Ingeborg Maus's contribution to this volume, "'Gesetzesbindung' der Justiz und die Struktur der nationalsozialistischen Rechtsnor-men," for a more differentiated account of the "judge as automaton" paradigm; see also Regina Ogorek, *Richterkönig oder Subsumtionsautomat? Zur Justiztheorie im 19. Jahrhundert* (Frankfurt a. M.: Klostermann, 1986).

make a "caricature" or an "anti-constitution" of the Weimar document (*HV*, 116). In the preface to the second edition of *Political Theology*, published in 1934 after he had joined the National Socialists, Schmitt remarks on the technocratic consequences of Kelsen's legal positivism: "[It] makes of law a mere mode of operation of a state bureaucracy" (*PT*, 3). Proceeding imma- nently to Schmitt's work, we will inquire whether Schmitt does not unwit- tingly describe himself in these statements, that is, whether his own jurispru- dence promotes only an authoritarian statism in place of Kelsen's liberal statism. We will observe that Schmitt criticizes positivists for accelerating arbitrary state activity at the hands of the bureaucracy, by avoiding, in the psychological sense, its empirical reality. But Schmitt himself would acceler- ate such arbitrary bureaucratic discretion by seizing hold of it and employ- ing it in activity that maintains and inflates the power of the state rather than intervention that depletes its "power reserve."

Positivism, Decisionism, and Sovereignty

Just as Schmitt argues in his early treatises on law that a judge must mediate the gaps between the law and a particular case (gaps whose existence legal formalism denies) with a personal decision, he argues in *Political Theology* that a sovereign must address the political exception – the situation for which the constitution does not provide explicit direction – with a personal decision as well. The infamous first line of the work discussed earlier points up both the decisionism and the personalism of Schmitt's conception of sovereignty, particularly with respect to the exception: "Sovereign is he who decides on the exception" (*PT*, 5). What is important for my purposes is the way the statement confronts Schmitt's legal-positivist contemporaries.[13]

According to Schmitt, the formalist, neo-Kantian, constitutional jurists who rose to prominence during and after the First World War sought pre- cisely to replace the personalist theory of sovereignty with "abstractly valid"

13 For an excellent account of the legal/methodological controversies of the period, see Helge Wendenburg, *Die Debatte um die Vefassungsgerichtsbarkeit und der Methodenstreit der Staatsrechtslehre in der Weimarer Republik* (Göttingen: Otto Schwartz, 1984). Peter C. Cald- well, David Dyzenhaus, and Ellen Kennedy have full-length studies under way that exam- ine Schmitt specifically in the context of other Weimar jurists, such as Kelsen, Hermann Heller, Richard Thoma, and Rudolph Smend. On Schmitt and Heller, see Paul Book- binder, "Hermann Heller vs. Carl Schmitt," *International Social Science Review* 62 (1987); as well as Scheuerman, *Between the Norm and the Exception*, for an account of Schmitt's intellec- tual relationship to "Frankfurt School" legal theorists, Neumann and Kirchheimer. There is great anticipation for the sourcebook edited by Arthur J. Jacobson and Bernhard Schlink, *Weimar: A Jurisprudence of Crisis* (Berkeley: University of California Press, 1998).

principles.[14] Kelsen, for instance, claims that "the concept of sovereignty must be radically repressed."[15] Impatient with the inherent subjectivity of the personal, decisionistic method of constitutional jurisprudence, and distrustful of the potential abuses to which sovereigns might tend in adjudicating or suspending the law, such distinguished jurists as Hugo Krabbe, Hugo Preuß, and particularly Kelsen, "agree[d] that all personal elements be eliminated from the concept of the state" (*PT,* 29). Because they associated personalism with the European monarchies of the previous centuries, norms, as expressed in the law, not the faulty or biased judgments of individual persons, were to be the focus of jurisprudence:

> According to Kelsen, the conception of the personal right to command is the intrinsic error in the theory of state sovereignty; because the theory is premised on the subjectivism of command rather than on the objectively valid norm, he characterized the theory of the primacy of the state's legal order as "subjectivistic" and as a negation of the legal idea. (*PT,* 29)

Schmitt of course scoffs at such "objectivity," as he does at the objectivity of economic and technological thought, in *Political Form,* or the search for truth by way of discussion, in *Parlamentarismus:* "The objectivity that [Kelsen] claimed for himself amounted to no more than avoiding everything personalistic and tracing the legal order back to the impersonal validity of an impersonal norm" (*PT,* 29). Free-floating norms or values are made no more real by severing them from their human expressions but, on the contrary, are left unattainable in Kelsen's scheme. Decisionism, according to Schmitt, had less to do with any complicity with the monarchy than with the simple legal reality that norms need to be expressed or enforced in order to be realized. The positivists, on their part,

> fail to recognize that the conception of personality and its connection with formal authority arose from a specific juristic interest, namely, an especially

---

14   On the subject of legal positivism in Weimar, see Peter C. Caldwell, "Legal Positivism and Weimar Democracy," *American Journal of Jurisprudence* 39:1 (spring 1995); and in the German context generally, see Dieter Grimm, "Methode als Machtfaktor," in *Recht und Staat der bürgerlichen Gesellschaft* (Frankfurt a. M.: Suhrkamp, 1987); and Ernst-Wolfgang Böckenförde, *Gesetz und gesetzgebende Gewalt: Von den Anfängen der deutschen Staatsrechtslehre bis zur Höhe des staatsrechtlichen Positivismus* (Berlin: Duncker & Humblot, 1981). On Kelsen's neo-Kantianism in particular, see Stanley L. Paulson, "The Neo-Kantian Dimension of Kelsen's Pure Theory of Law," *Oxford Journal of Legal Studies* 12 (1992).

15   Kelsen, *Das Problem der Souveränität und die Theorie des Völkerrechts: Beiträge zu einer Reinen Rechtslehre* ([1920] Aalen: Scientia, 1981), p. 120.

clear awareness of what the essence of the legal decision entails. Such a decision in the broadest sense belongs to every legal perception. Every legal
thought brings a legal idea, which in its purity can never become reality, into
another aggregate condition and adds an element that cannot be derived
either from the content of the legal idea or from the content of a general
positive legal norm that is to be applied. (*PT,* 30)

For Schmitt, Kelsen disregards the problem of the very "realization of that
law" (*PT,* 21) and refuses to see that, as Weber pointed out, judges must
contribute a part of themselves into every decision in order to adjudicate.
Thus Schmitt's critique of legal positivism is both descriptive and –
ironically, given his aversion to normativism – normative: The positivists,
according to Schmitt, do not recognize the factual reality of the *actual*
activity of judges *and* do not realize that this is precisely what judges *ought* to
be doing in a jurisprudential sense when adjudicating.

The legal positivists further demonstrate their flight from the personal
with their insistence on separating politics or sociology from jurisprudence.
According to Schmitt, Kelsen seeks to preserve the "purity" of the norms to
be expressed in the law by renouncing any interest in sociological or political reality (*PT,* 15, 21).[16] In Kelsen's scheme, "the highest competence
cannot be traceable to a person or to a socio-psychological power complex
but only to the sovereign order in the unity of the system of norms. For
juristic consideration there are neither real nor fictitious persons, only
points of ascription" (*PT,* 19). Because of this, in *Verfassungslehre* five years
later, Schmitt accuses Kelsenian legal positivism of constructing "the empty
shell of liberalism," by "compressing all expressions of the life of the state
into a series of prescriptions, and transferring all state activity into actions
performed within precisely articulated and in principle limited spheres of
competence" (*V,* 41). Echoing Weber's description of legal formalism,
Schmitt recounts the fantasy of the nature of the constitution in the positivists' scheme: "It is pretended first, that the constitution is nothing but a
system of legal norms and prescriptions; second that this system is a closed
one; and third, that it is 'sovereign' – i. e., that it can never be interfered
with, or indeed even influenced, for any reasons or necessities of political

16 See Kelsen, *Der soziologische und der juristische Staatsbegriff: Kritische Untersuchung des Ver-*
    hältnisses von Staat und Recht ([1922] Aalen: Scientia, 1981), and *Grenzen zwischen juris-*
    tischer und soziologischer Methode (Tübingen: J. C. B. Mohr [Paul Siebeck], 1911). See also
    Stanley L. Paulson, "Kelsen's Legal Theory: The Final Round," *Oxford Journal of Legal*
    Studies 12 (1992).

existence" (*V,* 131).[17] We will see that Schmitt argues that a constitution must be more than a collection of multitiered forms; that it must be open to external expressions of concrete reality, such as the exception; and that the piece of paper or the collection of norms that *is* the written constitution is not itself truly "sovereign" but must, on the contrary, allow for its own suspension when "the necessities of political existence" call for the stepping forth of the person who – ambiguously – either is or represents the popular sovereign.

Yet, by Kelsen's own account, his conception of "norm" *is* purely formal, composed of "nodal points" rather than human decision makers:

> A norm is valid qua legal norm only because it was arrived at in a certain way – created according to a certain rule, issued or set according to a specific method. The law is only valid as positive law, that is, only a law that has been issued or set. In this necessary requirement of being issued or set, and in what it assures us, namely, that the validity of the law will be independent of morality and comparable systems of norms – therein lies the positivity of laws.[18]

The norm is traced back through the constitutional system to a basic norm or "basic rule," which itself is based on "the will" of a constitutional majority, the only moment of human contact in the system.[19] Hence, the "norms" for which Kelsen's jurisprudence is named are founded insincerely, according to Schmitt. Kelsen's system seeks to be impersonal but grounds itself on a personal moment of will, whose memory it subsequently represses through its procedural apparatus. Because the moment of popular will is mediated quantitatively through majoritarianism, it grasps only the mathematical immediacy of a people and is hence insubstantial. These norms lack substance; they are "mechanical" in the sense that their contents shift in accord with a corresponding change in the results of parliamentary elections, and as such function as part of what Schmitt deems a "mathematical mythology" (*PT,* 20, translation amended). Although it feigns indifference to such political or social matters as elections, legal positivism, through the famous separa-

---

17 As Judith Shklar explains, "The idea of treating law as a self-contained system of norms that is 'there,' identifiable without any reference to the content, aim, and development of the rules that compose it, is the very essence of formalism. . . . It consists . . . of treating law as an isolated block of concepts that have no relevant characteristics or functions apart from their possible validity or invalidity within a hypothetical system." *Legalism: Law, Morals and Political Trials* (Cambridge, Mass.: Harvard University Press, 1964), pp. 33–4.
18 Kelsen, *Introduction to the Problems of Legal Theory,* trans. B. L. Paulson and S. L. Paulson (Oxford: Oxford University Press, 1992), p. 56.
19 Ibid. On this issue, see Joseph Raz, "The Purity of the Pure Theory," in *Essays on Kelsen,* ed. R. Tur and W. Twining (Oxford: Oxford University Press, 1986).

tion of law and morality, is willing to accept that whatever is legislated on the basis of these elections *is* necessarily correct, that is, right.[20] Legal positivism is famous for seeming to be indifferent to *what* the law says as opposed to the fact that it says it. Consequently, it is often backed into the corner of admitting that were a law passed through the proper legislative channels that called for the most heinous of actions, that law would by definition be valid. Kelsen admits that the majority principle is vaguely "mechanical"[21] but insists that it is a better political manifestation of democracy than the quasi-metaphysical, semireligious, and inherently dangerous substantive model that Schmitt would endorse.[22]

By defining validity solely in terms of quantitative majorities, however, Kelsen leaves himself and his theory open to charges of moral substancelessness – from the Left as well as the Right. As Habermas observes, what is called "normativist" is actually empty of norms in any meaningful sense: "The assumption . . . which sprang up with legal positivism and . . . social-scientific functionalism [was] that normative validity claims could be withdrawn, without any noteworthy consequences for the stability of the legal system."[23] But for Schmitt, the consequences for the legal system are devastatingly "noteworthy," not only morally but practically. In fact in *Political Theology*, Schmitt is actually less concerned with the ethical *source* of legal positivism's laws as with the practical *application*, or rather nonapplication, of those laws.

Even if the norms reflected in a formalist scheme of jurisprudence were to have some ethical resonance, Schmitt demonstrates that the system would nevertheless rob these norms of their substance in the process of application. Through their indifference and even hostility to certain fundamental means of applying the law, jurists like Kelsen and Krabbe so radically subvert the relationship between the substance of a law and its practice that they render the values in question substantial in name only. Krabbe's statement, as quoted by Schmitt, that "the state reveals itself only in the making of law. . . . [It] does not manifest itself in applying laws" (*PT*, 23), begs the

---

20 This position is most forcefully put forth by Anglo-American legal positivism: see H. L. A. Hart, "Positivism and the Separation of Law and Morals" (1958), in *Essays in Jurisprudence and Philosophy* (Oxford: Oxford University Press, 1983).

21 Kelsen, *Vom Wesen und Wert der Demokratie* ([1920] Aalen: Scientia, 1981), p. 9.

22 Ibid., pp. 99–100. Later Kelsen would turn the tables on Schmitt, suggesting that it is *his* jurisprudence that, in delivering law over to the whims of executive authority, is in fact "mechanical"; see "Wer soll der Hüter der Verfassung sein?" *Die Justiz* 6 (1930/31): 591–2.

23 Habermas, *The Theory of Communicative Action. Vol. 1: Reason and the Rationalization of Society*, trans. Thomas McCarthy (Boston: Beacon Press, 1984), p. 269.

question of how the norms these laws are supposed to reflect become realized. The values are not infused into society or politics but remain embedded, in Kelsen's phrase, "wholly in the formalism of law."[24] But as Schmitt would declare most bluntly a decade later, in *Legalität und Legitimität,* "no norm, neither higher nor lower, interprets and administers, protects nor defends itself; no normative validity makes itself valid; and there is also . . . no hierarchy of norms but rather only a hierarchy of men and instances" (*LL,* 311). This betrays his nostalgia for the concrete domination of persons over persons that is characteristic of traditional politics and part and parcel of his developing neoauthoritarianism, as much as it conveys his concern for jurisprudential praxis. I will return to this crucial issue later.

As a consequence of its excessive formalism, then, legal positivism can be judged equally guilty of the charge of "empty form" that we have already witnessed Schmitt level against technological and economic thought. In fact, these supposed shortcomings, like those identified with parliamentarism, are a result of the infiltration of the law with precisely these technically rational influences, as opposed to substantively rational ones.[25] And although Schmitt is quick to emphasize the positivist, valueless quality of a normativist jurisprudence invaded by the technical, he is simultaneously careful to distance his own decisionism from any link with positivism. Recall the two kinds of legal formalism that Weber describes in *Economy and Society.* Once removed from the realm of traditional religiocultural practices, the first mode of formal jurisprudence, which centers on the ritual act, such as a dance, a song, or affixing a seal, is just as empty of substance as the second mode of jurisprudence, which centers on formally abstract rules, because the former is no longer embedded in a particular cultural framework. Schmitt's "decision" is similarly unconstrained and is therefore potentially as "substanceless" as Kelsen's positivist formalism. In fact, Habermas asserts that Schmitt and Kelsen are opposite sides of the same coin and that ultimately their positions are mutually interchangeable: There is a concrete will

24 Quoted in Rupert Emerson, *State and Sovereignty in Modern Germany* (New Haven: Yale University Press, 1928), p. 170.
25 In a discussion of Weber's sociology of law, Habermas describes how what has been inextricably linked in Schmitt's thought to technology in earlier chapters, bureaucratization and excessive economic thinking – overly formalistic rationality – is identified as precisely the cause of the draining of morality from the law: "[T]he rationalization of law makes possible . . . both the institutionalization of purposive rational economic and administrative action and the detachment of subsystems of purposive rational action from their moral-practical foundations." *Theory of Communicative Action, vol. 1,* p. 243.

at the base of Kelsen's formalism and a purely formalistic tendency to Schmitt's emphasis on concrete will.[26]

Kelsen's oft-repeated claim that the sovereign will at the base of the constitutional order in his theory is only a hypothetical, epistemological, presupposition and not an ontological assertion of reality does as much to confirm Schmitt's charge of Kelsen's avoidance of, cum dependency on, a decisionistic element as it does to distance it from Schmitt's own legal philosophy of will.[27] Schmitt, for his part, at first takes note of the apparent affinities between a theory of decision and the technological-economic positivist theories he criticizes. Decisionism is in many obvious ways more *efficient* than the positivism he has charged as being overly concerned with efficiency, and it centers on an act – the decision – that Schmitt admits is in and of itself devoid of moral content, despite the supposed morality of what it may bring into being: "Every concrete juristic decision contains a moment of indifference from the perspective of content. . . . The certainty of the decision is, from the perspective of sociology, of particular interest in an age of intense commercial activity because in numerous cases commerce is less concerned with a particular content than with calculable certainty" (*PT,* 30). But as Schmitt goes on to write, despite such similarities, the legal decision stands quite apart from "commercial" indifference with "particular contents" and fixation on "calculable certainty," because of the way in which it makes principles "concrete":

> The legal interest in the decision as such should not be mixed up with this kind of calculability. It is rooted in the character of the normative and is derived from the necessity of judging a concrete fact concretely even though what is given as a standard for the judgment is only a legal principle in its general universality. Thus a transformation takes place every time. . . . [T]he legal idea cannot translate itself independently. (*PT,* 31)

We find Schmitt again searching for the means of mediating the form and content that is often artificially posited as separate in Enlightenment thought and that renders particularly difficult the task of jurisprudence. Indeed, Schmitt attributes Kelsen's inability to conceive of the proper rela-

---

26 See Habermas, "Dogmatism, Reason, and Decision: On Theory and Practice in Our Scientific Civilization," in *Theory and Practice,* trans. John Viertel (Boston: Beacon Press, 1973), pp. 253–82; and *Theory of Communicative Action, vol. 1,* p. 265. On the latent decisionism of legal positivism, see also Horst Dreier, *Rechtslehre, Staatssoziologie und Demokratietheorie bei Hans Kelsen* (Baden-Baden: Nomos, 1986), p. 196.

27 See Kelsen, *Das Problem der Souveränität,* pp. 8–9.

tionship of form and content to his infection with "natural-scientific" methodological influences, and ingenuously contrasts him with a Scholastic theory to which Schmitt himself, as we observed in the last chapter, no longer has theoretical recourse:

> [Kelsen] fails to see that the concept of substance in Scholastic thought is entirely different from that in mathematical and natural-scientific thinking. The distinction between the substance and the practice of law, which is of fundamental significance in the history of the concept of sovereignty, cannot be grasped with concepts rooted in the natural sciences and yet is an essential element of legal argumentation. (*PT*, 41–2)

The difference between the respective uses of the distinction in question, for Schmitt, lies in decisionism's ability to bring substance alive through the formal act of a decision rather than letting it lie stillborn in the letter of the law or the phraseology of the constitution. As he often states, forms or functions per se are not dangerous; they are necessary to make ideas realities.[28]

Schmitt faces a problem in jurisprudence similar to the one that, as we saw in Chapter 1, confronted Weber in sociology.[29] Weber was faced with the problem of drawing abstract observations from concrete facts so as to accurately "represent" reality. Weber's sociological method was a response to the question of how this is to be achieved without distortion or misinterpretation. Even in his earlier works, while he remained close to Weber and his methodology, Schmitt recognized in the decision the overcoming of this opposition between ideal and real in the law: "Between every abstraction and every concretion lies an unbridgeable gap. . . . [P]ositive law [must know] that law is concretized only in a judgment, not in a norm."[30]

28 In the sequel to *Political Theology*, published almost half a century later, Schmitt reemphasized the need for substances to be embodied in forms, only now adding the friend/enemy language of his late-Weimar "concept of the political" thesis and his National Socialist "concrete orders" doctrine: "A conflict is always a struggle between organizations and institutions in terms of concrete orders, a battle between 'competent authorities,' not between substances. Substances first need to find a form, they must organize themselves, in some way, before they can confront one another as agents capable of a battle; as *parties belligérantes*." *Politische Theologie II. Die Legende von der Erledigung jeder politischen Theologie* (Berlin: Duncker & Humblot, 1970), p. 106. Cf. Schmitt, *The Concept of the Political* (1932), trans. George Schwab (New Brunswick: Rutgers University Press, 1976); and *Ueber die drei Arten des rechtswissenschaftlichen Denkens* (Hamburg: Hanseatische Verlagsanstalt, 1934).
29 See also, G. L. Ulmen, "The Sociology of the State: Carl Schmitt and Max Weber," *State, Culture and Society* 1 (1985).
30 Schmitt, *Der Wert des Staates*, p. 79.

But the nature of the decision becomes something much more radical by 1922 and *Political Theology,* as does his criticism of Kelsen.

As in *Parlamentarismus,* it is not enough for Schmitt to simply illustrate the theoretical shortcomings in some aspect of liberalism's political philosophy; he seems compelled further to demonstrate that liberalism not only does not live up to its principles in practice but often betrays them outright. For instance, he observes that the attempt on the part of normativist jurisprudence to banish subjectivity from the adjudication of the law allows room for as much subjective judgment as was ever possible before:

> The normative science to which Kelsen sought to elevate jurisprudence in all purity cannot be normative in the sense that the jurist by his own free will makes value assessments; he can only draw on the given (positively given) values. Objectivity thus appears to be possible, but has no necessary connection with positivity. Although the values on which the jurist draws are given to him, he confronts them with relativistic superiority. (*PT,* 20–1)

Judges may be formally restricted by all the ironclad norms in the world, but at the moment of judgment there is always at least a slight leeway in how they apply the norms. Thus does subjectivity rear its supposedly suppressed head. The reliance on the scientific method ignores the personal, the human element, only to ultimately undermine precisely that scientific project.

In their revulsion to arbitrariness, the formalists sought to eliminate the state from jurisprudential concerns, just as they wished to eliminate the personal, subjective, decision from such matters, and, according to Schmitt, were equally unsuccessful in each endeavor. Kelsen sought to subsume the state under the law, in Schmitt's paraphrase, declaring that it is "neither the creator nor the source of the legal order. . . . [T]he state is nothing else but the legal order itself" (*PT,* 19).[31] Under this formulation, the state would seem inhibited to act, but act it must – albeit with the formalists' collective head turned the other way – if the judicial system is to function at all. And in this manner does Kelsen's formalism serve as an ideology that belies the deformalization of law that is brought about by state activity in the new era of interventionism:

> [W]hoever takes the trouble of examining the public law literature of positive jurisprudence for its basic concepts and arguments will see that the state

---

31 On Schmitt's exaggeration of Kelsen's position on this point and in general, see David Dyzenhaus, "'Now the Machine Runs Itself': Carl Schmitt on Hobbes and Kelsen," *Cardozo Law Review* 16:1 (August 1994): 11; and Peter C. Caldwell, "Legal Positivism and Weimar Democracy."

intervenes everywhere. At times it does so as a *deus ex machina*, to decide according to positive statute a controversy that the independent act of juristic perception failed to bring to a generally plausible solution; at other times it does so as the graceful and merciful lord who proves by pardons and amnesties his supremacy over the laws. There always exists the same inexplicable identity: lawgiver, executive power, police, pardoner, welfare institution. Thus to an observer who takes the trouble to look at the total picture of contemporary jurisprudence, there appears a huge cloak-and-dagger drama, in which the state acts in many disguises but always as the same invisible person. (*PT,* 38)

Schmitt implores the positivists to see the disjuncture pointed out by Weber in *Economy and Society:* Beside the ostensibly "objectively formal" operation of the legal system are the actual "subjectively concrete" moments that in reality characterize its practical functioning during judging or state administration. By repressing the state, the legal positivists not only do *not* prevent arbitrary state functioning, but they allow its activity to proliferate more extensively and undetected to an even greater degree. Later, in *Verfassungslehre,* Schmitt remarks, "mostly the treatment of the concept of sovereignty has suffered from this method of fiction and of ignoring [the state]. In practice apocryphal acts of sovereignty are carried out characteristically by non-sovereign state officials or institutions who make frequent and silently permitted sovereign decisions" (*V,* xii). As we will see, Schmitt's concern with this situation is not that the state will abuse its power through such functioning but rather that it will actually lose it.

Thus, as in the argument presented in *Parlamentarismus,* in which Schmitt suggests with relish that the principle of openness that had been formulated in the fight against tyranny has itself become a tool for coercion, he here intimates with his theologico-monarchical language that, in the flight from authority, the positivists have, in their suppression of the state, reinstituted, as it were, the divine right of kings in the twentieth-century welfare state. For Schmitt, this demonstrates no mere lack of consistency but a lack of fortitude as well. The Enlightenment's rebellion against authority is all the more contemptible given the feeble ways in which it sought to cling to some fabric of it. Like the Deists, who wished to cripple God yet assert his existence, the French liberals of the nineteenth century sought to "paralyze" the king but needed nonetheless to keep him on the throne (*PT,* 59). So, too, then are the legal positivists parasites on the very body that they would decapitate – the state.[32]

---

32 David Dyzenhaus criticizes later incarnations of legal positivism for a similar nonchalance

The decisionistic or personal element not only asserts itself with regard to the everyday workings of the law; the other component of Schmitt's theory of sovereignty, the exception, is the true occasion for the decision and the defining moment for "whoever [*wer*]" is sovereign. As it turns out, the notion of the exception, like the decision, has been clouded for Schmitt by the emphasis on natural-scientific methods and technological thought in the age of "intense commercial activity."

Science, Liberal Mechanisms, and the Exception

Schmitt locates the source of what he has thus far identified as Kelsen's jurisprudential rigidity: "At the foundation of his identification of state and legal order rests a metaphysic that identifies the lawfulness of nature and normative lawfulness. This pattern of thinking is characteristic of the natural sciences. It is based on the rejection of all 'arbitrariness,' and attempts to banish from the human mind every exception" (*PT,* 41). Kelsen and the legal theory he represents are a manifestation of Enlightenment thought's increasing indifference and even antagonism to the idea of the exception. But any attempt to draw attention to the exception – whatever form it takes, beneficial, banal, or, most important, dangerous – is considered irrational from the standpoint of the Enlightenment.[33] According to Schmitt, "in a positivistic age," such attempts are denounced as mere "metaphysics" or "theology" (*PT,* 38–9); anything that calls "the system" into question "is

regarding state application of law. Postwar legal positivists' attempt to preserve the "purity" of their "primary rules" of jurisprudence by being quite indulgent toward vast latitudes of discretion in the application of the law at a "secondary" level. Any semblance of determinacy – even according to the most highly formal criteria – is lost as bureaucracies freely apply law in innumerable ways at the "lower" level of quite diverse social realities. See Dyzenhaus, "The Legitimacy of Legality," *University of Toronto Law Journal* 46 (1994). Thus is borne out Schmitt's charge that the "sheer rationality" of positivism at the high level of theory collapses into arbitrary irrationality at the practical level of application. Dyzenhaus also suggests that Schmitt would have predicted the liberal *non*positivist attempt, exemplified by the work of Ronald Dworkin, at taking back the content-generating power for the constitutional judiciary. See "The Legitimacy of Legality" as well as, Dyzenhaus, "'Now the Machine Runs Itself,'" pp. 5, 17; Dworkin, *Taking Rights Seriously* (Cambridge, Mass.: Harvard University Press, 1977) and *Law's Empire* (Cambridge, Mass.: Harvard University Press, 1986). See also Gerald Frug, "The Ideology of Bureaucracy in American Law," *Harvard Law Review* 97 (1984), on how the gapless conception of law itself spawns discretion in adjudication.

33 Hannah Arendt, addressing a slightly different form of positivism, noted how the application of scientific and statistical methods did not demonstrate the existence of natural-scientific laws at work in human endeavors but rather ensured that these would be the only manifestations of reality considered worthy of reflection; see *The Human Condition* (Chicago: University of Chicago Press, 1958), pp. 42–3.

excluded as impure" (*PT*, 21). Yet Schmitt assures the reader that his conflict with positivist jurisprudence over the exception is not one of "radical
spiritualism" versus "radical materialism" (*PT*, 42); for such dichotomies are
themselves indications of a rationality that has been shrunken hideously. As
he emphasizes in *Political Form*, one need not argue with economic or technological rationality from an irrational, sentimental, or purely spiritual
standpoint but rather from the position of a more sophisticated rationality.
Schmitt's sociological-jurisprudential method has as its goal not the
denigration of science but the achievement of a more fully "scientific result"
(*PT*, 45).[34]

Schmitt in effect asks, how "positive" can positivism be if it ignores what it
is supposedly concerned with, namely, the "fact?" In this case, the *fact* is that
there will always, and inevitably, be an unforeseen or unexpected occurrence that can never be predicted or for which accounts or plans can never
be made: The exception "cannot be circumscribed factually and made to
conform to a preformed law. . . . [I]t defies general codification" (*PT*, 6,
13). How rational or scientific can Enlightenment rationality be if it ignores
such a facet of concrete reality, if it is too afraid to, as it were, face the facts of
life? "A philosophy of concrete life must not withdraw from the exception
and the extreme case, but must be interested in it to the highest degree"
(*PT*, 15).[35] Schmitt claims that this abstract universal application of form is
generated by a natural-scientific rationality.

34 Schmitt's student Leo Strauss, with whom I will deal in the next chapter, makes this same
    move in his own criticism of positivist political science: Political philosophy as defined by
    Strauss is not superior to positivist political science because it is *less* scientific but because it
    is "scientific" in "the original meaning of the term"; see "What Is Political Philosophy?" in
    What is Political Philosophy? and Other Studies (Chicago: University of Chicago Press, 1988),
    p. 14. The other comparison to make with Schmitt on this general critique of positivism is
    with Max Horkheimer and T. W. Adorno. Just as Schmitt detects the unreflected rejection
    by Enlightenment thinking of anything that defies its system as "metaphysics," "theology,"
    or "impure," Horkheimer and Adorno observe, "to the Enlightenment, that which does
    not reduce to numbers and ultimately, to the one becomes illusion; modern positivism
    writes it off as literature." *Dialectic of Enlightenment* [1944], trans. John Cummings (New
    York: Continuum, 1989), p. 7. Their critique of the "totalitarianism" of the Enlighten-
    ment does not, however, involve the valorization of what defies the totality but rather an
    understanding of the dialectical relationship between the two. As I demonstrated in Part
    One, this is something Schmitt himself attempts before ultimately lapsing into an irra-
    tional privileging of "unconquered" nature, either as "the political" or, here, "the
    exception."
35 According to Shklar's description, "abstract formalists" like Kelsen seem to be inten-
    tionally eliminating the possibility of an exception, by endeavoring "to find a set of
    categories so totally devoid of any specific content as to be applicable to all social institu-
    tions from the most primitive to the most overdeveloped." *Legalism*, p. 84.

Schmitt's source for the rationality to counter that of the natural sciences, in *Political Theology,* is not exclusively or even primarily Roman Catholicism, as in *Political Form,* but rather Thomas Hobbes. For Schmitt, Hobbes is the "classic representative" of the "decisionist" theory of sovereignty: Hobbes "advanced a decisive argument that connected . . . decisionism with personalism and rejected all attempts to substitute an abstractly valid order for a concrete sovereignty of the state" (*PT,* 33). But there is an inherent tension – a tension that runs through all of his work – in Schmitt's choosing as an alternative to the natural-scientific influence on modern law a figure who is himself so closely associated with the triumph of Enlightenment rationality: "Hobbes remained personalistic and postulated an ultimate concrete deciding instance. . . . [H]e also heightened his state, the Leviathan, into an immense person. . . . This he did despite his nominalism and natural-scientific approach and his reduction of the individual to an atom. For him [personalism] was . . . a methodical and systematic postulate of his juristic thinking" (*PT,* 47). I will further elaborate on the relationship between Hobbes and Schmitt in Chapter 6. Suffice it to say here that Schmitt's "Hobbesian moment," when personalism stood over and above natural science, was not to last.[36] Throughout the age of absolutism in the seventeenth and eighteenth centuries, the idea of the personal ruler held sway, until Rousseau and the succeeding century of mass democracy ensured that the natural-scientific overwhelmed the personalistic: According to Schmitt, since the French Revolution,

> the consistency of exclusively scientific thinking has permeated political ideas, repressing the essentially juristic-ethical thinking that had predominated in the age of the Enlightenment. The general validity of the legal prescription has become identified with the lawfulness of nature, which applies without exception. . . . The general will of Rousseau became identical with the will of the sovereign; but simultaneously the concept of the general will also contained a quantitative determination with regard to its subject, which means that the people became the sovereign. The decisionistic and personalistic element in the concept of sovereignty was thus lost. (*PT,* 48)

Schmitt sees this shift to the quantitative at the root of Kelsen's conception "of democracy as the expression of a relativistic and impersonal scientism"

---

36 In his *Leviathan* book of 1938, which I will discuss in Chapter 6, Schmitt again identifies Hobbes not only as the apex of decisionism and political thought itself but also the beginning of the end. There, the eventual downfall of the Leviathan state is attributed to its creator himself and to his succumbing to the influence of science and technology.

(*PT,* 49). The norms embodied in the laws of one geographically demarcated area within one nation, whose residents elected the legislators of those laws, are as "right" to Kelsen as are some different norms legislated in some other geographical area. As was clear in the analysis of *Parlamentarismus,* in having values determined by any number of territorial divisions and mere numerical majorities, the quantitative element strips those values of any substance. Kelsen is perhaps most famous for his discussion of whether it is correct for the majority of the people to decide between Christ and Barabbas. It is perhaps due to Schmitt's misunderstanding of Kelsen's taking the affirmative position on this question that Schmitt maintains that Kelsen "openly reveals the mathematical and natural-scientific character of his thinking" (*PT,* 42).

Exactly how does this natural-scientifically tainted constitutionalism hamper the ability to deal with the exception? As we know from Chapter 3, according to Schmitt, any attempt to define the exception or to describe what circumstances might constitute an exceptional case is a hindrance on the ability to manage it when it in fact arises to threaten a regime. For Schmitt, it is ridiculous to make plans or provisions for what one could not possibly foresee (*PT,* 6–7). This could easily be taken as a call for a perpetual state of "emergency," in which an authoritarian regime is required to stand guard at every moment for the possibility of the sudden appearance of the exception.[37] Any limit, legal or otherwise, to this government's functioning would jeopardize its vigil and would necessarily require suspension. Schmitt seemingly attempts to allay such fears. Just as the exceptional case by definition cannot be predicted, by definition neither can it exist at all times. Because of this, the exception can be *good* for the legal order, for it confirms its existence. There can be no "exceptional" situation without a normal one. "The exception appears in its absolute form when a situation in which legal prescriptions can be valid must first be brought about. Every general norm demands a normal, everyday frame of life to which it can be factually applied and which is subjected to its regulations" (*PT,* 6–7). Schmitt asserts that the rule, in effect, defines the exception and that the exception, in turn, draws attention to the rule, hence, ostensibly restoring confidence in the importance and primacy of the norm-bound regular situation.[38]

37 See George Schwab's note on the difference between an "exception" and an "emergency," *PT,* 5, n. 1.
38 As Ulmen explains the initial thrust of the argument, "a constitution without gaps necessarily presupposes a normative utopia wherein there is no exception. By definition the

Schmitt goes on, however, to suggest that the normal situation actually owes its legitimate existence, on the contrary, to the exception:

> The exception can be more important . . . than the rule, not because of a romantic irony for the paradox, but because the seriousness of an insight goes deeper than the clear generalizations inferred from what ordinarily repeats itself. The exception is more interesting than the rule. The rule proves nothing; the exception proves everything: *It confirms not only the rule but its existence, which derives only from the exception.* (*PT,* 15, emphasis added)

In the sentence that follows this passage, Schmitt reminds us of the foolhardy relationships among modern science, which theoretically expels the exception from nature; technology, which physically compels nature to abide by science's exceptionless rules; and liberalism, which enforces this banishment of the exception in the realm of politics: "In the exception the power of real life breaks through the crust of a mechanism that has become torpid by repetition" (*PT,* 15). "Real life" takes its revenge on liberalism, in *Political Theology,* for imposing similar political "mechanisms."

The exception shatters the iron cage of liberal constitutionalism in both the latter's jurisprudence and its institutional theory. Kelsen's positivist jurisprudence is explicitly grounded in the Kantian assumption that the ability to intuit causality is an a priori condition of human cognition. The laws function for Kelsen because citizens understand that under the stipulations of the law, *if* they behave in a certain manner that contradicts those stipulations, *then* the state will react in a certain way.[39] Schmitt, whose rancor against the notion of a universe governed solely by causality is matched only by Nietzsche's, disrupts the jurisprudence of cause and effect with his super-extrapolation on the idea of gaps – the exception. As we observed in Part One, Schmitt perceives a mechanical order of cause and effect as a meaningless order, and hence meaning is given to that order by the exception and the sovereign action called for by it. For Kelsen, conversely, the gapless, "closed" quality of such an order renders it *more* meaningful than one that could be interrupted by something as arbitrary as an exception.

---

norm precludes the exception, whereas the exception presupposes the norm and is bound by its definition. The exception cannot decide *for* the exception; it can only decide *for* the norm." *Politische Mehrwert,* p. 244.

39 Caldwell discusses the importance of Kantian "causality" for Kelsen's legal theory in *Popular Sovereignty and the Crisis of German Constitutional Law.*

The airtight equilibrium of liberalism's constitutionally prescribed institutional arrangements also arouses Schmitt's ire regarding rationalistic order. Again, the most obvious institutional "mechanisms" of this sort are checks and balances and the separation of powers (*PT,* 7). Although his argument emphasizes the harm that the exception can do to the liberal order, liberal constitutionalism's reliance on a system of checks and balances "hampers" (*PT,* 7) the state's ability to deal with the exception: "[T]he development and practice of the liberal constitutional state . . . attempts to repress the question of sovereignty by a division and mutual control of competences" (*PT,* 11). Jean Bodin's theory of sovereignty, on the other hand, was "indivisible," there could be no separating or mutual checking of power, especially in the case of an emergency (*PT,* 8). Hence, Schmitt depicts Bodin, as he does Hobbes, as free of the scientific-technical influence becoming so dominant in their age.

Under normal conditions, the sovereign could be bound by law, according to Bodin, because such law was dictated for him by natural law. But in the case of an exception, natural law is no longer binding for the sovereign, presumably because the law of nature itself has been suspended by the emergence of a miracle-like exception. For Bodin, because the possible conditions of the exceptional situation are innumerable and its ramifications potentially infinite, the sovereign's power in such a situation must be "unlimited" (*PT,* 10).[40] In opposition to this, liberalism avoids contemplating the necessary circumstances for unlimited authority, wishing instead to focus on "time *limits*" and *enumerating* "extraordinary powers" (*PT,* 12, emphasis added) in less-than-normal situations. Conceiving of exceptions only in terms of "disturbances," for which emergency provisions can to some degree be circumscribed, liberal constitutionalism refuses to imagine a situation in which its supposedly ironclad laws of politics, which derive from their counterparts in the natural sciences, do not apply. In the realm of politics, especially, nature does not respond passively to the domination of political technology. Because of the employment of the technique of separated powers, the uncertainty and the stalemate that result in a liberal

---

40 Stephen Holmes questions Schmitt's excessively absolutist interpretation of Bodin and discusses the full extent of the French state theorist's account of limited government; see "The Constitution of Sovereignty in Jean Bodin," in *Passions and Constraint: On the Theory of Liberal Democracy* (Chicago: University of Chicago Press, 1995). According to Holmes, Bodin understood quite well that a ruler's binding of himself could actually make him *more* powerful in the long run than the unrestrained wielding of unlimited power on short-term affairs. Schmitt apparently never took seriously the evidence presented by Weber to make a similar case (*ES,* 993).

regime from the confusion over who has authority, when the provisions made for an emergency prove inadequate, will lead to the destruction of such a government. Either the emergency itself or the strife it causes within the government will ensure that result. According to Schmitt, this is nature's political rebellion and revenge.

If it seems that the exception warrants more than analytical treatment, this is only because Schmitt presents it as something more than an analytical category. Of course both teachers and students of Schmitt have demonstrated the heuristic utility of focusing on the extreme case. As Weber remarks, "for the purpose of theoretical speculation, extreme examples are the most useful" (*ES*, 334). And despite his renunciation of the influence of Schmitt on his work, Franz Neumann suggests that "the study of . . . emergency situations will yield valuable hints as to where political power actually resides in 'normal' periods."[41] However, to ground a theory of sovereignty and constitutionalism on the primacy of exceptional situations is to invert and narrow the priorities of political and legal science.[42] Kelsen suggests that Schmitt's approach does just that, reducing the Weimar constitution to the emergency provisions of Article 48; Ingeborg Maus is slightly more generous in noting that Schmitt's radical appeals to popular sovereignty and exceptional situations reduce the constitution to the preamble *and* Article 48.[43] These issues bring us directly to Schmitt's interpretation of the Weimar constitution and his attempt to "save" it from the technical, mechanical, mathematical influences he associates with Kelsen's positivistic liberalism.

The constitution versus the Constitution

The more immediately practical elements of Schmitt's dissatisfaction with positivist jurisprudence are more apparent in his writings that deal directly with the Weimar constitution than in the quasi-metaphysical *Political Theology*. The overly formal and technocratic notion of constitutionalism that he associates with Kelsen has dangerous and even ludicrous implications for Schmitt in his mid- to late-Weimar writings, most notably *Verfassungslehre*

41 Neumann, *The Democratic and the Authoritarian State: Essays in Political and Legal Theory*, ed. Herbert Marcuse (New York: Free Press, 1957), p. 17.
42 See Bernard Manin, "Elections, Elites and Democracy," in *Principles of Representative Government* (Cambridge: Cambridge University Press, 1997) for a critique of Schmitt along these lines.
43 See Kelsen, "Wer soll der Hüter der Verfassung sein?" See also Ingeborg Maus, *Bürgerliche Rechtstheorie und Faschismus: Zur sozialen Funktion und aktuellen Wirkung der Theorie Carl Schmitts* (Munich: C. H. Beck, 1980), p. 121.

(*Constitutional Theory*), *Der Hüter der Verfassung* (*Guardian of the Constitution*), and *Legalität und Legitimität* (*Legality and Legitimacy*). We have observed above how Schmitt corners Kelsenian liberal constitutionalism on the formula of mathematical majorities equaling correctness. As a result, he has more weapons to wield against the parliamentary component of the Weimar constitution as he develops his own theory of constitutionalism than he had at his disposal in *Parlamentarismus,* in 1923. More emphatically and, at least apparently, more systematically, Schmitt urges the identification of the popular will *with* the office of the executive and *against* the institution of the legislature, after 1927. He collects and reduces the parliamentary, procedural, formal, written, *liberal* elements of the Weimar constitution to mere mathematicism, technicism, and functionalism, while promoting the presidential, substantive, spiritual, essentialist, supposedly *democratic* components to a position of ascendancy. In *Verfassungslehre,* Schmitt lays out specifically how plebiscitary, acclamation democracy can be seen as the answer to the invasion of constitutional law by "the functionalism of arithmetical-statistical methods" (*LL,* 298) and the mere "'technology' of political will-formation" (*LL,* 318) associated with legal positivism.

The first dozen or so pages of Schmitt's mammoth statement on the Weimar constitution and constitutionalism in general are devoted to explicating his theory of the sovereign popular will at the base of the constitution and extricating it from the, from his standpoint, bad-conscience relationship of will and constitution in the Kelsenian positivist conception. On the very first page of *Verfassungslehre,* he asserts the absolute identity of people, state, and constitution:

> If an understanding is to be possible, the word "constitution" must be confined to the constitution of the state, i. e., the political unity of a people. In this confinement can the state itself be defined – indeed the individual concrete state as political unity or as a specific concrete kind and form of stately existence. Then constitution signifies the comprehensive situation of political unity and order. (*V,* 3)

Schmitt appears to be theoretically parsimonious in "confining" or "delimiting" a definition of a constitution, but his definition actually ambiguously combines three elements that the positivist tradition had tried to keep logically distinct in order to better understand them. But his distance from that tradition is declared outright in the very next sentence, when he claims that a constitution might be defined as a "closed system of norms" and, as such, as a kind of "unity." He quickly dispenses with this definition, however, because it is merely indicative of an "intellectual" or "ideal" unity and not a sufficiently "existential one" (*V,* 3).

Abstractly formal notions of the constitution that separate the three elements of state, constitution, and people cannot ascertain the substantive, essential aspects of a constitution's existence:

> The state does not *have* a constitution, the "according to which" the stately will develops and functions, but rather the state *is* the constitution, in other words, the essential, at hand, situation, a status of unity and order. The state would cease to exist if this constitution, that is this unity and order, ceases. The constitution is its "soul," its concrete life and individual existence. (*V,* 4, emphasis added)

Refuting a technical-instrumentalist notion of constitutionalism, Schmitt asserts that a constitution is not a tool of state functioning but is the state itself or, more important, its life and soul.

In a recapitulation of his earlier arguments against Kelsen and legal positivism (*V,* 7–10), Schmitt distinguishes between the constitution defined as something solely normative, "a simple 'should'" (*V,* 7), from something actually present in the world: "[T]he [constitutional] will is existentially at hand, its power and authority reside in its being" (*V,* 9). Yet the reality of the constitution does not remain only or primarily in its obvious physical manifestations, the individual articles of the constitution or the statutes produced thereby (*V,* 11–12), or even the written document itself (*V,* 13), but rather elsewhere. Again, we find Schmitt straddling the distinction between the irrationally ephemeral and the vulgarly material, but his own solution is again less than rationally accountable.

He draws on the preamble of the Weimar constitution for support:

> The unity of the German Reich is not based in any of the 181 Articles [of the constitution] and their validity, but rather on the political existence of the German people. The will of the German people, thus something existential, grounds the political and constitutional unity despite all systemic contradictions, structural insufficiencies, and nebulous constitutional statutes. The Weimar constitution is valid because the German people has "given it to itself." (*V,* 10)

Schmitt is persistently unclear on how this political existence specifically "gives" the constitution "to itself" in the act of constitution making, betraying the fact that the three elements of state, constitution, and people may not be as logically identified as he would have it: "Political being is the precondition of constitutive power. What does not politically exist can also not consciously decide. With this fundamental procedure, in which a people act with political consciousness, political existence is presupposed and is the act by which to distinguish the people who create a constitution from the constitution of a state itself" (*V,* 50).

Does a popular unity make the constitution that merely confirms the prior political existence, or is this "political being" brought together as a unity or, at least, to a higher level of unity by the very act of constitution making?[44] Schmitt does not elaborate on this procedure but rather introduces his recently developed, polemical element of "the political" to define what the state–constitution–people configuration is *not.* It is *not* something that can be turned against itself or that can be self-negating, and this collectively personal presence that cannot logically account for the ambiguity of its own existence is nevertheless to account for the ambiguities of a real-world legal-constitutional order:

> The political decision, that means the constitution, can not be turned against its subject and supercede its existence. Next to and over the constitution does this will remain. Every real constitutional conflict, one that concerns the foundations of the political comprehensive decision itself, can thereby be decided only by the constitutional power. And every gap in the constitution – in contrast to constitutional-legislative obscurities and differences of opinion in detail – is filled by an act of constitutional power; it decides every unforeseen case whose decision concerns the foundational political decision. (*V,* 77)

Thus, what commentators have identified as an almost religious "fundamentalism" or a "communitarian existentialism" at the base of Schmitt's constitutionalism[45] culminates in the evocation of "the political." Once again, rather than energetically theorizing a particular intellectual-political constellation of modernity, we find Schmitt erupting into essentialist – here nationalist – excess. In the face of what is still today the very real difficulty of postulating the specific relationship of a popular will to a constitutional arrangement, Schmitt resorts to the ultimately *negative* definition of contrast with an external enemy.[46]

44   See Caldwell, *Popular Sovereignty and the Crisis of German Constitutional Law,* for an analysis of the circular reasoning of Schmitt's account of constitutional origins.

45   Caldwell, *Popular Sovereignty and the Crisis of German Constitutional Law;* and Dyzenhaus, *Truth's Revenge: Carl Schmitt, Hans Kelsen and Hermann Heller in Weimar* (Oxford: Oxford University Press, 1996), respectively.

46   Recent attempts at reconciling ostensibly opposed democratic and constitutional impera-

Why Schmitt does not promote a positive nationalist vision akin to other Weimar conservatives that revolves around Teutonic folklore, Wagner, or the Black Forest is not readily apparent. Whether his early Catholicism prevented him from adopting such primarily nineteenth-century, Prussian-hegemony myths, or whether such allusions came under the purview of what he had previously denounced as "political romanticism" is not clear.[47] But his refrain from such cultural vulgarities puts Schmitt in the awkward theoretical position of accusing liberal constitutionalism of neutrality and contentlessness, when his own nationalism is rather agnostic on what specifically makes up the content of the state–constitution–people unity. This refrain also ultimately pushes him, as we will see, into political vulgarity. The political, the postulation of an enemy, a *Volk* that is not one's own *Volk*, serves to distract from the discomfort, the "unspeakable confusion" mentioned in Chapter 2, of not knowing exactly what oneself, one's culture, or one's historical predicament is in modernity, in the age of technology. But, as we will see, the automatic formulation of an other to arrive at self-identification and thereby to forge meaning is as mechanical as anything in Kelsen's legal theory.[48]

tives in contemporary liberal democracy include Albert Weale, "The Limits of Democracy," in *The Good Polity: Normative Analysis of the State*, ed. Alan Hamlin and P. Pettit (Oxford: Basil Blackwell, 1989), and Walter F. Murphy, "Constitutions, Constitutionalism and Democracy," in *Constitutionalism and Democracy: Transitions in the Contemporary World*, ed. D. Greenberg, S. N. Katz et al. (Oxford: Oxford University Press, 1993). Two authors who frankly ought to know better, Sheldon Wolin and Bruce Ackerman, have each recently attempted to effectively separate – in almost Schmittian fashion – constitutional norms and democratic will such that the normative status of the latter is left indeterminate. Wolin distinguishes the democratic spirit from the legal letter of the constitution, in "Collective Identity and Constitutional Power," in *The Presence of the Past: Essays on the State and the Constitution* (Baltimore: Johns Hopkins University Press, 1989), and "Fugitive Democracy," *Constellations* 1:1 (April 1994). Ackerman differentiates "normal politics" from "constitutional politics" – the former which obtains in everyday circumstances of political pluralism and the latter during exceptional moments of popular unity – in *We the People. Vol. 1: Foundations* (Cambridge, Mass.: Harvard University Press, 1991). Stephen Holmes prescribes a more reasoned reconciliation of the democratic and constitutional impulses, in "Precommitment and the Paradox of Democracy," in *Constitutionalism and Democracy*, ed. Jon Elster and Rune Slagstad (Cambridge: Cambridge University Press, 1988). Ulrich K. Preuß establishes a typology of how this reconciliation plays itself out in the respective American, French, and British contexts, in "The Political Meaning of Constitutionalism," Austin Lecture, UK Association for Legal and Social Philosophy (University of East Anglia, Norwich, April 6–8, 1995).

47 On Schmitt's peculiar nationalism, see the chapter, "Der Nationalist," in Helmut Quaritsch, *Positionen und Begriffe Carl Schmitts* (Berlin: Duncker & Humblot, 1989).

48 On the role of the friend/enemy thesis in Schmitt's constitutionalism, see Ernst-Wolfgang Böckenförde, "Der Begriff des Politischen als Schlüssel zum staatsrechtlichen Werk Carl

According to Schmitt, Kelsen conceives of a preconstitutional will that constitutes the basis of the constitutional norms but then represses its substance under the weight of the formalism of the law. For Kelsen, then, the decisionist moment of will is the primal act that must subsequently be repressed; for Schmitt, however, it is perpetually present: "The people must be present and presupposed as a political unity to be the subject of a constitution-providing power" (*V,* 61). Even when the expression of will is reenacted for Kelsen during an election, he dismisses it as "sociological" or "political," even though it will determine the norms that make up the supposedly "pure" constitution. For Schmitt, through the act of popular acclamation in referenda, the popular will is continually expressed and explicitly recognized as such.[49]

Schmitt thus apparently wants to be more honest about the impact of elections on democratic will formation than Kelsen and seeks to protect the privileged, original, constitutionally decisive will from tampering by fleeting parliamentary majorities. With a distinction between *Verfassung,* that is, the constitution in a thick sense, the identity of state and popular will, on the one hand, and *Verfassungsgesetz,* the constitution in a formal sense, the statutes and written document, the mere letter of the law, on the other, Schmitt, not unproblematically, posits a transhistorical substance that lies outside the reach of momentary legislative whim.

For instance, Schmitt objects to the maintenance of an across-the-board minimum requirement of a two-thirds majority in the *Reichstag* for amending the constitution, for this means that fundamental constitutional principles, such as the status of the Weimar government as a *Republik,* based on "popular authority," is just as open to change as the protection of civil-service pensions (*V,* 99–112). Should the amendment process allow for the total reconstitution of the republic, a wholesale undermining of the state–constitution–people unity? As Schmitt declares in *Legalität und Legitimität,* in terms that will be better explained later, "Just because a constitution allows for the possibility of constitutional revision, this does not conse-

Schmitts," in *Complexio Oppositorum: Ueber Carl Schmitt,* ed. Helmut Quaritsch (Berlin: Duncker & Humblot, 1988). On the disturbing revival of "political" constitutionalism in contemporary Eastern Europe, see Ulrich K. Preuß, "Umrisse einer neuen konstitutionellen Form des Politischen," in *Revolution, Fortschritt und Verfassung* (Frankfurt a. M.: Fischer, 1994).

49 In Ulrich Preuß's words, for Schmitt the popular will "slumbers as a latent potential in the constitution." "Political Order and Democracy: Carl Schmitt and His Influence," in *Social System, Rationality and Revolution,* ed. L. Nowak and M. Paprzycki (Rodopi: Poznan Studies in the Philosophy of the Sciences and the Humanities 33 [1993]), p. 17.

quently mean that it provides the legal means for the abolition of its own legality, let alone the legitimate means for the destruction of its own legitimacy" (*LL*, 311). Majoritarianism, the ground rule of Kelsenian liberalism, makes for some rather unpleasant political results, according to Schmitt. The "neutral compromise of a value-free functionalism" that *is* Weimar constitutional law, for Schmitt, witnesses "the remarkable result that the fundamental bourgeois-constitutional principles of universal freedom and right of property have the 'inferior' legality of only 51% of the votes while the rights of the religious societies and officials (through better representation, the trade unions as well) have the 'superior' legality of 67%" (*LL*, 311). Whoever has greater numerical weight in the legislature, through votes or influence, has the greater legal power, regardless of what they espouse.

Part II, section 13 of *Verfassungslehre*, "The Constitutional Concept of Statute," describes how the parliament must be held in tow if mere majority-generated, legislative statutes are not to undermine the legal substance of the constitution (*V*, 139). The legislative administrators in the *Reichstag* were to be kept from striking back at the entity that granted them authority in the first place, the originary democratic will (*V*, 143–6). As Neumann points out, Schmitt is able to speak in the cautionary language of the American constitutional practice of "inherent limitations upon the amending power," wherein extramajoritarian measures are required to alter a constitutional core that is above mere statutes.[50] But Maus demonstrates how this gives Schmitt recourse to denounce all socially progressive change as unconstitutional, because such provisions were not part of the original decision of the constitution.[51] Moreover, Schmitt's appeal to the presidency to combat such legislative movement gives his constitutionalism not merely a conservatively reactive but an energetically reactionary character. The parliament may not act substantively against the original constitutional will, whereas the president may act unlimitedly in supposed accord with it.

The Schmittian distinction between *Verfassung* and *Verfassungsgesetz* – ultimately a distinction between spirit and letter of the law, however much Schmitt would object to such a reduction – although seemingly rather abstract, has dramatic institutional ramifications. This dichotomy can be played out in many ways by Schmitt. For instance, when he declares, in *Verfassungslehre*, that "the modern constitution rests on a combining and

50   See Neumann, "The Change in the Function of Law in Modern Society" (1937), in *The Democratic and the Authoritarian State*, pp. 53–4.
51   Maus, *Bürgerliche Rechtstheorie und Faschismus*, p. 107.

mixing of bourgeois-rule of law principles with political . . . principles" and declares that the former, which clearly correspond to the *Verfassungsgesetz,* have served as a kind of constraint on the latter, which constitute the substance of the *Verfassung* (*V,* 216), he draws on the arguments of two of his most famous treatises, which I dealt with earlier: the opposition of liberalism and democracy, from *Parlamentarismus;* and the friend/enemy thesis, from *The Concept of the Political.* Schmitt has declared an institutional war between the constitutional body that sustains the "democratic," "political," substantively constitutional essence, the *Reichspräsident,* on the one hand, and the constitutionally granted body that reflects only the liberal, compromising, letter of the law-inclined, functionally formal body, the *Reichstag,* on the other. Only in this way can the essence of the constitution be protected from the threat posed by the majoritarianism of Kelsenian liberalism. As he had since the metamorphosis from *Die Diktatur* to *Political Theology,* in 1921–22, Schmitt continues, in *Verfassungslehre,* to champion the *Reichspräsident* as the solution to the many woes brought on by parliamentary liberalism (*V,* 27, 111, 269, 292, 350).

But it is the crises of the early thirties that provide Schmitt with the opportunity to most vigorously wage war on behalf of the president versus his, and hence the people's, interconstitutional enemy, the parliament, in *Der Hüter der Verfassung* and *Legalität und Legitimität.* As Preuß remarks, capturing Schmitt's martial strategy, the decision, for Schmitt, "*mobilizes* the 'substance of the constitution' against its functional elements."[52] Although seeds of this war between parts of the constitution were sown in *Verfassungslehre,* there the issue of constitutional contradictions is described most famously in terms of the "dilatory formal compromise" among the kinds of rights incorporated into the document during its inception at the behest of interest groups, such as social democracy and political Catholicism (*V,* 31–2).[53] But as the social, political, and economic crises of Weimar grew more severe in the early thirties, the image of slapdash and hodgepodge components that are unable to coexist together comfortably

52 Preuß, "The Critique of German Liberalism," *Telos* 71 (spring 1987): 99, emphasis added. On this issue, see also Preuß, "Zum 95. Geburtstag von Carl Schmitt: Die latente Diktatur in Verfassungsstaat," *Tageszeitung* (Jul. 12, 1983); and "Aktuelle Probleme einer linken Verfassungstheorie," *Prokla: Zeitschrift für politische Oekonomie und sozialistishe Politik* (December 1985).

53 Consult the assessments of Schmitt's appraisal of the constitution's supposedly "compromised" character by his Weimar students: see Kirchheimer, "Weimar – and What Then?" (1930), in *Politics, Law and Social Change: Selected Essays of Otto Kirchheimer,* ed. F. S. Burin and K. L. Shell (New York: Columbia University Press, 1969), pp. 53–4; and Neumann, "The Changing Function of Law," p. 50.

within the constitution is supplanted by the image of mortal enemies whose very existence depends on the eradication of the other.

The Parliament versus the President

Schmitt radicalizes the assertion of a contradiction within the Weimar constitution, in *Der Hüter der Verfassung*. The paradigm of the "dualistic state," the nineteenth-century balance of a "governmental" state with a "legislative" one, has resulted, in practice, with the latter's predominance over the former (*HV*, 75). This dualism has been built into the Weimar document itself with "the balancing of parliamentary with plebiscitary democracy." And Schmitt's proposed solution to the harmful ascendancy of the parliament is to use the person of the president, who "stands at the center of the plebiscitary part of the constitution" not to reestablish the balance between the two components (*HV*, 116) but to purge the parliamentary role in the constitution, because the two are no longer compatible (*HV*, 156–7).

How does Schmitt justify abandoning the principle of the separation of powers that is clearly entailed by such a strategy? Rather than argue against the principle on the grounds that it is a hindrance to decisive emergency action, as he does in *Political Theology* (see Chapter 3), or that it is an illegitimate prism that refracts into splinters the solitary force of sovereign will, as he does in *Verfassungslehre* (see *V*, 182–99), in the midst of the crisis of the early thirties, Schmitt responds much more pragmatically. The separation of powers encourages each part of the constitutional order to view itself as the constitutionally primary part, to guard its sphere jealously, and to use such claims to political advantage vis-à-vis the other branches (*HV*, 10).[54] States that assign prominent roles for the legislature or the judiciary may function well in times of consensus but not in moments of political dissension like the present (*HV*, 78).

This pragmatic justification for the presently proposed presidential conjoining of the distinct powers separated by the bourgeois *Rechtsstaat*, however, contradicts the very heart of Schmitt's theory of constitutionalism as developed in *Verfassungslehre* and proposed for practice in *Der Hüter der Verfassung*: the eternal unitary will that is prior to, and present in, the thick definition of *Verfassung*. As Schmitt repeats in the work from 1931, "the democratic (not liberal) state conception must hold fast to the often-

---

54 Holmes argues that Schmitt's account here is quite accurate and expresses exactly why the separation of powers is *effective;* see "The Constitution of Sovereignty in Jean Bodin," in *Passions and Constraint.*

mentioned democratic basis that the state is an indivisible unity" (*HV,* 145). This transhistorical, ontological definition is nevertheless incompatible with the claim that a separation of powers would be appropriate at any point in time. And as we have observed in previous chapters, when Schmitt resorts to the transhistorical, he concomitantly resorts to a call for concrete domination as well, and this is the crux of the crisis works from the early thirties: a revival of personal domination of a concrete people embodied in a thereby legitimate president versus the abstract domination of impersonal, merely legal statutes. Hence, *Verfassungsgesetz* versus *Verfassung,* and *Reichstag* versus *Reichspräsident* mean legality versus legitimacy.

In *Legalität und Legitimität,* Schmitt is explicit from the outset that abstract, impersonal domination has replaced domination by concrete persons. He laments that power is wielded by "governing statutes" and no longer by "men, authorities or magistrates" (*LL,* 264). "More correctly," he adds, "the statutes do not govern, they are valid only as norms. Generally there is no longer domination and sheer power [at all]. Whoever exercises power and domination does so only 'on the basis of statutes' or 'in the name of statutes.' He does not according to the situation make valid law valid" (*LL,* 264). The absence of the personal element in applying the law that was evident in Schmitt's early responses to Weber and most dramatically in *Political Theology* are still apparent here but are now shaded a different hue. There was a quasi-normative element in the early works regarding the position of what is "human" in legal adjudication and an expressed desire to be more honest about the personal will – collective will in a people or individual will in a judge or executive – than is the Kelsenian jurisprudence that would hide the fact that it requires the personal for its own undertakings. In *Legalität und Legitimität,* the strategy is again much more pragmatic. As Schmitt states on the very first page, "the contemporary *domestic-*state crisis of Germany" lies with the "whole problematic of the concept of legality" (*LL,* 263, emphasis added). This reminds us that to Schmitt's mind Germany has an *external* state crisis as well and that the source of, as well as the solution to, *both* state crises is in fact the same:

> **the source:** class myth in the external form of the Soviet Union and in the
> internal form of domestic parties;
> **the solution:** a nationalist president.

The abstract domination by impersonal norms brought on by positivist jurisprudence is still in itself as intolerable for Schmitt as it was in *Political Theology,* but it is the new form of concrete domination whose way it paves that is the most dangerous aspect of such rule of norms here in *Legalität und Legitimität*. Abstract legality allows for seizing a state that is increasingly viewed as merely a power mechanism and not the site of the existential integration of the people. We will see that Schmitt's nostalgia for traditional, concrete domination will in fact lead to a strategy that offers a countertheory of abstract cum concrete domination. But first it is necessary to understand his elaboration of the "whole problematic of legality," in *Legalität und Legitimität*, to fully understand this strategy.[55]

Schmitt explicitly describes the first element in the title of his 1932 work, "legality," in terms of legal positivism: "[A] closed system of legality establishes the claim to obedience and justifies that every law in opposition is abolished. The specific form of appearance of law here is the statute, specifically the justification of state compulsion to legality" (*LL*, 264). But wherein lies the deciding will in such a system? – especially if the classifications of aristocracy, monarchy, and classical democracy, in which such a will was inherent in the regime's type or form, no longer obtain (*LL*, 266). If Kelsenian liberalism purports to be democratic, why does it suppress the immediacy of the sovereign popular will with elaborate formal mechanisms and repress the memory of the actual role of that will in its undertakings?

> Today the normative fiction of a closed legal system moves in striking and emphatic opposition to a real, present and lawful will; that is today the decisive opposition, not that of monarchy, aristocracy, oligarchy or democracy, which for the most part only obscure and mislead. In this we find the essence of our state in a transformation, one which can be characterized for the present moment as a "turn to the total state" with its unavoidable tendency toward "planning" (as opposed to the previous century's tendency toward "freedom") which seems today typically as the turn toward the administrative state . . . [in which all aspects of government] are viewed as instruments. (*LL*, 266)

Thus the permanent passing of the age of concrete governance by a particular concrete body, whether the demos, the nobles, or the king (the many, the few, or the one), and the thwarting of the contemporary mass-democratic governance through liberalism lead to rule by abstract, anonymous forces that blueprint the lives of citizens without their say. Schmitt alludes to his recently published essay on the "total state," which analyzes a

---

55 Schmitt again took up the issue of legality after the war, retaining his critique but ostensibly refraining from his earlier-proposed authoritarian solution; see "Das Problem der Legalität" (1950), in *Verfassungsrechtliche Aufsätze*. For a different approach to a similar problematic, see Ulrich K. Preuß, *Legalität und Pluralismus: Beiträge zum Verfassungsrecht der Bundesrepublik Deutschland* (Frankfurt a. M.: Suhrkamp, 1973).

new state–society relationship in the welfare state: The state's acceding to the many demands from the myriad of organized social interests fuses state and society together such that there is no longer a state authority that actually decides the organization of society nor an integrated society whose demands are at least consistent with itself and hence called for by itself. This state, deemed a "quantitative total state," is thereby weakened, and society is increasingly fragmented.[56]

Besides the abstract danger posed by this administrative total state fostered by naked constitutional legality is the greater danger posed by a new form of concrete domination should any one of the many social groups seize the state and put it solely toward its own designs. In fact, Schmitt suggests that the "abstract and disconnected formalism and functionalism" of pure legality actually provide the ready means for such a result:

> The essential presuppositions and the specific pathos of the legalistic statutory conception are revealed as such. . . . The illusion develops that all is conceivable, that a legal way and legal methods are open to radical and revolutionary attempts, goals and movements, that they can achieve their goal without violence and overthrow, through a procedure that functions at the same time in an orderly and fully "value-neutral" fashion. (*LL*, 270)

I will deal with this more elaborately in the next chapter's discussion of pluralism and the state in Schmitt's theory, but here it helps emphasize the mechanization and indeed mathematicization of the state that functions under the positivist conception of the constitution or, as Schmitt at his most adjectival describes it, "an absolutely 'neutral,' value and quality-free, contentless, formalistic, functionalistic, conception of legality" (*LL*, 280).

By emphasizing mathematics and functionality, Schmitt makes the expression "Herrschaft des Gesetzes," which could legitimately signify "rule of law," instead read "domination by statute." He ridicules the formulation that was uncontroversial to the Weimar document's framers: "law = statute; statute = the concurrence of the people's representatives according to state rules" (*LL*, 276), by semantically divorcing the people's representatives

---

56 Schmitt, "Die Wendung zum totalen Staat" (1931), in *Positionen und Begriffe im Kampf mit Weimar – Genf – Versailles: 1923–1939* (Hamburg: Hanseatische Verlagsanstalt, 1940). An account of this state of affairs that, in contrast to Schmitt's, seeks to preserve rather than dispense with the democratic elements of a state–society relationship under welfare-state conditions is Ernst-Wolfgang Böckenförde, "Die Bedeutung der Unterscheidung von Staat und Gesellschaft im demokratischen Sozialstaat der Gegenwart" (1972), in *Recht, Staat, Freiheit: Studien zur Rechtsphilosophie, Staatstheorie und Verfassungsgeschichte* (Frankfurt a. M.: Suhrkamp, 1991).

from the people themselves and emphasizing the numerical method of arriving at statute. *Recht* and *Gesetz* become mutually exclusive in Schmitt's hands: "Law" comes to equal "the people" not represented by parliament but embodied in the president; "statute" is what is mechanically manufactured by the parliamentary machine without, or even against, the popular will. Whoever holds the majority of seats in parliament becomes an illegitimate "legislator," ruling not on behalf of the people's will but on behalf of the solidification and expansion of its own power. This legislator holds the "monopoly of legality" in its hands, and makes "whatever it will" of statutory procedure, whose outcome is supposedly the equivalent of "law" (*LL*, 277–80). Through such a procedure, "all guarantees of fairness and reasonableness end and also the statutory conception of legality itself consequently deteriorates into the functionalistic substancelessness and contentlessness of an arithmetical majority concept," where 51 percent of the parliament equals law (*LL*, 284).

Of course, Schmitt observes that the majoritarian method of will formation is "sensible and endurable" when practiced under conditions of "substantive likeness of a whole people," because there is no permanent minority under such conditions (*LL*, 284). Under conditions of hostile social divisions, however, the combination of "majority mathematics" and the principle of an "equal chance" of participation for all parties leads to "a grotesque game and a mockery of the notion of fairness" because of an "indifference to every outcome's content," leading to a result that "brings the system itself to an end": the establishment of a "legally continuing power," one that could no longer "do anything unlawful," and acting in such a way that the term "tyranny" no longer has any meaning (*LL*, 285–6). According to Schmitt, "with such consequences the principles of a contentless, functionalistic concept of legality moves itself to absurdity," because the 51 percent can then make the 49 percent illegal and change the conditions whereby the minority might become a majority again (*LL*, 286–7). "Whoever has a majority makes valid statutes; moreover he makes anything which he makes itself valid. Validity and validity-making, sanction and production of legality is their monopoly" (*LL*, 287).

But Schmitt will not entertain the notion that the requirement of more than a simple majority would cure the ills of the tyranny of the majority of which he speaks, a tyranny in which "the sheerly mathematic becomes sheerly inhuman" (*LL*, 295). Perhaps the coalition building that would go into the creation of a two-thirds majority would prevent the kind of extremism he warns against; perhaps the simple fact of a percentage that large will ensure a broad base of support for any constitution amending. He dismisses such remedies as merely "technical-practical" and hence not relevant to the real problem:

> [C]ertainly 66% is quantitatively more than 51%, but the concrete problem of the constitution remains unapproached. The constitutionally theoretical question aims at something else, namely, the central magnitude of the statutory state, the legislator, the concept of statute and their legality. . . . Quantification [of majorities] which are thought of as only quantitative qualifications could be in a negative sense a practical means of checking; however they constitute neither a generally positive principle of fairness or reasonableness, nor a specific constitutional viewpoint, nor are they particularly democratic. (*LL*, 294–5)

To frame the problem in terms of mathematics is to exacerbate that very problem, because abstract forms, such as numbers, are what keep democratic substance, "the will of the constitution" (*LL*, 295), from full expression to begin with: Quantitative majoritarianism of any kind "is grounded not in democratic foundations and even less in the logic of fairness, humanity and reason, but rather in practical-technical considerations on the present situation" (*LL*, 295).

Here Schmitt in fact reveals himself to be totally unconcerned about the tyranny of the majority he has been railing against. The almost liberal arguments regarding persecution of minorities that Schmitt has been wielding against Weimar liberalism emerge as insincere, because his own definition of democracy excludes any such protection: "In truth the need for protection [of minorities] can be very great. But then one must be conscious of the fact that with such, democracy is already denied and it is then less useful to expect a 'lasting' and higher democracy than a lasting minority-protection" (*LL*, 296). Ingenuously criticizing liberalism for a principle he himself does not even take seriously, Schmitt reasserts the necessity of "homogeneity" as the "foundation of all democracies; even parliamentary ones" (*LL*, 295).

That homogeneity, that substantive element that binds a people together – ideology, class, religion, race, ethnicity, or language – must be the core that cannot be relativized or legislated away by some arbitrary, quantitative arrangement of a parliamentary body: "[T]he statutory state must for sure hold fast to definite qualities of statutory conception that is not materially-legally neutral, if it is not to be ruined in a senseless and abstract functionalism" (*LL*, 308). Because the parliament has proven itself thus far incapable of helping to realize this homogeneity in substantive as opposed to formal legislation – indeed, on the contrary, it has accelerated the deterioration thereof – the presidency, as the more explicit agent of such integration, must be called forth more extensively. With feigned resignation, Schmitt states that, although it might not be "true" to the hundred-year tradition of a dual, executive-legislative, constitutional state to tip the balance between the two facets of the constitution in favor of the executive, it is more appropriate to the present mass-democratic moment: "the plebiscitary immediacy of the deciding people [as] legislator" (*LL*, 314). Balance between the executive and the legislature is in fact no longer even a practical option, for each has evolved into "two completely different kinds of state" (*LL*, 315), which may no longer be able to "endure next to one another" (*LL*, 319): Between the two, "there is not only no concurrence of instance, but rather a struggle between two conceptions of what law is" (*LL*, 319).

As we have observed before, Schmitt shifts rather effortlessly between arguments about timely practical necessity and that of universal normative correctness, and in this regard his argument for the *Reichspräsident* over the *Reichstag* is no different: Because of the direct and immediate link between the people and the president, the plebiscitary-democratic aspect of the constitution makes "a qualitatively higher kind of statute" than the legislative system (*LL*, 331). Because parliament relies on quantitative majoritarianism it is inherently crippled by its own technicism: "[A] particular parliament with a particular majority is . . . only a plebiscitary in-between-circuit [*Zwischenschaltung*] . . . . and has parliamentary significance only on 'social-technical' grounds" (*LL*, 339). But Schmitt then lapses again into situation-specific justifications for his strategy: "The strong motive of every tendency toward *auctoritas* lies . . . in a constitutionally theoretical view in the situation itself and arises from the fact that presently the plebiscitary legitimacy remained as a last resort [*ist . . übriggeblieben*] as a singular acknowledged system of justification" (*LL*, 340).

Drawing again from the revolutionary tradition he is opposed to, Schmitt outlines both the procedures and the naïveté of his authoritarian vision for a plebiscitary system:

> [T]he formulations of the great constitutional architect Sieyés applies [*sic*] – authority from above, confidence from below. Plebiscitary legitimacy needs a government or some other instance of authority in which one can have confidence that it will frame the correct question correctly, and that it will not misuse the great power that lies in such a framing of questions. This is a very significant and rare kind of authority. (*LL*, 340–1)

So rare in fact that there has never been an authority like it – one that combines perfect wisdom with perfect benevolence. And unless one's con-

ception of democracy is akin to the clanging of swords on shields, Schmitt's
is perhaps not the most promising source for a substantive democratic
theory. By any conventional standards, the actual practice of electoral majoritarianism, even if its ideology is not one of "substance," may allow for a
more substantive democratic expression than the "yes or no" of
plebiscites.[57]

Form and Substance; Law and Democracy

Weber had predicted that the progress of mass democracy would increase
the demand for "substance" in welfare-state legislation as particular groups
asked for particular redress from the state – demands that would conflict
with the legal formalism that aided in the rise of democracy in the first place
(*ES*, 811). Weber chose to see this as an "insoluble conflict," another manifestation of his "warring gods" vision of modernity (*ES*, 893). Schmitt
thought that he could do better. By opting so unreflectively for the substantive notion of democracy – by attempting to unify into one homogeneous,
"democratic" acclamation all the pluralistic social demands for substantive
state intervention – Schmitt, for his part, endorses a democracy that accentuates not the people's power but precisely their lack of it.[58] Weber had
observed how mass-party democracy entailed intraparty charisma (of the
party leader) and intraparty plebiscitarianism (autocratic hierarchical control).[59] These phenomena engender a "soullessness" among the party following, an "intellectual-spiritual proletarianization."[60] Schmitt's attempt to
convert all the particular charismas and plebiscitarianisms of the many

57 Weber, for instance, well understood the limitations of plebiscites; see *ES*, 1455. Holmes
    argues that the Madisonian scheme of limitations on democracy is actually *more* "democra-
    tic" than the pure or direct theories of democracy associated with Rousseau and Jefferson;
    see "Precommitment and the Paradox of Democracy," in *Passions and Constraint*.
58 Preuß writes, "a democracy of the people actually assembled, acclaiming and complain-
    ing, one directly identified with itself. . . . is an absurdly radical concept that expresses
    nothing more than the people's powerlessness, whose acclamation only serves as the basis
    of legitimation for an otherwise illegitimate political elite." "The German Critique of
    Liberalism," p. 109; and also *Legalität und Pluralismus*. Despite Schmitt's rhetoric regard-
    ing substantive democracy, we should not forget that – apropos of Chapter 4 – Schmitt's
    "substantive" democracy is ineffectual democracy; and – apropos of Chapter 2 – it is the
    formation of a European *elite* that is his main concern. As Kirchheimer remarked of his
    Doktorvater along these lines, Schmitt's valorization of a politically diffuse popular sub-
    stance, on the one hand, and his rejection of abstract norms of validity, on the other, leave
    democracy either "unrealized or unjustified." See Kirchheimer and Nathan Leites, "Re-
    marks on Carl Schmitt's *Legalität und Legitimität*," in *Politics, Law and Social Change*, p. 186.
59 See "Politics as a Vocation," in *From Max Weber: Essays in Sociology*, ed., H. H. Gerth and C.
    Wright Mills (Oxford: Oxford University Press, 1958), p. 103.
60 Ibid., p. 113.

parties into the single office of the *Reichspräsident* entails the proletarianization of the nation as a whole – a soulless mass democracy.[61]

Even taken on its own terms, Schmitt's theory of democracy is again open to the criticism that it is as morally contentless as the Kelsenian liberalism it criticizes.[62] Just as Kelsen cannot account for the moral substance of the norms produced at the end of the constitutional process, Schmitt cannot account for the moral substance of the will at the outset of his theory of constitutionalism, except with the empty criteria of "the political":

> Every existing political unity has its value and "existential justification" not in the rightness or usefulness of norms but solely in its existence as such. That which exists as a political form, considered juridically, has value because it exists. From this alone originates its "right to self-preservation," the presupposition of any further consideration. It seeks ultimately to maintain its existence "*in suo esse preserverare.*" It protects "its existence, its integrity, its security, and its constitution" – all existential values. (*V,* 73)

Existence is not after all a particularly thick criterion of ethical content. Stripped of the resource of the traditional justifications of moral substance by the knowledge that they have been rendered perpetually inadequate historically, and unable to carry through the dialectical intuitions of much of his writings to sufficiently ground a theory of modernity, Schmitt is left with only an existential positivism that mirrors the logical positivism he so intensely despises.

Furthermore, in light of these considerations, Schmitt's strategy regarding the concrete predicament of law in the twentieth-century industrial welfare state becomes suddenly clearer and will be taken up more specifically in the next chapter: If the structural imperatives of the welfare state require the supercession of laissez-faire capitalism, then the institutional and normative developments of liberalism and the rule of law that accompany this economic state of affairs – most obviously and immediately, basic rights (*V,* 163) and the separation of powers established to protect them (*V,*

---

61   A process that was already occurring and to which Schmitt-like fascist alternatives were a response. See Siegfried Kracauer on "the proletarianization of the middle class" in his analysis of the circle around the journal *Die Tat,* which included Schmitt: "The Revolt of the Middle Classes" (1931), in *The Mass Ornament: Weimar Essays,* ed., Thomas Y. Levin (Cambridge, Mass.: Harvard University Press, 1995), p. 122.

62   Habermas and Maus both point out the "pseudopositivism" of Schmitt's antipositivism; see "Dogmatism, Reason and Decision," and *Bürgerliche Rechtstheorie und Faschismus,* respectively. See also Christian Graf von Krockow, *Die Entscheidung: Eine Untersuchung über Ernst Jünger, Carl Schmitt, Martin Heidegger* (Frankfurt a. M.: Campus, 1990).

126) – may consequently also be scrapped.[63] Schmitt therefore savagely attacks the ideology of the previous era and its "invisible-hand," abstract, notion of domination, while appropriating and redirecting the immediate social reality of the present era, namely, the "hands-on," concrete domination that both he and social scientists affiliated with the Frankfurt School identify as the emerging "primacy of the political."[64] Thus Schmitt's ability to discern contradictions between abstract and concrete manifestations of modernity, as well as ideology and social bases in industrial transformation, does not entail his rigorously tracing them back to their generative sources. On the contrary, he accepts them as automatically given, irreducible oppositions and, worse, seeks to arrange them strategically such that his authoritarian vision is the most reasonable solution to the theoretical-political impasse. We have observed how this vision is "necessitated" by the logic of liberalism's development and the specificity of the present historical moment but also sanctioned cryptonormatively in transhistorical terms as the most preferred political arrangement in general: liberalism then; fascism now; authoritarianism forever.[65] The hope of veiling the strategic manipula-

63 See Scheuerman, *Between the Exception and the Norm*, pp. 71–80, 126–33. Scheuerman also notes how Schmitt's refusal to engage in the anachronistic nostalgia for nineteenth-century market capitalism, in marked contrast to one of his most influential devotees, Friedrich Hayek, demonstrates that Schmitt is more theoretically sensitive to actual social structures and industrial transformations. But it also illustrates exactly how he is more politically dangerous through his willingness to abandon the normative liberal principles to which Hayekian neoconservatives insist on clinging as they attempt to revive the supposedly "free" market; see "The Unholy Alliance of Carl Schmitt and Friedrich A. Hayek," *Constellations* 4:2 (October 1997).

64 Cf. the essays by Friedrich Pollock of 1941: "State Capitalism: Its Possibilities and Limitations" and "Is National Socialism a New Order?" both reprinted in *The Essential Frankfurt School Reader*, ed. Andrew Arato and Eike Gebhardt (Oxford: Basil Blackwell, 1978). On the social-theoretical deficiencies and yet pervasive influence of Pollock's thesis, see Moishe Postone, *Time, Labor and Social Domination: A Reinterpretation of Marx's Critical Theory* (New York: Cambridge University Press, 1993), pp. 90–120.

65 Through such a strategy did Schmitt acquire the title: "Lenin of the Bourgeoisie." Kracauer points out in his analysis of the *Tat* circle how fascists like Schmitt generally practice a bad-faith orientation toward liberalism: "The manic need to harass and chase liberalism into the remote recesses allows one to conclude indisputably that this is, in psychoanalytic terms, something like a symptom of repression. People pursue liberalism with such hatred because it is something they discover within themselves. And indeed *Die Tat* unconsciously contains so much of it that it spews forth from all sides. It will not allow itself to be hidden: the liberalism turned away at the front gate is always graciously invited to enter through the back door. And even if it slips in under a different name, there is no way to mistake it. Its presence within a realm of thought hostile to it is, however, just further evidence of the latter's powerlessness. . . . Thus, if *Die Tat* on the one hand is advocating a state that arises through organic growth, yet on the other hand wants to achieve a kind of socialism by means of a planned economy, it is aiming at something that is simply impossible. It throws reason out of the temple of the *Volk*'s state and simultaneously invites it into the offices of

tion of twentieth-century socioeconomic realities into a more "stable" – that is, reactionary – orientation by denouncing the residual ideology of the last century's Kantian idealism is what drives the ever-escalating war between Schmittian concreteness and Kelsenian abstractness throughout his Weimar development.[66]

But if Schmitt accepts the twentieth-century necessity of state intervention into society and the economy, how will he keep his state from intervening in the manner that induces the development of what he characterizes in pejoratively technical terms as the "total quantitative state?" How will he theorize state intervention into society, state manipulation of socioeconomic forces, such that the state retains its status as a "total qualitative state," more specifically, an exception-executing, presidential, *sovereign* state that replaces the also situation-specific, legislative, *welfare* state and regulates economic equilibrium instead of social inequality?[67]

To do so, he must purge every residue of liberal normativity, even that which remains – in perhaps contradictory manner – as ethical justification for the liberal *Sozialstaat* that supersedes the liberal *Rechtsstaat*, and replace it with other criteria for state activity. At the base of Schmitt's new *Staatslehre*, I will argue in the next chapter, is the attempt to replace the liberal principles of freedom or equality with the element of fear. Thus, Schmitt seeks to formulate a mode of abstract domination that functions as if it were concrete domination but does not, as the latter so often does, require the state to overextend itself into society and necessarily make available its techniques and instruments of domination to partisans within society. Fear, mythic fear, is the abstract entity that acts as if it were concrete repression, that is, that keeps citizens, or in Schmitt's neo-Hobbesian terms, subjects, at bay without touching them bodily on a regular basis. This strategy of state restraint is guided not by normative, liberal principles of privacy or personal

---

the state economy. This is not *one* but two movements, and they are going in opposite directions. The first, the primary movement, is the reaction against liberalism; the second, which aims at a planned economy that can be realized only by means of rational organization, marks the appearance of the principle of reason, which is all too reductively designated 'liberalist.'" "The Revolt of the Middle Classes," pp. 119, 122–3.

66 Ernst Fraenkel detected this strategy in Schmitt's jurisprudence; he notes how Schmitt "stole from Hegel the tendency to use 'concreteness' as a weapon against 'abstraction.' According to Hegel the principle of reason must be conceived as concrete in order that true freedom may come to rule. Hegel characterizes the school of thought which clings to abstraction as liberalism and emphasizes that the concrete is always victorious against the abstract and that the abstract always becomes bankrupt against the concrete." *The Dual State: A Contribution to the Theory of Dictatorship* (1941), trans. E. A. Shils (New York: Octagon Books, 1969), p. 143.

67 See Schmitt's *Unabhängig der Richter: Gleichheit vor dem Gesetz und Gewährleistung des Privateigentums nach der Weimarer Verfassung* (Berlin: Walter de Gruyter, 1926).

space but by pragmatic principles of a neo–raison d'état. Thus, an ideology of abstract legality that allowed for an indiscriminately concrete reality of state activity, which weakens the state in positivist constitutional theory, is supplanted by Schmitt's state theory in which an ideology of almost total intervention into the realms of the social and the private – an ideology that necessarily arouses fear – allows for the state's restraint, selectivity, and prudence in its actual mode of intervention, thus preserving its own vitality. Such a state will not frivolously spend what Schmitt often calls the "political surplus value" necessary for its independence (e. g., *LL,* 288).

We will witness Schmitt's exhilaration at this renewed opportunity for myth-making elites in modernity, an opportunity afforded by the passing away of the socially and politically "self-regulating" ideologies of the nineteenth century and by the new "activist" moment in the twentieth. Schmitt, who had labored so hard for a political theory that spoke in the name of the mass-democratic moment but in fact made way for new elites, would obviously take a lead role in this new epoch. The age of "abstraction," of "belief in rationality and ideality," of "typically Cartesian belief" in "idées générales" is passed (*LL,* 270). And because the abstract rule of law, rule of norms, also must consequently pass, it is up to elites to shape the newly emerging rule of persons over persons. It must not take the form of soviet-style concrete rule, for that would lead to foreign domination; nor should it, however, stray too far from the powerful source of legitimacy to which foreign and domestic soviets appeal so successfully: the irresistible progress of mass democracy. Hence Schmitt's answer: nationalist-presidential democracy instead of class-party democracy. In this we see again that the "countermovement" (e. g., *HV,* 131) to which Schmitt often refers is less *counter*revolutionary than simply *cooptively* revolutionary, for Schmitt consistently seeks to appropriate the social, political, and historical thunder of what he opposes.

We will also witness how Schmitt's deconstruction of constitutionalism, necessarily liberal constitutionalism, made for the dissolution of any possible checks in the state theory he formulated to replace it. We will observe how the state–constitution–people constellation of political unity that Schmitt formulated in *Verfassungslehre,* which entailed undermining the *rechtsstaatliche* quality of the middle term, "constitution," more or less compels Schmitt to take up the new constellation of state–*movement*–people that he formulated in 1933 to justify the newly triumphant National Socialist regime.[68]

---

68   See Schmitt, *Staat, Bewegnung, Volk: Die Dreigliederung der politischen Einheit* (Hamburg: Hanseatische Verlagsanstalt, 1934).

6

THE STATE

Throughout his Weimar writings, Schmitt often asserts the existence of a dissociation between what is natural-scientific and what is "personalistic," "human," "specifically real," "alive" within the philosophy of Thomas Hobbes. For example,

> It is striking that one of the most consequential representatives of the abstract scientific orientation of the seventeenth century [Thomas Hobbes] became so personalistic. This is because as a juristic thinker he wanted to grasp the reality of societal life just as much as he, as a philosopher and a natural scientist, wanted to grasp the reality of nature. . . . [J]uristic thought in those days had not yet become so overpowered by the natural sciences that he, in the intensity of his scientific approach, should unsuspectingly have overlooked the specific reality of legal life.[1]

In this chapter, I discuss why Schmitt felt the need to emphasize this supposed distinction or opposition in the work of the great seventeenth-century English political theorist, particularly in his famous *Concept of the Political*. As Hobbes remarked, "The Passion to be reckoned upon, is Fear"

---

1 Carl Schmitt, *Political Theology: Four Chapters on the Concept of Sovereignty* (1922), trans. George Schwab (Cambridge, Mass.: MIT Press, 1986), p. 34.

(I, 14),[2] and Schmitt recognizes something vital, substantive, and fundamentally human in Hobbes's grounding of the state in the fear of death. On the eve of Weimar's collapse, Schmitt, with the intellectual aid of a young admirer named Leo Strauss, sought to retrieve this primal source of political order and free it from the elements that Hobbes himself had found necessary to employ to construct a state on this foundation: natural science and technology. Schmitt and Strauss saw in these latter elements the very cause of the breakdown or the "neutralization" of what they were intended to help build, the modern state. The particular sociopolitical situation of Weimar – violence exercised by private groups, a widespread perception of technology as a "runaway" phenomenon, and so on – rendered it a critical moment to reintroduce the issue of fear and the issue of science and consequently to reformulate Hobbes and the intellectual foundation of the state. I suggest, however, that the issues of fear, violence, technology, and the state could not be so easily distinguished within Hobbes's thought, and, in light of the emergence of National Socialism, Schmitt felt compelled in *The Leviathan in The State Theory of Thomas Hobbes* either to qualify significantly or abandon completely this approach to Hobbes – in retrospect, an approach with ominous implications.[3]

Fear and the Political

In *Der Begriff des Politischen*,[4] Schmitt sets forth his most famous thesis on the "essence" of politics: "The specific political distinction to which political actions and motives can be reduced is that between friend and enemy" (*CP*, 26). Yet despite the apparent novelty of this proposition, one finds the shadow of Thomas Hobbes cast quite prominently over this famous treatise.

2 All references to Hobbes are from the English version of *Leviathan,* with book and chapter citations appearing bracketed within the text.

3 This chapter differs from the studies by Strauss disciples, such as Heinrich Meier, *Carl Schmitt and Leo Strauss: The Hidden Dialogue,* trans. J. Harvey Lomax (Chicago: University of Chicago Press, 1995); and Susan Shell, "Meier on Strauss and Schmitt," *Review of Politics* 53:1 (winter 1991); as well as from that of Strauss critic John Gunnell, "Strauss before Straussianism: The Weimar Conversation," *Review of Politics* 52:1 (winter 1990), in that my interest is primarily with Schmitt as participant and with Hobbes as subject of this "dialogue."

4 Schmitt, *The Concept of the Political,* trans. George Schwab (New Brunswick: Rutgers University Press, 1976). References are to the 1932 edition, cited as *CP.* Schmitt's thesis was originally put forth in an article of the same title in 1927, and subsequently in a new version of the book in 1933. See Meier, *Carl Schmitt and Leo Strauss,* on the differences among the editions.

As Hobbes himself had maintained, in humanity's natural condition, in the state of nature, "every man to every man, for want of a common power to keep them all in awe is an Enemy" (I, 15).[5] Indeed, Schmitt's friend/enemy distinction is intended to serve a theoretical-political role analogous to Hobbes's "state of nature." If Hobbes predicated the modern state on the "state of nature," Schmitt declares that "the concept of the state presupposes the concept of the political." And any inquiries made into the "essence" of the state that do not first take this foundation into consideration would be premature (*CP*, 19). Questions of whether the state is "a machine or an organism, a person or an institution, a society or a community, an enterprise or a beehive" – questions in which Schmitt will eventually become quite interested, as we will see – must be provisionally set aside (*CP*, 19).

Schmitt thus conceives of his formulation of "the political" as an "Archimedean point," not unlike that which Hobbes sought to locate in the state of nature:

> Insofar as it is not derived from other criteria, the antithesis of friend and enemy corresponds to the relatively independent criteria of other antitheses: good and evil in the moral sphere, beautiful and ugly in the aesthetic sphere, and so on. In any event it is independent, not in the sense of a distinct new domain, but in that it can neither be based on any one antithesis or any combination of other antitheses, nor can it be traced to these. (*CP*, 26)

"The political" is irreducible to any other element. Indeed Schmitt envisions the friend/enemy distinction as so fundamental and elementary that in the course of his argument he feels compelled at particular points to remark on the self-evidence of his thesis: "nothing can escape this logical conclusion of the political" (*CP*, 36). Schmitt even resorts to the most questionable of Hobbes's arguments to demonstrate the actual existence of the state of affairs he describes: Like the state of nature, the political can be shown to exist on the basis of behavior of states in the arena of international affairs (*CP*, 28).[6]

These are interesting parallels between Schmitt and Hobbes, but they do

5 The language of "friend" and "enemy" is quite prevalent in *Leviathan*, for instance, "when either [a group of people] have no common *enemy*, or he that by one part is held for an *enemy*, is by another part held for a *friend*, they must needs by the difference of their interests dissolve, and fall again into a war among themselves" (II, 17, emphasis added).
6 The existence of such phenomena as the "balance of power" is often used to counter Hobbes's equation of the realm of international relations with the "state of nature."

not drive to the heart of Schmitt's neo-Hobbesian project.[7] Schmitt observes that Hobbes formulated his political theory "in the terrible times of civil war" when

> all legitimate and normative illusions with which men like to deceive themselves regarding political realities in periods of untroubled security vanish. If within the state there are organized parties capable of according their members more protection than the state, then the latter becomes at best an annex of such parties, and the individual citizen knows whom he has to obey. (*CP*, 52)

This is quite an apt description of Weimar Germany during its crisis years. Schmitt sees in the context of Hobbes's thought a parallel with his own and, relatedly, a parallel in their projects. In *Leviathan*, Hobbes sought "to instill in man again 'the mutual relation between Protection and Obedience'" (*CP*, 52) and so forestall the strife and chaos that arises when armed autonomous groups confront each other. This is not far removed from Schmitt's own intentions.[8] The "exceptional" situation of civil war reveals normally concealed political realities, such as human behavior in a "state of nature": "In it, states exist among themselves in a condition of continual danger, and their acting subjects are evil for precisely the same reasons as animals who are stirred by their drives (hunger, greediness, fear, jealousy)" (*CP*, 59). Therefore, argues Schmitt, all "genuine" political theories, that is, those that have observed the normally concealed "political realities," presuppose "man to be evil," meaning "dangerous and dynamic" (*CP*, 61).

---

7   Schmitt's debt to Hobbes is touched on in many commentaries; see Helmut Rumpf, *Carl Schmitt und Thomas Hobbes: Ideelle Beziehungen und aktuelle Bedeutung mit einer Abhandlung über: Die Frühschriften Carl Schmitts* (Berlin: Duncker & Humblot, 1972); Joseph Bendersky, *Carl Schmitt: Theorist for the Reich* (Princeton: Princeton University Press, 1983); David J. Levy, "The Relevance of Carl Schmitt," *The World and I* (March 1987); Herfried Münkler, "Carl Schmitt und Thomas Hobbes," *Neue Politische Literatur* 29 (1984); George Schwab, *The Challenge of the Exception* (Westport: Greenwood, 1989); Paul Edward Gottfried, *Carl Schmitt: Politics and Theory* (Westport: Greenwood, 1990); Stephen Holmes, "Carl Schmitt: The Debility of Liberalism," in *The Anatomy of Antiliberalism* (Cambridge, Mass.: Harvard University Press, 1993); Jeffrey Andrew Barash, "Hobbes, Carl Schmitt et les apories du décisionnisme politique," *Les Temps Modernes* (August–September 1993); Gershon Weiler, *From Absolutism to Totalitarianism: Carl Schmitt on Thomas Hobbes* (Durango: Hollowbrook Press, 1994). On the place of Schmitt's thesis in Western political thought in general, see Bernard Willms, "Politics as Politics: Carl Schmitt's Concept of the Political and the Tradition of European Political Thought," *History of European Ideas* 13:4 (1991).
8   As Meier perceptively notes, Schmitt's argument comes to focus more on civil war and an impending decline of liberalism in the 1932 book, revised in the midst of Weimar's most dramatic period of crisis, than he did in the 1927 essay, which was written during the relative calm of the Republic's middle period of the mid twenties. See *Carl Schmitt and Leo Strauss,* pp. 21–5.

Schmitt thus shares with Hobbes not only a similar historical context but a similar outlook on humanity as well. What are the ramifications of this? This particular outlook on humanity offers the way out of the problems of the state of nature, civil war, or impending civil war. Regarding the "genuine" political philosophers who take the view that the human being is essentially dangerous, Schmitt writes, "their realism can *frighten* men in need of security" (*CP*, 65, emphasis added). This is precisely the point. Schmitt recognizes, as did Hobbes, that by *frightening* people one can best "instill" in them that principle, "the *cogito ergo sum* of the state," *protego ergo obligo* [protection therefore obedience] (*CP*, 52). In other words, *fear* is the source of political order. Human beings once confronted with the prospect of their own dangerousness will be terrified into the arms of authority.

Thus, "For Hobbes, truly a powerful and systematic political thinker, the pessimistic conception of man is the elementary presupposition of a specific system of political thought" (*CP*, 65). But "systematic" does not mean for Schmitt "scientific" or "technical." Technology has helped foster the liberal conception of man that assumes that with wealth and abundance humanity's dangerousness can be ameliorated, and hence blinds humanity to the eternal reality of "the political" (*CP*, 61). Technology, according to Schmitt, as we know from Chapter 2, has facilitated the "neutralization" of the state and the European order of states, again concealing the nature of "the political." Schmitt chides Eduard Spranger for taking "too technical" a perspective on human nature, for viewing it in light of "the tactical manipulation of instinctive drives" (*CP*, 59). Hobbes's insight, on the contrary, is neither "the product of a frightful and disquieting fantasy nor of a philosophy based on free competition by a bourgeois society in its first stage . . . but is the fundamental presupposition of a specific political philosophy" (*CP*, 65). Schmitt's task then is to elaborate on Hobbes's view of humanity and revive the fear that is characteristic of man's natural condition in three ways: (1) by demonstrating the substantive affinity between his concept of the political and Hobbes's state of nature, (2) by making clear the ever-present possibility of a return to that situation in the form of civil war, and (3) by convincing individuals – partisans and nonpartisans alike – that only a state with a monopoly on decisions regarding what is "political" can guarantee peace and security. He must do all of this while avoiding the elements of natural science and technology, often associated with Hobbes, that undermined this project in the first place.[9]

9 Ingeborg Maus detects the opposition between "terror" and "technocratic rationality" in Schmitt's state theory; see *Bürgerliche Rechtstheorie und Faschismus: Zur sozialen Funktion und*

The radical subjectivity characteristic of the political heightens the danger regarding Schmitt's concept of the political and consequently intensifies the fear inspired by it. "Only the actual participants can correctly recognize, understand, and judge the concrete situation and settle the extreme case of conflict. Each participant is in a position to judge whether the adversary intends to negate his opponent's way of life and therefore must be repulsed or fought in order to preserve one's own form of existence" (*CP*, 27). The fact that in the absence of a centralized power there is no standard by which one can judge another as an enemy or be so judged by them clearly implies that one must always be ready to be attacked or, more reasonably, compels one to be the first to strike. This is obviously a revival of the Hobbesian scenario of "the condition of meer Nature" where all "are judges of their own fears" (I, 14). In this light, Pasquale Pasquino observes that it is exactly "the absence or epistemological impossibility of defining an objective criterion of what constitutes a threat to the individual's self preservation that transforms the natural right into the origin of the potential war of all against all."[10] Schmitt consistently drops the natural right and re-emphasizes the potential war. Hence, this radical subjectivity is the source of the danger in Schmitt's "political" and, according to Pasquino, "the essential reason why the Hobbesian state of nature is one of total uncertainty and lack of freedom."[11] This "potentiality" for war and the "uncertainty" that arise from this radical subjectivity intensify fear because they ensure the constancy of danger. In fact, the *threat* of danger is always present, even when the actual danger is not. As Hobbes remarks, the essence of the war that is the state of nature "consisteth not in actuall fighting; but in the known disposition thereto" (I, 13). Accordingly, Schmitt maintains that "to the enemy concept belongs the ever present *possibility* of combat" (*CP*, 32, emphasis added).

The continued existence of this sort of subjectivity within society implies the preservation of the state of war and the fear that it engenders. As Hobbes makes explicit, it is a "diseased" commonwealth that tolerates the doctrine "*That every private man is Judge of Good and Evil actions*" (I, 29) and, worse, one that allows persons to resort to violence to defend such judgments, "For those men that are so remissely governed, that they dare take up Armes, to defend, or introduce an Opinion, are still in Warre" (I, 18). Schmitt sees in

aktuellen Wirkung der Theorie Carl Schmitts (Munich: C. H. Beck, 1980), p. 125.

10   Pasquale Pasquino, "Hobbes: Natural Right, Absolutism, and Political Obligation," *Approches Cognitives Du Social* 90158 (September 1990): 9.

11   Ibid.

the pluralist theories of the early twentieth century a justification for just such behavior (*CP*, 52) and, like Hobbes, evaluates the outcome as state vulnerability both domestically and with regard to foreign powers:

> The intensification of internal antagonisms has the effect of weakening the common identity vis-à-vis another state. If domestic conflicts among political parties have become the sole political difference, the most extreme degree of internal political tension is thereby reached; i.e., the domestic, not the foreign friend-and-enemy groupings are decisive for armed conflict. The ever present possibility of conflict must always be kept in mind. If one wants to speak of politics in the context of the primacy of internal politics, then this conflict no longer refers to war between organized nations but to civil war. (*CP*, 32)

Hobbes adamantly maintains that the existence of violent factions, whether constituted by familial ties, religious affiliation, or economic status, is "contrary to the peace and safety of the people, a taking of the Sword out of the hand of the Sovereign" (II, 22). And it is precisely these kinds of armed antagonisms that had reemerged in late Weimar: trade unions versus company goons, communist mobs versus fascist gangs, political party versus political party, and so on.[12] Each had declared the right to evaluate self-protection in its own way and to act accordingly. Each had claimed the right to judge the political (*CP*, 37).

Schmitt wants desperately to demonstrate that this situation implies the likelihood of explosion into civil war and Hobbes's state of nature. He must revive the fear that led to the termination of the state of nature in order to prevent the reversion back to it. If groups other than the state, "counter-forces" as Schmitt describes them, have power, particularly such as that over declaring war, or worse if they do not possess such a power themselves but can prevent the state from exercising that power, the state disappears: "[T]hen a unified political entity would no longer exist" (*CP*, 39).

As he argues in his late Weimar essays on pluralism and the "total" state, even under seemingly normal conditions the practices of the former work to bring about the situation of civil war, because pluralism encourages

> a plurality of moral ties and duties, a "plurality of loyalties" through which the pluralist division becomes increasingly stronger and more destabilizing, and the solidity of a political unity becomes increasingly endangered. . . . [This]

12 See Eve Rosenhaft, "Working-Class Life and Working-Class Politics: Communists, Nazis, and the State Battle for the Streets of Berlin 1928–1932," in *Social Change and Political Development in Weimar Germany*, ed. Richard Bessel and E. J. Feuchtwanger (New York: Barnes & Noble, 1981), pp. 207–40, for a compelling account of this state of affairs.

destroys respect for the constitution and transforms the basis of the constitution into an uncertain terrain embattled from many sides.[13]

According to Schmitt, a constitutional order, which as we know from the previous chapter is identified by Schmitt explicitly with the state, must form some sort of unity within which plurality may obtain, but it must not be a modus vivendi in which one group is waiting to seize power from another:

> If the state becomes a pluralist party state, its unity can be maintained only as long as two or more parties recognize common premises. The unity then lies in the particular authority of a constitution recognized by all parties whereby the common basis must unequivocally be respected. The ethic of the state then becomes the ethic of the constitution. The stability, singularity of meaning, and authority of the constitution can then form a truly real unity. But if the constitution becomes nothing more than the mere rules of the game and its ethic degenerates into one of fair play then the unity is ultimately what the pluralists would make of it – merely a conglomerate of the changing appropriations by heterogeneous groups.[14]

Schmitt's implicit reading of Hobbes, therefore, is that a return to the state of nature is particularly an ever-present possibility for a society characterized by pluralism.

This reading of an impending return of the state of nature is generally countered by those who see Hobbes's state of nature as either merely a rhetorical device or an anthropological supposition about a very distant past. But as Pasquino persuasively argues, Hobbes viewed the state of nature not as a factually historical past but as a politically possible present: Hobbes conceived of this condition as one of "terror, that is to say a condition in which no individual is certain of his/her borders or even his physical identity, that is his life," and he was "anxious to show that the state of nature actually exists."[15] The state of nature as it exists in relationship to the *present*

13 Schmitt, "Die Wendung zum totalen Staat" (1931), in *Positionen und Begriffe im Kampf mit Weimar – Genf – Versailles: 1923–1939* (Hamburg: Hanseatische Verlagsanstalt, 1940), pp. 156–7.

14 Schmitt, "Staatsethik und pluralistisher Staat" (1930), in *Positionen und Begriffe*, pp. 144–5.

15 Pasquale Pasquino, "Hobbes On the Natural Condition of Mankind" (part 1 of the English manuscript of "Thomas Hobbes: la rationalité de l' obéissance à la loi, *La pensée politique* [spring 1994]), p. 3. Setting aside the view that the state of nature is a mere intellectual enterprise, Pasquino prefers to employ the term "subtraction" to describe it rather than "abstraction," for the state of nature is for Hobbes a stripping away from the empirical world rather than the product of imagination. There is of course the famous

is Hobbes's utmost concern, according to Pasquino: "It can happen at any time and must always be avoided. It is the face of the threat that political order must ward off."[16]

This buttressing of Schmitt's reading of Hobbes more clearly demonstrates his own project. Schmitt seeks to make real the terror of what is and what might be, so as to strengthen the existing order. The citizens of Weimar must reaffirm the pact that delivers human beings out of the state of nature and into civil society, by transferring their illegitimately exercised subjectivity regarding friend and enemy back to the sovereign state. "To the state as an essentially political entity belongs the *jus belli*, i.e., the real possibility of deciding in a concrete situation upon the enemy and the ability to fight him with the power emanating from the entity" (*CP,* 45). The state and the state alone decides on internal enemies (*CP,* 46) and external ones as well (*CP,* 28–9). Regarding internal enemies, Schmitt seeks to reverse the pluralist view of the state as merely one interest group among many others in society or even as a servant thereof (*CP,* 44). The state must stand above society as a quasi-objective entity, rather than help precipitate civil war by existing as one subjectivity among others. Regarding external enemies, just as Hobbes had Catholics in mind when he warned against allegiance to extranational powers, Schmitt surely thinks of the Communists when he writes that one should not "love and support the enemies of one's own people" (*CP,* 29). Moscow should come before Berlin no more than Rome before London or Paris. Only one's own state can ask one to surrender one's life for it (*CP,* 46), and Schmitt mocks liberal individualism for not being able to command this from citizens (*CP,* 71). But here he parts company with Hobbes, who is perhaps the most famous exponent of just this kind of right: *not* to lay down one's life in response to a political command. It is here that we should turn to Leo Strauss's critique and radicalization of Schmitt's project, for it is on this point and the issues surrounding it that Strauss's essay pivots.

What should be clear from my presentation thus far is that Schmitt seeks to make the threat of conflict, of war, felt and feared so as to make war's outbreak all the more unlikely domestically and its prosecution more easily facilitated abroad. In *Political Romanticism,* he declares that for romantics, "the state is a work of art."[17] A question that must be asked again is how

---

passage in which Hobbes asserts how close the "natural condition" really is to contemporary reality, by reminding his readers that they arm themselves when traveling, bolt their doors at night, and lock their chests even when at home (I, 13).

16 Pasquino, "Hobbes on the Natural Condition," p. 6.
17 Schmitt, *Political Romanticism,* trans. Guy Oakes (Cambridge, Mass.: MIT Press, 1985), p. 125.

much Schmitt himself aestheticized matters of state in his own *Staatslehre*. The issue of the aestheticization of violence is inherently conjoined with a subject that is only implicit in *The Concept of the Political* but that has arisen consistently in this study and is particularly relevant in Schmitt's later work on Hobbes: the question of myth. Recall from Chapter 2 that, in their respective analyses of myth, Max Horkheimer and T. W. Adorno, Ernst Cassirer, and Hans Blumenberg each focused on the element of fear.[18] According to these theorists of myth, humanity exchanges the fear of unordered and chaotic nature for the fear of something of their own contrivance, which is more certain and identifiable. This is very close to the kind of exchange that Hobbes offers: Subjects give up their epistemological uncertainty regarding the totality of *human* nature – their fear of everything and everyone at every moment – for the more tolerable knowledge that it is only the state that is to be feared, and then only under certain conditions. Indeed, Hobbes names his state after the mythic biblical monster, the Leviathan. The extent to which Schmitt's revival and reformulation of the Hobbesian exchange, in *The Concept of the Political*, succumbs to the element of myth and the question concerning the potential ramifications of this are subjects I will take up in later sections of the chapter.

Strauss's Commentary on *The Concept of the Political* (1932)

I address four aspects of the young Strauss's comments on Schmitt's thesis: his recognition of Schmitt's project as I have described it and its relationship to that of Hobbes; his confirmation of the necessity of such a project on the basis of "the present situation" of Weimar; his criticism of the project on the basis of Schmitt's own assumptions and aims; and finally, the manner in which he refashions, redirects, and radicalizes the project itself.[19]

Strauss realizes that Schmitt's inquiry into "the order of human things," into "the political," is necessarily an examination of the foundation of the state (*CP*, 81), for the state was founded with "the fundamental and extreme status of man" in mind (*CP*, 88). Indeed, as Strauss recognizes explicitly,

18 Horkheimer and Adorno, *Dialectic of Enlightenment* (1944), trans. John Cummings (New York: Continuum, 1989); Cassirer, *The Myth of the State* (New Haven: Yale University Press, 1946) and *Symbol, Myth and Culture: Essays and Lectures, 1935–1945*, ed. Donald Philip Verene (New Haven: Yale University Press, 1979); and Blumenberg, *Work on Myth*, trans. Robert Wallace, (Cambridge, Mass.: MIT Press, 1989).

19 Leo Strauss's "Anmerkungen zu Carl Schmitt, *Der Begriff des Politischen*" was originally published in *Archiv für Sozialwissenschaft und Sozialpolitik* 67:6 (August–September 1932). An English translation by E. M. Sinclair appears in the English edition of *The Concept of the Political*. Therefore, I will also cite Strauss's essay as *CP*.

"the political, which Schmitt brings out as fundamental, is 'the state of nature'. . . . Schmitt restores Hobbes's conception of the state of nature to a place of honor" (*CP*, 87–8). Just as "inspiring fear" is a primary characteristic of Hobbes's state of nature, the same can be said of Schmitt's political, according to Strauss's interpretation (*CP*, 95). As Strauss observed regarding Hobbes, in a work published only a few years earlier, in 1930,

> Fear is not only alarm and flight, but also distrust, suspicion, caution, care lest one fear. Now it is not death in itself that can be avoided, but only death by violence, which is the greatest of possible evils. For life itself can be of such misery that death comes to be ranked with the good. In the final instance what is of primary concern is ensuring the continuance of life in the sense of ensuring defense against other men. Concern with self-protection is the fundamental consideration, the one most fully in accord with the human situation. . . . The fear of death, the fear of death by violence, is [for Hobbes] the source of all right, the primary basis of natural right.[20]

Strauss thus acknowledges as justified Schmitt's revival of the image of the state of nature and the notion of fear that must accompany it. Echoing another of Schmitt's works, according to Strauss, the "present situation" in "the age of neutralizations and depoliticizing" calls for such a revival (*CP*, 82).[21] The prevailing pluralist and liberal theories of society and "culture," which view these entities as "autonomous" – that is, as legitimately separate from the state – have neutralized the political (*CP*, 86). Because such theories view culture as something "natural" in the sense that human beings develop it more or less spontaneously, they overlook that there is something that exists prior to culture. "This conception makes us forget that 'culture' always presupposes something which is cultivated: culture is always cultivation of nature" (*CP*, 86). Strauss makes explicit that nature in this sense also entails *human* nature and hence "the state of nature":

> Since we understand by 'culture' above all the culture of *human* nature, the presupposition of culture is, above all, human nature, and since man is by nature an *animal sociale*, the human nature underlying culture is the natural living together of men, i.e., the mode in which man – prior to culture – behaves towards other men. The term for the natural living together thus

20 Strauss, *Spinoza's Critique of Religion*, trans. E. M. Sinclair (New York: Schocken, 1965), p. 92.
21 Schmitt, "The Age of Neutralizations and Depoliticizations" (1929), trans. Matthias Konzett and John P. McCormick, *Telos* 96 (Summer 1993).

understood is the *status naturalis*. One may therefore say, the foundation of culture is the *status naturalis*. (*CP*, 87)

The cultivation of the state of nature is, as we know according to Hobbes and Schmitt, the state, not society initially. The state, by establishing order, makes possible the existence of society. Therefore, Strauss more firmly grounds the Schmittian thesis against the proponents of the theory of "autonomous" culture and society, namely, liberals and pluralists. The latter overlook the fact that the state of nature and the state itself exist prior to "culture" commonly understood as it exists within society. Consequently, behavior that weakens the state increases the risk of reviving the state of nature. The *status naturalis* and human nature as it exists within it – "the political" – do not go away simply because, according to Schmitt, liberalism has ignored it or even "negated" it. Strauss reiterates this Schmittian thesis; liberalism merely "conceals" the political:

> Liberalism has not killed the political, but merely killed understanding of the political, and sincerity regarding the political. To clear the obfuscation of reality which liberalism has caused, the political must be brought out and shown to be completely undeniable. Liberalism is responsible for having covered over the political, and the political must once again be brought to light, if the question of the state is to be put in full seriousness. (*CP*, 82–3)[22]

Strauss and Schmitt agree that liberalism has put the state into crisis by "obfuscating" the political, that the specter of the state of nature must be made apparent – with all the fear that accompanies it – and that "a different system" must be made the basis of the state "that does not negate the political, but brings the political into full recognition" (*CP*, 83). However, it is on the question of how to found this "different system" that the student challenges the master. The figure of Hobbes again proves central to the disagreement.

On the issue of how one cultivates nature – how the state is founded or how culture is developed – Strauss identifies two ways of proceeding. The first "means culture develops the natural disposition; it is careful cultivation of nature – whether of the soil or of the human mind; in this it obeys the

---

22   Several years later, in 1939, Walter Benjamin observed that one of the effects of technology – which Schmitt and Strauss in these works associate explicitly with liberalism – is to render a person "no longer capable of telling his proven friend from his mortal enemy." "On Some Motifs in Baudelaire," in *Illuminations*, ed. Hannah Arendt (New York: Schocken, 1968), p. 168. Whether Benjamin, who was quite familiar with Schmitt's work, is here explicitly alluding to "the political" is not clear.

indications that nature itself gives" (*CP,* 86). Strauss identifies the second
kind of cultivation with Bacon: "[C]ulture is not so much faithful cultivation
of nature as a harsh and cunning fight against nature" (*CP,* 87). This second, "specifically modern conception of nature" can also be located in
Hobbes, according to Strauss, a conception that associates culture with "a
disciplining of human will, as the *opposite* of the *status naturalis*"(*CP,* 87). In
terms of human nature, this means that Hobbes not only held the "pessimistic" view of humanity as "dangerous" and "dynamic" that Schmitt earlier
identifies but simultaneously a view of humanity as educable, prudent, and
capable of self-control for the sake of rational self-interest. This view fuels
the "autonomy" theory of society and gives it the justification for demanding
some degree of the subjectivity addressed in the previous section and, moreover, the justification for holding leverage against the state. Citizens must be
allowed to rule themselves in some sense, and society must be allowed to
remain free of the state to some degree. The first view of cultivation with
regard to human nature put forth by Strauss would, on the contrary, in line
with the empirical reality of the state of nature, deem humanity as "morally
depraved" and simply and unequivocally in "need of being ruled" (*CP,* 97).
The first definition would hence rule out any "autonomy" or "subjectivity"
for individuals, society, or culture, which instead must be kept under the
tight control of the state. Strauss faults Schmitt, following Hobbes, for not
being truly and exclusively pessimistic, for not identifying this more extreme
dangerousness of humanity.

In his book on Spinoza, Strauss explained how the "disciplining of human will," the second and less pessimistic type of cultivation of human
nature prescribed by Hobbes, necessarily requires the domination of nature
in general: "Physics," which Strauss identifies explicitly with "technology,"

> is concerned with man's happiness, anthropology [which Strauss identifies
> likewise with "political philosophy"] with man's misery. The greatest misfor-
> tune is death by violence; happiness consists in the limitless increase of power
> over men and over things. Fear of violent death, and the pursuit of domina-
> tion over things – it is basically these two determinants of willing which Hobbes
> accepts as justified.[23]

Instead of adopting the first kind of cultivation that "obeys the indications that nature itself gives" (which observes human beings in the state of
nature, recognizes them as incapable of ruling themselves, and governs

23 Strauss, *Spinoza's Critique of Religion*, p. 88.

them accordingly), Hobbes opts for the other kind of cultivation that eventually distracts human beings from their own nature by the conquest of
outer nature, by providing for their potential happiness with the promise of
a commodious life. The direct domination of humanity, suggested by "anthropology," is more "natural" than the direct domination of external nature, for the latter, relying more explicitly on "physics," is actually "the harsh
and cunning fight against nature" described earlier. According to Strauss,
Hobbes chooses "physics" over "anthropology," and hence ultimately "technology" over "political philosophy." Hobbes employs technology to neutralize precisely those characteristics that make humans dangerous, that create
the likelihood of violent death, and emphasizes that characteristic that
makes man capable of improvement, namely, reason:

> Reason, the provident outlook on the future, thus justifies the striving after
> power, possessions, gain, wealth, since these provide the means to gratify the
> underlying desire for pleasures of the senses. Reason does not justify, but
> indeed refutes, all striving after reputation, honor, fame: in a word and that
> word used in the sense applied by Hobbes, vanity. . . . The legitimate striving
> after pleasure is sublated into striving after power. What is condemned is the
> striving after reputation. Philosophy (or more accurately physics as distinct
> from anthropology) is to be understood as arising from the striving after
> power: *scientia propter potentiam.* Its aim is cultivation, the cultivation of nature.
> What nature offers to man without supplementary activity on the part of man
> is sufficient for no more than a life of penury. So that life may become more
> comfortable, human exertion is required, and the regulation of unregulated
> nature. . . . The purpose pursued by science is conquest over nature.[24]

Reason, science, and technology tame humanity by reducing vanity, physical
needs, and religion, by encouraging society's domination of nature at the
expense of the state's direct domination of human nature. Yet it is precisely
the continued existence of the somewhat freely exercised subjective reason
that accompanies this use of reason, science, and technology within civil
society that will undermine Hobbes's state.

Strauss focuses on the contradiction within Schmitt's thesis that we observed at the close of the last section. Schmitt maintains that the nature of
"the political" allows that the state, of which Hobbes is the founder, "may
'demand . . . from those belonging to a nation readiness to die,' and the
legitimacy of this demand is at least qualified by Hobbes: The man in the
battleranks who deserts by reason of fear for his life acts 'only' dishonorably,

24 Ibid., pp. 89–92.

but not unjustly" (*CP,* 88). It is precisely the reservation of such a right – subjectively determined by an individual's reason – regarding how and when and in what capacity one's life can be employed, that becomes a powerful weapon against the state. The normative consequences of Hobbes's grant of subjectivity (however narrow) to individuals for the question of what is right retains no real force, according to Strauss. Subjective freedom is maintained "at the price of the meaning of human life, for . . . when man abandons the task of raising the question regarding what is right, and when man abandons this question, he abandons his humanity" (*CP,* 101). Schmitt, to the extent that he models himself on Hobbes, betrays the fact that he is "under the spell" of the liberalism he criticizes. He defines his "political" as beyond objective normative standards, by defining it as if it were neutral (*CP,* 103). Schmitt's depiction of "the political" is hence reduced to a subjective interpretation characteristic of "the individualistic-liberal society" he wishes to replace (*CP,* 102). According to Strauss, Schmitt's project, as it stands, is hence "provisional," for it is "forced to make use of liberal elements" (*CP,* 83). Schmitt's critique "is detained on the plane created by liberalism. . . . [H]is critique of liberalism takes place within the horizon of liberalism" (*CP,* 104–5).[25] Unlike liberals, Schmitt advocates direct rule by the state over the lives of individuals; however, his view is much like liberalism's to the extent that he offers no account of the substance of that domination or the ends to which it is put besides the preservation of the lives of individuals. But at this point in his career, Strauss himself is less than fully forthcoming on what would be the substance of such nonliberal state rule.[26]

25 Strauss's assessment that Schmitt's project remains "within the horizon of liberalism" is sometimes exaggerated in an attempt to defend Schmitt's Weimar work from charges of latent Nazism. Yet just because Schmitt's work is not latently Nazi does not mean that it is not authoritarian or antiliberal. Strauss's comments can be seen to *emphasize* the point that Schmitt's theoretical shortcomings in his attack on liberalism are not for lack of trying; the intent and the attempt are quite apparent.

26 In *Carl Schmitt and Leo Strauss,* Meier suggests that Schmitt covertly sought the substance of such a prospective nonliberal regime in theology. This seems to be an unlikely possibility in Schmitt's case at this particular point given the diminished role of religion in his thought after his excommunication in 1926, something of which Meier makes no note. As I discussed in Chapters 1, 2, and 4, Roman Catholicism did serve as a potential source of political authority for the Schmitt of the early twenties. There is also reason to question Meier's claim that Strauss had already turned to classical philosophy as a substantively normative standpoint before his emigration. See Volker Reinecke and Jonathan Uhlaner, "The Problem of Leo Strauss: Religion, Philosophy and Politics," *Graduate Faculty Philosophy Journal* 16:1 (1992). However, as I will argue, to whatever extent Meier's claim is correct about the two authors' respective moral resuppositions, the result of the positive

Strauss gives ample evidence in his commentary of having read Schmitt's famous work of 1922, *Political Theology* (*CP,* 97, 103), cited at the opening of this chapter, and so he must have been familiar with Schmitt's attempt to separate the substantive Hobbes from the mechanistic Hobbes. Strauss is in full accord with this project to the extent that the substantive Hobbes recognizes what characterizes humanity's fundamental condition and the element with which to manage it: fear. But one must further distance this from the other Hobbes, who undermines his own insight by setting in motion the forces that will neutralize his system. Schmitt, in his failure to emphasize the radical dangerousness of man rather than what amounts to mere "liberal" dangerousness, is susceptible to the subjectivity and the tendency toward neutrality and technology that characterize the latter Hobbes. "A radical critique of liberalism," according to Strauss, "is therefore possible only on the basis of an adequate understanding of Hobbes" (*CP,* 105). This understanding is crucial for Strauss, citing the "Neutralizations" essay, if "the decisive battle between 'the spirit of technology,' the 'mass faith of an antireligious, this-worldly activism' and the opposite spirit and faith, which, it seems, does not yet have a name," is to be won (*CP,* 104). Hobbes negated the political; Schmitt affirms it (*CP,* 90). According to Strauss, he opens the possibility of starting the project over again. In a statement that seems alarmingly imprudent with the benefit of hindsight, in the Germany of 1932, Strauss exalts the possibility that "'the order of human things' may arise afresh" (*CP,* 101).

In this spirit, moreover, in the first incarnation of what would become *The Political Philosophy of Hobbes,* Strauss demonstrates how one would take up this "urgent task" (*CP,* 105) initiated by Schmitt, how one would move "beyond the horizon of liberalism."[27] In order to make the fear with which he is concerned more intense, Strauss makes the source of that fear more extreme than it appears in Hobbes himself, or even in Schmitt. It is not merely fear of death that serves as the foundation of Hobbesian politics and hence the politics of the modern state, but fear of *violent* death. Strauss

---

aestheticizing of the fear-evoking quality of domination by a deliberalized Hobbesian state renders such a state's normative "substance," whatever its implicit or explicit source, inconsequential relative to its naked ability to dominate.

27 Strauss, *The Political Philosophy of Hobbes: Its Basis and Genesis,* trans. E. M. Sinclair (Chicago: University of Chicago Press, 1952). See Meier, *Carl Schmitt and Leo Strauss,* pp. 11, 85. Despite the fact that Schmitt joined the National Socialist Party in May of 1933, as late as July of that year, Strauss, who certainly must have known of Schmitt's recent promotion to Prussian state counselor under Hitler, was still seeking a correspondence with Schmitt about the prospect of aiding in the compilation of a critical edition of Hobbes's work. See Meier, *Carl Schmitt and Leo Strauss,* pp. 127–8.

isolates Hobbes's thought from the forces of neutralization that will under-mine it: Once one adequately understands the basis of politics as fear of violent death, a fear based *not* on a somewhat dangerous, yet improvable and educable human nature but simply on an infinitely dangerous human nature, one no longer has any need for science. Once one corrects the mistakes of Hobbes's liberal successors, who take up the tasks of allowing citizens to rule themselves by providing them with the products of the conquest of nature and allaying their fears by showing them the orderliness of nature, one can set up a state more in accord with the natural condition of humanity, more in accord with "the political." The logical outcome of Strauss's turning of Schmitt's view of humanity to one that views it simply as in need of "being ruled" is a theory of state that consistently instills in citizens the fear of the "human situation" by constantly reminding them of its proximity. If this is to be achieved without technology, without the appa-ratus of physical domination, something else must hold sway.[28]

The myth of the state – the Leviathan, the horrible sea monster after which Hobbes named his greatest work on the state – must invoke in a uniform and controlled manner the terror that each citizen felt individually and overwhelmingly in the state of nature. Myth is the element that can maintain the state's separation from society while keeping it in check. Thus, for the state to keep from integrating too extensively into society and hence weakening itself in the manner discussed in the previous chapter, myth must hold sway.[29] Despite the mythic title of *Leviathan*, Hobbes was to emphasize myth more heavily in his later writings. In his commentary on Hobbes's *Behemoth*, Stephen Holmes describes how Hobbes came to realize that "the ultimate source of political authority is not coercion of the body, but captiva-tion of the mind."[30] It is to this issue in Hobbes that Strauss's work points and to which Schmitt himself turns in his later work on Hobbes, although, as we will see, his attitude toward the project as a whole has become signifi-cantly less sanguine.

28 For a more detailed account of the relationship of Strauss's book on Hobbes to Schmitt's Weimar project, see my "Fear, Technology and the State: Carl Schmitt, Leo Strauss and the Revival of Hobbes in Weimar and National Socialist Germany," *Political Theory* 22:4 (November 1994): 631–6.

29 It is interesting that the two historians of modern myth who do deal with Hobbes at all, Cassirer and Blumenberg, focus solely on the myth of the state of nature and not that of the Leviathan.

30 Stephen Holmes, introduction, to Thomas Hobbes, *Behemoth* (Chicago: University of Chicago Press, 1991), p. xi. Cf. George Kateb, "Hobbes and the Irrationality of Politics," *Political Theory* 17:3 (August 1989).

Schmitt, National Socialism, and Anti-Semitism

As noted before, during the Republic Schmitt had lent his intellectual support to the attempts of successive authoritarian chancellors, Brüning, Papen, and Schleicher, to usurp the authority of the parliament and govern through the "charismatically" and "plebiscitarily" elected office of *Reichspräsident* Hindenburg. Schleicher, the figure Schmitt was most closely aligned to personally, had hoped to carry out such a scheme while outmaneuvering the Nazis, who were gaining popular support – a strategy that Schmitt supported publicly.[31] After failing in this endeavor, Schleicher resigned in January of 1933. When Hitler subsequently became chancellor, Schmitt was invited by Papen, who himself had always been less wary of the Nazis than Schleicher was, to help legalize the new coalition fascist regime. As the regime became more exclusively National Socialist, Schmitt stood by as his leftist and Jewish friends and colleagues in the universities were dismissed from their positions, starting in April of that year.[32] Schmitt himself became a member of the National Socialist party on May 1, quickly assuming party leadership roles in academia and accepting the professorship that he had sought for so long at the prestigious Friedrich-Wilhelms-Universität, in Berlin. He revised his previous written work to conform with party dogma and authored treatises that, sometimes clumsily but always enthusiastically, integrated his Weimar theories into a justification for the power-consolidating National Socialist regime.[33]

Schmitt's former mentor Schleicher and his wife were murdered, as were over one hundred potential enemies from within Hitler's own party in the wake of the Night of the Long Knives, June 30, 1934. Schmitt did not flee Germany, nor did he retire into private life in response to the new regime's liquidation of the person who introduced him to practical politics. Instead, he authored an article that "legally" justified these actions, an article with

---

31   See Schmitt, "Der Mißbrauch der Legalität," *Tägliche Rundschau* (Jul. 19, 1932).

32   Schmitt was either completely silent about, or actively involved in, Hans Kelsen's expulsion from the Law Faculty at Cologne. Kelsen was decisive in securing Schmitt's own position there only months before. See Klaus Günther, "Hans Kelsen (1881–1973): Das nüchterne Pathos der Demokratie," in *Streitbare Juristen: Eine Andere Tradition,* ed. Thomas Blanke et al. (Baden-Baden: Nomos, 1988), p. 367; Frank Golczewski, *Kölner Universitätslehrer und der Nationalsozialismus* (Cologne: Böhlau, 1988), p. 117; and Hans Meyer, *Ein Deutscher auf Widerruf: Erinnerungen,* vol. 1 (Frankfurt a. M.: Suhrkamp, 1982), p. 144.

33   See, for instance, Schmitt, "Das Gesetz zur Behebung der Not von Volk und Reich," *Deutsche Juristen-Zeitung* 38 (1933); *Staat, Bewegung, Volk: Die Dreigliederung der politischen Einheit* (Hamburg: Hanseatische Verlagsanstalt, 1934); and *Ueber der drei Arten des Rechtswissenschaftlichen Denkens* (Hamburg: Hanseatische Verlagsanstalt, 1934).

the absurdly horrifying title "The Führer Protects the Law."[34] This is really all that needs to be said about Carl Schmitt the man and his involvement with National Socialism. But there is actually more: Tantalized by the favors of such power-wielding party dignitaries as Hermann Göring and Hans Frank, Schmitt accepted the position of chief counselor of Prussia and sought to become the preeminent architect of National Socialist law.[35]

But by 1936, Schmitt's academic rivals were able to use his unorthodox National Socialism, his past connection with political Catholicism, his earlier close associations with Jews, and his previous denunciations of the party to arouse the suspicions of the SS.[36] Apparently fearing for his life as a result of the ensuing investigation, he unofficially retired, maintaining his position in Berlin but choosing to publish essays exclusively focused on issues in the less controversial realm of international affairs.[37]

It is a curiosity of the postwar German intellectual scene that Schmitt is remembered as *the* legal theorist of National Socialism, when he actually failed in his attempt to attain such a status. Others ultimately better served National Socialism in this capacity than Schmitt and still managed to integrate themselves rather easily into the academic milieu of the Federal Republic after the war by undergoing the "de-Nazification" process that Schmitt himself spurned.[38] This refusal to publicly recant his devotion to

34   Schmitt, "Der Führer schützt das Recht," in *Positionen und Begriffe*. To whatever extent this is a "defense" of Schmitt, he more explicitly condones eliminating the paramilitary threats to Hitler's power than the execution of civilians murdered during the purge.

35   On the fierce competition to become the "Crown Jurist of the Third Reich," see Peter C. Caldwell, "National Socialism and Constitutional Law: Carl Schmitt, Otto Koellreutter, and the Debate over the Nature of the Nazi State, 1933–1937," *Cardozo Law Review* 16:2 (December 1994); and Bernd Rüthers, *Entartetes Recht: Rechtslehren und Kronjuristen im Dritten Reich* (Munich: C. H. Beck, 1988).

36   Raphael Gross critically examines the exact extent of Schmitt's fall from grace with the party, in "Politische Polykratie 1936: Die legendenumwobene SD-Akte Carl Schmitt," *Tel Aviver Jahrbuch für deutsche Geschichte* 23 (1994).

37   Schmitt's English and German biographies chronicle his involvement with National Socialism; see Bendersky, *Carl Schmitt: Theorist for the Reich;* and Paul Noack, *Carl Schmitt: Eine Biographie* (Berlin: Propyläen, 1993). However, there are dissenters against Bendersky's and Noack's presentations; see, Stephen Holmes, "Review: *Theorist for the Reich*," *American Political Science Review* 77:4 (December 1983); and Bernd Rüthers, "Wer war Carl Schmitt? Bausteine zu einer Biographie," *Neue Juristische Wochenschrift* 27 (July 1994). See also Rüthers, *Carl Schmitt im Dritten Reich: Wissenschaft als Zeitgeist-Verstärkung?* (Munich: C. H. Beck, 1989). A balanced and accessible account of Schmitt's life and career is offered by Manfred H. Wiegandt, "The Alleged Unaccountability of the Academic: A Biographical Sketch of Carl Schmitt," *Cardozo Law Review* 16 (1995).

38   Ulrich K. Preuß makes this point quite articulately; see "Political Order and Democracy: Carl Schmitt and His Influence," in *Social System, Rationality and Revolution*, ed. L. Nowak and M. Paprzycki (Rodopi: Poznan Studies in the Philosophy of the Sciences and the

the Third Reich may account for both his identification as the *preeminent* Nazi lawyer, by his critics, and as one of the very few *authentic* intellectual figures in his generation, by both his devotees and even some of his detractors.[39]

A related issue that ought to be addressed even more carefully than that of Schmitt's Nazism is his anti-Semitism. There are two main interpretations, with hard-liners on both sides. The first claims that Schmitt's work was always anti-Semitic and that his antipathy to Jews simply became more explicit when he joined the Nazis. The second claims that Schmitt only opportunistically took up anti-Semitism initially to ingratiate himself with, and later to protect himself from, the party.[40] What cannot be challenged is the *fact* of Schmitt's active anti-Semitism in the Third Reich: most notoriously exemplified by his organizing and hosting a conference called "German Jurisprudence at War with the Jewish Spirit," in 1936.[41]

The problem with the first argument asserting Schmitt's Weimar anti-Semitism is that there is little or no textual evidence to support it. On the basis of what I have presented in this book, during the late teens and most of the twenties, Schmitt seems to be most personally preoccupied by Protestantism and most politically preoccupied by socialism. Indeed, rather than characterize the latter as part of some "Jewish conspiracy" in the manner of many right-wing anti-Semites, Schmitt rather idiosyncratically identifies socialism's external manifestation in the Soviet Union with secularized Eastern Orthodox Christianity![42] Whether he identified German socialism with

---

Humanities 33 [1993]), p. 15. Reinhard Mehring lists Otto Koellreutter, Werner Best, and Reinhard Höhn as examples of those who "better served National Socialism ideologically." See *Carl Schmitt: Zur Einführung* (Hamburg: Junius, 1992), p. 103.

39 As Jürgen Habermas has recently suggested; see "Das Bedürfnis nach deutschen Kontinuitäten," *Die Zeit* (Dec. 3, 1993). See also Theo Rasehorn, "Der Kleinbürger als politischer Ideologe: Zur Entmythologisierung von Carl Schmitt," *Die Neue Gesellschaft, Frankfurter Hefte* (1986).

40 As representatives of these two respective positions, see Holmes, "Carl Schmitt: The Debility of Liberalism," p. 50; and Bendersky, *Carl Schmitt: Theorist for the Reich*, pp. 281–2.

41 Schmitt, "Die deutsche Rechtswissenschaft im Kampf gegen den jüdischen Geist," *Deutsche Juristen-Zeitung* 20 (Oct. 15, 1936). See Holmes, "Carl Schmitt: The Debility of Liberalism," pp. 38–9; and Schwab, *The Challenge of the Exception*, pp. 135–6, for accounts of Schmitt's vitriolic attacks on Jewish lawyers at this conference.

42 Recall the discussions of *Political Form* in Chapters 2 and 4: Schmitt considers Dostoyevsky as much as Trotsky as the source of Soviet Russia's dangerousness, and he squarely and singularly places the blame for the corruption of public order at the expense of private belief on Protestants, an indictment he will transfer over to Jews in his National Socialist work, as we will observe. See *Roman Catholicism and Political Form* (1923), trans. G. L. Ulmen (Westport: Greenwood, 1996), respectively, pp. 27, 32, 36 and 10,11, 20, 28; hereafter cited as *RC*, and referred to as *Political Form*.

Jews is certainly not explicit in his writings, whereas the call for Western socialists, liberals, and conservatives – Jews and non-Jews alike – to unite as Europeans against the Soviet threat in the East is in fact explicit.[43]

Moreover, it was the Protestant establishment in Germany, not Jews, who in Schmitt's experience had kept him out of the better law schools. There are indeed traces of resentment against Protestants whose prejudice confined, in Schmitt's own estimation, the greatest legal mind in Germany to a position in a business school.[44] Did Schmitt's excommunication by the Catholic Church in 1926 change his theological orientation such that Judaism replaced Protestantism as his cultural *bête noire?* Perhaps, but if so it does not manifest itself in the texts written between 1926 and 1933.[45]

Furthermore, at a time when anti-Semitism was rather freely expressed, particularly on the Right, and especially by his own acquaintances, such as Catholics like Hugo Ball and Protestants like Werner Sombart and Wilhelm Stapel, why did Schmitt refrain from participating in such displays if he in fact hated Jews during the twenties?[46] A final observation against the "life-long anti-Semitism" thesis is the apparent fact that Schmitt's attacks on Jews after 1933 seem to begin and then intensify only as he himself comes under increasing assault from enemies within the party, particularly the SS.[47]

On the other hand, the problem with the "opportunistic anti-Semitism" thesis is the fact that after the war Schmitt did not give up the fear and

43 *RC,* 36–9.
44 On Schmitt's career at the *Handelshochschule Berlin,* see Noack, *Carl Schmitt: Eine Biographie,* pp. 97–102; and Bendersky, *Carl Schmitt: Theorist for the Reich,* pp. 107–8. Schmitt probably would not have attained even this position without the help of liberal lawyer Moritz Julius Bonn, who was a Jew.
45 I would like to refrain as much as possible from psychologizing about Schmitt, as he has been the subject of some rather bizarre analyses along these lines. An example that focuses extensively on anti-Semitism is the work of Nicolaus Sombart, which is, however, problematic in its vulgar deployment of psychoanalysis and its questionable establishment of Schmitt, a paranoid post-*Kulturkampf* Catholic, as the paradigmatic example of the "German man" in a Germany still dominated in no small way by Prussia. See *Die deutschen Männer und ihre Feinde: Carl Schmitt – ein deutsches Schicksal zwischen Männerbund und Matriarchatsmythos* (Munich: Hanser, 1991), and *Jugend in Berlin, 1933–43: ein Bericht* (Frankfurt a. M.: Fischer, 1991). On the predicament of Catholics in a unified Germany, see Helen Lovell Evans, *The German Center Party, 1870–1933: A Study in Political Catholicism* (Carbondale: Southern Illinois Press, 1981). Sombart is also unhelpful in determining Schmitt's attitude toward Jews before 1933.
46 On the importance of Christianity in promoting anti-Semitism in Germany, see *Central European History* 27:3 (August 1994), Symposium: Christian Religion and Anti-Semitism in Modern German History.
47 A claim made most strongly by Bendersky, *Carl Schmitt: Theorist for the Reich,* pp. 281–2; and Schwab, *The Challenge of the Exception,* pp. 135–6; but not necessarily refuted by Rüthers, *Carl Schmitt im Dritten Reich,* pp. 81–95. See also, Gross, "Politische Polykratie, 1936."

hatred of the Jews that he expressed for purportedly cosmetic reasons under National Socialism. His diary, written well after he would any longer need to abide by a party line, is filled with anti-Semitic expressions, perhaps the most unnerving of which reads as follows: "Verily, the assimilated Jew is the true enemy."[48] There is some evidence that Schmitt's postwar attitude toward Jews stems from his perception that his former students, many of whom fled Germany because they were Jews, had betrayed him by encouraging his fall from grace with the Nazis, by disseminating within the Reich information unfavorable to him. Apparently, materials were smuggled into, and distributed throughout, Germany that depicted Schmitt as a former Nazi critic, a still-faithful Catholic, a Hobbesian, and a Jew lover – again, all qualities incompatible with orthodox National Socialism.[49] That Schmitt managed to hold a grudge against people who threatened his career and supposed security while he endorsed a regime that threatened their very existence speaks as much about Schmitt's hubris as it does about his anti-Semitism. Nevertheless, the fact that he left behind as his final thoughts on the Jewish question the despicable sentiments expressed in his postwar diary and not instead some attempt at an apology for, or at least a retraction of, his National Socialist words and deeds ultimately necessitates classifying him as an anti-Semite and a figure who must be held to some degree culpable in the Third Reich's destruction of European Jewry.

Technology and the Mortality of Myth

By 1938, the publication date of *The Leviathan in the State Theory of Thomas Hobbes: Meaning and Failure of a Political Symbol*,[50] Schmitt no longer held a

48   Schmitt, *Glossarium: Aufzeichnungen der Jahre 1947–51* (Duncker & Humblot, 1991), p. 18. See the discussions of the anti-Semitism of this volume by Mehring, in *Carl Schmitt: Zur Einführung*, and Heinrich Meier, "The Philosopher as Enemy: On Carl Schmitt's *Glossarium*," *Graduate Faculty Philosophy Journal* 17:1–2 (1994). Raphael Gross analyzes the relationship of anti-Semitism to Schmitt's post-Weimar work in "Carl Schmitts '*Nomos*' und die 'Juden,'" *Merkur* 47:5 (May 1993).

49   The main figures include Waldemar Gurian and Otto Kirchheimer, who smuggled literature subversive to the regime under Schmitt's auspices, thus embarrassing their former teacher. See Bendersky, *Carl Schmitt: Theorist for the Reich*, pp. 223–6; and Manfred Lauerman, "Exkurs Carl Schmitt 1936," in *Die Autonomie des Politischen: Carl Schmitts Kampf um einen beschädigten Begriff*, ed. Hans-Georg Flickinger (Wein: VCH Acta humaniora, 1990).

50   Schmitt, *Der Leviathan in der Staatslehre des Thomas Hobbes: Sinn und Fehlschlag eines politischen Symbols* ([1938] Cologne: Klett-Cotta, 1982). English renderings are from the translation by George Schwab and Erna Hilfstein, *The Leviathan in the State Theory of Thomas Hobbes: Meaning and Failure of a Political Symbol* (Westport: Greenwood, 1996), cited hereafter as *L*. Schmitt had originally formulated much of the argument of the book, particu-

place of prominence in the National Socialist regime. Moreover, he had not
taken up the Weimar-Hobbesian project he had shared with Strauss since
1933. Perhaps he thought he had found a solution in the political choice he
made in May of that year. But after the political and personal events of the
ensuing years, he returned to Hobbes and his Leviathan, which Schmitt
declared was the "earthly" and "mortal" god that must time and time again
bring humanity out of the "*chaos*" of the "natural condition" (*L*, 11). This
statement highlights a theme of Schmitt's treatise that was previously only
implicit to the project, myth, and one that is completely new, myth's mor-
tality. Fear, however, remains a central concern:

> [The Leviathan is] the *deus mortalis* . . . who, because of the fright that his
> power evokes, imposes peace on everyone. (*L*, 19)
> The starting point of Hobbes' construction of the state is fear of the state of
> nature; the goal and terminus is the security of the civil, the stately condi-
> tion. . . . The terror of the state of nature drives anguished individuals to
> come together; their fear rises to an extreme; a spark of reason flashes and
> suddenly there stands in front of them a new god. (*L*, 31)
> Fear brings atomized individuals together [and] a consensus emerges about
> the necessity of submitting to the strongest power. (*L*, 33)

Schmitt observes that for Hobbes there are three images of this strongest
power, three Leviathans, in the book of that name: the mythical monster,
the representative person, and the machine (*L*, 19). Schmitt's thesis is that
Leviathan as mythical monster, or even as representative person – images
that can sufficiently keep humanity peaceably in awe – historically becomes
superseded by Leviathan the machine, which is eventually viewed as a mere
tool to be used by various groups of citizens (*L*, 35). In other words, Schmitt
admits that the Weimar attempt to completely divorce the "mechanistic"
from the "vital" in Hobbes has proven to be historically impossible. In the
Leviathan book, we still find Schmitt defending Hobbes against those who
would interpret him "superficially" as strictly a "rationalist, mechanist, sen-
sualist, individualist" (*L*, 11). However, Schmitt is more forthright in admitting that these elements, particularly the mechanistic, are present (*L*, 19),
even if they did not initially dominate Hobbes's theory as a whole.[51]

larly its emphasis on technology, in an article from 1936, "The State as Mechanism in
Hobbes and Descartes" ("Der Staat als Mechanismus bei Hobbes und Descartes," *Archiv
für Rechts und Sozialphilosophie* 39 [1937]), included as an appendix to the Greenwood
edition of Schmitt's *Der Leviathan*.
51 Both Schmitt and Strauss completely abandon the attempt to divorce the "human" from

According to Schmitt, Hobbes did not intend his Leviathan state to serve as the merely sum/aggregate of all the individual wills of the state of nature but as something that transcends such merely mechanical or mathematical formulations, which would, in the end, simply render it a machine. Drawing on his theory of representation, as elaborated in Chapter 4, Schmitt empha- sizes how Hobbes intends the Leviathan to be a personally embodied "sovereign-representative" whose wholeness is greater than the particulars he represents; and drawing on his theory of myth, as examined in Chapters 2 and 4, he emphasizes how Hobbes presents the Leviathan as a mythic monster that will keep subjects in a peacefully stupefied state.[52] The book is the historical account of how the mechanical component of the Hobbesian trinity wins out over the other two and the political consequences of such a victory: "[T]he Leviathan becomes none other than a huge machine, a gigantic mechanism in the service of ensuring the physical protection of the governed" (*L*, 35). Yet ultimately, Schmitt suggests, the tool cannot perform even this particular task.[53]

The "neutralization" of Hobbes's state, argues Schmitt – referring to one of the few Weimar works explicitly mentioned in *Der Leviathan* – begins, with good reason, as a response to the wars of religion but leads inevitably to "the basic neutralization of every truth" (*L*, 43). Not only religious but metaphys- ical, juristic, and political considerations eventually come to mean nothing to the "clean" and "exact" workings of the state mechanism, in "a logical

the "scientific" Hobbes in their treatments of the philosopher after World War II. In 1953, Strauss portrays Hobbes as the *bearer* of the latter formally profane element: "The man who was the first to draw the consequences for natural right from this momentous change ["the emergence of modern science, of nonteleological natural science"] was Thomas Hobbes. . . . To Hobbes we must turn if we desire to understand the specific character of modern natural right." Strauss, *Natural Right and History* (Chicago: University of Chicago Press, 1953), p. 166; see also pp. 170–4. In 1965, Schmitt remarks that Hobbes inaugu- rates "a process of gradual neutralization that culminates finally in the methodical athe- ism and 'value-free' science concomitant with the scientific, the technical and the indus- trial age." "Die vollendete Reformation: Bemerkungen und Hinweise zu neuen Leviathan Interpretationen," *Der Staat: Zeitschrift für Staatslehre, öffentliches Recht und Ver- fassungsgeschichte* 4:1 (1965): 61.

52 Despite frequent allusions to some of his most important Weimar works, Schmitt never cites many of them explicitly in *Der Leviathan*. For instance, according to Ernst Fraenkel, Schmitt had prevented the reprinting of *Political Form* under the Third Reich; see Ernst Fraenkel, *The Dual State: A Contribution to the Theory of Dictatorship*, trans. E. A. Shils (New York: Octagon Books, 1969). The possible significance of this treatment of his Weimar work will be discussed later.

53 On the extrarationalistic or neotheological underpinnings of Hobbesian authority, see Tracy Strong, "How to Write Scripture: Words, Authority and Politics in Thomas Hobbes," *Critical Inquiry* 20:1 (autumn 1993).

process that culminates in a general technologization" (*L*, 42). Liberals and Communists both agree that the state is a machine, an apparatus that the most "varied political constellations can utilize as a technically neutral instrument" (*L*, 42). In hindsight, writes Schmitt, reversing his argument in *The Concept of the Political*, the state can be viewed as "the first product of the age of technology" (*L*, 34): "Hobbes' concept of the state became an essential factor in the four-hundred-year-long process of mechanization, a process that, with the aid of technical developments brought about a general 'neutralization' and especially the transformation of the state into a technically neutral instrument" (*L*, 41–2).

The fault does not lie fully with Hobbes, according to Schmitt, for he expected his state to continue to inspire awe as a myth that stood above society, maintaining peace through the fear it engendered, as much as he expected it to function as a finely tuned machine. Schmitt elaborates on an insight by Strauss noted earlier, that Spinoza perpetrates the radical technicizing of Hobbesian politics. Resorting to an anti-Semitism that is not apparent in his Weimar writings, Schmitt here blames Spinoza and subsequent Jewish authors, such as Moses Mendelssohn and Friedrich Julius Stahl, for accelerating the neutralizing process of turning the Leviathan from a myth into a machine.[54] Hobbes, the religious insider (nominally Christian Englishman), formulated the state/civil society relationship in the following *stable* manner:

public peace and sovereign power
ensures
individual freedom

Spinoza, the religious outsider (a Jew), changes the priorities so as to render the relationship fundamentally *unstable:*

individual freedom
is ensured by
public peace and sovereign power

54 See Holmes, "The Debility of Liberalism," pp. 50–3, for an extensive discussion of the gratuitous anti-Semitism expressed in the book, particularly Schmitt's professed disgust at Hobbes's choice of mythic symbol: a monster from the *Jewish* tradition. What goes unacknowledged in most treatments of anti-Semitism in the book is its explicit anti-Christian standpoint, whose significance I will discuss later in the chapter.

Thus, the dangerous subjectivity that was the concern of Schmitt in his reformulation of Hobbes, in *The Concept of the Political,* is historically given a place of primacy over the state that was founded precisely to keep it in check. The fact that Hobbes allowed subjective, private freedom of belief and the choice to disobey the sovereign over the deployment of one's life is subsequently exploited into a subversion of the objective state: "What is of significance is the seed planted by Hobbes regarding his reservation about private belief and his distinction between inner belief and outer confession. As it unfolded, it became an irresistible and all governing conviction" (*L,* 59).[55]

As the subjectivities proliferated and gained in power, they demanded of the state *objectivity* – objectivity toward its own existence – whose logical result is the complete neutrality of the state. According to Schmitt, Kant is guilty of finally sapping the state of any substantive content of its own, of disentangling the "organism" from the "mechanism"; but in Hobbes, these elements were all together, and hence the Leviathan state, in this awesome totality, was potentially mythical (*L,* 41). After Kant, the reigning image for jurisprudence is no longer a personal judge pronouncing decisions but a mechanism dispensing rules: "The *legislator humanus* becomes a *machina legislatoria*" (*L,* 65). Because the government has no moral content, neither do the laws it thereby produces: "For technically represented neutrality the laws of the state must become independent from substantive content, including religious tenets or legal justifications and propriety, and should be accorded validity only as the result of the positive determinations of the state's decision-making apparatus in the form of commands" (*L,* 44). The purely formal legal positivism that Hobbes unequivocally founds in *Leviathan* (*L,* 67), which Weber so perspicaciously analyzes in "Sociology of Law" (*L,* 66) and which Kelsen, whom Schmitt no longer mentions, most famously practices in the first part of this century, becomes lethally dangerous without the myth that Hobbes also deployed to undergird it. It ultimately places itself at the disposal of tyranny:

---

55 As Reinhart Koselleck, himself a student of Schmitt, explains it, the slightest trace of subjectivity that Hobbes granted to his citizens as compensation for giving up the "natural right" of the state of nature, later takes its revenge on the state itself: "The State created a new order, but then – in genuinely historic fashion – fell prey to that order. As evident in Hobbes, the moral inner space that had been excised from the State and reserved for man as a human being meant (even rudimentarily) a source of unrest. . . . The authority of conscience remained an unconquered remnant of the state of nature, protruding into the formally perfected State." Koselleck, *Critique and Crisis: Enlightenment and the Pathogenesis of Modern Society* (Cambridge, Mass.: MIT Press, 1988), pp. 38–9.

The technologyzing neutralization that resides in the general neutrality tinged construct of the state already contains in it the technologization and neutraliz- ation of right into law and constitution into constitutional law. . . . Law be- came a means of compulsory psychological motivation and calculable func- tioning that can serve different aims and contradictory contents. That is why, according to Hobbes, every legally calculable functioning compulsory system is a state and insofar as there can be state law, the state is also a constitutional state. The process of formalizing and neutralizing the concept of the "constitu- tional state" into a calculable functioning legal system of the state indifferent to aims, intrinsic truths and justice is known by the name of "legal positivism" and had become in the nineteenth century the generally dominant juristic doctrine. The embarrassment of bourgeois constitutional jurists was therefore great when between the years 1917 and 1920, a bolshevist state apparatus was constructed and insofar as it functioned according to calculable means, could claim for itself the name "constitutional state." (*L*, 68–9)

A state that is purely mechanical and has no value content whatsoever other than efficiency has *no* boundary, not even the Hobbesian one of the protection of individual life. "A technically neutral state can be tolerant as well as intolerant; in both instances it remains equally neutral. Its values, its truth and justice reside in its technical perfection. . . . The state machine either functions or does not function" (*L*, 45). Ironically, it is the state's granting both a subjective realm and the right to resist the state in the protection of one's life that come to endanger the lives of citizens, accord- ing to Schmitt. Had the state recognized, as Schmitt and Strauss wished, that humanity simply "needed to be ruled" and that to grant it any subjective determination of self-preservation was dangerous to order, peace, and life, it could have held for itself the rudimentary moral content of protecting the lives of its citizens. As the subjective entities of civil society demanded more objectivity from the state, they drained it of even this content. If any of these subjective entities, "autonomous" (*L*, 46) as they are from the state, should, in their guaranteed subjective freedom of conscience, choose not to recog- nize the boundary of the state in the safety of the people, and also seize the neutralized, efficient, but weakened state, the results would be horrific. It would be the state of nature, in which all are *not* equal in their ability to kill and be killed. It would be an entity with the unpredictable subjectivity of the state of nature and the irresistible objective efficiency of the sovereign state. As Schmitt so masterfully describes the predicament of late Weimar in Hobbesian terms, in *The Concept of the Political*, he has here, perhaps, set forth just such a Hobbesian depiction of National Socialism.

In his Weimar writings, Schmitt warns against the appropriation of the state by nonneutral forces who would "seize" the apparatus of "state will-formation" for themselves, "without themselves ceasing to be social and non-state entities."[56] He even described such a seizing of the state in terms of the dethroning of the Leviathan: "When the 'mortal god' falls from his throne and the kingdom of objective reason and civil society becomes 'a great gang of thieves,' then the parties slaughter the powerful Leviathan and slice pieces from the flesh of his body.' "[57] As we know from these Weimar writings on pluralism, Schmitt notes that a state that is integrated into every facet of society is hardly a state at all but rather a *quantitative* total state. A state worthy of the name, for Schmitt, must stand over and above society, governing it, no doubt firmly and vigilantly, as a separate entity – as a *qualitative* total state.[58] His emphasis on the mechanical or technological character of the modern state, on nearly every page of the text of *Der Leviathan,* and his account of how the "subjective," "indirect," and "social" forces demythify and commandeer the machine for themselves draw attention to these texts that he apparently feels he cannot cite under the present regime. But the suggestion is that Schmitt's "qualitative" fascism, one steeped in the early-modern state-building/mythmaking project of Hobbes and Machiavelli, could have better navigated the choice between the unordered terror of the state of nature and the overly ordered terror of the mechanistic state than did the "quantitative" fascism of National Socialism: "Considering the Leviathan as a great command mechanism of just or unjust states would ultimately be the same as 'discriminating' between just and unjust machines. . . . [Machiavelli's work] *The Prince* . . . still rings as very humane in comparison to the commands that are made in conformity to the consummate impartiality of the technically perfect machine" (*L,* 50).[59]

56   Schmitt, *Der Hüter der Verfassung* (Tübingen: J. C. B. Mohr [Paul Siebeck], 1931), p. 73.
57   Schmitt, "Staatsethik und pluralistisher Staat," pp. 28–9.
58   See Schmitt, "Weiterentwicklung des totalen Staats in Deutschland" (January 1933), in *Positionen und Begriffe.* For a cogent analysis of the distinction, which is often ignored or misunderstood in the literature, see Jean Cohen and Andrew Arato, *Civil Society and Political Theory* (Cambridge, Mass.: MIT Press, 1992), pp. 204, 237, 239. A study of authoritarianism that draws on the distinction is Abbott Gleason, *Totalitarianism* (Oxford: Oxford University Press, 1996).
59   One need not adhere to the interpretive methods of the school affiliated with Leo Strauss to find evidence of this reading of Schmitt's critique of the National Socialist regime. The method that Strauss discusses in *Persecution and the Art of Writing* (Glencoe, Ill.: Free Press, 1952) and practices throughout his postwar writings is perhaps most appropriately discerned under conditions of political tyranny like those that governed in the Third Reich. Schmitt speaks several times of Hobbes's resorting to "esoteric coverups" (e.g., *L,* 26), and Schmitt himself deploys them: by furtively referring to his early analysis of

It is the liberal state and the seizure and destruction of its machine by parties encouraged by pluralism that Schmitt ostensibly criticizes in *Der Leviathan:* "The institutions and concepts of liberalism, on which the positivist statute state rested, became weapons and power positions in the hands of the most illiberal forces. In this fashion, party pluralism has perpetrated the destruction of the state by using methods inherent in the liberal statutory state" (*L,* 74, translation amended).[60] But his implicit allusions, if not explicit references, to his quantitative/qualitative total-state distinction and his surprising restraint from praising National Socialism for overcoming the historical dilemma of the liberal state leave one to wonder whether the former is not an equally relevant target of his critique:

> It is in the interest of an indirect power to veil the unequivocal relationship between state command and political danger, power and responsibility, protection and obedience and the fact that the absence of responsibility associated with indirect rule allows the indirect powers to enjoy all the advantages and suffer none of the risks entailed in the position of political power. Furthermore, this typically indirect method *à deux mains* enables them to carry out their actions under the guise of something other than politics, namely religion, culture, economy, or private matter and still derive the advantages of the state. They were thus able to combat the Leviathan and still avail themselves of the animal until they destroyed the big machine. (*L,* 74)

Even in Hobbesian terms, the National Socialist state is no sovereign state but a pervertedly powerful form of the state of nature, where *no one* is sure if he or she is friend or enemy to fellow citizens or to the regime, constituted as it is by an irresponsibly destructive, particularist group of fanatics.

> Hobbes in *Political Theology* only by mentioning the year of its original publication (*L,* 44); by drawing on his own friend/enemy thesis only through an explication of Hobbes (Chap. 3); and by drawing attention to his conspicuously uncited essays on the qualitative versus quantitative total state in a footnote in which he remarks that "total" can have multiple meanings (*L,* 76, n. 7). What is clear is that the standpoint of this critique is not a quasi-liberal one, as Schmitt would later claim (see "Die vollendete Reformation") but an alternatively fascist one. In this vein, perhaps Schmitt's invocation of Machiavelli's *Prince* emphasizes *not* the fact that both it and Schmitt's *Der Leviathan* were written under conditions of exile, one external and the other internal, but rather that they are both ambiguous attempts to somewhat undermine, while garnering favor from, the reigning powers that punished their authors, through both subtle criticism and ostensible advice about more effective governance.

60 In order to demonstrate that the Weimar distinction between "law" and "statute" in Schmitt's thought, discussed in the previous chapter, is still significant for Schmitt here in *Der Leviathan,* I translate *Gesetzesstaat* as "statute state" rather than "law state," as does Schwab.

Schmitt refuses to acknowledge that the other moment within his fascist project besides neoabsolutism, namely, myth, may contribute to the abuses of the state in his day.[61] Schmitt insists, for instance, on distinguishing the myths preferred by Hobbes and himself to the nineteenth-century-style ones characteristic of Nietzsche (L, 5). I discussed in Chapter 2 the affinities between Schmitt's neoabsolutist and Nietzsche's *Lebensphilosophische* myths. However, as far as Schmitt is concerned, myth as such is not the problem. The aspect of myth in Hobbes could have kept the elements of society from becoming autonomous and from making demands against the state; according to Schmitt, it could have ruled not through the apparatuses of technical efficiency but by "captivating minds": "No clear chain of thought can withstand the force of genuine, mythical images" (L, 81). Hobbes erred in his choice of myth not in his deployment of it. The biblical image of the Leviathan itself already anticipates its disenchantment and instrumental operationalization by indirect, subjective, social forces. In both Jewish and Christian lore, the Leviathan monster is defeated by the triumphant religiously devout: The Jews feast on Leviathan's flesh; the Christians lure it in on a cross-shaped hook (L, 7–9). The religious prophecy of the subduing of the Leviathan by ideologically fanatical particularist groups would be fulfilled in the twentieth century:

> Hobbes' thought prevailed in the positivist statute state of the nineteenth century, but only in a rather apocryphal manner. The old adversaries, the "indirect" powers of the church and of interest groups, reappeared in that century as modern political parties, trade unions, social organizations, in a phrase, as "forces of society." They seized the legislative arm of parliament and the statute state and thought that they had placed the Leviathan in a harness. Their ascendancy was facilitated by a constitutional system that enshrined a catalogue of individual rights. The "private" sphere was thus withdrawn from the state and handed over to the "free," that is, uncontrolled and invisible forces of "society." . . . From the duality of state and state-free society arose a social pluralism in which the "indirect powers" could celebrate effortless triumphs. (L, 73)

Schmitt begins the work with the question of "whether the Leviathan withstood the test of being the politico-mythical image battling the Judeo-Christian destruction of natural unity, and whether he was equal to the

61   For a more reliable account than Schmitt's of developments within early-modern state theory, see Maurizio Viroli, *From Politics to Reason of State: The Acquisition and Transformation of the Language of Politics, 1250–1600* (Cambridge: Cambridge University Press, 1992).

severity and malice of such a battle" (L, 11). The answer is clearly no; the image of the Leviathan was an insufficiently strong myth to combat the historical forces of technologically equipped pluralism: "The image of an all-powerful animal taken from the Hebrew Bible that had been rendered harmless would not convey an intelligible symbol for a totality produced by modern technology" (L, 82). By constituting his Leviathan with an even partly machinelike character, Hobbes was fulfilling the prophecy of its demise by providing the means whereby it would be demystified as a mere tool for whoever was strong enough to exploit the subjective right to self-defense into a ploy to seize the machine. In this way, Hobbes was a flawed mythmaker: "With the image of the Leviathan did he only approximate a myth" (L, 126). Thus the awesome, multitude-embodying, sea king that adorns the frontispiece of Hobbes's 1651 edition of the work is reduced to the "failure [Fehlschlag]" that Schmitt's title suggests.

Protection and Obedience; Myth and Rationality

We must not, however, accept at face value Schmitt's self-understanding as the historically legitimated prophet of doom he implicitly presents himself to be in Der Leviathan. Rather, he is unquestionably also a contributor to the state of affairs he criticizes under National Socialism. He had promoted the Reichspräsident as the "neutral" force to keep the social elements at bay in Weimar, a neutral force only with regard to the competing parties but not neutral toward its own power. Yet as Schmitt's Weimar theoretical adversary, Hans Kelsen, so presciently asked at the time, what is to prevent the supposedly neutral entity from being a participant in the social conflict Schmitt describes?[62] Put in more abstract Hobbesian terms, what is to keep the "strongest power," ordained as Leviathan in the transition from the state of nature to the state, from being a force of indiscriminate domination instead of objective neutrality? Schmitt had no real answer in Weimar circa 1932, and he still has no answer under National Socialism after 1936.

Schmitt's own conception of the state's duty to protect subjects is grounded not in the "right to protection" of those subjects (L, 68) but in the state's "responsibility" to do so (L, 72). The onus is on the state, and hence the initiative to act (when and how) is its own prerogative and not a response to the demands of or manipulation by particular social forces. Schmitt thereby effectively stands liberalism on its head in the formulation of his antiliberalism – with all the theological force that prefix implies. But

---

62 Hans Kelsen, "Wer soll der Hüter der Verfassung sein?" Die Justiz 6 (1930/31).

his formulation still begs the question of how to secure state protection and how to prevent the state from becoming the agent of a particular social interest once the subjective right to protection is abolished.

Thus, the stance of Hobbesian neutrality that Schmitt maintains throughout the twenties and thirties turns out to be somewhat misleading. An important difference between the "state of nature" and the "friend/enemy" distinction is that in the former, despite some occasional references by Hobbes to families or professions, there are *no* friends and hence no antagonistic *groupings.* The abstract individualism of Hobbes's "war of all against all" points up his ultimate agnosticism regarding the respective combatants in the English Civil War: *Leviathan* was written, for the most part, in support of the king but was easily converted by Hobbes into a justification for Cromwell.[63] Schmitt had much stronger preferences regarding the participants in Weimar's near–civil war. It *did* matter to him, for instance, that the Social Democrats *not* gain victory, let alone the Communists. Groups who would be the "enemies" of these groups would necessarily be, according to Schmitt's "concept of the political," better "friends" of the state. Should these "friends" gain control of the state, it would be appropriate for them to suppress the enemies of that state. This is in fact what the National Socialists did, albeit more ruthlessly than Schmitt could have imagined. To this effect, Schmitt's theory encouraged, as much as it forewarned against, the seizure of the Leviathan state by radically "subjective" social forces.

In fact, the potentially lethal results of such a seizure are compounded by Schmitt's theoretical tampering with the Hobbesian formula of *protego ergo obligo.* Had Hobbes originally formulated the state in the way Schmitt and Strauss wished in 1932 – by *not* granting to the individual the subjective right of self-protection, even for the sake of better ensuring that individual's life – the logic of the Leviathan would have broken down. It is only the retention of some of that subjectivity regarding self-preservation that rules completely in the state of nature that encourages "Hobbesian man" to make a compact and submit to the state. Schmitt was correct to recognize, in *Der Leviathan,* that the state was, in a way, ultimately the product of the age of technology; it was an *instrument,* a *tool.* It served as a *means* to something else, namely, security and stability, preservation and peace.[64] The state itself could not,

63   See Hobbes, "A Review, and Conclusion," in *Leviathan;* as well as Quentin Skinner, "Conquest and Consent: Thomas Hobbes and the Engagement Controversy," in *The Interregnum,* ed. G. E. Aylmer (London: Macmillan, 1972), on the dating of the book.

64   As Perry Anderson rightly observes regarding both Schmitt's and Michael Oakeshott's

without most unfortunate results, be what he, and Strauss for that matter, wanted: the *embodiment* of these things, and *not* the means to them. Such a formulation is as dangerous as it is incoherent. The state could not be expected to absorb all of the right to self-preservation from the state of nature and at the same time guarantee it. The radical subjectivity, the dangerous right to "judge," accruing to the state as it does in Schmitt's and Strauss's interpretation of Hobbes, only increases that subjectivity's volatility exponentially. Schmitt briefly reconsiders the economy of fear that governs the Hobbesian pact; that is, the total fear of the state of nature exchanged for only qualified fear of the sovereign Leviathan might not in fact result in such a peaceful outcome: "Hobbes' theory of state would certainly have been a peculiar philosophy of state if its entire chain of thought had consisted in propelling poor human beings from the utter fear of the state of nature only into the similarly total fear of a domination by a Moloch or a Golem" (*L*, 71). He immediately dismisses the traditional Lockean-liberal objections to such logic and suggests that such a pact made to a non-technologically tainted sovereign would solve that problem. Formulated nontechnologically, or in terms of the Weimar project pursued with Strauss, this means not granting the right to resist and not granting the technological means to threaten the state through unrestricted commerce in civil society, and substituting in place of this direct rule, concrete domination. A state founded on "unconditional obedience" (*L*, 53) would prevent one of the "subjective" social groups from seizing it. But the state is already by definition the "strongest" power within the state of nature, and hence submission to this "new god" settles the liberal objections of neither Kelsen nor, for that matter, Locke:

> I desire to know what kind of Government that is, and how much better it is than the State of Nature, where one Man commanding a multitude, has Liberty to be Judge in his own Case, and may do to all his Subjects whatever he pleases, without the least liberty to anyone to question or controle those who Execute his Pleasure? And in whatsoever he doth, whether led by Reason, Mistake or Passion, must be submitted to? Much better it is in the State of Nature wherein Men are not bound to submit to the unjust will of another.[65]

views of Hobbes, "It would be difficult to think of a more incongruous authority for any *'non-instrumental'* . . . understanding of the state. The pact of civil association between individuals in *Leviathan* is supremely an *instrument* to secure common ends – the aims of security and prosperity, 'mutual peace' and 'commodious living.'" "The Intransigent Right at the End of the Century," *London Review of Books* (Sept. 24, 1992), p. 7, emphasis added.

65 Locke, *The Second Treatise on Government*, II, § 13, 19–27.

In Locke's reformulation of Hobbes, it is absolute rule, not the state of nature, that is the actual state of "Warre." The state of nature in which each individual has an equal chance of remaining alive must surely be better than a situation in which one has completely given over one's right *to*, and capacity *for*, self-protection to an inordinately stronger force that offers no guarantee, no assurance of protecting one's life. Did Schmitt ever come to understand that Weimar, for all his criticisms of it, if not as desirable as the "qualitative" total state that he tried to aid Schleicher and Papen in constructing, was certainly preferable to National Socialism? In the Republic, whatever the social disturbances and economic fluctuations, Schmitt's academic controversies did not cause him to fear for his life.[66]

If, in *Der Leviathan*, Schmitt at least implicitly comes close to recognizing his earlier mistake in attempting to reformulate the Hobbesian protection/obedience relationship in so dangerous a fashion, he does not recognize at all the mistake in his earlier calling for the rule of "myth" over the rule of *Technik* in the art of statecraft. Like Martin Heidegger, but for different reasons, Schmitt must have originally seen in National Socialism a myth that could serve as an alternative and antidote to the age of technology.[67] He views myth as an element of the Hobbesian project that had faded but could be revived to supplant the presently predominant element, technology, which threatened to bring down the whole structure. And like Heidegger, Schmitt must have realized somewhat late that in modernity myth can be revived only very carefully, particularly in relationship to technology. As we now know, and as Walter Benjamin had already observed in his masterpiece of 1936, "The Artwork in the Age of Its Technological Reproducibility," in National Socialism myth and technology were fatefully bound:

> The logical result of Fascism is the introduction of aesthetics into political life. The violation of the masses, whom Fascism, with its *Führer* cult, forces to its knees, has its counterpart in the violence of an apparatus which is pressed into the production of ritual values. . . . All efforts to render politics aesthetic culminate in one thing: war. . . . "*Fiat ars – pereat mundus*," says Fascism, and . . . expects war to supply the artistic gratification of a sense perception that has been changed by technology. . . . Mankind['s] self-alienation has reached

66   On the subject of Schmitt's perception of his precarious position in the Reich after his fall from favor with the regime, see Bendersky, *Carl Schmitt: Theorist for the Reich*, 263–4; and Schwab, *The Challenge of the Exception*, p. 142; a more skeptical view is offered by Rüthers, *Carl Schmitt im Dritten Reich*.

67   On Heidegger's "faith" in the NSDAP, see Richard Wolin, "'Over the Line': Reflections on Heidegger and National Socialism," in *Labyrinths: Explorations in the Critical History of Ideas* (Amherst: University of Massachusetts Press, 1995), pp. 124, 127.

such a degree that it can experience its own destruction as an aesthetic pleasure of the first order.[68]

As 1932 became 1933, how did Strauss and Schmitt expect to revive that
primal substance, that link to myth, the fear of violent death? Did they not
realize, as did Benjamin, that "an apparatus" would be needed to change
"sense perception" by "technology" and "press into production" such "ritual
values?"[69]

In a later discussion of Hobbes, Strauss disparages the concept of "phantasmagoria," to which the world is reduced under a certain reductionist
interpretation of Hobbes.[70] But if phantasmagoria can be described, according to Susan Buck-Morss, as "an appearance of reality that tricks the
senses through technical manipulation," as a "technoaesthetics" that serves
as "a means of social control," this is precisely what Hobbes had in mind for
his Leviathan.[71] The Leviathan is intended as a phantasmagoria; the technology and the myth are for Hobbes intrinsically linked from the start.
Schmitt might have paid better attention to the opening lines of Hobbes's
introduction to *Leviathan,* in which he describes how humans can manufacture a political machine, the state, in the way that "God" created a natural
machine, the human being.[72] And it is this technical construction that

68 Benjamin, "Das Kunstwerk im Zeitalter seiner technischen Reproduzierbarkeit," origi-
    nally published in *Zeitschrift für Sozialforschung,* 5:1 (1936); translated by Harry Zohn as
    "The Work of Art in the Age of Mechanical Reproduction," in *Illuminations,* p. 241. For a
    recent consideration of this issue, see Martin Jay, "'The Aesthetic Ideology' as Ideology:
    Or What Does it Mean to Aestheticize Politics?" in *Force Fields: Between Intellectual History
    and Cultural Critique* (New York: Routledge, 1993).
69 In her article on Benjamin's "Artwork" essay, Susan Buck-Morss recounts how, in 1932,
    Hitler rehearsed his facial expressions in front of a mirror under the supervision of an
    opera singer. Buck-Morss compares photographs of Hitler's subsequent speeches with
    psychopictorial studies of faces expressing different emotional states. What she finds,
    surprisingly, is that Hitler's expressions correspond not to representations of aggression,
    anger, or rage but to depictions of fear and pain. See "Aesthetics and Anaesthetics: Walter
    Benjamin's Artwork Essay Reconsidered," *October* 62 (fall 1992): 39–40. Thus "the fear of
    violent death" that Schmitt and Strauss wished to revive, divorced from the influence of
    technology, was already being communicated technically and mechanically through loud-
    speakers, newsreels, motion pictures, photographs, and radios. Such a divorce was, in
    short, already unlikely.
70 Strauss, "On the Basis of Hobbes's Political Philosophy," in *What Is Political Philosophy? and
    Other Studies* (Chicago: University of Chicago Press, 1988), pp. 178–9.
71 Buck-Morss, "Aesthetics and Anaesthetics," pp. 22–3.
72 Hobbes writes in his introduction, "Nature (the Art whereby God hath made and gov-
    ernes the World) is by the *Art* of man, as in many other things, so in this also imitated, that
    it can make an Artificial Animal. For seeing life is but a motion of Limbs, the begining
    whereof is in some principall part within; why may we not say, that all Automata (Engines

necessarily underlies the Leviathan preferred by Schmitt and Strauss: the "Mortall God," which "hath the use of so much Power and Strength conferred on him, that by terror thereof, he is enabled to conforme the wills of them all, to Peace at home, and mutuall ayd against their enemies abroad" (II, 17).[73]

In Hobbes, and consequently in modernity, the result of this entwinement of myth and technology is the tragic fact that the former can serve to intensify rather than diminish the threat posed by the latter. Perhaps an attempt to exalt myth over science and technology beyond Hobbes's original balance between the two spheres paradoxically leads only to a greater predominance of the latter within the former, as a result of their intrinsic link. The way to disengage the mutual relationship of myth and technology, or, in the more familiar phrasing of Horkheimer and Adorno, myth and enlightenment, would perhaps be through the threshold of reason and not that of myth.[74] This would of course necessitate abandoning fear as a contributing element to politics. The potential result of the opposite strategy, of subordinating rationality to myth, as Benjamin points out so well, is war. At what better site in the twentieth century could "fear," "pain," "violence," "aesthetics," and "technology" gather?[75]

---

that move themselves by springs and wheeles as doth a watch) have an artificiall life? . . . *Art* goes yet further, imitating that Rationall and most excellent worke of Nature, *Man*. For by Art is created that great LEVIATHAN called a COMMON-WEALTH, or STATE, (in Latine CIVITAS) which is but an Artificiall Man."

73   According to Buck-Morss, phantasmagoria have "the effect of anaesthetizing the organism, not through numbing, but through flooding the senses. These simulated sensoria alter consciousness, much like a drug, but they do so through sensory distraction rather than chemical alteration, and – most significantly – their effects are experienced collectively rather than individually" (p. 23). We must not forget that Hobbes intended his automaton, his man–monster–machine to be a "*visible* Power to keep *them* in *awe*" (II, 17, emphasis added), in other words, a sense-induced distraction of the masses.

74   See particularly the first two essays of Horkheimer and Adorno, *Dialectic of Enlightenment:* "The Concept of Enlightenment," and "Odysseus or Myth and Enlightenment." Although Blumenberg recognizes the intrinsic relationship between myth and Enlightenment rationality, in *Work on Myth*, Cassirer, a renowned Kantian, insists on their distinction. However, Cassirer comes very close to acknowledging the "dialectic of enlightenment" when he remarks on the "strategic," "technical," and "artificial" quality of myth in relationship to modern technology and politics – what he calls "the technique of political myth." *Symbol, Myth and Culture*, pp. 235–7.

75   As noted earlier, Benjamin claimed that, "All efforts to render politics aesthetic culminate in one thing: war." Furthermore, as Michael Geyer reminds us, in terms that recall Benjamin *and* Schmitt, "war" was indeed the essence of National Socialism: "The direction of the Third Reich was toward *war*. War was essential to regain the 'autonomy of the political' and to recenter the stage by giving politics at least the appearance of purposeful and unified action which it otherwise lacks. In the counterrevolutionary Third Reich, war,

We observed that, in *The Concept of the Political*, Schmitt finds it necessary to aestheticize – to elevate to mythic proportions – conflict in order to generate the salutary fear that could restore order to society. But such aestheticization, such mythmaking, on the contrary, contributed to the generation of far-from-salutary fear and the intensification of disorder. Rather than, in Hobbes's words, ensuring "Peace at home," and simply fostering "mutuall ayd" against external enemies, the aestheticization and elevation of conflict to the status of myth inspired a war, ghastly in manner and scale, on Germany's own citizens and, in unprecedented global terms, on other nations. Schmitt's student, Franz Neumann, in fact describes the National Socialist state not as the Leviathan but as its opposite, the Behemoth: "a non-state, a situation of lawlessness, disorder and anarchy."[76]

Schmitt criticizes Hobbes's choice of myth in the foundation of his state theory but not the enterprise of mythmaking itself. It is not clear, however, whether any mythmaking is free of the faults Schmitt finds with Hobbes's Leviathan. Hobbes's formulation of the Leviathan myth caused him to lose control of the apparatus that was simultaneously technical and mythical: "Whoever utilizes such images, easily glides into the role of the magician who summons forces that cannot be matched by his arm, his eye, or any other measure of his human ability. He runs the risk that instead of encountering an ally he will meet a heartless demon who will deliver him into the

---

victorious war, was meant to achieve more than that. War not only happened to be Hitler's main and ultimate goal in the creation of a new German society, it also made the Third Reich an 'exceptional state.' War permits the 'autonomy of the political' to reach its extreme in the age of imperialism. In an 'exceptional state' war is neither simply the predatory instinct of special interests, nor the manifestation of atavistic sentiments. Rather, war is fought to create and recreate a society *and* a state which 'habitually lives on war.' War recenters state and society in combat, domination, and direct exploitation." "The State in National Socialist Germany," in *Statemaking and Social Movements: Essays in History and Theory*, ed. Charles Bright and Susan Harding (Ann Arbor: University of Michigan Press, 1984), p. 198.

In 1933, Schmitt sought to overcome the state of nature, the friend/enemy distinction, in domestic politics so that the state could take part in these in the realm in which, according to Schmitt, they could *never* be overcome, the realm of international relations. Thus, for Schmitt, war had to be suppressed at home in order to prepare for it abroad, specifically against the Soviet Union. National Socialism, therefore, defies Schmitt's own "concept of the political" by as vigorously making war at home as on foreign soil, by maintaining, in Geyer's words, "an escalating system of domestic terror and violence abroad." Geyer, "The Stigma of Violence: Nationalism and War in Twentieth Century Germany," *German Studies Review* (winter 1992): 97.

76 Neumann, *Behemoth: The Structure and Practice of National Socialism, 1933–1944* (New York: Harper & Row, 1944), p. xii. Schmitt understands Behemoth exclusively as a symbol of religious fanaticism and revolution (*L*, 21).

hands of his enemies" (*L*, 82). This is what becomes of Hobbes, whose state was commandeered by the social forces it was designed to keep at bay; to the participants in the state of nature, whose fate at the hands of the "new god" they effectively create may be far worse than their precarious natural freedom; and to Schmitt himself, whose vainglorious attempt to institute his qualitative total state under the auspices of the National Socialist party myth in the end compelled him to submit to the party's will within the domain of its quantitative total state.

Thus, Schmitt's and Strauss's Weimar attempt to supplant liberalism by reinterpreting Hobbes is a catastrophic failure in two ways. First, they tamper with one Hobbesian formula, the protection/obedience relationship, that had already been improved by the liberalism that succeeded Hobbes. Second, they experiment with another Hobbesian formula, the myth/technology relationship, to which post-Hobbesian liberalism continues to be oblivious. In both cases, they render the reformulation more dangerous than the original supposedly unstable proposition, and the historical reality with which it corresponds is undeniably disastrous.

Liberalism, Fascism, and Conservatism

In his commentary on Schmitt's *Concept of the Political*, Strauss expresses the need to "disregard the question whether it is possible to speak of any conception of culture [and nature] except the modern one" (*CP*, 87). He obviously feels that the modern conception of these entities that led to the crisis of the state requires a modern solution. This is expressed at the conclusion of his commentary on Schmitt and in the first several chapters of his book on Hobbes. Strauss later remarks that his writings in the dwindling days of Weimar were "based on the premise, sanctioned by powerful prejudice, that a return to pre-modern philosophy is impossible."[77] That changes, however, with the publication of the full text of *The Political Philosophy of Hobbes*, in 1936, and especially *Natural Right and History*, in 1953. Modern philosophical-political expressions, particularly as reflected in Hobbes, are in these later works cast in a particularly unfavorable comparison with the classical tradition. In light of ensuing events, perhaps Strauss was – to use a word that has figured prominently in this chapter – "frightened" into this stance by the implications of the earlier project he shared with Carl Schmitt. In his "second sailing," he no longer so explicitly

---

77 See the so-called autobiographical preface, included in Strauss, *Spinoza's Critique of Religion*, p. 30.

voices "modern" solutions to modern political problems. Strauss, as is well known, went on to achieve cult status in the United States, to a large degree because he had learned to keep his political inclinations hidden behind both a religion he did not believe in and an "ancient" form of esoteric writing that he supposedly rediscovered but perhaps just as likely contrived.[78]

Walter Benjamin, on the other hand, did not have the good fortune to have his exit from Germany or the continent procured for him by a soon-to-be member of the National Socialist party in 1933. A Jew who did *not* flirt

---

[78] In a review of Heinrich Meier's *Schmitt and Strauss,* Paul Gottfried describes how Meier and other Straussians attempt to artificially separate Strauss's Weimar views from those of Schmitt. See "Schmitt and Strauss," *Telos* 96 (summer 1993). Meier himself admits that "both seem to agree in their political positions or in fact agree in their political critique of a common opponent [liberalism]." Meier, *Carl Schmitt and Leo Strauss,* p. 43. And other admirers of Strauss leave open the question of how much, if at all, Strauss changed his mind after emigrating. As Volker Reinecke and Jonathan Uhlaner remark, "Leaving Europe behind, Strauss began to rearrange his attitude toward philosophy. He abandoned none of the positions with which he had worked for over a decade, but transformed their coordination." "The Problem of Leo Strauss: Religion, Philosophy and Politics," p. 196. There is of course the assessment of young Strauss's political predilections that Hannah Arendt conveyed to her biographer; see Elisabeth Young-Bruehl, *Hannah Arendt: For Love of the World* (New Haven: Yale University Press, 1982), pp. 98, 169. Such commentators as Stephen Holmes and Shadia Drury have recently elucidated the postwar esoteric writing method deployed by Strauss whereby a "philosopher" does not overtly and immediately reveal what he or she means for fear of political consequences. The content of these supposedly unbearable truths are, among others, the moral anarchy of a universe absent of the divine, the illegitimacy of all national borders, the ultimate amorality of political action and the brute reality of the strong over the weak. Strauss invokes classical standards of truth, beauty, and justice to keep these "terrible" truths from the ears of the vulgar masses, who would purportedly otherwise run amok, and instead preserves them in the hands of "philosophers," who prudently and strategically put them at the service of politicians in order to moderate their potential tyranny. Hence, Strauss appropriated Schmitt's call for rule by an intellectual elite by turning to the Platonic model of rule by philosopher kings. See Shadia Drury, *The Political Ideas of Leo Strauss* (New York: St. Martin's Press, 1988); and Holmes, "Strauss: Truth for Philosophers Alone," in *The Anatomy of Antiliberalism.*

Just as Plato and Xenophon portray a Socrates who only too late learned the mortal dangers of speaking so blatantly about the amoral truths of the political, Strauss tried to change his tune before the damage to philosophers, such as himself, in the twentieth century became irreparable. Learning from the mistakes of his mentor, Strauss subsequently sought to textually conceal nihilistic political "truths" within his nearly impenetrable ruminations on the "right" and the "good" in classical philosophy rather than, like Schmitt, easily putting such dangerous truths at the disposal of the practitioners of political tyranny. Although Strauss would indeed become an inspiration to right-wing intellectuals and Republican party think-tankers in the United States, his new philosophical approach attempted to make political engagement better serve the *philosopher* rather than the *politician.* See Strauss, *What Is Political Philosophy? and Other Studies.*

with a political philosophy that now sounds painfully close to the ideology that would very soon make "war" on Jews, Benjamin, rather, was one of its most brilliant critics and ultimately became one of the millions of its victims seven years later.[79]

Schmitt himself later attempted to justify his collaboration with National Socialism by appealing to the Hobbesian standard of "obedience for protection": He merely offered allegiance to a new regime that he assumed would in turn protect him.[80] It is almost fitting, then, that this "Hobbesian" who sought to theorize into oblivion the "protection" component of the "protection/obedience" formula, may have come rather close several times during the Third Reich to paying with his life for making that unforgivable political choice.[81] Instead, Schmitt lived well into his nineties, claiming until the end that he was simply misconstrued. Fond of comparing himself with the likes of Machiavelli and Hobbes, who were discredited in their times and immediately after their deaths for their particular political endorsements, Schmitt often repeated the concluding lines of *Der Leviathan*,[82] which referred as much in his mind to "that lonely philosopher from Malmesbury" (*L*, 82) as to that perhaps even more lonely philosopher from Plettenberg:

> Today we grasp the undiminished force of his polemics, understand the intrinsic honesty of his thinking, and admire the imperturbable spirit who fearlessly thought through man's existential anguish, and as a true champion, destroyed the murky distinctions of indirect powers. To us he is a true teacher of a great political experience; lonely as every pioneer; misunderstood as is everyone

79 On Benjamin's aborted attempt to flee the Nazis and his subsequent suicide as a response to his fear of being captured by them, see Susan Buck-Morss, *The Origin of Negative Dialectics: Theodor W. Adorno, Walter Benjamin and the Frankfurt Institute* (New York: Free Press, 1977), pp. 162–3. Despite the existential flavor of the early Benjamin's engagement with Schmitt's work, it did not lean so precariously toward political authoritarianism as did Strauss's treatment of Schmitt's thesis. See Benjamin's letter to Schmitt, in Benjamin's *Gesammelte Schriften*, vol. 1. ed. R. Tiedemann and H. Scheppenhäuser (Frankfurt a. M.: Suhrkamp, 1974). On Benjamin and Schmitt, see Michael Rumpf, "Radikale Theologie: Benjamins Beziehung zu Carl Schmitt," in *Walter Benjamin – Zeitgenosse der Moderne*, ed. Peter Gebhardt et al. (Kronberg: Scriptor, 1976); Norbert Bolz, "Charism and Souveränität: Carl Schmitt und Walter Benjamin im Schatten Max Webers," in *Der Fürst dieser Welt: Carl Schmitt und die Folgen*, ed. Jacob Taubes (Munich: Wilhelm Fink, 1983); and Samuel Weber, "Taking Exception to Decision: Walter Benjamin and Carl Schmitt," *Diacritics* 22:3–4 (fall/winter 1992).

80 Bendersky, *Carl Schmitt: Theorist for the Reich*, p. 204.

81 Ibid., pp. 230–42.

82 See G. L. Ulmen, "Anthropological Theology/Theological Anthropology," *Telos* 93 (Fall 1992): 73, n. 15.

whose political thought does not gain acceptance among his own people; unrewarded, as one who opened a gate through which others marched on; and yet in the immortal community of the great scholars of the ages, "a sole retriever of an ancient prudence." Across the centuries we reach out to him: Now you do not teach in vain, Thomas Hobbes! (*L*, 86)

III

LIBERALISM AND FASCISM/TECHNOLOGY AND POLITICS

EPILOGUE AND SUMMARY

Schmitt's major theoretical statement under National Socialism in the years following *Der Leviathan* of 1938 is "The Plight of European Jurisprudence," originally delivered as a lecture throughout the Reich in 1943–44.[1] Although there is a question as to how much of the subtly brazen criticisms of National Socialism were added to the text only after the war,[2] it is indeed possible that Schmitt intended the essay to serve as a kind of apology, if only in the classical sense of the term. In the wake of the arrest and hanging of Schmitt's surviving political mentor, Johannes Popitz, for his role in the plot to assassinate Hitler in July of 1944, Schmitt may have felt sufficiently threatened to leave behind a "testament."[3] Or with the end of the war not an unforeseeable possibility at this point and the outcome not boding particularly well for Germany, Schmitt may have felt the need to put on his best face for the civilized world.

The object of Schmitt's criticism in the essay is again the legal positivism that he still views as a jurisprudence infected by technology: The "widespread opinion that only a positivist jurisprudence is feasible is a product of

---

1 Schmitt, "The Plight of European Jurisprudence," trans. G. L. Ulmen, *Telos* 83 (spring 1990); hereafter *PJ*.
2 See Bernd Rüthers, *Carl Schmitt im Dritten Reich: Wissenschaft als Zeitgeist-Verstärkung?* (Munich: C. H. Beck Verlag, 1989).
3 For an account of the historical context of the essay, see Paul Piccone and G. L. Ulmen, "Schmitt's 'Testament' and the Future of Europe," *Telos* 83 (spring 1990).

the late nineteenth century. In this narrowing [of jurisprudence] into mere technique, the progress of law is confused with the increasing promptness of the legislative machine" (*PJ*, 56). However, the jurisprudence that Schmitt seeks to protect from this positivist "motorization" of law (*PJ*, 53) is defended in a manner quite different from that which we observed Schmitt employ in his Weimar works. Using the great nineteenth-century German jurist, F. C. Savigny, as a resource in his mission to defend jurisprudence, Schmitt gives a particularly historical bent to his endeavor, one that ignores the "decision" so crucial to his earlier critique of legal positivism:

> Law as concrete order must not be separated from its history. True law is not imposed; it arises from unintentional elements. It reveals itself in the concrete form of jurisprudence, through which it becomes conscious of its development. For Savigny, the jurisprudential concept of the positive is bound to a particular type of "source" protected by jurists. Law emerges from this "source" in a specific way, as something not merely legislated but given. The later positivism knows no origin and has no home. It recognizes only causes or basic norms. It seeks to be the opposite of "unintended" law. Its ultimate goal is control and calculability. (*PJ*, 56–7)

To be sure, Schmitt still defends the concreteness of the law against an encroaching abstractness associated with positivism. But the importance of the concrete is no longer exemplified by a lightning bolt out of the sky like the exception, or the decision over it, but rather it is justified by the more sober force of jurisprudentially preserved historical continuity. Schmitt still has not forsworn his emphasis on elites, but the agent of the substantively concrete is no longer a deciding sovereign or a plebiscitarily legitimated executive but rather the more mundane personage of the jurist. With Savigny – that "ill-starred historical figure" who was disgraced by practical political involvement with the King of Prussia (*PJ*, 62) – as his mouthpiece and alter ego, Schmitt heralds a change or a reversion in his legal philosophy and his political theory. Recall from Chapter 5 how Schmitt abandoned the merely "conservative" position of the consensus of a particular community of judges as the mediation between formal law and concrete case,[4] just as in Chapters 1 and 2 he rejected a Burkean "conservative" interpretation of history as traditional continuity.[5] In this late National Socialist work

4   See Schmitt, *Gesetz und Urteil: Eine Untersuchung zum Problem der Rechtspraxis* ([1912] Munich: C. H. Beck, 1969).
5   See Schmitt, *Political Romanticism*, trans. Guy Oakes (Cambridge, Mass.: MIT Press, 1985), pp. 61–2.

on "European Jurisprudence," he has apparently retreated to both of these less radically conservative positions.

Whereas Schmitt had previously resorted to existential mythology and quasi theology to defend his legal and constitutional theory from the colonization of technopositivism in the majority of his Weimar work, he now claims that the task of the jurist is to defend jurisprudence from *both* theology *and* technology. Schmitt describes in familiar terms the *technical* threat to jurisprudence: the "untrammeled technicism," the "subaltern instrumentalization" of positivism that he identifies as "the danger inherent in the spirit of mechanization, runaway technology and mass society" (*PJ*, 66–7). Yet he now also notes a traditional threat posed to jurisprudence by *theology:* "Jurisprudence would cease to be an autonomous science with its own specific character if it surrendered of its own volition to theology" (*PJ*, 64). It is the jurist's task to maintain jurisprudence as "a science . . . against both sides" – against technology *and* theology (*PJ*, 66).

As we observed in Chapter 6, Schmitt explicitly champions myth against technology, in the *Leviathan* book of 1938, and laments its defeat in the service of the sovereign state. In the five or six years that had elapsed, did Schmitt change his mind regarding the mythic and the neotheological? The answer is inconclusive, but this new stance that purports to mediate between mythology and technology does not in the end ecstatically shift to the former element, as his previous stances so often did. It is a stance, moreover, that Schmitt was to maintain for the rest of his life. Concomitant with his more grandiose self-associations with the *Kathechon,* mentioned at the conclusion of Chapter 2, or the great state philosophers, such as Machiavelli and Hobbes, discussed in Chapter 3 and the last chapter, Schmitt's self-presentation from now on would also be that of the bookish jurist, the humble clerk, whose commentaries would defend the law from fanatical religiosity, on one side, and technocratic manipulation, on the other. In fact, Schmitt would also encourage a reading of his Weimar works in precisely this light. Schmitt goes on to suggest that those writings be read in their "juridical context" and that such categories as "the political" or "the exception" be read as purely "juristic categories."[6] But his explicit endorsement of myth in *Der Leviathan* and his adamant opposition to it in "The Plight of European Jurisprudence" as well as in his postwar works are shifts

6 See Schmitt, *Der Nomos der Erde im Völkerrecht des Jus Publicum Europaeum* ([1950] Berlin: Duncker & Humblot, 1974); *Ex Captivitate Salus: Erfahrungen der Zeit 1945/47* (Cologne: Greven, 1950), and, most outrageously, the preface to the 1963 edition of *Der Begriff des Politischen: Text von 1932 mit einem Vorwort und drei Corollarien* (Berlin: Duncker & Humblot), pp. 13, 14–16.

away from what I have demonstrated as a persistent and implicit deployment of myth in his Weimar works.

Schmitt's position in "European Jurisprudence," although unquestionably conservative, is at least closer to the methodology expected of a theorist
so sensitive to the antinomial poles of modernity, which I elucidated in Part
One. The instrumental rationality and the romantic irrationality discerned
by Schmitt in his early work as entwined, poles that crystallize in the terms of
"technology" and "theology" deployed in the "European Jurisprudence"
essay, can only be understood in relationship to their historical situation, as
Schmitt himself declares in *"Northern Lights," Political Romanticism,* and *Political Form.* When Schmitt observes that these poles "are in complete harmony
with the spirit [*Geist*] of our epoch because their intellectual structure corresponds to a reality," and that their "point of departure is actually a real
cleavage and division: an antithesis that requires a synthesis,"[7] it is incumbent on him to interrogate that structure more rigorously than he ever
actually does.

Schmitt's flawed notion of what constitutes this "real structure" generating the antitheses is bound with his ultimately inadequate notion of history
that itself prevents him from overcoming these oppositions and actually
encourages him to exalt one moment of it – the romantic one – into a false
"higher third" as a solution. This is precisely the kind of artificial and
ineffectual move that he detected and criticized in the romantics who would
posit, for instance, "true soul" as the supercession of the opposition "body
and soul." He is equally guilty of the charge, which he leveled against the
romantics, of relying on rhetorical cleverness, "pithy and striking" assertions, that deflect attention from his moments of theoretical inadequacy.

In the end, Schmitt is guilty of merely radicalizing instead of actually
transcending Weber's conception of history as rationalization and the relationship of political practice to it. As we know from Chapter 1, Weber
establishes an irresistible march of technological rationalization as the
course of modern history to which political practice must respond with
responsible, if not necessarily effectual, stands. Schmitt does not refute
Weber's account of modern history up to this century, but he suggests that
from an activist, initially Catholic- and subsequently secular-elitist perspective, these political stands, which already waver on the brink of irrationality
in Weber, can actually effectively seize control of the "wheel of history." If

7 Schmitt, *Römischer Katholizismus und politische Form* (Stuttgart: Klett-Cotta, 1984), p. 16. See
   Roman Catholicism and Political Form (1923), trans. G. L. Ulmen (Westport: Greenwood,
   1996).

measured not by the Protestant criteria of "inwardly experience" but by the criteria of a more activist stance, such praxis could reappropriate history. For Schmitt, after all, the rationalization process that Weber describes and Schmitt reconstructs as a neutralization process was actually authored by such intellectual elites as Descartes, Newton, and Hobbes; now that this process has run its course through all the neutralizing experiments of the previous century, especially the liberalism of the nineteenth, it is their turn to reclaim it. For both Weber and Schmitt, the result of rationalization and neutralization in modernity is a multitude of bearers of incommensurable worldviews – a pluriverse of warring gods – competing to take hold of state power apparatuses across the globe. Schmitt's solution is to foster a self-conscious and active elite that can tame these social groups by constructing the appropriate myths to fortify the potentially terrifying but allegedly neutral state.

Thus the "real structure" underlying the antitheses of modernity in Schmitt's mind was set in place by the conscious practice of elites, which was subsequently sublimated by the general populace into the anonymous workings of economy and society and out of the hands of such elites. However, these elites, according to Schmitt throughout his mid- to late-Weimar writings, can and must retake the reins of this process. His false "higher third" in all the works we have examined is intended to facilitate an active romantic orientation toward this reappropriation of history by elites and shake them from their passively romantic disposition toward it. This culminates in the fantasy of a culturally or nationally legitimated elitist authoritarianism in Europe that confronts an economically legitimated elitist authoritarianism in the East.

As I elaborated in Chapter 1, despite his careful elucidation of the apparent antinomies that accompany technology – abstract rationality versus substantive irrationality; reduction of qualitatively different entities to quantitative sameness versus arbitrary valorization of concrete qualities, and so on – Schmitt does not interrogate the question of authenticity, meaning, or "realness" far enough. In Chapter 2, we observed how he compares the epistemological uncertainty aroused by technology to that inspired by the Antichrist: the inability to decide what is real, the inability to discover whether this entity that ostensibly brings so much good is *in fact* good or is the worst incarnation of evil. He recognizes the fear inspired by the Antichrist-like technology but succumbs to it himself. His own latent fear of not knowing what he is as an elite or "cleric," or what the "West" is as a cultural entity, causes him to grasp for such a meaning in the definition of a mythic enemy, an opposite, Soviet Russia.

In the successive chapters of this book, I have shown how Schmitt consistently opts for the mythic, what he would call in 1944 the "theological," over the technically rational, because his attempt to ground a rationality that is neither of these poles ultimately fails. Chapter 3 attempts to explain why he shifts from the moderate position suggesting the constitutionally bound Roman dictatorship as a model for emergency powers, in *Dictatorship*, to the extreme position of the charismatically imbued and constitutionally unlimited figure of the "sovereign," in *Political Theology*, only a year later. I demonstrate in Chapter 4 how Schmitt, after undertaking a painstakingly careful analysis of the technification of the principles and practices of liberal representative government, in *Parlamentarismus*, ultimately endorses the politics of nationalist myth. After finding the liberal representative scheme lacking in comparison with the medieval model, he neither offers the latter as an alternative nor suggests how the former could be made more "substantive." Instead he destroys the very idea of representation by endorsing a plebiscitary leader who "embodies" the nation as a whole. In Chapter 5, I suggest that what begins as a probing analytical observation on Schmitt's part – specifically, that a liberal legal theory and constitutional law overly influenced by modern natural science is insufficiently attentive to the possibility of contingency, indeterminacy, the exception – lapses into an aestheticization of that exception as an extrarational force. The decisive judgment required to adjudicate a particular case or the sovereign power needed to address the exceptional situation become the triumph of executive action over the paralyzing equilibrium of liberal constitutional mechanisms.

In Chapter 6, we observed Schmitt's response to the merging of the state and civil society in twentieth-century welfare-state Germany. For the state to re-attain its sovereignty and free itself from the greedy hands of the social forces who increasingly make demands of it, and who become more and more dangerous to each other and to the state itself, the state must instill *fear* in its citizens. In Hobbesian fashion it must first arouse citizens' boundless fear of each other – the myth of the state of nature – and replace it with the tempered fear of the state – the myth of the Leviathan. Because Schmitt perceives the twentieth-century crisis of state and society as attributable to Hobbes's granting citizens limited subjective freedom – to be expressed in science and commerce – Schmitt seeks to revive Hobbes's mythic state without the reliance on individual freedom, science, and technology.

In fact it might be argued, as Schmitt reveals most tellingly in *Der Leviathan*, his perfect state *combines* myth and technical rationality, in such a way that he expects to overcome the opposition. If one could marry the thoroughly positivist and, as Schmitt identifies it, "mechanistic" equation of positive command and law, as Hobbes does, with a myth that would ward off particular groups from attempting to appropriate that command mechanism, one would have the authoritarian, "qualitative" state *par excellence*. The problem with Kelsenian or liberal positivism is that it is too democratic; it offers the mechanism of lawmaking to pluralist factions within the general populace, thus inviting the state's own destruction. Romanticism, despite its proclivity toward irrationality, cannot be an adequate source of myth to protect the state from such forces in Schmitt's understanding, because it is subjectively passive and does not actively seek to serve politics, that is, authority. The phenomenon of myth, understood by Schmitt as distinct from romanticism, can serve authority in such a way. Schmitt's utopic qualitative, rather than quantitative, total state is hence no substantive mediation of rationalization and romanticism but rather a merging of the two. However, his mourning over the dead myth of Hobbes's Leviathan state suggests that it is the mythic component for which Schmitt held the highest hopes in his own state theory.[8]

Furthermore, Schmitt's lack of faith in even the most remote possibility that people can democratically govern themselves without collapsing into factious partisans who promote different "gods" and "demons" fuels the fixation on elites we have observed throughout his work: an intellectual elite that defines the "West" against the Russians, the plebiscitary dictator who embodies the homogeneous nation, the deciding sovereign who confronts the exception, the law professor and his philosophy-student admirer who would revive Hobbesian myth and save the state. The elites can rule the people by exploiting these various myths. Schmitt indeed takes a "democratic" turn when confronted with the technocratic tendencies of modern liberalism, but it is to an authoritarian democracy not a more substantively popular one. His cynically radicalized Weberianism affords him no vision of a populace as something other than a potentially homogenized unity or a hopelessly pluralized multitude of factions.[9] Although Schmitt never conveys an outright contempt for the masses, as do many of his contemporary rightist colleagues, he never relinquishes the position that the masses must be guided and ruled by a supposedly knowing elite.

8 Siegfried Kracauer and Herbert Marcuse criticize the stunted dialectics practiced by theorists, such as Schmitt, that come very close to ascertaining the nature of the abstract and concrete modes of domination in modernity only to place those dialectics in the service of a more violent, concrete, and mythic domination. See Kracauer, "The Mass Ornament" (1927), in *The Mass Ornament: Weimar Essays*, ed. T. Levin (Cambridge, Mass.: Harvard University Press, 1995); and Marcuse, "The Struggle against Liberalism in the Totalitarian View of the State" (1934), in *Negations: Essays in Critical Theory*, trans. Jeremy Shapiro (Boston: Beacon Press, 1968).

9 An outlook that he did not abandon even later in his life; see Schmitt, *Theorie des Partisanen: Zwischenbemerkung zum Begriff des Politischen* (Berlin: Duncker & Humblot, 1963).

Thus, Schmitt the avowed historicist is an odd one indeed, for his is a historicism that excludes theorists themmselves as intellectual elites and potential makers of history from being determined by their own historical moment. In this particular sense, Schmitt's historicism is more like that associated with existentialism – like that of Nietzsche and Heidegger, who see the changes that history inscribes on "Being" but not on *their* being – than the Hegelianism within which I have often situated him. Whether inspiring his only slightly less-enlightened fellow elites in the "Neutraliza-tions" essay to confront the Eastern menace, or planning the revival of the Leviathan state, Schmitt's is the mind that stands outside of history. Al-though he is adamant, throughout his Weimar writings, in his claim that modern history is driven by elites, he makes no attempt to explain how they know exactly what they purportedly know. Confidence in such knowledge certainly inflates the expectations concerning what such a mind that stands outside of history can achieve when intervening actively in history. The folly of such intellectual-political bravado is all too well documented throughout the history of the twentieth century. If this way of thinking does not make for theoretical rigor or desirable political success, it makes for even less as a potentially viable source for democratic theory. In a certain way, the kind of elitism professed by Schmitt as well as the aestheticization to which he frequently resorts – aestheticization of conflict, of the exception, of execu-tive power, and so on – are the unconquered remnants of the primal will to domination that is never fully exorcised from his thought.[10]

In the Introduction, I claimed that I would not criticize Schmitt from a standpoint outside of his own thought. I did not want to conclude that he was "wrong" simply on the basis of the fact that he happened not to be a liberal or a leftist. However, according to the "Plight of European Jurispru-dence" lecture of 1944, a kind of liberalism is all that Schmitt ever really wanted for his jurisprudence:

> We [jurists] preserve the basis of a rational human existence that cannot do without legal principles such as: a recognition of the individual based on mutual respect even in a conflict situation; a sense for the logic and con-sistency of concepts and institutions; a sense for reciprocity and the minimum of an orderly procedure, due process, without which there can be no law. That we defend this indestructible core of all law against all destructive enactments

---

10   In this light, critics have pointed out the regressive-infantile quality – in the Freudian sense – of, for instance, the friend/enemy distinction; see, T. W. Adorno, *Minima Moralia: Reflections from Damaged Life*, trans. E. F. N. Jephcott (London: Verso, 1978), pp. 131–2; and J. Huizinga, *In the Shadow of Tomorrow* (New York: W. W. Norton, 1936), pp. 125–6.

means that we maintain a dignity which today in Europe is more critical than at any other time and in any other part of the world. (*PJ*, 67).

Whether Schmitt was sufficiently courageous or foolish to deliver these words when he lectured in 1944 or inserted them later, so that he might better posture for posterity, is ultimately an irrelevant question. We know that he often spoke of the "dignity" of humanity in his Weimar writings: a dignity that was threatened by a technology that cannot distinguish between humanity and other material matter, and that seeks to manipulate both to the same grindingly efficient degree; he also spoke of the dignity that was threatened by a scheme of liberal political representation that, under the thrall of the technological, only mechanically reproduced the quantitatively material aspect of people, and nothing more substantive than that. Never, however, does Schmitt associate "dignity" with these liberal principles of individual rights, due process, and orderly procedure he mentions in the "European Jurisprudence" essay. He never attempts to theorize how these might be distinguished from the decidedly technical in liberalism or how they might be preserved through a truly rigorous critique of the very real technocratic aspects of liberal political theory and practice. Liberalism was ultimately a resource for Schmitt only insofar as he could demonstrate that his authoritarian future was necessitated by the recent liberal past that preceded it. In the passage just quoted, he only inverts what was his consistent orientation to liberalism, namely, jettisoning its abstract normativity and appropriating its sociohistorical reality for which he constructed an authoritarian answer.

I certainly do not endorse an "if not us then fascism" legitimation of liberalism, but, as Schmitt at least implicitly comes to realize through his late National Socialist and postwar work, there are worse intersections of myth and technology than that found in liberalism and the positivism/ romanticism dichotomy that accompanies it – hence his eventual stand against technology and theology. As suggested in Chapter 6, one cannot elevate myth over technology without results potentially far worse than those associated with liberal theory and practice. However, the point is neither to criticize liberalism on the issue of technology in such a way as to make such other alternatives possible or likely, nor to be so frightened by such ramifications that one blindly endorses the liberal principles Schmitt mentions and forsakes an interrogation of liberalism and technology. The contemporary dilemma of political liberalism and technology as a site of historical change – still very much a Weberian dilemma – is the central topic of my concluding reflections.

CONCLUSION

By so extensively discussing the relationship of the early work of Leo Strauss to the Weimar writings of Carl Schmitt in the final major chapter of this work, I intended to build a bridge between past and present, between interwar German fascism and post–World War II North American conservatism. Strauss continues to be an intellectual resource for conservatism in the United States long after his death in 1973. Strauss managed to exert a profound effect in American academia by inspiring a whole generation of intellectuals, often right-leaning, of whom the late Allan Bloom would be the most famous example.[1] His influence is now also felt at the highest levels of American national politics in the recently reinvigorated Republi-

---

1   See Allan Bloom, *The Closing of the American Mind* (New York: Basic Books, 1987). After Strauss's emigration, his philosophical-political task became the search for an alternative source by which to temper the "corrosive" modern influences of science and technology. Since myth promulgated in the *modern* manner by Strauss's Weimar influences, Schmitt, and, of course, Martin Heidegger, proved so disastrous, Strauss turns to the ancients and the more sublime mythmaking of the likes of Plato as a resource. See Luc Ferry, *The New Quarrel between the Ancients and the Moderns,* trans. F. Philip (Chicago: University of Chicago Press, 1990). Strauss attempts to rein in the abstract, formal, and dynamic workings of the market and technological progress by appeals to the "natural law" of the ancient Greeks and the Judeo-Christian fathers: "law" that is passed off as "truth" to the many but regarded by the few as "salutary myth." See the essays included in Leo Strauss, *The Rebirth of Classical Rationalism,* ed. Thomas Pangle (Chicago: University of Chicago Press, 1989).

can party, through the person of policy advisor William Kristol, an acknowledged "Straussian."[2]

Yet accompanying the Straussian appeal to "traditional values," voiced by Bloom in the academy and Kristol in the broader popular culture, is a market-centered, futuristic, technoeconomic ideology of progress and "freedom" perhaps best represented by the views of the incumbent Speaker of the House, Newt Gingrich,[3] but in no small degree inspired by Austrian political economist and Schmitt devotee Friedrich Hayek.[4] The seemingly incompatible conjunction of "traditional" values and technological determinism is now the dominant motif of the conservative agenda in the United States. Just as in the Federal Republic of Germany, members of the right who had previously valorized technology in ecstatic positive or negative tones came to treat it after the war as a sober fact to which all demands for emancipatory policy must capitulate,[5] the American Right now combines market-oriented technoeconomic progress with an active promotion of potentially regressive cultural policies.[6]

A third component of contemporary conservatism in the United States, foreign policy, has not solidified into a coherent ideology since the end of the Cold War. Yet two competing options – a nationalist, anti-immigrant, isolationist one, characteristic of perennial Republican presidential candi-

2   Kristol is one of the new "young conservatives" featured in James Atlas, "The Countercounterculture," *New York Times Magazine* (Feb. 12, 1995). See also, Jacob Weisberg, "The Family Way: How Irving Kristol, Gertrude Himmelfarb and Bill Kristol Made Tormenting Liberals a Home Industry," *New Yorker* (Oct. 21 and 28, 1996). Consult the discussion in the *New York Times* by Brent Staples of Strauss's contemporary political influence: "Undemocratic Vistas: The Sinister Vogue of Leo Strauss," *New York Times* (Nov. 28, 1994); as well as Richard Bernstein, "A Very Unlikely Villain (or Hero)," *New York Times* (Jan. 29, 1995); and also the response to these pieces by Laurence Berns, "Correcting the Record on Leo Strauss," *PS: Political Science and Politics* 28:4 (December 1995). Strauss's daughter, Jenny Strauss Clay, defends her father against Staples's charges of a surreptitious anti-Enlightenment bias by citing passages from her father's work; the sincerity of these passages, however, Strauss's own hermeneutic method would question (*New York Times* [Nov. 30, 1994]).
3   On the technofuturist aspects of Gingrich's political agenda, see Hendrik Hertzberg, "Marxism: The Sequel," *New Yorker* 70:49 (1995).
4   See Bill Scheuerman, "The Unholy Alliance of Carl Schmitt and Friedrich A. Hayek," *Constellations* 4:2 (October 1997) on the full extent of Hayek's debt to, and admiration for, Schmitt; as well as Renato Cristi, "Hayek and Schmitt on the Rule of Law," *Canadian Journal of Political Science* 17:3 (1984).
5   The best example is the work of Schmitt protégé Ernst Forsthoff; see Peter C. Caldwell, "Ernst Forsthoff and the Legacy of Radical Conservative State Theory in the Federal Republic of Germany," *History of Political Thought* 15:4 (1994).
6   For an analysis of these issues in the German context, see the essays included in Jürgen Habermas, *The New Conservatism: Cultural Criticism and the Historians' Debate,* trans. S. Weber Nicholsen (Cambridge, Mass.: MIT Press, 1989).

date, Patrick Buchanan, and a neoimperialist xenophobic quest for a world-historical enemy advocated by Samuel Huntington – both exhibit signs of what may be identified as Schmittianism. Buchanan's championing of a homogeneous national culture and a reassertion of U.S. political and economic sovereignty, on the one hand, and Huntington's cynical search for a postcommunist enemy in what he constructs as the "Islamic-Confucian" alliance, on the other, ring uncomfortably familiar in light of what has been discussed in previous chapters of this work.[7] There is in fact a potential link between Huntington's international "realism" and Schmitt's own through the conduit of Schmitt student and émigré Cold War foreign-policy architect Hans Morgenthau.[8]

Thus, there are clear lines of succession back to Schmitt in all of the major components of contemporary American conservatism: cultural conservatism via Strauss; technoeconomic conservatism via Hayek; and foreign-policy conservatism via Morgenthau. The historical phenomenon of the Cold War allowed the earlier representatives of these strands to be viewed as nothing more extreme or radical than simply conservative. Moreover, the staunch opposition to the Soviet Union exhibited by advocates of these positions generally enabled them to be viewed as merely friendly critics of liberal democracy. In the absence of the Soviet enemy, these conservative tendencies may become less moderate than the word "conservative" connotes, and they may – and in fact already have, at least rhetorically – set their sights on "liberalism" itself as an enemy.[9]

In short, defense of classical republican virtue, advocacy of market capitalism, and opposition to the Soviet Union are no longer adequate

7   See Samuel Huntington, "The Clash of Civilizations?" *Foreign Affairs* 72:3 (Summer 1993). Consult the responses to Huntington's somewhat sinister thesis by Fouad Ajami, Kishore Mahbubani, Robert Bartley, Lin Binyan, and Jeane Kirkpatrick in the following issue, *Foreign Affairs* 72:4 (September/October 1993), as well as the full-length version of the thesis, Huntington, *The Clash of Civilizations and the Remaking of World Order* (New York: Simon & Schuster, 1996).

8   See Hans J. Morgenthau, "Fragment of an Intellectual Autobiography," in *Truth and Tragedy: A Tribute to Hans J. Morgenthau*, ed. Kenneth Thompson and Robert Myers (New Brunswick: Transaction, 1984); Stanley Hoffmann, "The Case of Dr. Kissinger," *New York Review of Books* (Dec. 6, 1979), pp. 14–18, 21–5, 27–9; and Alfons Söllner, "German Conservatism in America: Morgenthau's Political Realism," *Telos* 72 (summer 1987).

9   On the future of neoconservatism's relationship to liberalism, see Mark Gerson, *The Neoconservative Vision: From the Cold War to the Culture Wars* (New York: Rowman and Littlefield, 1995); on its past, see Charles W. Dunn and J. David Woodward, *The Conservative Tradition in America* (New York: Rowman & Littlefield, 1996); Godfrey Hodgson, *The World Turned Right Side Up: A History of the Conservative Ascendancy in America* (Boston: Houghton Mifflin, 1996).

litmus tests of one's relative disposition toward liberal democracy.[10] We have witnessed the political path that the godfather of these strands of contemporary conservatism, Carl Schmitt, chose in the midst of a radical socioeconomic transformation earlier in this century. We can only speculate at this juncture what paths will be followed in the midst of this present structural transformation, not only in North America and Europe but in the "second" and "third" worlds as well. Preliminary indicators, however – neo-Nazism, militia movements, "Christian identity" ideologies, ethnic cleansing, racially motivated mass rape, violent attacks on emigrant workers and foreigners, bombings of abortion clinics and state administrative buildings, and assignations of the proponents of peace – certainly give cause for alarm.

If firmly established or newly emerging democracies are not to succumb to a kind of fascism reminiscent of Schmitt's, then the philosophy of history and sociological assumptions of a Weberian worldview ought not to remain unchallenged in liberal political theory. The tenets of an absolute "pluriverse of values," on the one hand, and a technoeconomic determinist notion of progress as a process that cannot be fully controlled and that cannot be significantly changed, on the other, must be called into question, if they are not to be subverted by those on the Right in the name of nationalist, culturalist, or worst of all, pseudo-"populist" alternatives.[11] Just as "pluralism" – the apparent fact of a heterogeneity of incommensurable perspectives within society that some formal arrangement of procedures, legal or otherwise, may contain – was the preferred liberal sociopolitical solution to "rationalization" in Weber's context, "complexity" is the complement to notions of "differentiation" in our own.[12] Contemporary liberals

10 See Michael Walzer, "What's Going On?: Notes on the Right Turn," *Dissent* (winter 1996).
11 Rawls declares pluralism a "fact," in *Political Liberalism* (New York: Columbia University Press, 1993), pp. 56–7; and Charles Larmore declares the inevitability of "reasonable disagreement" to be a "truth," something that can be expected to occur "naturally," in *The Morals of Modernity* (Cambridge: Cambridge University Press, 1996), pp. 153, 12. These may indeed be correct assessments, but they ought not to be accepted dogmatically as an unquestioned and unquestionable sociological given, as they so often are in much of liberal political theory. On the Kantian roots of notions of value pluralism, or as he refashions it, "reasonable disagreement," see Larmore, *The Morals of Modernity*, pp. 28–34. As noted in Chapter 1, it is this Kantian origin that decidedly influenced Weber's thinking on pluralism. The rationalization thesis has been reconstructed and updated by the differentiation theory best represented by the highly influential work of Niklas Luhmann; see e.g., *Social Systems* (Stanford: Stanford University Press, 1995).
12 Sophisticated versions of a "complexity" approach to contemporary democracy include Bernhard Peters, *Die Integration moderner Gesellschaften* (Frankfurt a. M.: Suhrkamp, 1993); Danilo Zolo, *Democracy and Complexity* (University Park: Pennsylvania State University,

persistently subscribe to an understanding of modernity as driven by processes of subsystem differentiation and societal rationalization.[13] However, instead of the invocation of a palpable empirical reality, "complexity" can be understood in some sense as the refuge into which Kantian rationality hides, or against which it rebels, when faced with the incommensurability of "ideal" categories and the "real world" in changing historical contexts.

One of the traditional differences between liberal- and social-democratic theoretical orientations has been over the question of the exact extent to which the conditions of modernity can be actively changed without disadvantageous consequences. Just as social-democratic political theory, to its credit, has absorbed much of liberal institutional, legal, and ethical theory in recent years,[14] liberals must take seriously the arguments regarding transforming social practices advocated by progressive scholars to their left.[15] Only then might the somewhat schizophrenic liberal worldviews of Rawlsian normative philosophy and deterministic, positivist empirical research be

1992); James Bohman, *Public Deliberation: Pluralism, Complexity and Democracy* (Cambridge, Mass.: MIT Press, 1995); and Amy Gutmann and Dennis Thompson, *Democracy and Disagreement* (Cambridge, Mass.: Harvard University Press, 1996).

13   The oft-ignored interrelationship between the social-philosophical systems theory of a Luhmann and the political-philosophical liberal theory of a Rawls is reflected in Stephen Holmes, "Differenzierung und Arbeitsteilung im Denken des Liberalismus," in *Soziale Differenzierung: Zur Geschichte einer Idee*, ed. Niklas Luhmann (Opladen: Westdeutscher, 1985); and Charles Larmore, *Patterns of Moral Complexity* (Cambridge; Cambridge University Press, 1987).

14   Of which Jürgen Habermas' *Between Facts and Norms: Contributions to a Discourse Theory of Law and Democracy* (Cambridge, Mass.: MIT Press, 1996) is something of a culminating moment.

15   A recent attempt at navigating new historical waters from a liberal standpoint is Stephen Holmes, "Liberalism for a World of Ethnic Passions and Decaying States," *Social Research* 61:3 (fall 1994). It would be something of a mistake for leftists to dismiss the possibility of liberalism's ability to adapt to the changing circumstances for the state in the international realm, as does Immanuel Wallerstein, *After Liberalism* (New York: New Press, 1996). Holmes explains the manner in which liberalism previously adapted to the realities and responsibilities of the welfare state, in *Passions and Constraint: On the Theory of Liberal Democracy* (Chicago: University of Chicago Press, 1995). Unfortunately, Wallerstein's is a move reminiscent of the kind made by many socialist and social-democratic intellectuals in the midst of the last transformation from laissez-faire to welfare-state arrangements. This rendered liberalism vulnerable to historicizing assaults by the likes of Schmitt and often rendered leftists with impoverished institutional and principled resources in formulating their own political strategies. This tendency is characteristic of the early works of Otto Kirchheimer and Franz Neumann, a tendency that they later sought to redress in their postemigration work. See Bill Scheuerman, ed., *The Rule of Law Under Siege: Selected Essays of Franz L. Neumann and Otto Kirchheimer* (Berkeley: University of California Press, 1996).

brought back together and transcended in a way that both resolves the problems inherent in its Weberian incarnation and inoculates it against appropriation and exploitation by the forces of reaction.[16] As explained earlier, especially in Chapter 1, Weberian liberalism is vulnerable to manipulation on two counts: Subjectively, it provides for little common ground among the many value differences within modernity and may even encourage irrational responses to the ostensibly incommensurable nature of such value pluralism; objectively, it provides for the viability of no effectual practice by which the processes of modern rationalization may be brought under the control of conscious, rational, human choice and activity. The still generally widespread dissatisfaction with the Rawlsian solution to contemporary pluralism and the manner in which "complexity" is often unreflectively invoked as a social-scientific fact today in a way that seems only to confirm the inevitability of things as they are, suggest that these Weberian problems have yet to be resolved.[17] As witnessed earlier, their lack of resolution in the Weimar Republic facilitated irrefutably disastrous results.[18]

16 This is one of the explicit goals of Habermas's *Between Facts and Norms*. Whether the work is successful in this regard is the subject of debate; for different conclusions, see David M. Rasmussen, "How Is Valid Law Possible?: A Review of *Faktizität und Geltung* by Jürgen Habermas," *Philosophy and Social Criticism* 20:4 (1994); and James Bohman, "Complexity, Pluralism and the Constitutional State: On Habermas' *Faktizität und Geltung*," *Law and Society Review* 28 (November 1994).

17 Two strikingly Schmittian critiques of Rawlsian pluralism, the first of which draws on Schmitt explicitly and the second that does not mention his name, are Chantal Mouffe, *The Return of the Political* (London: Verso, 1993); and Bonnie Honig, *Political Theory and the Displacement of Politics* (Ithaca, N.Y.: Cornell University Press, 1993). On the limits of "complexity" as a progressive social theoretical category, see Thomas McCarthy, "Complexity and Democracy: Or the Seducements of Systems Theory," and Hans Joas, "The Unhappy Marriage of Hermeneutics and Functionalism," both in *Communicative Action*, ed. Axel Honneth and Hans Joas (Cambridge, Mass.: MIT Press, 1991).

18 David Dyzenhaus, in particular, has rightfully identified the Weberian character of recent debates over liberalism and diversity, and the Schmittian threat that looms over the results; see "The Legitimacy of Legality," *University of Toronto Law Journal* 46 (1996); and "Liberalism after the Fall: Schmitt, Rawls and the Problem of Justification," *Philosophy and Social Criticism* 22:3 (1996). In the latter piece, Dyzenhaus discerns how Schmitt delineates the manner in which liberals, when under criticism, will waver between value-affirming, rights-based and value-neutral, rules-based positions – between concrete substance and abstract form – and describes how Schmitt would alternately set his sights on each one in an equally devastating manner. Another progressive theorist, Charles Larmore, disagrees with judgments like Dyzenhaus's regarding the actual perspicacity of Schmitt's critique of liberalism; see Larmore, "Carl Schmitt's Critique of Liberal Democracy," in *The Morals of Modernity*. Perhaps precisely because Larmore is somewhat less sensitive to the Weberian antinomial dilemma of contemporary liberalism, he underestimates the full force of Schmitt's critique. Larmore explicitly defends the viability of a balance between romantic, subjective dispositions within society and an objective, recon-

To be more specific, should "multiculturalism" and "globalization" – two discourses central to recent social change – be misconstrued and misrepresented by the Right in the way that party pluralism (mass democracy) and internationalism (of either Soviet or League of Nations varieties) were so treated in the first third of this century, democracy as a political principle would become more easily manipulated within a nationalist, integrationist, and homogeneous strategy.[19] The perceived double threat of, on the one

structed notion of formal liberalism in politics, a balance that cannot be sustained in times of crisis like that of Weimar. Moreover, Larmore's conception of a "political liberalism," which he shares with Rawls, is to some extent guilty of the charge of wavering between value-affirming and value-neutral positions that Dyzenhaus extracts from Schmitt. On the one hand, Larmore seeks to defend liberalism against charges of normative emptiness by recasting it in terms that render it "minimally moral" (p. 145); conversely, he seeks to rescue the latest expression of Rawlsian liberalism, in *Political Liberalism*, from affirming, in a potentially dogmatic manner, pluralism as a *value* by asserting instead the *fact* of "reasonable disagreement" (p. 153). It remains less than clear how Larmore's "minimally moral" conception of liberalism would be sufficiently "thick" to ensure a normative content that would satisfy liberal critics of Aristotelian, civic-republican or communitarian stripes. More important, Larmore's opting for a *descriptive* account of "reasonable disagreement" over a *normative* preference for pluralism degenerates into a merely semantical distinction when reasonable disagreement ceases to be "reasonable" in a qualitatively changing and crisis-ridden social reality. There seems to be a lack of the kind of sociological guidelines in Larmore's account that would prevent "political liberalism" from, as Schmitt claimed, on the one hand, veering toward moral bankruptcy, on the other, veering toward a Hobbesian/Weberian battle of warring gods and value stances. As discussed earlier, especially in Part One, if history is actually constituted by a kind of change more dynamic than that described in theories of rationalization, differentiation, increasing complexity, and ever-more-likely disagreement – all presupposed by contemporary liberalism – then the arguments of Schmitt, and Lukács for that matter (notwithstanding the excesses of their own proposed solutions), against the propensity toward philosophical insufficiency, social instability, and latent political authoritarianism found in Weber's thought are still to a significant degree valid against contemporary liberal pluralism. The opposition of a plurality of incommensurable value stances, on the one hand, and a social reality determined by an irresistibly unfolding process of rationalization, on the other, becomes unstable when reality suddenly comes to be seen as potentially under the immediate control of human activity, and particular groups view themselves as the legitimate agents of such change and go about attempting to accelerate it through regressively irrational, instead of progressively rational, means.

19   For a critique of the cynical abuse of multiculturalism and for a serious attempt to articulate a progressive vision of it, see Will Kymlicka, *Multicultural Citizenship: A Liberal Theory of Minority Rights* (Oxford: Oxford University Press, 1995). On the exploitation of the theme of "globalization," see Paul Hirst and Grahame Thompson, "Globalization and the Future of the Nation-State," *Economy and Society* 24:3 (1995); and Frances Fox Piven, "Is It Global Economics or Neo-Laissez-Faire?" *New Left Review* 213 (September/October 1995). The racist and xenophobic strategy of exaggerating the dangers of multiculturalism is fairly transparent. However, globalization is deployed less uniformly: as an unassailable reality that must be accepted by proponents of market capitalism, on the one hand, and as a sinister phenomenon that must be resisted by protectionist nationalists, on the other.

hand, supranational schemes by the United Nations, the World Bank, the International Monetary Fund, and the like – quite frequently communicated in unmistakably anti-Semitic terms – and, on the other, sub- or transnational groups like emigrant workers, ethnic minorities, gender coalitions, and so on, who are often unfairly labeled as "particularist" or "special" interests, is again a powerful tool of conservative rhetoric.

Moreover, the oft-referred-to diminishing of state capabilities associated with recent worldwide socioeconomic changes[20] cannot be interpreted as insurance against the severity of abusive state power, as recent events in Rwanda and the former Yugoslavia attest.[21] Simply because the first transformation of state and society in this century served to inflate the power of the state, despite sly protestations to the contrary by the likes of Schmitt, this does not mean that a new vulnerability of the state will not elicit violent retrenchist or consolidationist state activity, particularly if legitimated by the new nationalist, xenophobic, and "our patria first" mentality so rampant around the globe today.[22] At the risk of descending into what might be perceived as hysterical, naive, or simply foolish conjecture in these concluding reflections, I believe that recent trends, both popular (e.g., the social phenomena mentioned earlier) and academic (witness *les affaires* Heideg-

---

20 See Susan Strange, *The Retreat of the State: The Diffusion of Power in the World Economy* (Cambridge: Cambridge University Press, 1996); as well as *Daedalus* 124:2 (spring 1995), special issue: "What Future for the State?"

21 On these questions, see Peter Anderson, *The Global Politics of Power, Justice and Death* (London: Routledge, 1996); and Philip McMichael, *Development and Social Change: A Global Perspective* (London: Sage, 1996).

22 Perhaps a reliable indication that the sovereignty of the state must be diminishing is the degree to which the contemporary Right, in genuine "owl of Minerva" fashion, attacks it as "totalitarian." There is good reason to be wary of those who rhetorically beat the carcass of the decaying state but who would be happy to resuscitate it and employ it as a weapon against their enemies should they be successful in seizing hold of it. This is an issue about which we can learn much from Schmitt, as long as we keep in mind, in light of Chapters 5 and 6, that Schmitt's own solution involved making the state into the tool of a preferred particularist interest. Schmitt depicted the "quantitative total state" of liberal democracy as weak in order to supplant it with his supposedly strong, authoritarian "qualitative total state." Contemporary rightist critics of the liberal democratic state invoke descriptive *and* normative claims regarding the supposedly strong and coercive totalitarian nature of such regimes. What they would do with such a state should they have more influence over its operation remains an open but crucial question. On the new nationalisms, see Michael Ignatieff, *Blood and Belonging: Journeys into the New Nationalism* (New York: Farrar, Straus and Giroux, 1994); Rogers Brubaker, "Nationhood and the National Question in the Soviet Union and Post-Soviet Eurasia: An Institutional Account," *Theory and Society* 23:1 (February 1994); and Ted Robert Gurr, *Minorities at Risk: A Global View of Ethnopolitical Conflicts* (Washington, D.C.: United States Institute of Peace Press, 1993).

ger, de Man, Schmitt, etc.) render such risks worthy and such cautionary remarks valid.[23]

The prevailing notions of "pluralism," whether in its existential warring-gods, Weberian manifestation or its more mundane American post–World War II variety, are rightfully challenged today for their insensitivity to concrete cultural, economic, or gender-based specificity.[24] But the advocates of identity and difference qua concrete otherness ought not to leave wholly unexamined their own potential essentializing of themselves or others in their challenges to traditional pluralism. When both sides foreclose the possibility of commonality and mutual rational exchange, they consequently leave the public sphere vulnerable to those who would seek to enforce a stable and unifying order from above and who would exploit concrete otherness, not on behalf of those unjustly marginalized or banished from the redistributive picture but rather in a strategy aimed at naked political gain. Although I cannot elaborate here, the movement to take into account diversity, difference, and the attempt to practice a multiculturalism that appreciates concrete otherness does not necessarily preclude, as some critics on both sides would suggest, universality, consensual agreement, and the possibility of fully democratic legitimacy.[25]

23 On the popular and the academic trends, respectively, see Mabel Berezin, "Fascism/ Antiliberalism: Some New Thoughts on an Old Idea," Department of Sociology, University of Pennsylvania, unpublished manuscript, 1996; and the essays in Richard Wolin, *Labyrinths: Explorations in the Critical History of Ideas* (Amherst: University of Massachusetts Press, 1995). In general, see Walter Laquer, *Fascism: Past, Present and Future* (Oxford: Oxford University Press, 1995).

24 See William Connolly, *The Ethos of Pluralism* (Minneapolis: University of Minnesota Press, 1996). Poststructuralists celebrate the multiplicity of the supposedly permanently inscribed identities of the social world that in their understanding liberals barely tolerate and in fact attempt to coercively coordinate into orderly sociopolitical arrangements. On the drawbacks inherent in such criticisms of liberalism, see George Kateb, "Notes on Pluralism," *Social Research* 61:3 (fall 1994).

25 In particular, the dialogue between feminists of a critical-theoretic inclination, such as Seyla Benhabib and Nancy Fraser, and those of a more poststructuralist/postmodernist perspective, such as Iris Marion Young, has generated perhaps the most clarifying and potentially most fruitful theoretical results. The former defend universalistic Enlightenment principles from a standpoint that has for some time extensively worked through its deficiencies, whereas the latter pursues a more particularist agenda, but nevertheless with a quite serious commitment to democracy, as such. See Seyla Benhabib, *Situating the Self* (New York: Routledge, 1992); Benhabib, "In Defense of Universalism – Yet Again!" *New German Critique* 62 (spring/summer 1992); Nancy Fraser, "Recognition or Redistribution?: A Critical Reading of Iris Young's *Justice and the Politics of Difference*," *Journal of Political Philosophy* 3:2 (June 1995); Fraser, *Justice Interruptus: Rethinking Key Concepts of a "Postsocialist" Age* (London: Routledge, 1996); Iris Marion Young, *Justice and the Politics of Difference* (Princeton: Princeton University Press, 1990); Young, "Comments on Seyla Benhabib,

Turning to the other side of the Weberian dilemma, that of the "objective" social reality of increasing rationalization, we will recall from Chapter 2 how both Schmitt and Heidegger pointed out the "anxiety" over "mastery" engendered by modern technology. As we may observe today, such pathologies do not always manifest themselves in the highly aestheticized manner that they did in Weimar Germany. For instance, Daniel Bell's influential considerations on technology from the seventies that foreshadow contemporary conservative rhetoric are a more sober yet ultimately no more theoretically rigorous case in point: His technological determinism that posits an apparently autonomously generated technology leads him to call for the revival of a Protestant ethic–like asceticism with which to conform to it.[26] An appropriate engagement with technology ought not lapse into a neoconservative fatalism that suggests we must resign ourselves and the possibilities for sociopolitical justice to irresistible technological imperatives – the contemporary manifestation of the passivity that Schmitt so despised in Weimar.[27] Nor is it to *will* oneself or one's culture beyond this position by seizing hold of the instruments of technology in some mythical, supratechnological political project, such as Soviet Communism, or as demonstrated in this work, the authoritarian national- or continental-conflict theory that Schmitt so vigorously championed in the twenties and

Situating the Self," New German Critique 62 (spring/summer 1992). See also Fraser's comments on Benhabib, "False Antitheses: A Response to Seyla Benhabib and Judith Butler," *Praxis International* 11:2 (July 1991).

There is at least some cause for optimism on the sociological level as well, as the work of Yasemin Soysal demonstrates that in contemporary practices of social membership in Europe, "universalist" or "particularist" claims are not opted for by, for instance, emigrant workers, in an either/or fashion, but are intermingled in novel, potentially emancipatory strategies; see Yasemin Nuhoglu Soysal, *Limits of Citizenship: Migrants and Postnational Membership in Europe* (University of Chicago Press: Chicago, 1994). The lesson to be learned from both Schmitt's efforts and the virulent new nationalisms from around the globe is that multiculturalism is not politically dangerous as a democratic discursive or institutional practice but rather as an object for cynical co-opting by power consolidating elites.

26 See Daniel Bell, *The Coming of Post-Industrial Society* (New York: Basic Books, 1972), and *The Cultural Contradictions of Capitalism* (New York: Basic Books, 1978). Bell even suggests the return to traditional religion; see Bell, "The Return of the Sacred?" in *The Winding Passage* (New York: Basic Books, 1980).

27 For an analysis of this position taken up by Schmitt's own students after the war, see Claus Offe, *Contradictions of the Welfare State*, ed. John Keane (Cambridge, Mass.: MIT Press, 1984). Studies of "technocracy" concerned with Schmitt's influence in the postwar German context are Ingeborg Maus, *Bürgerliche Rechtstheorie und Faschismus: Zur sozialen Funktion und aktuellen Wirkung der Theorie Carl Schmitts* (Munich: C. H. Beck, 1980); and Thomas Vesting, *Politische Einheitsbildung und technische Realisation: Ueber die Expansion der Technik und die Grenzen der Demokratie* (Baden-Baden: Nomos, 1990).

thirties.[28] There is indeed a "confusion" surrounding technology but a confusion that is clarified by neither *resignation* nor *resoluteness*.

Technology will continue to serve as a particularly acute source of fear, anxiety, discomfort, and also potential exhilaration, as economic stability, ecological viability, and geopolitical security remain bound with its development. This will prove especially true as the state's control over national economic policy becomes increasingly tenuous in the transition from the welfare state to socioeconomic arrangements that are apparently beyond the regulation of the nation state,[29] and as its control over weapons of mass destruction significantly depreciates as the realities of a bipolar Cold War scenario give way to a less stable multipolar political one.[30] However, apprehending the specificities of what constitutes technology in the contemporary postindustrial world will reveal what technology is: not a horrible fate nor a key to a utopic kingdom but rather the social practices that reflexively *structure* and are *structured by* social life, and that in their particular workings often obscure their own genesis. The delineation and elucidation of the specificities that constitute these practices are notoriously difficult to ascertain.[31] Nevertheless, the task is a necessary one if we are to move away from the ever-immanent propensity toward mythology associated with technology in modernity that has been discussed at length in this work and, instead, to reiterate the title of an early work of Jürgen Habermas, to move toward a *truly* rational society.

This work began with an examination of the efforts of Lukács and Schmitt, two particularly engaged intellectuals of the Left and the Right

28   Positions that academic poststructuralist critics of Enlightenment reason come dangerously close to replicating, despite their progressive self-understandings; see Wolin, "Antihumanism in the Discourse of French Postwar Theory," "Deconstruction at Auschwitz: Heidegger, de Man, and the New Revisionism," and "Afterword: Derrida on Marx, or the Perils of Left Heideggerianism," in *Labyrinths*.

29   See Bob Jessop, "Post-Fordism and the State," in *Post-Fordism: A Reader,* ed. Ash Amin (London: Blackwell, 1994).

30   See Daniel Deudney, "Nuclear Weapons and the Waning of the *Real*-State," *Daedalus* 124:2 (spring 1995).

31   Serious attempts to properly situate technology within the practices of structurally transforming societies have been set forth previously by Jürgen Habermas, *Toward a Rational Society: Student Protest, Science and Politics,* trans. Jeremy Shapiro (Boston: Beacon Press, 1970); and Pierre Bourdieu, *Outline of a Theory of Practice,* trans. R. Nice (Cambridge: Cambridge University Press, 1977); and more recently by Andrew Feenberg, *Critical Theory of Technology* (Oxford: Oxford University Press, 1991); and Moishe Postone, *Time, Labor and Social Domination: A Reinterpretation of Marx's Critical Theory* (New York: Cambridge University Press, 1993). See also the essays included in Merritt Roe Smith and Leo Marx, eds., *Does Technology Drive History?: The Dilemma of Technological Determinism* (Cambridge, Mass.: MIT Press, 1994).

coming to terms with the methodological-political framework of Weberian social science in the midst of a radical transition in the relationship of state and society in early-twentieth-century central Europe. In the present second crisis of the state in this century – this moment of decline in national sovereignty and increased globalization of economic power – the tension between the "subjective" and "objective" poles in culture and philosophy is again becoming acute and the need to overcome it urgent.[32] To sum up what has already been dealt with implicitly, and often explicitly, in the preceding analysis of Weimar intellectual controversies in which Schmitt participated, now reigning in the fields of the human sciences are the debates in law between formalism and antiformalism, in ethics between transcendental and immanent moralities, in the social sciences between positivist and interpretavist approaches, and in political theory between universalist and particularist conceptions of justice. As mentioned before, we may also observe in popular and political culture in the United States and abroad an intensifying fundamentalism, in many respects frighteningly reminiscent of Schmitt's fascism: attempts to stake secure positions against the rapidly changing socioeconomic landscape in the supposedly timeless entities of family, nation, and faith. Another side of popular and political culture seems occupied by projects not unlike that of Lukács (even if their adherents would most likely dismiss his universalist faber-centric "metanarrative"): a desperate search for the marginalized concrete, qualitative essence from whose standpoint (of race, gender, ethnicity, etc.) the very real metaphysical *aporiai* of liberal theory and the even more real injustices of liberal-democratic society can be overcome.

One of the tasks of critical social and political theory today, one that would escape the drawbacks of Weberian social science, as well as the dangers exhibited by the work of its most radical discontented practitioners, especially Schmitt, should be an attempt to understand the relationships among the transformation, the academic debates and the cultural stands, as well as the persistence of the oppositions, the antinomies, the dualisms, explicated earlier, within them.[33] It would certainly not be to aesthetically

32 See Moishe Postone, "Contemporary Historical Transformations: Some Theoretical Considerations," Department of History, University of Chicago, unpublished manuscript (1995).

33 On, for instance, the poststructuralist or postmodernist misrecognition of the socioeconomic, as opposed to simply ideological, character of contemporary transformations, see David Harvey, *The Condition of Postmodernity* (Oxford: Blackwell, 1989); Fredric Jameson, *Postmodernism, or, The Cultural Logic of Late Capitalism* (Durham, N.C.: Duke University Press, 1991); Krishnan Kumar, *From Post-Industrial to Post-Modern Society: New Theories of the*

attach oneself to any particular aspect of this constellation, placing a rather heavy wager that it will serve as the door to a new consciousness. The fates of some of the best minds of this century who put themselves at the disposal of tyranny attest to this. These endeavors are necessary in order to exorcise the still-haunting ghost of Carl Schmitt or – rather than capitulate to his cryp-totheological and hence inherently regressive mode of discourse – adequately address the intellectual-structural realities of the modern world that make his authoritarian strategy a viable contemporary political agenda as well as an obstruction to free and just alternatives. What should be most clear after an extensive examination of the efforts of one of the most brilliant critics of the Weberian worldview and several of its liberal incarnations is that it is only after the most careful theorization of contemporary contradictions that progressive practice is really possible.

Solche festgewordene Gegensätze aufzuheben, ist das einzige Interesse der Vernunft. (Hegel, *Phänomenologie des Geistes, Werke* I, 173)

Contemporary World (Oxford: Blackwell, 1995); and Craig Calhoun, "Postmodernism as Pseudohistory: The Trivialization of Epochal Change," in *Critical Social Theory: Culture, History and the Challenge of Difference* (Oxford: Blackwell, 1995). Two recent attempts to formulate democratic possibilities under presently changing socioeconomic conditions are David Held, *Democracy and the Global Order: From the Modern State to Cosmopolitan Governance* (Oxford: Polity Press, 1995); and Paul Hirst, *Associative Democracy* (Amherst: University of Massachusetts Press, 1994).

WORKS CITED

Works by Schmitt (in German)

Schmitt, Carl. *Der Wert des Staates und die Bedeutung des Einzelnen.* Tübingen: J. C. B. Mohr (Paul Siebeck), 1914.

"Die Sichtbarkeit der Kirche: Eine scholastische Erwägung." *Summa: Eine Vierteljahresschrift* (1917).

"Die Tyrannei der Werte." In *Der Tyrannei der Werte.* Edited by Carl Schmitt et al. Hamburg: Lutherisches Verlagshaus, 1979.

"Diktatur und Belagerungszustand: Eine staatsrechtliche Studie." *Zeitschrift für die gesamte Strafrechtswissenschaft* 38 (1917).

Politische Romantik. Munich: Duncker & Humblot, 1925.

Die geistesgeschichtliche Lage des heutigen Parlamentarismus. Munich: Duncker & Humblot, 1926.

Unabhängig der Richter: Gleichheit vor dem Gesetz und Gewährleistung des Privateigentums nach der Weimarer Verfassung. Berlin: Walter de Gruyter, 1926.

Hugo Preuß: Sein Staatsbegriff und seine Stellung in der deutschen Staatslehre. Tübingen: J. C. B. Mohr (Paul Siebeck), 1930.

Der Hüter der Verfassung. Tübingen: J. C. B. Mohr (Paul Siebeck), 1931.

Legalität und Legitimität. Munich: Duncker & Humblot, 1932.

"Der Mißbrauch der Legalität," *Tägliche Rundschau* (Jul. 19, 1932).

"Das Gesetz zur Behebung der Not von Volk und Reich," *Deutsche Juristen-Zeitung* 38 (1933).

Politische Theologie: Vier Kapitel zur Lehre von der Souveränität. Munich: Duncker & Humblot, 1934.

Staat, Bewegnung, Volk: Die Dreigleiderung der politischen Einheit. Hamburg: Hanseatische Verlagsanstalt, 1934.

Ueber der drei Arten des Rechtswissenschaftlichen Denkens. Hamburg: Hanseatische Verlagsanstalt, 1934.

"Die deutsche Rechtswissenschaft im Kampf gegen den jüdischen Geist." *Deutsche Juristen-Zeitung* 20 (Oct. 15, 1936).

"Der Staat als Mechanismus bei Hobbes und Descartes." *Archiv für Rechts- und Sozialphilosophie* 39 (1937).

Positionen und Begriffe im Kampf mit Weimar – Genf – Versailles: 1923–1939. Hamburg: Hanseatische Verlagsanstalt, 1940.

Donoso-Cortés in gesamteuropäischer Interpretation: Vier Aufsätze. Köln: Greven, 1950.

Ex Captivitate Salus: Erfahrungen der Zeit 1945/47. Cologne: Greven, 1950.

"Die Einheit der Welt." *Merkur* 6:1 (January 1952).

"Der Neue Nomos der Erde." *Gemeinschaft und Politik* 3:1 (1955).

"Die andere Hegel-Linie: Hans Freyer zum 70. Geburtstag." *Christ und Welt* 30 (Jul 25, 1957).

Verfassungsrechtliche Aufsätze aus den Jahren 1924–1954: Materialien zu einer Verfassungslehre. Berlin: Duncker & Humblot, 1958.

Der Begriff des Politischen: Text von 1932 mit einem Vorwort und drei Corollarien. Berlin: Duncker & Humblot, 1963.

Theorie des Partisanen: Zwischenbemerkung zum Begriff des Politischen. Berlin: Duncker & Humblot, 1963.

"Die vollendete Reformation: Bemerkungen und Hinweise zu neuen Leviathan Interpretationen." *Der Staat: Zeitschrift für Staatslehre, öffentliches Recht und Verfassungsgeschichte* 4:1 (1965).

Gesetz und Urteil: Eine Untersuchung zum Problem der Rechtspraxis. Munich: C. H. Beck, 1969.

Politische Theologie II. Die Legende von der Erledigung jeder politischen Theologie. Berlin: Duncker & Humblot, 1970.

Der Nomos der Erde im Völkerrecht des Jus Publicum Europaeum. Berlin: Duncker & Humblot, 1974.

"Der Dichter des 'Nordlicht' der aus dem Süden kam." *Deutsches Allgemeine Sonntagsblatt* 15:33 (August 1976).

Der Leviathan in der Staatslehre des Thomas Hobbes: Sinn und Fehlschlag eines politischen Symbols. Cologne: Klett-Cotta, 1982.

Römischer Katholizismus und politische Form. Stuttgart: Klett-Cotta, 1984.

Die Diktatur: Von den Anfängen des modernen Souveränitätsgedankens bis zum proletarischen Klassenkampf. Berlin: Duncker & Humblot, 1989.

Verfassungslehre. Berlin: Duncker & Humblot, 1989.

Glossarium: Aufzeichnungen der Jahre 1947–51. Duncker & Humblot, 1991.

Theodor Däublers "Nordlicht": Drei Studien über die Elemente, den Geist und die Aktualität des Werkes. Berlin: Duncker & Humblot, 1991.

Works by Carl Schmitt (in English)

Schmitt, Carl. *The Concept of the Political*. Translated by George Schwab. New Brunswick: Rutgers University Press, 1976.

The Crisis of Parliamentary Democracy. Translated by Ellen Kennedy. Cambridge, Mass.: MIT Press, 1985.

Political Romanticism. Translated by Guy Oakes. Cambridge, Mass.: MIT Press, 1985.

Political Theology: Four Chapters on the Concept of Sovereignty. Translated by George Schwab. Cambridge, Mass.: MIT Press, 1985.

"The Legal World Revolution." Translated by G. L. Ulmen. *Telos* 72 (summer 1987).

"The Plight of European Jurisprudence." Translated by G. L. Ulmen. *Telos* 83 (spring 1990).

"The Constitutional Theory of Federation." Translated by G. L. Ulmen. *Telos* 91 (spring 1992).

"Appropriation/Distribution/Production: Toward a Proper Formulation of the Basic Questions of Any Social and Economic Order." Translated by G. L. Ulmen. *Telos* 95 (spring 1993).

"The Age of Neutralizations and Depoliticizations." Translated by M. Konzett and J. P. McCormick. *Telos* 96 (summer 1993).

The Leviathan in the State Theory of Thomas Hobbes: Meaning and Failure of a Political Symbol. Translated by G. Schwab and E. Hilfstein. Westport: Greenwood, 1996.

Roman Catholicism and Political Form. Translated by G. L. Ulmen. Westport: Greenwood, 1996.

Other Works

Ackerman, Bruce. *We the People, Vol. 1. Foundations*. Cambridge, Mass.: Harvard University Press, 1991.

Adorno, Theodor W. *The Jargon of Authenticity*. Translated by K. Tarnowski and F. Will. Evanston, Ill.: Northwestern University Press, 1973.

Minima Moralia: Reflections from Damaged Life. Translated by E. F. N. Jephcott. London: Verso, 1978.

Amin, Ash, ed. *Post-Fordism: A Reader*. Oxford: Blackwell, 1994.

Anderson, Benedict. *Imagined Communities: Reflections on the Origins and Spread of Nationalism*. London: Verso, 1983.

Anderson, Perry. "The Intransigent Right at the End of the Century." *London Review of Books* (Sept. 24, 1992).

Anderson, Peter. *The Global Politics of Power, Justice and Death*. London: Routledge, 1996.

Arato, Andrew, and Paul Breines. *The Young Lukács and the Origins of Western Marxism.* New York: Pluto Press, 1979.

Arato, Andrew, and Eike Gebhardt, eds. *The Essential Frankfurt School Reader.* Oxford: Blackwell, 1978.

Arendt, Hannah. *The Human Condition.* Chicago: University of Chicago Press, 1958.

The Origins of Totalitarianism. New York: Harcourt, Brace & Jovanovich, 1973.

The Life of the Mind. New York: Harcourt, Brace & Jovanovich, 1978.

Aschheim, Steven E. *The Nietzsche Legacy in Germany.* Berkeley: University of California Press, 1992.

Atlas, James. "The Countercounterculture." *New York Times Magazine.* (Feb. 12, 1995).

Bader, Veit-Michael. "Viel Geltung und immer weniger Faktizität: Zur Kritik an Jürgen Habermas' diskurstheoretischer Rechts- und Demokratietheorie," in *Produktion und Klassentheorie: Festschrift für Sebastion Herkommer.* Edited by H. Ganßmann and S. Krüger. Hamburg: VSA, 1993.

Baldwin, Peter. "Social Interpretations of Nazism: Renewing a Tradition." *Journal of Contemporary History* 25 (1990).

Barash, Jeffrey Andrew. "Hobbes, Carl Schmitt et les apories du décisionnisme politique." *Les Temps Modernes* (August–September 1993).

Barret, William. *Irrational Man: A Study in Existential Philosophy.* Garden City: Doubleday Anchor, 1958.

Beetham, David. "Weber and the Liberal Tradition." In *The Barbarism of Reason: Max Weber and the Twilight of Enlightenment.* Edited by A. Horowitz and T. Maley. Toronto: University of Toronto Press, 1994.

Bell, Daniel. *The Coming of Post-Industrial Society.* New York: Basic Books, 1972.

The Cultural Contradictions of Capitalism. New York: Basic Books, 1978.

The Winding Passage. New York: Basic Books, 1980.

Bellamy, Richard, and Peter Baehr. "Carl Schmitt and the Contradictions of Liberal Democracy." *European Journal of Political Research* 23 (February 1993).

Benda, Julien. *La trahison des clercs.* Paris: Grasset, 1981.

Bendersky, Joseph. *Carl Schmitt: Theorist for the Reich.* Princeton: Princeton University Press, 1983.

"Carl Schmitt and the Conservative Revolution." *Telos* 72 (summer 1987).

"Review: Andreas Koenen, *Der Fall Carl Schmitt: Sein Aufsteig zum 'Kronjuristen des Dritten Reiches,'* and Heinrich Meier, *Carl Schmitt, and Leo Strauss: The Hidden Dialogue.*" *Journal of Modern History* (1997).

Benhabib, Seyla. *Critique, Norm and Utopia: A Study of the Foundations of Critical Theory.* New York: Columbia University Press, 1986.

Situating the Self. New York: Routledge, 1992.

"In Defense of Universalism – Yet Again!" *New German Critique* 62 (spring/summer 1992).

Benjamin, Walter. *Illuminations.* Edited by Hannah Arendt. New York: Schocken, 1968.

Gesammelte Schriften. Vol. 1. Edited by R. Tiedemann & H. Scheppenhäuser. Frankfurt a. M.: Suhrkamp, 1974.

"Konvolut N [Re the Theory of Knowledge, Theory of Progress]." In *Benjamin: Philosophy, Aesthetics, History.* Edited by Gary Smith. Chicago: University of Chicago Press, 1989.

Berezin, Mabel. *Communities of Feeling: Culture, Politics and Identity in Fascist Italy.* Ithaca, N.Y.: Cornell University Press, 1996.

"Fascism/Antiliberalism: Some New Thoughts on an Old Idea." Department of Sociology, University of Pennsylvania, unpublished manuscript, 1996.

Berns, Laurence. "Correcting the Record on Leo Strauss." *PS: Political Science and Politics.* 28:4 (December 1995).

Bernstein, Richard. "A Very Unlikely Villain (or Hero)." *New York Times.* (Jan. 29, 1995).

Bernstein, Richard J. *Beyond Objectivism and Relativism: Science, Hermeneutics and Praxis.* Philadelphia: University of Pennsylvania Press, 1988.

The New Constellation: The Ethical/ Political Horizons of Modernity/Postmodernity. Cambridge, Mass.: MIT Press, 1992.

ed. *Habermas and Modernity.* Cambridge, Mass.: MIT Press, 1985.

Berthold, Lutz. "Wer hält zur Zeit den Satan auf? – Zur Selbstglossierung Carl Schmitts." *Leviathan: Zeitschrift für Sozialwissenschaft* 21:2 (1993)

Blackbourn, David, and Geoff Eley. *The Peculiarities of German History: Bourgeois Society and Politics in Nineteenth-Century Germany.* Oxford: Oxford University Press, 1984.

Bloom, Allan. *The Closing of the American Mind.* New York: Basic Books, 1987.

Blumenberg, Hans. *The Legitimacy of the Modern Age.* Translated by Robert Wallace. Cambridge, Mass.: MIT Press, 1985.

Work on Myth. Translated by Robert Wallace. Cambridge, Mass.: MIT Press, 1989.

Bobio, Norberto. *Democracy and Dictatorship: The Nature and the Limits of State Power.* Translated by Peter Kenealy. Minneapolis: University of Minnesota Press, 1987.

The Future of Democracy: A Defense of the Rules of the Game. Translated by Roger Griffin. Minneapolis: University of Minnesota Press, 1987.

Which Socialism? Marxism, Socialism and Democracy. Translated by Roger Griffin. Minneapolis: University of Minnesota Press, 1987.

Böckenförde, Ernst-Wolfgang. *Staat, Gesellschaft, Freiheit: Studien zur Staatstheorie und zum Verfassungsrecht.* Frankfurt a. M.: Suhrkamp, 1976.

Gesetz und gesetzgebende Gewalt: Von den Anfangen der deutschen Staatsrechtslehre bis zur Höhe des staatsrechtlichen Positivismus. Berlin: Duncker & Humblot, 1981.

"Der Begriff des Politischen als Schlüssel zum staatsrechtlichen Werk Carl Schmitts." In *Complexio Oppositorum: Ueber Carl Schmitt.* Edited by Helmut Quaritsch. Berlin: Duncker & Humblot, 1988.

Recht, Staat, Freiheit: Studien zur Rechtsphilosophie, Staatstheorie und Verfassungsgeschichte. Frankfurt a. M.: Suhrkamp, 1991.

Bohman, James. "Complexity, Pluralism and the Constitutional State: On Habermas' *Faktizität und Geltung.*" *Law and Society Review* 28 (November 1994).

Public Deliberation: Pluralism, Complexity and Democracy. Cambridge, Mass.: MIT Press, 1995.

Bohrer, Karl Heinz. *Die Aesthetik des Schreckens: Die pessimistische Romantik und Ernst Jüngers Frühwerk.* Munich: Carl Hanser, 1978.

    ed. *Mythos und Moderne: Begriff und Bild einer Rekonstruktion.* Frankfurt a. M.: Suhrkamp, 1983.

Boldt, Hans. "Article 48 of the Weimar Constitution, Its Historical and Political Implications." In *German Democracy and the Triumph of Hitler.* Edited by Anthony Nicholls and Erich Matthias. London: Unwin & Allen, 1971.

Bolz, Norbert. *Auszug aus der entzauberten Welt.* Munich: Wilhelm Fink Verlag, 1989.

    "Charism and Souveränität: Carl Schmitt und Walter Benjamin im Schatten Max Webers." In *Der Fürst dieser Welt: Carl Schmitt und die Folgen.* Edited by Jacob Taubes. Munich: Wilhelm Fink, 1983.

Bookbinder, Paul. "Hermann Heller vs. Carl Schmitt." *International Social Science Review* 62 (1987).

Bourdieu, Pierre. *Outline of a Theory of Practice.* Translated by R. Nice. Cambridge: Cambridge University Press, 1977.

Bracher, Karl Dietrich. *Die Auflösung der Weimarer Republik: Eine Studie zum Problem des Machtverfalls in der Demokratie.* Düsseldorf: Droste, 1984.

Brenner, Neil. "The Limits of Civil Society in the Age of Global Capital: A Critique of Jürgen Habermas' Mature Social Theory." Department of Political Science, University of Chicago, master's thesis, 1993.

    "State Territorial Restructuring and the Production of Spatial Scale: Urban and Regional Planning in the Federal Republic of Germany, 1960–1990," *Political Geography* 15:1 (1996).

Breuer, Stefan. "The Illusion of Politics: Politics and Rationalization in Max Weber and Georg Lukács." *New German Critique* 26 (summer 1982).

    "Nationalstaat und pouvoir constitutant bei Sieyés und Carl Schmitt." *Archiv für Rechts- und Sozialphilosophie* 70 (1984).

    "Der letzte Ritter der heiligen Johanna. Ein Anti-Hobbes: Günter Meuter legt die Fundamente von Carl Schmitts Zeitkritik frei." *Frankfurter Allgemeine Zeitung* (Feb. 27, 1995).

Brubaker, Rogers. "Nationhood and the National Question in the Soviet Union and Post-Soviet Eurasia: An Institutional Account." *Theory and Society* 23:1 (February 1994).

Buck-Morss, Susan. *The Origin of Negative Dialectics: Theodor W. Adorno, Walter Benjamin, and the Frankfurt Institute.* New York: Free Press, 1977.

    "Aesthetics and Anaesthetics: Walter Benjamin's Artwork Essay Reconsidered." *October* 62 (fall 1992).

Bürger, Peter. "Carl Schmitt oder die Fundierung der Politik auf Aesthetik." In *Zerstörung, Rettung des Mythos durch Licht.* Edited by Christa Bürger. Frankfurt a. M.: Suhrkamp, 1986.

Caldwell, Peter. "Ernst Forsthoff and the Legacy of Radical Conservative State Theory in the Federal Republic of Germany." *History of Political Thought* 15:4 (winter 1994).

"National Socialism and Constitutional Law: Carl Schmitt, Otto Koellreutter, and the Debate over the Nature of the Nazi State, 1933–1937." *Cardozo Law Review* 16:2 (December 1994).

"Legal Positivism and Weimar Democracy." *American Journal of Jurisprudence* 39:1 (spring 1995).

Popular Sovereignty and the Crisis of German Constitutional Law: The Theory and Practice of Weimar Constitutionalism. Durham, N. C.: Duke University Press, 1997.

Calhoun, Craig. "Postmodernism as Pseudohistory: The Trivialization of Epochal Change." In *Critical Social Theory: Culture, History and the Challenge of Difference.* Oxford: Blackwell, 1995.

——— ed. *Habermas and the Public Sphere.* Cambridge, Mass.: MIT Press, 1992.

Cassirer, Ernst. *The Myth of the State.* New Haven: Yale University Press, 1946.

——— *Symbol, Myth and Culture: Essays and Lectures, 1935–1945.* Edited by Donald Philip Verene. New Haven: Yale University Press, 1979.

Cohen, Jean, and Andrew Arato. *Civil Society and Political Theory.* Cambridge, Mass.: MIT Press, 1992.

Connolly, William. *The Ethos of Pluralism.* Minneapolis: University of Minnesota Press, 1996.

Craig, Gordon A. *Germany, 1866–1945.* Oxford: Oxford University Press, 1980.

Cristi, Renato. "Hayek and Schmitt on the Rule of Law." *Canadian Journal of Political Science* 17:3 (1984).

——— "Carl Schmitt on Liberalism, Democracy and Catholicism." *History of Political Thought* 14 (1993).

——— "Carl Schmitt on Sovereignty and Constituent Power." *Canadian Journal of Law and Jurisprudence* 10:1 (January 1997).

Daedalus 124:2 (spring 1995). Special issue: "What Future for the State?"

dal Lago, Alessandro. "Gloria e disperazione: il cattolcesimo polemico di Carl Schmitt e il politeismo di Max Weber." *Fenomenologia e Societa* 2:2 (1988).

Del Rosso, Stephen J., Jr. "The Insecure State: Reflections on 'the State' and 'Security' in a Changing World." *Daedalus* 124:2 (spring 1995).

Deudney, Daniel. "Nuclear Weapons and the Waning of the Real-State." *Daedalus* 124:2 (spring 1995).

Dicey, A. C. *Introduction to the Study of the Law of the Constitution.* Indianapolis: Liberty Classics, 1982.

Diggins, John Patrick. *Max Weber: Politics and the Spirit of Tragedy.* New York: Basic Books, 1996.

Dreier, Horst. *Rechtslehre, Staatssoziologie und Demokratietheorie bei Hans Kelsen.* Baden-Baden: Nomos, 1986.

Dreier, R., and W. Sellert, eds. *Recht und Justiz im "Dritten Reich."* Frankfurt a. M.: Suhrkamp, 1989.

Drury, Shadia. *The Political Ideas of Leo Strauss.* New York: St. Martin's Press, 1988.

Dunn, Charles W., and J. David Woodard. *The Conservative Tradition in America*. New York: Rowman & Littlefield, 1996.

Dworkin, Ronald. *Taking Rights Seriously*. Cambridge, Mass.: Harvard University Press, 1977.

  A Matter of Principle. Cambridge, Mass.: Harvard University Press, 1985.

  Law's Empire. Cambridge, Mass.: Harvard University Press, 1986.

Dyzenhaus, David Ludovic. "'Now the Machine Runs Itself': Carl Schmitt on Hobbes and Kelsen." *Cardozo Law Review* 16:1 (August 1994).

  "The Legitimacy of Legality." *University of Toronto Law Journal* 46 (1996).

  "Liberalism after the Fall: Schmitt, Rawls and the Problem of Justification," *Philosophy and Social Criticism* 22:3 (1996).

  Truth's Revenge: Carl Schmitt, Hans Kelsen and Hermann Heller in Weimar. Oxford: Oxford University Press, 1997.

  ed. *Canadian Journal of Law and Jurisprudence* 10:1 (January 1997). Special issue: "Sovereignty in the Pluriverse of Ideologies: Carl Schmitt's Challenge to the Liberal Ideal of the Rule of Law."

Eagleton, Terry, *The Illusions of Postmodernism* (Oxford: Blackwell, 1996).

Eberl, Matthias. *Die Legitimität der Moderne: Kulturkritik und Herrschaftskonzeption bei Max Weber und Carl Schmitt*. Marburg: Tectum, 1994.

Eley, Geoff. *Reshaping the German Right: Radical Nationalism and Political Change after Bismarck*. New Haven: Yale University Press, 1980.

  "What Produces Fascism: Preindustrial Traditions or a Crisis of Capitalism?" *Politics and Society* 12:1 (1983).

  ed. *Society, Culture, and the State in Germany, 1870–1930*. Ann Arbor: University of Michigan Press, 1996.

Elster, Jon, and Rune Slagstad, eds. *Constitutionalism and Democracy*. Cambridge: Cambridge University Press, 1988.

Ely, John. "The Polis and 'The Political': Civic and Territorial Views of Association." *Thesis Eleven* 46 (August 1996).

Emerson, Rupert. *State and Sovereignty in Modern Germany*. New Haven: Yale University Press, 1928.

Evans, Helen Lovell, *The German Center Party, 1870–1933: A Study in Political Catholicism*. Carbondale: Southern Illinois Press, 1981.

Farias, Victor. *Heidegger and the Nazis*. Philadelphia: Temple University Press, 1989.

Feenberg, Andrew. *Lukács, Marx, and the Sources of Critical Theory*. New York: Oxford University Press, 1986.

  Critical Theory of Technology. Oxford: Oxford University Press, 1991.

  and Alastair Hannay, eds. *Technology and The Politics of Knowledge*. Bloomington: Indiana University Press, 1995.

Fellows, Roger, ed. *Philosophy and Technology*. Cambridge: Cambridge University Press, 1995.

Ferry, Luc. *The New Quarrel between the Ancients and the Moderns*. Translated by F. Philip. Chicago: University of Chicago Press, 1990.

Fijalkowski, Jürgen. *Die Wendung zum Führerstaat: Ideologische Komponenten in der politischen Philosophie Carl Schmitts.* Cologne: Westdeutscher, 1958.

Finn, John E. *Constitutions in Crisis: Political Violence and the Rule of Law.* Oxford: Oxford University Press, 1991.

Foreign Affairs 72:4 (September/October 1993). Special issue on Samuel Huntington.

Forsthoff, Ernst. *Rechtsstaat im Wandel: Verfassungsrechtliche Abhandlungen, 1954–1973.* Munich: C. H. Beck, 1976.

Fraenkel, Ernst. *The Dual State: A Contribution to the Theory of Dictatorship.* Translated by E. A. Shils. New York: Octagon Books, 1969.

Frank, Manfred. *Der kommende Gott: Vorlesungen über die neue Mythologie.* Frankfurt a. M.: Suhrkamp, 1982.

Fraser, Nancy. "False Antitheses: A Response to Seyla Benhabib and Judith Butler." *Praxis International.* 11:2 (July 1991).

Justice Interruptus: Rethinking Key Concepts of a "Postsocialist" Age. London: Routledge, 1996.

"Recognition or Redistribution?: A Critical Reading of Iris Young's *Justice and the Politics of Difference.*" *Journal of Political Philosophy* 3:2 (June 1995).

Freud, Sigmund. "The Uncanny." In *The Complete Psychological Works of Sigmund Freud.* Vol. 22. Edited and translated by James Strachey. London: Hogarth Press, 1963.

Friedrich, Carl Joachim. "The Issue of Judicial Review in Germany." *Political Science Quarterly* 42 (1928).

"Dictatorship in Germany." *Foreign Affairs* 9:1 (1930).

"The Development of Executive Power in Germany." *American Political Science Review* 27 (1933).

Constitutional Government and Democracy: Theory and Practice in Europe and America. New York: Ginn, 1950.

Constitutional Reason of State: The Survival of the Constitutional Order. Providence: Brown University Press, 1957.

The Philosophy of Law in Historical Perspective. Chicago: The University of Chicago Press, 1958.

Frug, Gerald. "The Ideology of Bureaucracy in American Law." *Harvard Law Review* 97 (1984).

Gaus, Gerald F. "Public Reason and the Rule of Law." In *The Rule of Law* (*Nomos* 36). Edited by Ian Shapiro. New York: New York University Press, 1994.

Gay, Peter. *Weimar Culture: The Outsider as Insider.* London: Penguin, 1992.

Germain, Gilbert G. *A Discourse on Disenchantment: Reflections on Politics and Technology.* Albany: State University of New York Press, 1995.

Gerson, Mark. *The Neoconservative Vision: From the Cold War to the Culture Wars.* New York: Rowman and Littlefield, 1995.

Geuss, Raymond. *The Idea of a Critical Theory: Habermas and the Frankfurt School.* Cambridge: Cambridge University Press, 1981.

Geyer, Michael. "The State in National Socialist Germany." In *Statemaking and Social*

Movements: Essays in History and Theory. Edited by Charles Bright and Susan Harding. Ann Arbor: University of Michigan Press, 1984.

"The Stigma of Violence: Nationalism and War in Twentieth Century Germany." *German Studies Review* (winter 1992).

Gleason, Abbott. *Totalitarianism.* Oxford: Oxford University Press, 1996.

Gluck, Mary. *Georg Lukács and His Generation: 1900–1918.* Cambridge, Mass.: Harvard University Press, 1985.

Golczewski, Frank. *Kölner Universitätslehrer und der Nationalsozialismus.* Cologne: Böhlau, 1988.

Goldman, Harvey. *Politics, Death and the Devil: Self and Power in Max Weber and Thomas Mann.* Berkeley: University of California Press, 1992.

Goldmann, Lucien. *Lukács and Heidegger: Towards a New Philosophy.* Translated by W. Q. Boelhower. London: Routledge & Kegan Paul, 1979.

Gottfried, Paul Edward. *Carl Schmitt: Politics and Theory.* Westport: Greenwood, 1990.

"Confronting the Challenge of the Exception: George Schwab as an Interpreter of Carl Schmitt." *The Political Science Reviewer* 20 (spring 1991).

The Conservative Movement. New York: Twayne, 1993.

"Schmitt and Strauss." *Telos* 96 (summer 1993).

Greenberg, D., and S. N. Katz et al., eds. *Constitutionalism and Democracy: Transitions in the Contemporary World.* Oxford: Oxford University Press, 1993.

Griffin, Roger. *The Nature of Fascism.* New York: St. Martin's Press, 1991.

ed. *Fascism.* Oxford: Oxford University Press, 1996.

Grimm, Dieter. *Recht und Staat der bürgerlichen Gesellschaft.* Frankfurt a. M.: Suhrkamp, 1987.

Die Zukunft der Verfassung. Frankfurt a. M.: Suhrkamp, 1991.

Gross, Raphael. "Carl Schmitts 'Nomos' und die 'Juden.'" *Merkur* 47:5 (May 1993).

"Politische Polykratie 1936: Die legendenumwobene SD-Akte Carl Schmitt." *Tel Aviver Jahrbuch für deutsche Geschichte* 23 (1994).

Güde, Fritz. "Der Schiffbrüchige und der Kapitän: Carl Schmitt und Walter Benjamin auf stürmischer See." *Kommune* 61 (1985).

Gunnell, John. "Strauss Before Straussianism: The Weimar Conversation." *Review of Politics* 52:1 (winter 1990).

Günther, Klaus. "Hans Kelsen (1881–1973): Das nüchterne Pathos der Demokratie." In *Streitbare Juristen: Eine Andere Tradition.* Edited by Thomas Blanke et al. Baden-Baden: Nomos, 1988.

Gurr, Ted Robert. *Minorities at Risk: A Global View of Ethnopolitical Conflicts.* Washington, D.C.: United States Institute of Peace Press, 1993.

Gutmann, Amy, and Dennis Thompson. *Democracy and Disagreement.* Cambridge, Mass.: Harvard University Press, 1996.

Habermas, Jürgen. *Toward a Rational Society: Student Protest, Science and Politics.* Translated by Jeremy Shapiro. Boston: Beacon Press, 1970.

Theory and Practice. Translated by John Viertel. Boston: Beacon Press, 1973.

Philosophical-Political Profiles. Translated by Frederick Lawrence. Cambridge, Mass.: MIT Press, 1983.

The Theory of Communicative Action. Vol. 1. *Reason and the Rationalization of Society*. Translated by Thomas McCarthy. Boston: Beacon Press, 1984.

The Theory of Communicative Action. Vol. 2. *Lifeworld and System: A Critique of Functionalist Reason*. Translated by Thomas McCarthy. Boston: Beacon Press, 1987.

The Philosophical Discourse of Modernity. Translated by Frederick Lawrence. Cambridge, Mass.: MIT Press, 1987.

The New Conservatism: Cultural Criticism and the Historians' Debate, Translated by Shierry Weber Nicholsen (Cambridge, Mass.: MIT Press, 1989).

The Structural Transformation of the Public Sphere. Translated by T. Burger with the assistance of F. Lawrence. Cambridge, Mass.: MIT Press, 1989.

"Das Bedürfnis nach deutschen Kontinuitäten." *Die Zeit* (Dec. 3, 1993).

Between Facts and Norms: Contributions to a Discourse Theory of Law and Democracy. Cambridge, Mass.: MIT Press, 1996.

Habermas, Jürgen, and Niklas Luhmann. *Theorie der Gesellschaft oder Sozialtechnologie*. Frankfurt a. M.: Suhrkamp, 1971.

Hager, Carol J. *Technological Democracy: Bureaucracy and Citizenry in the German Energy Debate*. Ann Arbor: University of Michigan Press, 1995.

Halperin, S. William. *Germany Tried Democracy: A Political History of the Reich from 1918 to 1933*. New York: W. W. Norton, 1965.

Hamilton, Alexander, James Madison, and John Jay. *The Federalist Papers*. New York: Mentor, 1961.

Hamlin, Alan, and P. Pettit, eds. *The Good Polity: Normative Analysis of the State*. Oxford: Blackwell, 1989.

Hansen, Miriam. "Introduction to Adorno's 'Transparencies on Film' (1966)." *New German Critique* 24–5 (fall/winter 1981–82).

"Unstable Mixtures, Dilated Spheres." *Public Culture* 5 (1993).

Hart, H. L. A. *Essays in Jurisprudence and Philosophy*. Oxford: Oxford University Press, 1983.

Harvey, David. *The Condition of Postmodernity*. Oxford: Blackwell, 1989.

Hastedt, Heiner. *Aufklärung und Technik*. Frankfurt a. M.: Suhrkamp, 1991.

Havel, Václav. *Living in Truth*. London: Faber & Faber, 1987.

Heidegger, Martin. *An Introduction to Metaphysics*. Translated by Ralph Manheim. Garden City, N.Y.: Doubleday Anchor, 1961.

Discourse on Thinking. Translated by J. M. Anderson and E. H. Freund. New York: Harper & Row, 1966.

The End of Philosophy. Translated by Joan Stambaugh. New York: Harper & Row, 1973.

Basic Writings. Edited by David Farrell Krell. New York: Harper & Row, 1977.

The Question Concerning Technology and Other Essays. Translated by William Lovitt. New York: Harper & Row, 1977.

The Metaphysical Foundations of Logic. Translated by Michael Heim. Bloomington: Indiana University Press, 1984.

Held, David. *Introduction to Critical Theory: Horkheimer to Habermas.* Berkeley: University of California Press, 1980.

Democracy and the Global Order: From the Modern State to Cosmopolitan Governance. Oxford: Polity Press, 1995.

Heller, Agnes. "The Concept of the Political Revisited." In *Political Theory Today.* Edited by D. Held. Stanford: Stanford University Press, 1991.

et al., eds. *Die Seele und das Leben: Studien zum frühen Lukács.* Frankfurt a. M.: Suhrkamp, 1977.

ed. *Lukács Reappraised.* New York: Columbia University Press, 1983.

Herf, Jeffrey. *Reactionary Modernism: Technology, Culture and Politics in Weimar and the Third Reich.* New York: Cambridge University Press, 1984.

Paul Piccone, and G. L. Ulmen. "Reading and Misreading Schmitt: An Exchange." *Telos* 74 (winter 1987–88).

Hertzberg, Hendrik. "Marxism: The Sequel." *New Yorker* 70:49 (1995).

Herz, John. "Looking at Carl Schmitt from the Vantage Point of the 1990s." *Interpretation* 19:3 (spring 1992).

Hess, David J. *Science and Technology in a Multicultural World: The Cultural Politics of Facts and Artifacts.* New York: Columbia University Press, 1995.

Hirst, Paul. *Law, Socialism and Democracy.* London: Routledge, 1986.

"Carl Schmitt's Decisionism." *Telos* 72 (summer 1987).

"Carl Schmitt – Decisionism and Politics." *Economy and Society* 17:2 (May 1988).

The Pluralist Theory of the State. London: Routledge, 1989.

Representative Democracy and Its Limits. Cambridge: Polity Press, 1990.

"The State, Civil Society and the Collapse of Soviet Communism." *Economy and Society* 20:2 (May 1991).

Associative Democracy. Amherst: University of Massachusetts Press, 1994.

Hirst, Paul, and Grahame Thompson. "Globalization and the Future of the Nation-State." *Economy and Society.* 24:3 (1995).

Hobbes, Thomas. *Leviathan.* Edited by Richard Tuck. Cambridge: Cambridge University Press, 1991.

Hobsbawm, Eric J. *Nations and Nationalism since 1780: Programme, Myth, Reality.* Cambridge: Cambridge University Press, 1995.

Hodgson, Godfrey. *The World Turned Right Side Up: A History of the Conservative Ascendancy in America.* Boston: Houghton Mifflin, 1996.

Hoffmann, Stanley. "The Case of Dr. Kissinger," *New York Review of Books* (Dec. 6, 1979).

Hofmann, Hasso. *Legitimität gegen Legalität: Der Weg der politischen Philosophie Carl Schmitts.* Berlin: Hermann Luchterhand, 1964.

Hohendahl, Peter. "The Dialectic of Enlightenment Revisited: Habermas's Critique of the Frankfurt School." *New German Critique* 35 (summer 1985).

Holmes, Stephen. "Review: *Carl Schmitt; Theorist for the Reich.*" *American Political Science Review* 77:4 (December 1983).

Benjamin Constant and the Making of Modern Liberalism. New Haven: Yale University Press, 1984.

"Differenzierung und Arbeitsteilung im Denken des Liberalismus." In *Soziale Differenzierung: Zur Geschichte einer Idee.* Edited by Niklas Luhmann. Opladen: Westdeutscher, 1985.

"Precommitment and the Paradox of Democracy." In *Constitutionalism and Democracy.* Edited by J. Elster and R. Slagstad. Cambridge: Cambridge University Press, 1988.

"The Scourge of Liberalism." *New Republic* 199 (Aug. 22, 1988).

The Anatomy of Antiliberalism. Cambridge, Mass.: Harvard University Press, 1993.

"Liberalism for a World of Ethnic Passions and Decaying States." *Social Research* 61:3 (fall 1994).

Passions and Constraint: On the Theory of Liberal Democracy. Chicago: University of Chicago Press, 1995.

Honig, Bonnie. *Political Theory and the Displacement of Politics.* Ithaca, N.Y.: Cornell University Press, 1993.

Honneth, Axel. *The Critique of Power: Reflective Stages in a Critical Social Theory.* Translated by Kenneth Baynes. Cambridge, Mass.: MIT Press, 1991.

Honneth, Axel, and Hans Joas, eds. *Communicative Action.* Cambridge, Mass.: MIT Press, 1991.

Horkheimer, Max, and T. W. Adorno. *Dialectic of Enlightenment.* Translated by John Cummings. New York: Continuum, 1989.

Horowitz, A., and T. Maley, eds. *The Barbarism of Reason: Max Weber and the Twilight of Enlightenment.* Toronto: University of Toronto Press, 1994.

Hughes, H. Stuart. *Consciousness and Society: The Reorientation of European Social Thought, 1890–1930.* New York: Vintage Books, 1977.

Huizinga, J. *In the Shadow of Tomorrow.* New York: W. W. Norton, 1936.

Huntington, Samuel. "The Clash of Civilizations?" *Foreign Affairs* 72:3 (summer 1993).

The Clash of Civilizations and the Remaking of World Order. New York: Simon & Schuster, 1996.

Huyssen, Andreas. *After the Great Divide: Modernism, Mass Culture, Postmodernism.* Bloomington: Indiana University Press, 1986.

Ignatieff, Michael. *Blood and Belonging: Journeys into the New Nationalism.* New York: Farrar, Straus and Giroux, 1994.

Jacobson, Arthur, J., and Bernhard Schlink, eds. *Weimar: A Jurisprudence of Crisis.* Berkeley: University of California Press, 1998.

Jameson, Fredric. *Postmodernism, or, The Cultural Logic of Late Capitalism.* Durham, N. C.: Duke University Press, 1991.

Jay, Martin. *The Dialectical Imagination: A History of the Frankfurt School and the Institute of Social Research, 1923–1950*. Boston: Little, Brown, 1973.

    Marxism and Totality: The Adventures of a Concept from Lukács to Habermas. Berkeley: University of California Press, 1984.

    "Reconciling the Irreconcilable? Rejoinder to Kennedy." *Telos* 71 (spring 1987).

    "The Reassertion of Sovereignty in a Time of Crisis: Carl Schmitt and Georges Bataille." In *Force Fields: Between Intellectual History and Cultural Critique*. New York: Routledge, 1993.

    "'The Aesthetic Ideology' as Ideology: Or What Does It Mean to Aestheticize Politics?" In *Force Fields: Between Intellectual History and Cultural Critique*. New York: Routledge, 1993.

Jessop, Bob. "Post-Fordism and the State." In *Post-Fordism: A Reader*. Edited by Ash Amin. Oxford: Blackwell, 1994.

Joerges, Christian. "On the Context of German-American Debates over Sociological Jurisprudence and Legal Criticism: A History of Transatlantic Misunderstandings and Missed Opportunities." In *European Yearbook in the Sociology of Law*. Edited by A. Febbrajo and D. Nelken. Brussels: Giuffrè, 1993.

Kadarkay, Arpad. *Georg Lukács: Life, Thought and Politics*. Oxford: Blackwell, 1991.

Kantorowicz, Hermann (a. k. a., Gnaeus Flavius). *Der Kampf um die Rechtswissenschaft*. Heidelberg: Carl Winter, 1906.

Kateb, George. "Hobbes and the Irrationality of Politics." *Political Theory* 17:3 (August 1989).

    "Notes on Pluralism." *Social Research* 61:3 (fall 1994).

Kaufmann, Walter. *From Shakespeare to Existentialism*. Garden City, N.Y.: Doubleday Anchor, 1960.

    Nietzsche: Philosopher, Psychologist, Antichrist. Princeton: Princeton University Press, 1974.

Keane, John. *Democracy and Civil Society*. London: Verso, 1988.

Kelsen, Hans. *Grenzen zwischen juristischer und soziologischer Methode*. Tübingen: J. C. B. Mohr (Paul Siebeck), 1911.

    "Wer soll der Hüter der Verfassung sein?" *Die Justiz* 6 (1930/31).

    Das Problem der Souveränität und die Theorie des Völkerrechts: Beiträge zu einer Reinen Rechtslehre. Aalen: Scientia, 1981.

    Der soziologische und der juristische Staatsbegriff: Kritische Untersuchung des Verhältnisses von Staat und Recht. Aalen: Scientia, 1981.

    Vom Wesen und Wert der Demokratie. Aalen: Scientia, 1981.

    Introduction to the Problems of Legal Theory. Translated by B. L. Paulson and S. L. Paulson. Oxford: Oxford University Press, 1992.

Kennedy, Ellen. "Carl Schmitt's *Parlamentarismus* in Its Historical Context." In Carl Schmitt, *The Crisis of Parliamentary Democracy*. Cambridge, Mass.: MIT Press, 1985.

"Carl Schmitt and the Frankfurt School." *Telos* 71 (spring 1987).

Keohane, Robert O., and Helen V. Miller, eds. *Internationalization and Domestic Politics*. Cambridge: Cambridge University Press, 1996.

Kitschelt, Herbert, and Anthony McGann. *The Radical Right in Western Europe: A Comparative Analysis*. Ann Arbor: University of Michigan Press, 1995.

Koenen, Andreas. *Der Fall Carl Schmitt: Sein Aufsteig zum "Kronjuristen des Dritten Reiches."* Darmstadt: Wissenschaftlichen Buchgesellschaft, 1995.

Kolb, Eberhard. *The Weimar Republic*. Translated by P. S. Falla. London: Unwin Hyman, 1988.

Koselleck, Reinhart. *Futures Past: On the Semantics of Historical Time*. Translated by Keith Tribe. Cambridge, Mass.: MIT Press, 1985.

Critique and Crisis: Enlightenment and the Pathogenesis of Modern Society. Cambridge, Mass.: MIT Press, 1988.

Kracauer, Siegfried. *The Mass Ornament: Weimar Essays*. Translated and Edited by Thomas Y. Levin. Cambridge, Mass.: Harvard University Press, 1995.

Kumar, Krishnan. *From Post-Industrial to Post-Modern Society: New Theories of the Contemporary World*. Oxford: Blackwell, 1995.

Kymlicka, Will. *Multicultural Citizenship: A Liberal Theory of Minority Rights*. Oxford: Oxford University Press, 1995.

Lampert, Laurence. *Nietzsche and Modern Times: A Study of Bacon, Descartes, and Nietzsche*. New Haven: Yale University Press, 1993.

Laquer, Walter. *Fascism: Past, Present and Future*. Oxford: Oxford University Press, 1995.

Larmore, Charles. *Patterns of Moral Complexity*. Cambridge: Cambridge University Press, 1987.

The Morals of Modernity. Cambridge: Cambridge University Press, 1996.

Lash, Scott, and John Urry. *The End of Organized Capitalism*. Madison: University of Wisconsin Press, 1987.

Latour, Bruno. *Aramis, or The Love of Technology*. Cambridge, Mass.: Harvard University Press, 1996.

Lauerman, Manfred. "Exkurs Carl Schmitt 1936." In *Die Autonomie des Politischen: Carl Schmitts Kampf um einen beschädigten Begriff*. Edited by Hans-Georg Flickinger. Wein: VCH Acta humaniora, 1990.

Lehman, Hartmut, and Guenther Roth, eds. *Weber's Protestant Ethic: Origins, Evidence, Contexts*. Cambridge: Cambridge University Press, 1995.

Lenk, Hans. *Zur Sozialphilosophie der Technik*. Frankfurt a. M.: Suhrkamp, 1983.

Levy, David J. "The Relevance of Carl Schmitt." *The World and I* (March 1987).

Lietzmann, Hans. "Vater der Verfassungsväter?: Carl Schmitt und die Verfassungsgründung in der Bundesrepublik Deutschland." In *Carl Schmitt und die Liberalismuskritik*. Opladen: Laske & Budrich, 1988.

Lipietz, Alain. *Towards a New Economic Order. Postfordism, Ecology and Democracy*. New York: Oxford University Press, 1992.

LoBel, Jules. "Emergency Powers and the Decline of Liberalism." *Yale Law Review* 98 (1989).

Locke, John. *Two Treatises on Government*. Edited by Peter Laslett. Cambridge: Cambridge University Press, 1988.

Löwith, Karl. *Meaning in History*. Chicago: University of Chicago Press, 1949.

"Max Weber und Carl Schmitt." *Frankfurter Allgemeine Zeitung* (Jun. 27, 1964).

"The Occasional Decisionism of Carl Schmitt." In *Heidegger and European Nihilism*. Translated by Gary Steiner. New York: Columbia University Press, 1995.

Luhmann, Niklas. *A Sociological Theory of Law*. London: Routledge & Kegan Paul, 1985.

Social Systems. Stanford: Stanford University Press, 1995.

Lukács, Georg. "Zur Soziologie des modernen Drama." *Archiv für Sozialwissenschaft und Sozialpolitik*. (1914).

Georg Lukács Werke. Vol. 2: *Frühschriften II*. Berlin: Hermann Luchterhand, 1964.

Lenin: A Study of the Unity of His Thought. Translated by N. Jacobs. Cambridge, Mass.: MIT Press, 1971.

Theory of the Novel. Translated by A. Bostock. Cambridge, Mass.: MIT Press, 1971.

Tactics and Ethics. Translated by M. McColgan and edited by R. Livingstone. New York: Harper & Row, 1972.

Soul and Form. Translated by A. Bostock. Cambridge, Mass.: MIT Press, 1974.

The Young Hegel. Translated by R. Livingstone. Cambridge, Mass.: MIT Press, 1976.

The Destruction of Reason. Translated by Peter Palmer. Atlantic Highlands, N. J.: Humanities Press, 1980.

"Gelebtes Denken: Notes Toward an Autobiography." In *Record of a Life: An Autobiographical Sketch*. Edited by I. Eörsi and Translated by R. Livingstone. London: Verso, 1983.

History and Class Consciousness. Translated by Rodney Livingstone. Cambridge, Mass.: MIT Press, 1988.

Machiavelli, Niccolò. *Il Principe*. Milan: Rizzoli, 1950.

Discorsi sopra la prima deca di Tito Livio. Milan: Rizzoli, 1984.

The Prince. Translated by Harvey C. Mansfield. Chicago: University of Chicago Press, 1985.

Discourses on the First Decade of Titus Livy. Translated by Harvey C. Mansfield and Nathan Tarcov. Chicago: University of Chicago Press, 1995.

MacIntyre, Alasdair. *After Virtue*. South Bend, Ind.: University of Notre Dame Press, 1984.

MacKinnon, Catherine. *Toward a Feminist Theory of the State*. Cambridge, Mass.: Harvard University Press, 1989.

Maier, Charles S. "Between Taylorism and Technocracy: European Ideologies and the Vision of Industrial Productivity in the 1920s." *Journal of Contemporary History* 5 (1970).

Recasting Bourgeois Europe: Stabilization in France, Germany, and Italy in the Decade after World War I. Princeton: Princeton University Press, 1975.

The Unmasterable Past: History, Holocaust and German Identity. Cambridge, Mass.: Harvard University Press, 1988.

Maier, Joseph B. "Georg Lukács and the Frankfurt School: A Case of Secular Messianism." In *Georg Lukács: Theory, Culture and Politics.* Edited by J. Marcus and Z. Tarr. Oxford: Transaction, 1989.

Manin, Bernard. "On Legitimacy and Political Deliberation." *Political Theory* 15:3 (August 1987).

"Checks, Balances and Boundaries: The Separation of Powers in the Constitutional Debate of 1787." In *The Invention of the Modern Republic.* Edited by Biancamaria Fontana. Cambridge: Cambridge University Press, 1994.

"The Metamorphoses of Representative Government." *Economy and Society* 23:2 (May 1994).

Principles of Representative Government. Cambridge: Cambridge University Press, 1997.

Marcuse, Herbert. "The Struggle Against Liberalism in the Totalitarian View of the State." In *Negations: Essays in Critical Theory.* Translated by Jeremy Shapiro. Boston: Beacon Press, 1968.

"Industrialization and Capitalism." In *Max Weber and Sociology Today.* Edited by Otto Stammer. Translated by K. Morris. New York: Harper & Row, 1971.

Marx, Karl. *Capital: A Critique of Political Economy.* Translated by Ben Fowkes. Vol. 1. London: Vintage, 1976.

Maus, Ingeborg. *Bürgerliche Rechtstheorie und Faschismus: Zur sozialen Funktion und aktuellen Wirkung der Theorie Carl Schmitts.* Munich: C. H. Beck, 1980.

Rechtstheorie und politische Theorie im Industriekapitalismus. Munich: Wilhelm Fink, 1986.

"Zur 'Zäsur' von 1933 in der Theorie Carl Schmitts." In *Rechtstheorie und politische Theorie im Industriekapitalismus.* Munich: Fink, 1986.

McCarthy, Thomas. *The Critical Theory of Jürgen Habermas.* Cambridge, Mass.: MIT Press, 1978.

McCormick, John P. "Addressing the Political Exception: Machiavelli's 'Accidents' and the Mixed Regime." *American Political Science Review* 87:4 (December 1993).

"Introduction to Schmitt's 'The Age of Neutralizations and Depoliticizations.'" *Telos* 96 (summer 1993).

"Fear, Technology and the State: Carl Schmitt, Leo Strauss and the Revival of Hobbes in Weimar and National Socialist Germany." *Political Theory* 22:4 (November 1994).

"Dangers of Mythologyzing Technology and Politics: Nietzsche, Schmitt and the Antichrist." *Philosophy and Social Criticism* 21:4 (July 1995).

"The Dilemmas of Dictatorship: Carl Schmitt and Constitutional Emergency Powers." *Canadian Journal of Law and Jurisprudence* 10:1 (January 1997).

"Transcending Weber's Categories of Modernity?: The Early Lukács and Schmitt on the Rationalization Thesis." *New German Critique* (1997).

McMichael, Philip. *Development and Social Change: A Global Perspective.* London: Sage, 1996.

Mehring, Reinhard. *Pathetisches Denken: Carl Schmitts Denkweg am Leitfaden Hegels: Katholische Grundstellung und antimarxistische Hegelstrategie.* Berlin: Duncker & Humblot, 1989.

Carl Schmitt: Zur Einführung. Hamburg: Junius, 1992.

"Der philosophische Führer und der Kronjurist: Praktisches Denken und geschichtliche Tat von Martin Heidegger und Carl Schmitt." *Deutsches Vierteljahrsschrift für Literaturwissenschaft und Geistesgeschichte* 68 (1994).

"Raffinierter Meister des Anstößigen. Versuch jenseits von Apologie und Polemik: Carl Schmitts Werk und seine Wirkung." *Die Welt* (May 21, 1994).

"Carl Schmitt und die Verfassungslehre unserer Tage." *Archiv des öffentlichen Recht* 55 (1995).

"Liberalism as a 'Metaphysical System': The Methodological Structure of Carl Schmitt's Critique of Political Rationalism," *Canadian Journal of Law and Jurisprudence* 10:1 (January 1997).

Meier, Heinrich. *Carl Schmitt, Leo Strauss und "Der Begriff des Politischen."* Stuttgart: J. B. Metzlersche Buchhandlung, 1988.

"The Philosopher as Enemy: On Carl Schmitt's *Glossarium.*" *Graduate Faculty Philosophy Journal* 17:1–2 (1994).

Carl Schmitt and Leo Strauss: The Hidden Dialogue. Translated by J. Harvey Lomax. Chicago: University of Chicago Press, 1995.

Melzer, Arthur M., J. Weinberger, and M. R. Zinman, eds. *Technology in the Western Political Tradition.* Ithaca, N.Y.: Cornell University Press, 1993.

Meuter, Günter. *"Der Katechon": Zu Carl Schmitts fundamentalistischer Kritik der Zeit.* Berlin: Duncker & Humblot, 1994.

Meyer, Hans. *Ein Deutscher auf Widerruf: Erinnerungen.* Vol. 2 Frankfurt a. M.: Suhrkamp, 1982.

Mitzman, Arthur. *The Iron Cage: An Historical Interpretation of Max Weber.* New Brunswick: Transaction Books, 1985.

Mommsen, Hans. *The Rise and Decline of Weimar Democracy.* Chapel Hill: University of North Carolina Press, 1996.

Mommsen, Wolfgang. "The Antinomian Structure of Max Weber's Thought." *Current Perspectives in Social Theory* 4 (1983).

Max Weber and German Politics, 1890–1920. Translated by M. S. Steinberg. Chicago: University of Chicago Press, 1984.

Montesquieu, Charles de Secondat, Baron de. *The Spirit of the Laws.* Edited and translated by A. M. Cohler, B. C. Miller, and H. S. Stone. Cambridge: Cambridge University Press, 1989.

Morgenthau, Hans J. "Fragment of an Intellectual Autobiography." In *Truth and*

Tragedy: A Tribute to Hans J. Morgenthau. Edited by Kenneth Thompson and Robert Myers. New Brunswick: Transaction, 1984.

Mosca, Gaetano. *The Ruling Class.* Translated by A. Livingston. New York: McGraw-Hill, 1939.

Mosse, George L. *The Crisis of German Ideology: Intellectual Origins of the Third Reich.* New York: Grosset & Dunlap, 1964.

Mouffe, Chantal. *The Return of the Political.* London: Verso, 1993.

Muller, Jerry Z. *The Other God that Failed: Hans Freyer and the Deradicalization of German Conservatism.* Princeton: Princeton University Press, 1987.

"Carl Schmitt, Hans Freyer and the Radical Conservative Critique of Liberal Democracy in the Weimar Republic." *History of Political Thought* 12:4 (winter 1991).

Münkler, Herfried. "Carl Schmitt und Thomas Hobbes." *Neue Politische Literatur* 29 (1984).

Murphy, Walter F. "Constitutions, Constitutionalism and Democracy." In *Constitutionalism and Democracy: Transitions in the Contemporary World.* Edited by D. Greenberg, S. N. Katz et al. Oxford: Oxford University Press, 1993.

Mußgnug, R. "Carl Schmitts verfassungsrechtliches Werk und sein Fortwirken im Staatsrecht der Bundesrepublik Deutschland." In *Complexio Oppositorum: Ueber Carl Schmitt.* Edited by Helmut Quaritsch. Berlin: Duncker & Humblot, 1988.

Neely, Mark E., Jr. *The Fate of Liberty: Abraham Lincoln and Civil Liberties.* Oxford: Oxford University Press, 1991.

Negt, Oskar, and Alexander Kluge. *Public Sphere and Experience: Toward an Analysis of the Bourgeois and Proletarian Public Sphere.* Translated by P. Labanyi, J. O. Daniel, and A. Oksiloff. Minneapolis: Minnesota University Press, 1993.

Nehamas, Alexander. *Nietzsche: Life as Literature.* Cambridge, Mass.: Harvard University Press, 1985.

Neumann, Franz. *Behemoth: The Structure and Practice of National Socialism, 1933–1944.* New York: Harper & Row, 1944.

The Democratic and the Authoritarian State: Essays in Political and Legal Theory. Edited by Herbert Marcuse. New York: Free Press, 1957.

Neumann, Volker. *Der Staat im Bürgerkrieg: Kontinuität und Wandlung des Staatsbegriffs in der politischen Theorie Carl Schmitts.* Frankfurt a. M.: Campus, 1980.

"Verfassungstheorien politischer Antipoden: Otto Kirchheimer und Carl Schmitt." *Kritische Justiz* 3 (1981).

Nichols, A. J. *Weimar and the Rise of Hitler.* London: Macmillan, 1991.

Nietzsche, Friedrich. *The Portable Nietzsche.* Edited and translated by Walter Kaufmann. New York: Viking, 1954.

Basic Writings of Nietzsche. Edited and translated by Walter Kaufmann. New York: Random House, 1968.

Selected Letters of Friedrich Nietzsche. Edited and translated by Christopher Middleton. Chicago: University of Chicago Press, 1969.

The Gay Science. Translated by Walter Kaufmann. New York: Vintage, 1974.

On the Advantage and Disadvantage of History for Life. Translated by Peter Preuss. Indianapolis: Hackett, 1980.

Philosophy and Truth: Selections from Nietzsche's Notebooks of the Early 1870's. Translated by Daniel Breazeale. New Jersey: Humanities Press, 1990.

Noack, Paul. *Carl Schmitt: Eine Biographie.* Berlin: Propyläen, 1993.

Nozick, Robert. *Anarchy, State, and Utopia.* New York: Basic Books, 1974.

Offe, Claus. *Contradictions of the Welfare State.* Edited by John Keane. Cambridge, Mass.: MIT Press, 1984.

Disorganized Capitalism: Contemporary Transformations of Work and Politics. Edited by John Keane. Cambridge, Mass.: MIT Press, 1985.

"The Utopia of the Zero-Option: Modernity and Modernization as Normative Political Criteria." *Praxis International* 7:1 (April 1987).

and Ulrich K. Preuß. "Democratic Institutions and Moral Resources." In *Political Theory Today.* Edited by David Held. Stanford: Stanford University Press, 1991.

Ogorek, Regina. *Richterkönig oder Subsumtionsautomat? Zur Justiztheorie im 19. Jahrhundert.* Frankfurt a. M.: Klostermann, 1986.

Ostrogoski, Mosei. *Democracy and the Organization of Political Parties.* New York: Haskell, 1970.

Palaver, Wolfgang. "A Girardian Reading of Schmitt's *Political Theology.*" *Telos* 93 (fall 1992).

Pan, David. "Political Aesthetics: Carl Schmitt on Hamlet." *Telos* 72 (summer 1987).

Pareto, Vilfredo. *The Mind and Society.* Translated by A. Livingston and A. Bongioro. New York: Harcourt, Brace & Jovanovich, 1935.

Parkinson, G. H. R. *Georg Lukács.* London: Routledge & Kegan Paul, 1977.

Pasquino, Pasquale. "Politische Einheit, Demokratie und Pluralismus: Bemerkungen zu Carl Schmitt, Hermann Heller und Ernst Fraenkel." In *Der Soziale Rechtsstaat.* Edited by C. Müller and I. Staff. Baden-Baden: Nomos, 1984.

"Die Lehre vom pouvoir constituant bei Abbe Sieyés und Carl Schmitt: Ein Beitrag zur Untersuchung der Grundlagen der modernen Demokratietheorie." In *Complexio Oppositorum: Ueber Carl Schmitt.* Edited by Helmut Quaritsch. Berlin: Duncker & Humblot, 1988.

"Hobbes: Natural Right, Absolutism, and Political Obligation." *Approches Cognitives Du Social,* 90158 (September 1990).

"Hobbes on the Natural and Legal Conditions of Mankind." English manuscript of "Thomas Hobbes: la rationalité de l' obéissance à la loi." *La pensée politique* (spring 1994).

Paulson, Stanley L. "The Neo-Kantian Dimension of Kelsen's Pure Theory of Law." *Oxford Journal of Legal Studies* 12 (1992).

"Kelsen's Legal Theory: The Final Round." *Oxford Journal of Legal Studies* 12 (1992).

"The Reich President and Weimar Constitutional Politics: Aspects of the Schmitt-Kelsen Dispute on the 'Guardian of the Constitution.'" Paper presented at the annual meeting of the American Political Science Association, Chicago, August 31–September 3, 1995.

Pensky, Max. *Melancholy Dialectics: Walter Benjamin and the Play of Mourning.* Amherst: University of Massachusetts Press, 1993.

Peters, Bernhard. *Die Integration moderner Gesellschaften.* Frankfurt a. M.: Suhrkamp, 1993.

Peukert, Detlev. *The Weimar Republic: The Crisis of Classical Modernity.* Translated by Richard Deveson. New York: Hill & Wang, 1992.

Piccone, Paul, and G. L. Ulmen. "Schmitt's 'Testament' and the Future of Europe." *Telos* 83 (spring 1990).

Piore, Michael, and Charles Sabel. *The Second Industrial Divide: Possibilities for Prosperity* New York: Basic Books, 1984.

Pippin, Robert B. *Kant's Theory of Form: An Essay on the* Critique of Pure Reason. New Haven: Yale University Press, 1982.

Hegel's Idealism: The Satisfactions of Self-Consciousness. Cambridge: Cambridge University Press, 1989.

Modernism as a Philosophical Problem: On the Dissatisfactions of European High Culture. Oxford: Blackwell, 1991.

"On the Notion of Technology as Ideology: Prospects." In *Technology, Pessimism and Postmodernism.* Edited by Y. Ezrahi, E. Mendelsohn, and H. Segal. Boston: Kluwer, 1994.

Pitkin, Hanna. *The Concept of Representation.* Berkeley: University of California Press, 1967.

Piven, Frances Fox. "Is It Global Economics or Neo-Laissez-Faire?" *New Left Review* 213 (September/October 1995).

Poggi, Gianfranco. *Calvinism and the Capitalist Spirit: Max Weber's* Protestant Ethic. Amherst: University of Massachusetts Press, 1983.

Postone, Moishe. *Time, Labor and Social Domination: A Reinterpretation of Marx's Critical Theory.* New York: Cambridge University Press, 1993.

"Contemporary Historical Transformations: Some Theoretical Considerations." Department of History, University of Chicago, unpublished manuscript (1995).

Preuß, Ulrich K. *Legalität und Pluralismus: Beiträge zum Verfassungsrecht der Bundesrepublik Deutschland.* Frankfurt a. M.: Suhrkamp, 1973.

"Zum 95. Geburtstag von Carl Schmitt: Die latente Diktatur in Verfassungsstaat." *Tageszeitung* (Jul. 12, 1983).

Politische Verantwortung und Bürgerloyalität: Von den Grenzen der Verfassung und des Gehorsams in der Demokratie. Frankfurt a. M.: Fischer, 1984.

"Aktuelle Probleme einer linken Verfassungstheorie." *Prokla: Zeitschrift für politische Oekonomie und sozialistishe Politik.* (December 1985).

"The Concept of Rights and the Welfare State." In *Dilemmas of Law in the Welfare State.* Edited by Günther Teubner. New York: Walter de Gruyter, 1986.

"The Critique of German Liberalism: Reply to Kennedy." *Telos* 71 (spring 1987).

"The Politics of Constitution Making: Transforming Politics into Constitutions." *Law & Policy* 13:2 (April 1991).

"Political Order and Democracy: Carl Schmitt and His Influence." In *Social System, Rationality and Revolution*. Edited by L. Nowak and M. Paprzycki. Rodopi: Poznan Studies in the Philosophy of the Sciences and the Humanities, 1993.

"Constitutional Powermaking for the New Polity: Some Deliberations on the Relations between Constituent Power and the Constitution." *Cardozo Law Review* 14:3–4 (January 1993).

"Vater der Verfassungsväter?: Carl Schmitts Verfassungslehre und die verfassungspolitische Diskussion der Gegenwart." In *Politisches Denken Jahrbuch 1993*. Edited by V. Gerhardt, H. Ottman, and M. Thompson. Stuttgart: J. B. Metzler, 1993.

Revolution, Fortschritt und Verfassung. Frankfurt a. M.: Fischer, 1994.

"The Political Meaning of Constitutionalism," Austin Lecture, UK Association for Legal and Social Philosophy, University of East Anglia, Norwich (April 6–8, 1995).

"Problems of a Concept of European Citizenship." *European Law Journal* 1:3 (November 1995).

Quaritsch, Helmut, ed. *Complexio Oppositorum: Ueber Carl Schmitt*. Berlin: Duncker & Humblot, 1988.

Positionen und Begriffe Carl Schmitts. Berlin: Duncker & Humblot, 1989.

Rabinbach, Anson. "Between Enlightenment and Apocalypse: Benjamin, Bloch and Modern Jewish Messianism." *New German Critique* 34 (winter 1985).

Rasehorn, Theo. "Der Kleinbürger als politischer Ideologe: Zur Entmythologisierung von Carl Schmitt." *Die Neue Gesellschaft, Frankfurter Hefte* (1986).

Rasmussen, David M. "How Is Valid Law Possible?: A Review of *Faktizität und Geltung* by Jürgen Habermas." *Philosophy and Social Criticism* 20:4 (1994).

Rawls, John. *A Theory of Justice*. Cambridge, Mass.: Harvard University Press, 1971.

Political Liberalism. New York: Columbia University Press, 1993.

Raz, Joseph. "The Purity of the Pure Theory." In *Essays on Kelsen*. Edited by R. Tur and W. Twining. Oxford: Oxford University Press, 1986.

Reinecke, Volker, and Jonathan Uhlaner. "The Problem of Leo Strauss: Religion, Philosophy and Politics." *Graduate Faculty Philosophy Journal* 16:1 (1992).

Rose, Gillian. *Judaism and Modernity: Philosophical Essays*. Oxford: Blackwell, 1993.

Rosenhaft, Eve. "Working-Class Life and Working-Class Politics: Communists, Nazis, and the State Battle for the Streets of Berlin 1928–1932." In *Social Change and Political Development in Weimar Germany*. Edited by R. Bessel and E. J. Feuchtwanger. New York: Barnes & Noble, 1981.

Rossiter, Clinton. *Constitutional Dictatorship: Crisis Government in Modern Democracies*. Princeton: Princeton University Press, 1948.

Ruggie, John Gerard, ed. *Multilateralism Matters: The Theory and Praxis of an Institutional Form*. New York: Columbia University Press, 1993.

Rumpf, Helmut. *Carl Schmitt und Thomas Hobbes: Ideelle Beziehungen und aktuelle Bedeutung mit einer Abhandlung über: Die Frühschriften Carl Schmitts.* Berlin: Duncker & Humblot, 1972.

Rumpf, Michael. "Radikale Theologie: Benjamins Beziehung zu Carl Schmitt." In *Walter Benjamin–Zeitgenosse der Moderne.* Edited by Peter Gebhardt et al. Kronberg: Scriptor, 1976.

Rüthers, Bernd. *Entartetes Recht: Rechtslehren und Kronjuristen im Dritten Reich.* Munich: C. H. Beck, 1988.

Carl Schmitt im Dritten Reich: Wissenschaft als Zeitgeist-Verstärkung? Munich: C. H. Beck, 1989.

"Wer war Carl Schmitt? Bausteine zu einer Biographie." *Neue Juristische Wochenschrift* 27 (July 1994).

Rutsky, R. L. "The Mediation of Technology and Gender: *Metropolis,* Nazism, Modernism." *New German Critique* 60 (fall 1993).

Sartori, Giovanni. "The Essence of the Political in Carl Schmitt." *Journal of Theoretical Politics* 1:1 (January 1989).

Scaff, Lawrence A. *Fleeing the Iron Cage: Culture, Politics and Modernity in the Thought of Max Weber.* Berkeley: University of California Press, 1989.

Scheuerman, William E. "Carl Schmitt and the Nazis." *German Politics and Society* 23 (summer 1991).

Between the Norm and the Exception: The Frankfurt School and the Rule of Law. Cambridge, Mass.: MIT Press, 1994.

"Is Parliamentarism in Crisis?: A Response to Carl Schmitt." *Theory and Society* 24:1 (February 1995).

"The Unholy Alliance of Carl Schmitt and Friedrich A. Hayek." *Constellations* 4:2 (October 1997).

ed. *The Rule of Law Under Siege: Selected Essays of Franz L. Neumann and Otto Kirchheimer.* Berkeley: University of California Press, 1996.

Schürmann, Reiner. *Heidegger on Being and Acting: From Principles to Anarchy.* Bloomington: Indiana University Press, 1987.

"Technicity, Topology, Tragedy: Heidegger on 'That Which Saves' in the Global Reach." In *Technology in the Western Political Tradition.* Edited by A. M. Melzer, J. Weinberger, and M. R. Zinman. Ithaca, N.Y.: Cornell University Press, 1993.

Schutz, Gerhard. *Zwischen Demokratie und Diktatur: Verfassungspolitik und Reichsreform in der Weimar Republik.* Vol. 1. *Die Periode der Konsolidierung und der Revision des Bismarckschen Reichsaufbaus 1919–1930.* Berlin: Walter De Gruyter, 1963.

Schwab, George. "Carl Schmitt: Through a Glass Darkly." *Schmittiana – Eclectica* 71–2 (1988).

The Challenge of the Exception: An Introduction to the Political Ideas of Carl Schmitt between 1921 and 1936. Westport: Greenwood, 1989.

Sharpe, R. J. *The Law of Habeas Corpus.* Oxford: Oxford University Press, 1991.

Shell, Susan. "Meier on Strauss and Schmitt." *Review of Politics* 53:1 (winter 1991).

Shklar, Judith N. *Legalism: Law, Morals and Political Trials.* Cambridge, Mass.: Harvard University Press, 1964.

Skinner, Quentin. "Conquest and Consent: Thomas Hobbes and the Engagement Controversy." In *The Interregnum.* Edited by G. E. Aylmer. London: Macmillan, 1972.

    et al., eds. *Machiavelli And Republicanism.* Cambridge: Cambridge University Press, 1990.

Slagstad, Rune. "Liberal Constitutionalism and Its Critics: Max Weber and Carl Schmitt." In *Constitutionalism and Democracy.* Edited by J. Elster and R. Slagstad. Cambridge: Cambridge University Press, 1988.

Smith, Gary, ed. *Benjamin: Philosophy, Aesthetics, History.* Chicago: University of Chicago Press, 1989.

Smith, Merritt Roe, and Leo Marx, eds. *Does Technology Drive History?: The Dilemma of Technological Determinism.* Cambridge, Mass.: MIT Press, 1994.

Söllner, Alfons. "Leftist Students of the Conservative Revolution: Neumann, Kirchheimer and Marcuse." *Telos* 61 (fall 1984).

"Beyond Carl Schmitt: Political Theory in the Frankfurt School." *Telos* 71 (spring 1987).

"German Conservatism in America: Morgenthau's Political Realism." *Telos* 72 (summer 1987).

Sombart, Nicolaus. *Die deutschen Männer und ihre Feinde: Carl Schmitt – ein deutsches Schicksal zwischen Männerbund und Matriarchatsmythos.* Munich: Hanser, 1991.

Jugend in Berlin, 1933–43: Ein Bericht. Frankfurt a. M.: Fischer, 1991.

Somers, Margaret R. "What's Political or Cultural about Political Culture and the Public Sphere? Toward an Historical Sociology of Concept Formation." *Sociological Theory* 13:2 (1995).

"Narrating and Naturalizing Anglo-American Citizenship Theory: The Place of Political Culture and the Public Sphere." *Sociological Theory* 13:3 (1996).

Soysal, Yasemin Nuhoglu. *Limits of Citizenship: Migrants and Postnational Membership in Europe.* Chicago: University of Chicago Press, 1994.

Stammer, Otto, ed. *Max Weber and Sociology Today*. Translated by K. Morris. New York: Harper & Row, 1971.

Staples, Brent. "Undemocratic Vistas: The Sinister Vogue of Leo Strauss." *New York Times* (Nov. 28, 1994).

Sternberger, Dolf. "Machiavelli's *Principe* und der Begriff des Politischen." In *Schriften.* Vol. 3. Frankfurt: Fischer, 1980.

Sternhell, Zeev. *The Birth of Fascist Ideology.* Translated by David Maisel. Princeton: Princeton University Press, 1994.

Strange, Susan. *The Retreat of the State: The Diffusion of Power in the World Economy.* Cambridge: Cambridge University Press, 1996.

Strauss, Leo. *The Political Philosophy of Hobbes: Its Basis and Genesis.* Translated by Elsa M. Sinclair. Chicago: University of Chicago Press, 1952.

Persecution and the Art of Writing. Glencoe: Free Press, 1952.

Natural Right and History. Chicago: University of Chicago Press, 1953.

Thoughts On Machiavelli. Glencoe: Free Press, 1958.

Spinoza's Critique of Religion. Translated by Elsa M. Sinclair. New York: Schocken, 1965.

What Is Political Philosophy? and Other Studies. Chicago: University of Chicago Press, 1988.

The Rebirth of Classical Rationalism. Edited by T. Pangle. Chicago: University of Chicago Press, 1989.

Strong, Tracy. *Friedrich Nietzsche and the Politics of Transfiguration*. Berkeley: University of California Press, 1988.

"How to Write Scripture: Words, Authority and Politics in Thomas Hobbes." *Critical Inquiry* 20:1 (autumn 1993).

"Max Weber and the Bourgeoisie." In *The Barbarism of Reason: Max Weber and the Twilight of Enlightenment*. Edited by A. Horowitz and T. Maley. Toronto: University of Toronto Press, 1994.

"Foreword: Dimensions of the New Debate around Carl Schmitt." In Carl Schmitt, *The Concept of the Political*. Translated by George Schwab. Chicago: University of Chicago Press, 1996.

Struve, Walter. *Elites Against Democracy: Leadership Ideals in Bourgeois Political Thought in Germany, 1890–1933*. Princeton: Princeton University Press, 1973.

Sunstein, Cass R. *After the Rights Revolution: Reconceiving the Regulatory State*. Cambridge, Mass.: Harvard University Press, 1990.

Taubes, Jacob. *Die Politische Theologie des Paulus*. Munich: Fink, 1993.

ed. *Der Fürst dieser Welt: Carl Schmitt und die Folgen*. Munich: Wilhelm Fink, 1983.

Telos 72 (summer 1987). Special issue: "Carl Schmitt: Enemy or Foe?"

Thiele, Leslie Paul. *Friedrich Nietzsche and the Politics of the Soul*. Princeton: Princeton University Press, 1990.

Tribe, Keith, ed. *Social Democracy and the Rule of Law: Otto Kirchheimer and Franz Neumann*. London: Allen & Unwin, 1987.

Ulmen, G. L. "The Sociology of The State: Carl Schmitt and Max Weber." *State, Culture and Society* 1 (1985).

Politische Mehrwert: Eine Studie über Max Weber und Carl Schmitt. Weinheim: VCH Acta humaniora, 1991.

"Anthropological Theology/Theological Anthropology: Reply to Palaver." *Telos* 93 (fall 1992).

Unger, Roberto. *Law in Modern Society*. New York: Free Press, 1976.

van Laaks, Dirk. *Gespräche in der Sicherheit des Scheigens – Carl Schmitt in der Geistesgeschichte der frühen Bundesrepublik*. Berlin: Akademie, 1993.

Vesting, Thomas. *Politische Einheitsbildung und technische Realisation: Ueber die Expansion der Technik und die Grenzen der Demokratie*. Baden-Baden: Nomos, 1990.

Vile, M. J. C. *Constitutionalism and the Separation of Powers*. Oxford: Oxford University Press, 1967.

Viroli, Maurizio. *From Politics to Reason of State: The Acquisition and Transformation of the Language of Politics, 1250–1600*. Cambridge: Cambridge University Press, 1992.

Vivarelli, Roberto. "Interpretations of the Origins of Fascism." *Journal of Modern History* 63 (March 1991).

von Gierke, Otto. *Political Theories of the Middle Ages*. Translated by F. W. Maitland. Boston: Beacon Press, 1958.

    Community in Historical Perspective. Edited by Antony Black. Translated by Mary Fischer. Cambridge: Cambridge University Press, 1990.

von Krockow, Christian Graf. *Die Entscheidung: Eine Untersuchung über Ernst Jünger, Carl Schmitt, Martin Heidegger*. Frankfurt a. M.: Campus, 1990.

Wacker, Bernd. *Die eigentlich katholische Verschärfung . . . : Konfession, Theologie und Politik im Werk Carl Schmitts*. Munich: Wilhelm Fink, 1994.

Wallerstein, Immanuel. *After Liberalism*. New York: New Press, 1996.

Walzer, Michael. "What's Going On?: Notes on the Right Turn." *Dissent* (winter 1996).

Wank, Ulrich, ed. *The Resurgence of Right-Wing Radicalism in Germany: New Forms of an Old Phenomenon?* Atlantic Highlands, N.J.: Humanities Press, 1996.

Warren, Mark. *Nietzsche and Political Thought*. Cambridge, Mass.: MIT Press, 1990.

Watkins, Frederick Mundell. *The Failure of Constitutional Emergency Powers under the German Republic*. Cambridge, Mass.: Harvard University Press, 1939.

Weale, Albert. "The Limits of Democracy." In *The Good Polity: Normative Analysis of the State*. Edited by Alan Hamlin and P. Pettit. Oxford: Blackwell, 1989.

Weber, Marianne. *Max Weber: A Biography*. Translated by Harry Zohn. New York: Wiley, 1975.

Weber, Max. *The Methodology of the Social Sciences*. Translated and Edited by G. Roth and C. Wittich. New York: Free Press, 1949.

    From Max Weber: Essays in Sociology. Edited and translated by H. H. Gerth and C. Wright Mills. Oxford: Oxford University Press, 1958.

    The Protestant Ethic and the Spirit of Capitalism. Translated by Talcott Parsons. New York: Scribner's, 1958.

    Economy and Society: An Outline of Interpretive Sociology. Edited by Guenther Roth and Claus Wittich. 2 vols. Berkeley: University of California Press, 1978.

    "The President of the Reich." In *Weber: Political Writings*. Edited by Peter Lassman and Ronald Speirs. Cambridge: Cambridge University Press, 1994.

Weber, Samuel. "Taking Exception to Decision: Walter Benjamin and Carl Schmitt." *Diacritics* 22:3–4 (fall/winter 1992).

Weiler, Gershon. *From Absolutism to Totalitarianism: Carl Schmitt on Thomas Hobbes*. Durango: Hollowbrook Press, 1994.

Weisberg, Jacob. "The Family Way: How Irving Kristol, Gertrude Himmelfarb and Bill Kristol Made Tormenting Liberals a Home Industry." *New Yorker* (October 21,28, 1996).

Wendenburg, Helge. *Die Debate um die Verfassungsgerichtsbarkeit und der Methodensteit der Staatsrechtslehre in der Weimarer Republik*. Göttingen: Otto Schwartz, 1984.

White, Stephen K. *Edmund Burke and the Dangers of Modernity: Modernity, Politics and Aesthetics.* London: Sage, 1994.

Wiegandt, Manfred H. "The Alleged Unaccountability of the Academic: A Biographical Sketch of Carl Schmitt." *Cardozo Law Review* 16 (1995).

Willey, Thomas. *Back to Kant: The Revival of Kantianism in German Social and Historical Thought, 1860–1914.* Detroit: Wayne State University Press, 1978.

Willms, Bernard. "Politics as Politics: Carl Schmitt's Concept of the Political and the Tradition of European Political Thought." *History of European Ideas* 13:4 (1991).

Winckelmann, Johannes. *Legitimität und Legalität im Max Webers Herrschaftssoziologie.* Tübingen: J. C. B. Mohr (Paul Siebeck), 1952.

Winkler, Heinrich August. *Weimar 1918–1933: Die Geschichte der Ersten Deutschen Demokratie.* Munich: C. H. Beck, 1994.

Wolin, Richard. *The Politics of Being: The Political Thought of Martin Heidegger.* New York: Columbia University Press, 1990.

   The Terms of Cultural Criticism: The Frankfurt School, Existentialism, Poststructuralism. New York: Columbia University Press, 1992.

   "Carl Schmitt, the Conservative Revolutionary: Habitus and the Aesthetics of Horror." *Political Theory* 20:3 (August 1992).

   Walter Benjamin: An Aesthetic of Redemption. Berkeley: University of California Press, 1994.

   Labyrinths: Explorations in the Critical History of Ideas. Amherst: University of Massachusetts Press, 1995.

   ed. *The Heidegger Controversy.* Cambridge, Mass.: MIT Press, 1993.

Wolin, Sheldon. *The Presence of the Past: Essays on the State and the Constitution.* Baltimore: Johns Hopkins University Press, 1989.

   "Fugitive Democracy." *Constellations* 1:1 (April 1994).

Young, Iris Marion. *Justice and the Politics of Difference.* Princeton: Princeton University Press, 1990.

   "Comments on Seyla Benhabib, *Situating the Self.*" *New German Critique* 62 (spring/summer 1992).

   "Reason in Exile: Critical Theory and Technological Society." In *Technology in the Western Political Tradition.* Edited by A. M. Melzer, J. Weinberger, and M. R. Zinman. Ithaca, N.Y.: Cornell University Press, 1993.

Young-Bruehl, Elisabeth. *Hannah Arendt: For Love of the World.* New Haven: Yale University Press, 1982.

Zimmerman, Michael E. *Heidegger's Confrontation with Modernity: Technology, Politics, Art.* Bloomington: Indiana University Press, 1990.

Zolo, Danilo. *Democracy and Complexity.* University Park: Pennsylvania State University, 1992.

INDEX

Abraham, 55
Ackerman, Bruce, 233n
Adorno, T. W., 5n, 8, 22, 23n, 26,
    68n, 90–2, 109, 113–5, 224n,
    258, 284, 300
Ajami, Fouad, 304n
Alighieri, Dante, 46, 55
Amin, Ash, 9n, 11n, 312n
Anderson, Benedict, 204n
Anderson, J. M., 115n
Anderson, Perry, 280n
Anderson, Peter, 309n
Antichrist, the, 19, 27, 67, 82, 83,
    86–9, 91, 93, 96, 103, 106,
    111–13, 115–17, 297; *see also*
    devil, Mephistopheles, Satan
Apostles, the, 163n
Arato, Andrew, 1n, 17n, 33n, 35n,
    56n, 61n, 74n, 76n, 144n,
    158n, 183n, 246n, 276n
Archenholtz, J. W., von, 150n
Arendt, Hannah, 2, 22, 109n,
    158n, 223n, 260n, 287n

Aristotle, 129n, 130
Aschheim, Steven E., 84n
Atlas, James, 303n
Aylmer, G. E., 280n

Bacon, Francis, 261
Bader, Veit-Michael, 23n
Baehr, Peter, 6n, 171n
Bakunin, Mikhail, 16, 94–5, 106,
    191–2
Baldwin, Peter, 11n
Ball, Hugo, 269
Barash, Jeffery A., 252n
Bartley, Robert, 304n
Baynes, Kenneth, 8n, 114n
Beetham, David, 8n
Behrends, Otto, 212n
Bell, Daniel, 3n, 311
Bellamy, Richard, 6n, 170n
Benda, Julien, 99n
Bendersky, Joseph, 1n, 15n, 24n,
    35n, 36n, 42n, 83n, 114n,
    123n, 129n, 252n, 267n,